OECD Institutional Investors Statistics 2014

OECD
BETTER POLICIES FOR BETTER LIVES

Please cite this publication as:
OECD (2014), *OECD Institutional Investors Statistics 2014*, OECD Publishing.
http://dx.doi.org/10.1787/instinv-2014-en

ISBN 978-92-64-22582-4 (print)
ISBN 978-92-64-22583-1 (PDF)

Annual: OECD Institutional Investors Statistics
ISSN 2225-2061 (print)
ISSN 2225-207X (online)

Table of contents

Conventional signs and abbreviations 9

International comparisons 11
1. Financial assets of open-end investment funds, as a percentage of GDP 12
2. Financial assets of insurance corporations, as a percentage of GDP 13
3. Financial assets of autonomous pension funds, as a percentage of GDP 14

Country tables 15

Australia
1. Financial assets of institutional investors, 2012 16
2. Financial assets of investment funds 17
3. Financial assets of insurance corporations and autonomous pension funds ... 19
4. Portfolio composition by type of investor 21

Austria
1. Financial assets of institutional investors, 2012 22
2. Financial assets of investment funds 23
3. Financial assets of insurance corporations and autonomous pension funds ... 25
4. Portfolio composition by type of investor 27

Belgium
1. Financial assets of institutional investors, 2012 28
2. Financial assets of investment funds 29
3. Financial assets of insurance corporations and autonomous pension funds ... 31
4. Portfolio composition by type of investor 33

Canada
1. Financial assets of institutional investors, 2013 34
2. Financial assets of investment funds 35
3. Financial assets of insurance corporations and autonomous pension funds ... 37
4. Portfolio composition by type of investor 39

Chile
1. Financial assets of institutional investors, 2013 40
2. Financial assets of investment funds 41
3. Financial assets of insurance corporations and autonomous pension funds ... 43
4. Portfolio composition by type of investor 45

Czech Republic
1. Financial assets of institutional investors, 2012 46
2. Financial assets of investment funds 47

3. Financial assets of insurance corporations and autonomous pension funds ... 49
4. Portfolio composition by type of investor ... 51

Denmark
1. Financial assets of institutional investors, 2013 ... 52
2. Financial assets of investment funds ... 53
3. Financial assets of insurance corporations and autonomous pension funds ... 55
4. Portfolio composition by type of investor ... 57

Estonia
1. Financial assets of institutional investors, 2013 ... 58
2. Financial assets of investment funds ... 59
3. Financial assets of insurance corporations and autonomous pension funds ... 61
4. Portfolio composition by type of investor ... 63

Finland
1. Financial assets of institutional investors, 2012 ... 64
2. Financial assets of investment funds ... 65
3. Financial assets of insurance corporations and autonomous pension funds ... 67
4. Portfolio composition by type of investor ... 69

France
1. Financial assets of institutional investors, 2013 ... 70
2. Financial assets of investment funds ... 71
3. Financial assets of insurance corporations and autonomous pension funds ... 73
4. Portfolio composition by type of investor ... 75

Germany
1. Financial assets of institutional investors, 2012 ... 76
2. Financial assets of investment funds ... 77
3. Financial assets of insurance corporations and autonomous pension funds ... 79
4. Portfolio composition by type of investor ... 81

Greece
1. Financial assets of institutional investors, 2013 ... 82
2. Financial assets of investment funds ... 83
3. Financial assets of insurance corporations and autonomous pension funds ... 85
4. Portfolio composition by type of investor ... 87

Hungary
1. Financial assets of institutional investors, 2013 ... 88
2. Financial assets of investment funds ... 89
3. Financial assets of insurance corporations and autonomous pension funds ... 91
4. Portfolio composition by type of investor ... 93

Iceland
1. Financial assets of institutional investors, 2013 ... 94
2. Financial assets of investment funds ... 95
3. Financial assets of insurance corporations and autonomous pension funds ... 97
4. Portfolio composition by type of investor ... 99

Ireland

1. Financial assets of institutional investors, 2013 100
2. Financial assets of investment funds 101
3. Financial assets of insurance corporations and autonomous pension funds ... 103
4. Portfolio composition by type of investor 105

Israel

1. Financial assets of institutional investors, 2012 106
2. Financial assets of investment funds 107
3. Financial assets of insurance corporations and autonomous pension funds ... 109
4. Portfolio composition by type of investor 111

Italy

1. Financial assets of institutional investors, 2012 112
2. Financial assets of investment funds 113
3. Financial assets of insurance corporations and autonomous pension funds ... 115
4. Portfolio composition by type of investor 117

Japan

1. Financial assets of institutional investors, 2012 118
2. Financial assets of investment funds 119
3. Financial assets of insurance corporations and autonomous pension funds ... 121
4. Portfolio composition by type of investor 123

Korea

1. Financial assets of institutional investors, 2011 124
2. Financial assets of investment funds 125
3. Financial assets of insurance corporations and autonomous pension funds ... 127
4. Portfolio composition by type of investor 129

Luxembourg

1. Financial assets of institutional investors, 2013 130
2. Financial assets of investment funds 131
3. Financial assets of insurance corporations and autonomous pension funds ... 133
4. Portfolio composition by type of investor 135

Mexico

1. Financial assets of institutional investors, 2013 136
2. Financial assets of investment funds 137
3. Financial assets of insurance corporations and autonomous pension funds ... 139
4. Portfolio composition by type of investor 141

Netherlands

1. Financial assets of institutional investors, 2013 142
2. Financial assets of investment funds 143
3. Financial assets of insurance corporations and autonomous pension funds ... 145
4. Portfolio composition by type of investor 147

Norway

1. Financial assets of institutional investors, 2013 148
2. Financial assets of investment funds 149

3. Financial assets of insurance corporations and autonomous pension funds ... 151
4. Portfolio composition by type of investor ... 153

Poland
1. Financial assets of institutional investors, 2013 ... 154
2. Financial assets of investment funds ... 155
3. Financial assets of insurance corporations and autonomous pension funds ... 157
4. Portfolio composition by type of investor ... 159

Portugal
1. Financial assets of institutional investors, 2013 ... 160
2. Financial assets of investment funds ... 161
3. Financial assets of insurance corporations and autonomous pension funds ... 163
4. Portfolio composition by type of investor ... 165

Slovak Republic
1. Financial assets of institutional investors, 2011 ... 166
2. Financial assets of investment funds ... 167
3. Financial assets of insurance corporations and autonomous pension funds ... 169
4. Portfolio composition by type of investor ... 171

Slovenia
1. Financial assets of institutional investors, 2013 ... 172
2. Financial assets of investment funds ... 173
3. Financial assets of insurance corporations and autonomous pension funds ... 175
4. Portfolio composition by type of investor ... 177

Spain
1. Financial assets of institutional investors, 2013 ... 178
2. Financial assets of investment funds ... 179
3. Financial assets of insurance corporations and autonomous pension funds ... 181
4. Portfolio composition by type of investor ... 183

Sweden
1. Financial assets of institutional investors, 2013 ... 184
2. Financial assets of investment funds ... 185
3. Financial assets of insurance corporations and autonomous pension funds ... 187
4. Portfolio composition by type of investor ... 189

Switzerland
1. Financial assets of institutional investors, 2013 ... 190
2. Financial assets of investment funds ... 191
3. Financial assets of insurance corporations and autonomous pension funds ... 193
4. Portfolio composition by type of investor ... 195

Turkey
1. Financial assets of institutional investors, 2012 ... 196
2. Financial assets of investment funds ... 197
3. Financial assets of insurance corporations and autonomous pension funds ... 199
4. Portfolio composition by type of investor ... 201

United Kingdom

1. Financial assets of institutional investors, 2012 202
2. Financial assets of investment funds 203
3. Financial assets of insurance corporations and autonomous pension funds ... 205
4. Portfolio composition by type of investor 207

United States

1. Financial assets of institutional investors, 2013 208
2. Financial assets of investment funds 209
3. Financial assets of insurance corporations and autonomous pension funds ... 211
4. Portfolio composition by type of investor 213

Russian Federation

1. Financial assets of institutional investors, 2013 214
2. Financial assets of investment funds 215
3. Financial assets of insurance corporations and autonomous pension funds ... 217
4. Portfolio composition by type of investor 219

Conventional signs and abbreviations

Signs and abbreviations

.. Not available

. Decimal point

0 Nil or negligible

Concepts and definitions

Metadata (data):

http://stats.oecd.org/OECDStat_Metadata/ShowMetadata.ashx?Dataset=7IA_A_Q

Metadata (indicators):

http://stats.oecd.org/OECDStat_Metadata/ShowMetadata.ashx?Dataset=7II_INDIC

On-line database

OECD Institutional Investors Statistics (*http://dx.doi.org/10.1787/instinv-data-en*).

System of National Accounts

Commission of the European Communities, International Monetary Fund, Organisation for Economic Co-operation and Development, United Nations, World Bank, Brussels/Luxembourg, New York, Paris, Washington, DC., 1993, *System of National Accounts 1993*, *http://unstats.un.org/unsd/nationalaccount/docs/1993sna.pdf.*

European Commission, International Monetary Fund, Organisation for Economic Co-operation and Development, United Nations, World Bank, New York, 2009, *System of National Accounts 2008*, *http://unstats.un.org/unsd/nationalaccount/docs/SNA2008.pdf.*

ISO currency abbreviations

Abbreviation	Country	Currency
AUD	Australia	dollar
EUR	Austria	euro
EUR	Belgium	euro
CAD	Canada	dollar
CLP	Chile	peso
CZK	Czech Republic	koruna
DKK	Denmark	krone
EUR	Estonia	euro
EUR	Finland	euro
EUR	France	euro
EUR	Germany	euro
EUR	Greece	euro
HUF	Hungary	forint
ISK	Iceland	krona
EUR	Ireland	euro
ILS	Israel	new shekel
EUR	Italy	euro
JPY	Japan	yen
KRW	Korea	won
EUR	Luxembourg	euro
MXN	Mexico	peso
EUR	Netherlands	euro
NOK	Norway	krone
PLN	Poland	zloty
EUR	Portugal	euro
EUR	Slovak Republic	euro
EUR	Slovenia	euro
EUR	Spain	euro
SEK	Sweden	krona
CHF	Switzerland	franc
TRY	Turkey	new lira
GBP	United Kingdom	pound
USD	United States	dollar
RUB	Russian Federation	ruble

OECD Institutional Investor Statistics 2014

International comparisons

Table 1. Financial assets of open-end investment funds, as a percentage of GDP

Per cent

	2006	2007	2008	2009	2010	2011	2012	2013
Australia	38.0	35.2	21.3	25.6	22.4	16.1	16.8	..
Austria	63.4	58.2	44.8	49.5	50.7	44.1	46.0	..
Belgium	37.9	36.0	25.4	27.8	26.3	22.0	22.5	..
Canada	52.7	55.0	43.4	54.7	58.0	56.9	62.3	72.0
Chile	11.7	13.5	12.1	18.2	16.3	14.1	13.9	15.0
Czech Republic	..	..	..	..	..	..	..	..
Denmark	55.0	58.7	43.0	50.5	71.5	77.8	89.8	100.5
Estonia	..	..	..	..	3.3	2.2	2.2	2.3
Finland	35.8	36.3	21.8	30.4	33.7	28.8	34.6	..
France	..	..	67.3	76.9	74.0	64.3	66.8	66.1
Germany	44.4	43.2	37.2	43.6	45.7	43.4	48.7	..
Greece	10.7	9.1	3.5	3.5	2.8	1.9	2.3	2.5
Hungary	9.1	11.5	7.2	10.4	12.9	10.2	10.6	14.1
Iceland	37.8	50.7	13.7	12.3	17.5	17.9	18.5	19.1
Ireland	393.4	406.7	357.1	458.4	610.7	649.5	762.2	832.3
Israel[1]	16.4	16.6	12.8	16.4	18.0	15.4	17.2	..
Italy	19.4	15.3	12.4	13.0	11.5	8.9	8.7	..
Japan	..	..	..	..	..	..	..	..
Korea	..	..	..	..	..	..	..	..
Luxembourg	5 706.7	6 021.3	4 622.3	5 546.8	6 052.1	5 513.1	6 012.6	6 407.2
Mexico	6.7	7.5	6.4	7.9	9.3	..	..	..
Netherlands	..	..	..	..	..	..	..	..
Norway	17.7	19.9	12.5	19.0	21.4	19.3	21.0	24.0
Poland	9.0	11.2	5.5	6.3	7.5	5.6	6.5	7.9
Portugal	17.4	14.6	7.8	9.7	7.8	6.2	7.2	7.2
Slovak Republic	6.4	6.9	4.4	5.4	5.7	4.6	..	..
Slovenia	6.1	8.3	4.0	5.1	5.7	4.9	5.1	5.1
Spain	30.0	26.8	18.3	18.5	16.0	14.6	14.2	17.8
Sweden	47.0	47.3	32.5	46.5	50.9	44.9	51.4	62.7
Switzerland	69.4	72.5	53.9	66.2	69.7	70.8	78.4	86.3
Turkey	3.0	3.2	2.5	3.1	2.8	2.1	2.1	..
United Kingdom	32	34	29	35	42	39	44	..
United States	70.6	79.2	65.7	76.0	77.6	74.5	82.3	94.8
Russian Federation	0.6	0.6	0.2	0.2	0.3	0.2	0.2	0.2

Note: Detailed metadata at: http://metalinks.oecd.org/instinv/20141203/f18e

Information on data for Luxembourg: http://metalinks.oecd.org/instinv/20141203/2954

1. Information on data for Israel: http://oe.cd/israel-disclaimer.

Table 2. Financial assets of insurance corporations, as a percentage of GDP

Per cent

	2006	2007	2008	2009	2010	2011	2012	2013
Australia	34.9	34.1	27.8	29.1	27.8	26.3	28.2	..
Austria	32.4	31.1	31.0	34.1	34.3	32.5	32.8	..
Belgium	63.1	63.7	60.7	67.4	67.9	67.3	73.1	..
Canada	36.3	35.4	31.6	36.6	37.6	38.2	39.3	39.6
Chile	15.9	16.3	18.0	18.0	17.0	16.9	17.5	17.8
Czech Republic	9.7	9.8	10.0	11.0	11.8	11.2	11.9	..
Denmark	68.8	69.0	69.8	79.1	83.3	90.2	98.2	100.1
Estonia	..	..	..	..	7.2	6.0	5.7	5.4
Finland	26.8	24.8	21.7	25.7	27.1	24.3	27.9	..
France	83.5	85.6	79.7	90.8	94.8	91.1	99.3	103.2
Germany	58.7	56.9	54.0	57.6	57.7	56.2	60.8	..
Greece	5.4	5.7	5.4	5.8	6.2	6.4	7.2	8.2
Hungary	8.3	9.0	8.0	9.0	9.0	8.4	8.6	8.4
Iceland	14.1	11.5	7.8	8.1	8.4	8.5	8.6	8.7
Ireland	..	..	..	..	..	..	..	..
Israel[1]	28.7	29.5	27.2	31.9	33.4	32.7	34.2	..
Italy	35.2	31.5	29.6	34.2	32.4	31.1	33.7	..
Japan	76.5	73.2	71.2	77.3	78.3	82.4	87.9	..
Korea	36.1	37.9	38.5	42.2	43.1	45.3	..	..
Luxembourg	224.5	228.4	216.8	280.4	307.4	288.1	305.8	325.8
Mexico	2.8	3.1	3.3	3.8	3.9	4.1	4.3	4.6
Netherlands	58.5	57.4	53.8	57.5	61.4	64.5	68.6	66.1
Norway	35.9	37.1	34.2	38.6	39.4	38.6	39.8	42.8
Poland	10.0	10.6	10.6	10.0	9.9	9.2	9.9	9.9
Portugal	30.2	31.2	31.7	36.1	36.6	33.8	34.9	34.8
Slovak Republic	7.5	8.5	7.5	8.5	8.9	8.5	..	..
Slovenia	11.6	13.1	11.8	13.7	14.8	14.4	17.3	18.1
Spain	22.2	20.8	20.7	22.2	22.0	23.0	24.4	26.4
Sweden	81.1	79.4	71.7	83.2	83.8	80.1	85.6	89.8
Switzerland	81.1	82.5	73.1	80.7	80.7	82.8	86.9	86.6
Turkey	1.3	1.5	1.5	1.7	1.4	1.3	1.5	..
United Kingdom	94	95	83	91	88	85	89	..
United States	43.5	43.8	39.5	43.0	43.6	43.3	43.7	44.8
Russian Federation	2.3	2.1	1.9	2.2	1.9	1.7	1.7	1.8

Note: Detailed metadata at: http://metalinks.oecd.org/instinv/20141203/5fdb

Information on data for Luxembourg: http://metalinks.oecd.org/instinv/20141203/0bb5

1. Information on data for Israel: http://oe.cd/israel-disclaimer.

Table 3. Financial assets of autonomous pension funds, as a percentage of GDP

Per cent

	2006	2007	2008	2009	2010	2011	2012	2013
Australia	86.4	97.4	74.6	87.1	85.9	81.8	92.3	..
Austria	4.6	4.6	4.0	4.8	5.1	4.8	5.2	..
Belgium	3.8	3.9	2.9	3.6	3.8	3.5	3.5	..
Canada	61.8	60.8	50.2	58.3	62.7	61.8	65.4	70.1
Chile	57.5	61.0	49.8	62.0	62.6	58.0	59.8	62.2
Czech Republic	3.9	4.3	4.6	5.3	5.7	6.0	6.6	..
Denmark	48.5	48.4	55.4	63.5	71.5	75.4	75.5	69.2
Estonia	..	..	..	..	7.9	7.4	8.9	10.0
Finland	3.0	3.0	2.3	2.8	2.2	2.9	1.7	..
France	..	..	..	..	..	..	..	..
Germany	11.0	11.6	11.7	13.3	13.7	14.0	14.6	..
Greece	..	..	..	..	..	..	..	..
Hungary	9.7	10.9	9.8	13.6	15.1	4.0	4.1	4.1
Iceland	124.2	122.7	102.6	111.1	117.0	123.0	134.5	141.7
Ireland	..	..	..	..	..	..	..	..
Israel[1]	29.7	27.0	30.1	34.6	35.7	35.0	37.2	..
Italy	1.2	1.4	1.3	1.6	1.9	1.9	2.1	..
Japan	25.4	23.8	22.6	24.7	23.7	24.4	26.3	..
Korea	3.7	3.7	3.4	3.8	4.0	3.9	..	..
Luxembourg	1.1	1.1	1.0	2.3	2.3	2.3	2.5	2.7
Mexico	7.0	7.6	7.6	9.5	10.4	..	14.1	14.8
Netherlands	120.5	115.2	95.3	110.5	119.2	125.7	146.7	149.3
Norway	6.9	7.2	6.2	7.7	8.0	7.5	7.8	8.2
Poland	11.0	11.9	10.9	13.4	15.6	14.7	17.0	18.2
Portugal	11.9	12.2	10.9	12.0	10.4	8.4	8.1	8.3
Slovak Republic	1.7	1.3	4.7	6.2	7.7	8.2	..	..
Slovenia	3.8	4.0	3.8	4.8	5.5	6.0	5.7	5.8
Spain	9.9	9.8	8.7	9.7	9.8	9.8	10.4	11.1
Sweden	13.6	14.2	10.7	15.0	15.2	15.0	17.4	20.8
Switzerland	98.1	94.0	80.3	91.0	92.5	91.6	97.2	103.2
Turkey	0.5	0.6	0.6	0.7	0.7	0.7	0.7	..
United Kingdom	77	74	62	74	81	87	95	..
United States	87.9	88.6	82.2	91.3	97.2	96.1	97.3	100.7
Russian Federation	1.9	1.8	1.4	1.9	1.9	2.1	2.5	3.3

Note: Detailed metadata at: http://metalinks.oecd.org/instinv/20141203/2abf

1. Information on data for Israel: http://oe.cd/israel-disclaimer.

OECD Institutional Investors Statistics 2014

Country tables

Table 1. Financial assets of institutional investors, 2012

Million AUD

		Total	Investment funds			
			Open-end companies (mutual funds)			Closed-end companies
			Total	Money market funds	Other mutual funds	Total
2	Financial assets	270 283	256 066	31 604	224 462	69 826
2.1	Currency and deposits	20 466	18 003	9 253	8 750	2 463
2.2	Securities other than shares, except financial derivatives	84 498	85 061	19 233	65 828	2 672
2.2.1	Short-term securities	30 054	29 928	17 831	12 097	374
2.2.2	Long-term securities	54 444	55 133	1 402	53 731	2 298
2.2.3	Securities issued by residents	66 641	67 345	19 233	48 112	2 531
2.2.4	Securities issued by non-residents	17 857	17 716	0	17 716	141
2.3	Loans	22 765	3 532	3	3 529	19 331
2.3.1	Short-term loans	0	0	0	0	0
2.3.2	Long-term loans	22 765	3 532	3	3 529	19 331
2.3.3	Loans granted to residents	19 063	2 670	3	2 667	16 491
2.3.4	Loans granted to non-residents	3 702	862	0	862	2 840
2.4	Shares and other equity	139 567	147 720	3 072	144 648	44 123
2.4.1	Shares issued by residents	113 850	129 415	3 072	126 343	36 711
2.4.2	Shares issued by non-residents	25 717	18 305	0	18 305	7 412
2.5	Other, not elsewhere classified	2 987	1 750	43	1 707	1 237

		Total	Insurance corporations and autonomous pension funds			
			Insurance corporations			Autonomous pension funds
			Total	Life insurance corporations	Non-life insurance corporations	Total
2	Financial assets	1 644 720	428 861	249 347	179 514	1 403 716
2.1	Currency and deposits	240 937	29 719	12 949	16 770	211 218
2.2	Securities other than shares, except financial derivatives	292 869	115 334	42 198	73 136	177 628
2.2.1	Short-term securities	76 886	23 496	8 365	15 131	53 390
2.2.2	Long-term securities	215 983	91 838	33 833	58 005	124 238
2.2.3	Securities issued by residents	225 556	101 451	34 949	66 502	124 198
2.2.4	Securities issued by non-residents	67 313	13 883	7 249	6 634	53 430
2.3	Loans	19 437	9 252	2 537	6 715	10 185
2.3.1	Short-term loans	4	4	0	4	0
2.3.2	Long-term loans	19 433	9 248	2 537	6 711	10 185
2.3.3	Loans granted to residents	18 028	7 862	2 283	5 579	10 166
2.3.4	Loans granted to non-residents	1 409	1 390	254	1 136	19
2.4	Shares and other equity	1 045 939	239 390	187 028	52 362	818 940
2.4.1	Shares issued by residents	794 826	214 254	177 628	36 626	592 963
2.4.2	Shares issued by non-residents	251 113	25 136	9 400	15 736	225 977
2.5	Other, not elsewhere classified	45 538	35 166	4 635	30 531	185 745

Note: Detailed metadata at: http://metalinks.oecd.org/instinv/20141203/9e9f

AUSTRALIA

Table 2. Financial assets of investment funds

Million AUD

		2006	2007	2008	2009	2010	2011	2012	2013
	Investment funds								
2	Financial assets	376 984	414 974	303 297	341 053	323 531	264 121	270 283	..
2.1	Currency and deposits	18 321	19 635	23 681	17 633	22 072	19 014	20 466	..
2.2	Securities other than shares, except financial derivatives	112 159	128 200	109 980	95 322	84 991	87 409	84 498	..
2.2.1	Short-term securities	60 264	74 702	54 899	43 552	34 993	34 697	30 054	..
2.2.2	Long-term securities	51 895	53 498	55 081	51 770	49 998	52 712	54 444	..
2.2.3	Securities issued by residents	97 668	113 991	94 937	80 623	69 849	72 345	66 641	..
2.2.4	Securities issued by non-residents	14 491	14 209	15 043	14 699	15 142	15 064	17 857	..
2.3	Loans	29 442	35 507	35 177	30 195	29 425	24 462	22 765	..
2.3.1	Short-term loans	0	0	0	0	0	0	0	..
2.3.2	Long-term loans	29 442	35 507	35 177	30 195	29 425	24 462	22 765	..
2.3.3	Loans granted to residents	25 659	30 083	28 821	25 752	25 662	20 594	19 063	..
2.3.4	Loans granted to non-residents	3 783	5 424	6 356	4 443	3 763	3 868	3 702	..
2.4	Shares and other equity	214 449	228 589	131 001	194 246	183 231	130 260	139 567	..
2.4.1	Shares issued by residents	181 286	184 125	102 182	154 276	147 949	104 209	113 850	..
2.4.2	Shares issued by non-residents	33 163	44 464	28 819	39 970	35 282	26 051	25 717	..
2.5	Other, not elsewhere classified	2 613	3 043	3 458	3 657	3 812	2 976	2 987	..
	Open-end companies (mutual funds)								
2	Financial assets	413 104	415 183	268 489	331 351	315 512	239 270	256 066	..
2.1	Currency and deposits	16 690	17 645	20 666	13 678	18 668	17 053	18 003	..
2.2	Securities other than shares, except financial derivatives	114 500	128 578	109 335	94 704	84 425	87 927	85 061	..
2.2.1	Short-term securities	62 326	75 664	55 328	43 350	34 823	35 491	29 928	..
2.2.2	Long-term securities	52 174	52 914	54 007	51 354	49 602	52 436	55 133	..
2.2.3	Securities issued by residents	100 480	114 997	95 216	80 650	69 657	73 187	67 345	..
2.2.4	Securities issued by non-residents	14 020	13 581	14 119	14 054	14 768	14 740	17 716	..
2.3	Loans	10 826	11 669	9 905	8 251	6 445	5 335	3 532	..
2.3.1	Short-term loans	0	0	0	0	0	0	0	..
2.3.2	Long-term loans	10 826	11 669	9 905	8 251	6 445	5 335	3 532	..
2.3.3	Loans granted to residents	9 267	9 877	8 280	7 035	5 222	4 168	2 670	..
2.3.4	Loans granted to non-residents	1 559	1 792	1 625	1 216	1 223	1 167	862	..
2.4	Shares and other equity	269 758	255 982	126 851	212 326	203 908	127 265	147 720	..
2.4.1	Shares issued by residents	255 863	236 668	121 596	186 009	180 297	112 063	129 415	..
2.4.2	Shares issued by non-residents	13 895	19 314	5 255	26 317	23 611	15 202	18 305	..
2.5	Other, not elsewhere classified	1 330	1 309	1 732	2 392	2 066	1 690	1 750	..
	Money market funds								
2	Financial assets	50 310	57 346	54 053	40 799	32 281	29 954	31 604	..
2.1	Currency and deposits	7 303	7 749	10 812	5 410	7 292	6 388	9 253	..
2.2	Securities other than shares, except financial derivatives	39 660	46 225	40 087	32 423	22 492	21 027	19 233	..
2.2.1	Short-term securities	36 829	43 155	37 365	30 034	21 268	19 742	17 831	..
2.2.2	Long-term securities	2 831	3 070	2 722	2 389	1 224	1 285	1 402	..
2.2.3	Securities issued by residents	39 660	46 225	40 087	32 423	22 492	21 027	19 233	..
2.2.4	Securities issued by non-residents	0	0	0	0	0	0	0	..
2.3	Loans	5	7	9	476	0	3	3	..
2.3.1	Short-term loans	0	0	0	0	0	0	0	..
2.3.2	Long-term loans	5	7	9	476	0	3	3	..
2.3.3	Loans granted to residents	5	7	9	476	0	3	3	..
2.3.4	Loans granted to non-residents	0	0	0	0	0	0	0	..
2.4	Shares and other equity	3 239	3 269	3 054	2 437	2 433	2 485	3 072	..
2.4.1	Shares issued by residents	3 239	3 269	3 054	2 437	2 433	2 485	3 072	..
2.4.2	Shares issued by non-residents	0	0	0	0	0	0	0	..
2.5	Other, not elsewhere classified	103	96	91	53	64	51	43	..
	Other mutual funds								
2	Financial assets	362 794	357 837	214 436	290 552	283 231	209 316	224 462	..
2.1	Currency and deposits	9 387	9 896	9 854	8 268	11 376	10 665	8 750	..
2.2	Securities other than shares, except financial derivatives	74 840	82 353	69 248	62 281	61 933	66 900	65 828	..
2.2.1	Short-term securities	25 497	32 509	17 963	13 316	13 555	15 749	12 097	..
2.2.2	Long-term securities	49 343	49 844	51 285	48 965	48 378	51 151	53 731	..
2.2.3	Securities issued by residents	60 820	68 772	55 129	48 227	47 165	52 160	48 112	..
2.2.4	Securities issued by non-residents	14 020	13 581	14 119	14 054	14 768	14 740	17 716	..
2.3	Loans	10 821	11 662	9 896	7 775	6 445	5 332	3 529	..
2.3.1	Short-term loans	0	0	0	0	0	0	0	..
2.3.2	Long-term loans	10 821	11 662	9 896	7 775	6 445	5 332	3 529	..
2.3.3	Loans granted to residents	9 262	9 870	8 271	6 559	5 222	4 165	2 667	..
2.3.4	Loans granted to non-residents	1 559	1 792	1 625	1 216	1 223	1 167	862	..
2.4	Shares and other equity	266 519	252 713	123 797	209 889	201 475	124 780	144 648	..
2.4.1	Shares issued by residents	252 624	233 399	118 542	183 572	177 864	109 578	126 343	..
2.4.2	Shares issued by non-residents	13 895	19 314	5 255	26 317	23 611	15 202	18 305	..
2.5	Other, not elsewhere classified	1 227	1 213	1 641	2 339	2 002	1 639	1 707	..

Table 2. Financial assets of investment funds *(cont.)*

Million AUD

		2006	2007	2008	2009	2010	2011	2012	2013
	Closed-end companies								
2	Financial assets	86 371	111 133	96 178	88 093	86 295	77 542	69 826	..
2.1	Currency and deposits	1 631	1 990	3 015	3 955	3 404	1 961	2 463	..
2.2	Securities other than shares, except financial derivatives	2 937	3 752	3 756	2 959	3 158	2 571	2 672	..
2.2.1	Short-term securities	493	476	665	574	720	84	374	..
2.2.2	Long-term securities	2 444	3 276	3 091	2 385	2 438	2 487	2 298	..
2.2.3	Securities issued by residents	2 466	3 124	2 832	2 314	2 784	2 247	2 531	..
2.2.4	Securities issued by non-residents	471	628	924	645	374	324	141	..
2.3	Loans	20 115	25 603	26 078	22 597	23 129	19 348	19 331	..
2.3.1	Short-term loans	0	0	0	0	0	0	0	..
2.3.2	Long-term loans	20 115	25 603	26 078	22 597	23 129	19 348	19 331	..
2.3.3	Loans granted to residents	17 891	21 971	21 347	19 370	20 589	16 647	16 491	..
2.3.4	Loans granted to non-residents	2 224	3 632	4 731	3 227	2 540	2 701	2 840	..
2.4	Shares and other equity	60 405	78 054	61 603	57 317	54 858	52 376	44 123	..
2.4.1	Shares issued by residents	41 137	52 904	38 039	43 664	43 187	41 527	36 711	..
2.4.2	Shares issued by non-residents	19 268	25 150	23 564	13 653	11 671	10 849	7 412	..
2.5	Other, not elsewhere classified	1 283	1 734	1 726	1 265	1 746	1 286	1 237	..

Note: Detailed metadata at: http://metalinks.oecd.org/instinv/20141203/9e9f

AUSTRALIA

Table 3. Financial assets of insurance corporations and autonomous pension funds

Million AUD

		2006	2007	2008	2009	2010	2011	2012	2013
	Insurance corporations and autonomous pension funds								
2	Financial assets	1 127 379	1 351 049	1 130 406	1 324 271	1 416 705	1 432 038	1 644 720	..
2.1	Currency and deposits	89 594	124 879	150 045	165 306	173 590	205 348	240 937	..
2.2	Securities other than shares, except financial derivatives	201 549	218 315	225 011	248 948	241 315	253 781	292 869	..
2.2.1	Short-term securities	59 665	65 655	58 494	72 446	58 924	63 637	76 886	..
2.2.2	Long-term securities	141 884	152 660	166 517	176 502	182 391	190 144	215 983	..
2.2.3	Securities issued by residents	157 972	167 831	173 562	194 017	186 983	196 936	225 556	..
2.2.4	Securities issued by non-residents	43 577	50 484	51 449	54 931	54 332	56 845	67 313	..
2.3	Loans	15 141	17 732	18 718	16 586	17 583	18 168	19 437	..
2.3.1	Short-term loans	212	431	443	0	0	4	4	..
2.3.2	Long-term loans	14 929	17 301	18 275	16 586	17 583	18 164	19 433	..
2.3.3	Loans granted to residents	12 584	15 703	16 322	14 958	15 799	16 337	18 028	..
2.3.4	Loans granted to non-residents	2 557	2 029	2 396	1 628	1 784	1 831	1 409	..
2.4	Shares and other equity	800 322	965 259	707 004	867 998	949 295	913 326	1 045 939	..
2.4.1	Shares issued by residents	629 213	757 191	534 329	685 906	746 887	694 717	794 826	..
2.4.2	Shares issued by non-residents	171 109	208 068	172 675	182 092	202 408	218 609	251 113	..
2.5	Other, not elsewhere classified	20 773	24 864	29 628	25 433	34 922	41 415	45 538	..
	Insurance corporations								
2	Financial assets	379 608	401 587	349 319	377 827	390 755	390 852	428 861	..
2.1	Currency and deposits	14 690	15 157	21 781	23 007	21 337	24 964	29 719	..
2.2	Securities other than shares, except financial derivatives	83 742	80 997	96 095	96 549	94 569	102 801	115 334	..
2.2.1	Short-term securities	25 883	24 735	21 790	23 869	22 797	25 199	23 496	..
2.2.2	Long-term securities	57 859	56 262	74 305	72 680	71 772	77 602	91 838	..
2.2.3	Securities issued by residents	75 969	73 169	88 338	88 200	86 786	93 374	101 451	..
2.2.4	Securities issued by non-residents	7 773	7 828	7 757	8 349	7 783	9 427	13 883	..
2.3	Loans	9 319	11 116	11 496	8 911	8 977	9 024	9 252	..
2.3.1	Short-term loans	212	431	443	0	0	4	4	..
2.3.2	Long-term loans	9 107	10 685	11 053	8 911	8 977	9 020	9 248	..
2.3.3	Loans granted to residents	6 782	9 102	9 129	7 296	7 218	7 210	7 862	..
2.3.4	Loans granted to non-residents	2 537	2 014	2 367	1 615	1 759	1 814	1 390	..
2.4	Shares and other equity	258 874	279 837	200 118	234 592	240 752	222 211	239 390	..
2.4.1	Shares issued by residents	240 862	260 927	182 455	215 093	221 030	200 051	214 254	..
2.4.2	Shares issued by non-residents	18 012	18 910	17 663	19 499	19 722	22 160	25 136	..
2.5	Other, not elsewhere classified	12 983	14 480	19 829	14 768	25 120	31 852	35 166	..
	Life insurance corporations								
2	Financial assets	250 528	260 360	209 126	234 617	240 051	233 050	249 347	..
2.1	Currency and deposits	5 528	5 398	8 622	9 296	7 850	10 067	12 949	..
2.2	Securities other than shares, except financial derivatives	39 238	35 940	37 606	35 655	36 123	38 704	42 198	..
2.2.1	Short-term securities	12 960	12 363	9 770	10 169	9 049	9 451	8 365	..
2.2.2	Long-term securities	26 278	23 577	27 836	25 486	27 074	29 253	33 833	..
2.2.3	Securities issued by residents	35 777	32 449	35 182	32 655	33 469	34 381	34 949	..
2.2.4	Securities issued by non-residents	3 461	3 491	2 424	3 000	2 654	4 323	7 249	..
2.3	Loans	4 266	4 655	4 951	3 821	3 561	2 983	2 537	..
2.3.1	Short-term loans	0	0	0	0	0	0	0	..
2.3.2	Long-term loans	4 266	4 655	4 951	3 821	3 561	2 983	2 537	..
2.3.3	Loans granted to residents	3 705	4 411	4 542	3 421	3 000	2 346	2 283	..
2.3.4	Loans granted to non-residents	561	244	409	400	561	637	254	..
2.4	Shares and other equity	199 201	211 383	154 254	182 439	188 630	176 795	187 028	..
2.4.1	Shares issued by residents	191 347	203 362	147 392	175 176	181 793	168 815	177 628	..
2.4.2	Shares issued by non-residents	7 854	8 021	6 862	7 263	6 837	7 980	9 400	..
2.5	Other, not elsewhere classified	2 295	2 984	3 693	3 406	3 887	4 501	4 635	..
	Non-life insurance corporations								
2	Financial assets	129 080	141 227	140 193	143 210	150 704	157 802	179 514	..
2.1	Currency and deposits	9 162	9 759	13 159	13 711	13 487	14 897	16 770	..
2.2	Securities other than shares, except financial derivatives	44 504	45 057	58 489	60 894	58 446	64 097	73 136	..
2.2.1	Short-term securities	12 923	12 372	12 020	13 700	13 748	15 748	15 131	..
2.2.2	Long-term securities	31 581	32 685	46 469	47 194	44 698	48 349	58 005	..
2.2.3	Securities issued by residents	40 192	40 720	53 156	55 545	53 317	58 993	66 502	..
2.2.4	Securities issued by non-residents	4 312	4 337	5 333	5 349	5 129	5 104	6 634	..
2.3	Loans	5 053	6 461	6 545	5 090	5 416	6 041	6 715	..
2.3.1	Short-term loans	212	431	443	0	0	4	4	..
2.3.2	Long-term loans	4 841	6 030	6 102	5 090	5 416	6 037	6 711	..
2.3.3	Loans granted to residents	3 077	4 691	4 587	3 875	4 218	4 864	5 579	..
2.3.4	Loans granted to non-residents	1 976	1 770	1 958	1 215	1 198	1 177	1 136	..
2.4	Shares and other equity	59 673	68 454	45 864	52 153	52 122	45 416	52 362	..
2.4.1	Shares issued by residents	49 515	57 565	35 063	39 917	39 237	31 236	36 626	..
2.4.2	Shares issued by non-residents	10 158	10 889	10 801	12 236	12 885	14 180	15 736	..
2.5	Other, not elsewhere classified	10 688	11 496	16 136	11 362	21 233	27 351	30 531	..

Table 3. Financial assets of insurance corporations and autonomous pension funds *(cont.)*

Million AUD

		2006	2007	2008	2009	2010	2011	2012	2013
	Autonomous pension funds								
2	Financial assets	939 951	1 148 584	939 214	1 129 550	1 208 460	1 215 106	1 403 716	..
2.1	Currency and deposits	74 904	109 722	128 264	142 299	152 253	180 384	211 218	..
2.2	Securities other than shares, except financial derivatives	118 168	137 649	129 033	152 452	146 777	151 045	177 628	..
2.2.1	Short-term securities	33 782	40 920	36 704	48 577	36 127	38 438	53 390	..
2.2.2	Long-term securities	84 386	96 729	92 329	103 875	110 650	112 607	124 238	..
2.2.3	Securities issued by residents	82 364	94 993	85 341	105 870	100 228	103 627	124 198	..
2.2.4	Securities issued by non-residents	35 804	42 656	43 692	46 582	46 549	47 418	53 430	..
2.3	Loans	5 832	6 627	7 234	7 675	8 606	9 144	10 185	..
2.3.1	Short-term loans	0	0	0	0	0	0	0	..
2.3.2	Long-term loans	5 832	6 627	7 234	7 675	8 606	9 144	10 185	..
2.3.3	Loans granted to residents	5 812	6 612	7 205	7 662	8 581	9 127	10 166	..
2.3.4	Loans granted to non-residents	20	15	29	13	25	17	19	..
2.4	Shares and other equity	561 618	700 562	521 103	649 994	720 207	703 075	818 940	..
2.4.1	Shares issued by residents	408 521	511 404	366 091	487 401	537 521	506 626	592 963	..
2.4.2	Shares issued by non-residents	153 097	189 158	155 012	162 593	182 686	196 449	225 977	..
2.5	Other, not elsewhere classified	179 429	194 024	153 580	177 130	180 617	171 458	185 745	..

Note: Detailed metadata at: http://metalinks.oecd.org/instinv/20141203/9e9f

Table 4. Portfolio composition by type of investor

Percentage of total financial assets

Per cent

		2006	2007	2008	2009	2010	2011	2012	2013
	Investment funds								
2	Financial assets	100.0	100.0	100.0	100.0	100.0	100.0	100.0	..
2.1	Currency and deposits	4.9	4.7	7.8	5.2	6.8	7.2	7.6	..
2.2	Securities other than shares, except financial derivatives	29.8	30.9	36.3	27.9	26.3	33.1	31.3	..
2.2.1	Short-term securities	16.0	18.0	18.1	12.8	10.8	13.1	11.1	..
2.2.2	Long-term securities	13.8	12.9	18.2	15.2	15.5	20.0	20.1	..
2.2.3	Securities issued by residents	25.9	27.5	31.3	23.6	21.6	27.4	24.7	..
2.2.4	Securities issued by non-residents	3.8	3.4	5.0	4.3	4.7	5.7	6.6	..
2.3	Loans	7.8	8.6	11.6	8.9	9.1	9.3	8.4	..
2.3.1	Short-term loans	0.0	0.0	0.0	0.0	0.0	0.0	0.0	..
2.3.2	Long-term loans	7.8	8.6	11.6	8.9	9.1	9.3	8.4	..
2.3.3	Loans granted to residents	6.8	7.2	9.5	7.6	7.9	7.8	7.1	..
2.3.4	Loans granted to non-residents	1.0	1.3	2.1	1.3	1.2	1.5	1.4	..
2.4	Shares and other equity	56.9	55.1	43.2	57.0	56.6	49.3	51.6	..
2.4.1	Shares issued by residents	48.1	44.4	33.7	45.2	45.7	39.5	42.1	..
2.4.2	Shares issued by non-residents	8.8	10.7	9.5	11.7	10.9	9.9	9.5	..
2.5	Other, not elsewhere classified	0.7	0.7	1.1	1.1	1.2	1.1	1.1	..
	Insurance corporations								
2	Financial assets	100.0	100.0	100.0	100.0	100.0	100.0	100.0	..
2.1	Currency and deposits	3.9	3.8	6.2	6.1	5.5	6.4	6.9	..
2.2	Securities other than shares, except financial derivatives	22.1	20.2	27.5	25.6	24.2	26.3	26.9	..
2.2.1	Short-term securities	6.8	6.2	6.2	6.3	5.8	6.4	5.5	..
2.2.2	Long-term securities	15.2	14.0	21.3	19.2	18.4	19.9	21.4	..
2.2.3	Securities issued by residents	20.0	18.2	25.3	23.3	22.2	23.9	23.7	..
2.2.4	Securities issued by non-residents	2.0	1.9	2.2	2.2	2.0	2.4	3.2	..
2.3	Loans	2.5	2.8	3.3	2.4	2.3	2.3	2.2	..
2.3.1	Short-term loans	0.1	0.1	0.1	0.0	0.0	0.0	0.0	..
2.3.2	Long-term loans	2.4	2.7	3.2	2.4	2.3	2.3	2.2	..
2.3.3	Loans granted to residents	1.8	2.3	2.6	1.9	1.8	1.8	1.8	..
2.3.4	Loans granted to non-residents	0.7	0.5	0.7	0.4	0.5	0.5	0.3	..
2.4	Shares and other equity	68.2	69.7	57.3	62.1	61.6	56.9	55.8	..
2.4.1	Shares issued by residents	63.5	65.0	52.2	56.9	56.6	51.2	50.0	..
2.4.2	Shares issued by non-residents	4.7	4.7	5.1	5.2	5.0	5.7	5.9	..
2.5	Other, not elsewhere classified	3.4	3.6	5.7	3.9	6.4	8.1	8.2	..
	Autonomous pension funds								
2	Financial assets	100.0	100.0	100.0	100.0	100.0	100.0	100.0	..
2.1	Currency and deposits	8.0	9.6	13.7	12.6	12.6	14.8	15.0	..
2.2	Securities other than shares, except financial derivatives	12.6	12.0	13.7	13.5	12.1	12.4	12.7	..
2.2.1	Short-term securities	3.6	3.6	3.9	4.3	3.0	3.2	3.8	..
2.2.2	Long-term securities	9.0	8.4	9.8	9.2	9.2	9.3	8.9	..
2.2.3	Securities issued by residents	8.8	8.3	9.1	9.4	8.3	8.5	8.8	..
2.2.4	Securities issued by non-residents	3.8	3.7	4.7	4.1	3.9	3.9	3.8	..
2.3	Loans	0.6	0.6	0.8	0.7	0.7	0.8	0.7	..
2.3.1	Short-term loans	0.0	0.0	0.0	0.0	0.0	0.0	0.0	..
2.3.2	Long-term loans	0.6	0.6	0.8	0.7	0.7	0.8	0.7	..
2.3.3	Loans granted to residents	0.6	0.6	0.8	0.7	0.7	0.8	0.7	..
2.3.4	Loans granted to non-residents	0.0	0.0	0.0	0.0	0.0	0.0	0.0	..
2.4	Shares and other equity	59.7	61.0	55.5	57.5	59.6	57.9	58.3	..
2.4.1	Shares issued by residents	43.5	44.5	39.0	43.2	44.5	41.7	42.2	..
2.4.2	Shares issued by non-residents	16.3	16.5	16.5	14.4	15.1	16.2	16.1	..
2.5	Other, not elsewhere classified	19.1	16.9	16.4	15.7	14.9	14.1	13.2	..

Note: Detailed metadata at: http://metalinks.oecd.org/instinv/20141203/f729

AUSTRIA

Table 1. Financial assets of institutional investors, 2012

Million EUR (1999 ATS euro)

			Investment funds			
		Total	Open-end companies (mutual funds)			Closed-end companies
			Total	Money market funds	Other mutual funds	Total
2	Financial assets	125 008	145 932	400	145 532	..
2.1	Currency and deposits	8 083	8 083	0	8 083	..
2.2	Securities other than shares, except financial derivatives	81 189	81 189	397	80 792	..
2.2.1	Short-term securities	689	689	6	683	..
2.2.2	Long-term securities	80 500	80 500	391	80 109	..
2.2.3	Securities issued by residents	17 527	17 527	76	17 451	..
2.2.4	Securities issued by non-residents	63 662	63 662	321	63 341	..
2.3	Loans	0	0	0	0	..
2.3.1	Short-term loans	0	0	0	0	..
2.3.2	Long-term loans	0	0	0	0	..
2.3.3	Loans granted to residents	0	0	0	0	..
2.3.4	Loans granted to non-residents	0	0	0	0	..
2.4	Shares and other equity	35 657	56 581	3	56 578	..
2.4.1	Shares issued by residents	3 697	24 621	3	24 618	..
2.4.2	Shares issued by non-residents	31 960	31 960	0	31 960	..
2.5	Other, not elsewhere classified	78	78	0	78	..

			Insurance corporations and autonomous pension funds			
		Total	Insurance corporations			Autonomous pension funds
			Total	Life insurance corporations	Non-life insurance corporations	Total
2	Financial assets	114 256	104 051	76 272	27 778	16 407
2.1	Currency and deposits	4 262	3 687	2 292	1 396	575
2.2	Securities other than shares, except financial derivatives	46 400	46 851	37 698	9 153	375
2.2.1	Short-term securities	10	4	4	1	6
2.2.2	Long-term securities	46 389	46 846	37 694	9 152	369
2.2.3	Securities issued by residents	18 812	19 414	15 621	3 793	224
2.2.4	Securities issued by non-residents	27 588	27 437	22 076	5 360	151
2.3	Loans	4 027	7 433	5 749	1 684	31
2.3.1	Short-term loans	247	2 829	2 188	641	0
2.3.2	Long-term loans	3 780	4 604	3 561	1 043	31
2.3.3	Loans granted to residents	2 379	5 785	4 475	1 311	31
2.3.4	Loans granted to non-residents	1 647	1 647	1 274	373	0
2.4	Shares and other equity	56 055	42 072	29 693	12 378	15 373
2.4.1	Shares issued by residents	46 546	34 297	24 206	10 091	13 639
2.4.2	Shares issued by non-residents	9 509	7 774	5 487	2 287	1 734
2.5	Other, not elsewhere classified	3 513	4 009	841	3 168	52

Note: Detailed metadata at: http://metalinks.oecd.org/instinv/20141203/842c

AUSTRIA

Table 2. Financial assets of investment funds

Million EUR (1999 ATS euro)

		2006	2007	2008	2009	2010	2011	2012	2013
	Investment funds								
2	Financial assets	141 515	137 307	110 172	119 288	125 916	115 841	125 008	..
2.1	Currency and deposits	6 279	8 923	13 932	10 276	10 042	9 410	8 083	..
2.2	Securities other than shares, except financial derivatives	91 183	84 426	72 993	78 291	77 731	75 377	81 189	..
2.2.1	Short-term securities	313	482	545	667	774	1 118	689	..
2.2.2	Long-term securities	90 871	83 944	72 448	77 625	76 957	74 259	80 500	..
2.2.3	Securities issued by residents	17 361	14 374	15 127	16 062	16 012	16 682	17 527	..
2.2.4	Securities issued by non-residents	73 823	70 053	57 866	62 230	61 719	58 695	63 662	..
2.3	Loans	0	0	0	0	0	0	0	..
2.3.1	Short-term loans	0	0	0	0	0	0	0	..
2.3.2	Long-term loans	0	0	0	0	0	0	0	..
2.3.3	Loans granted to residents	0	0	0	0	0	0	0	..
2.3.4	Loans granted to non-residents	0	0	0	0	0	0	0	..
2.4	Shares and other equity	44 011	43 868	23 122	30 721	38 055	30 965	35 657	..
2.4.1	Shares issued by residents	4 555	4 839	2 555	3 591	4 181	3 396	3 697	..
2.4.2	Shares issued by non-residents	39 456	39 029	20 567	27 129	33 874	27 569	31 960	..
2.5	Other, not elsewhere classified	42	89	125	0	89	89	78	..
	Open-end companies (mutual funds)								
2	Financial assets	169 065	164 219	130 866	141 721	149 230	136 192	145 932	..
2.1	Currency and deposits	6 279	8 923	13 932	10 276	10 042	9 410	8 083	..
2.2	Securities other than shares, except financial derivatives	91 183	84 426	72 993	78 291	77 731	75 377	81 189	..
2.2.1	Short-term securities	313	482	545	667	774	1 118	689	..
2.2.2	Long-term securities	90 870	83 944	72 448	77 625	76 957	74 259	80 500	..
2.2.3	Securities issued by residents	17 360	14 374	15 127	16 062	16 012	16 682	17 527	..
2.2.4	Securities issued by non-residents	73 823	70 053	57 866	62 230	61 719	58 695	63 662	..
2.3	Loans	0	0	0	0	0	0	0	..
2.3.1	Short-term loans	0	0	0	0	0	0	0	..
2.3.2	Long-term loans	0	0	0	0	0	0	0	..
2.3.3	Loans granted to residents	0	0	0	0	0	0	0	..
2.3.4	Loans granted to non-residents	0	0	0	0	0	0	0	..
2.4	Shares and other equity	71 559	70 781	43 815	53 153	61 368	51 315	56 581	..
2.4.1	Shares issued by residents	32 102	31 751	23 249	26 024	27 494	23 746	24 621	..
2.4.2	Shares issued by non-residents	39 456	39 029	20 567	27 129	33 874	27 569	31 960	..
2.5	Other, not elsewhere classified	44	89	125	0	89	89	78	..
	Money market funds								
2	Financial assets	2 645	3 562	3 672	2 613	2 400	1 190	400	..
2.1	Currency and deposits	0	0	0	0	0	0	0	..
2.2	Securities other than shares, except financial derivatives	2 645	3 562	3 564	2 526	2 330	1 179	397	..
2.2.1	Short-term securities	12	0	31	34	22	66	6	..
2.2.2	Long-term securities	2 634	3 562	3 533	2 493	2 308	1 113	391	..
2.2.3	Securities issued by residents	298	426	582	609	539	260	76	..
2.2.4	Securities issued by non-residents	2 347	3 137	2 982	1 918	1 791	919	321	..
2.3	Loans	0	0	0	0	0	0	0	..
2.3.1	Short-term loans	0	0	0	0	0	0	0	..
2.3.2	Long-term loans	0	0	0	0	0	0	0	..
2.3.3	Loans granted to residents	0	0	0	0	0	0	0	..
2.3.4	Loans granted to non-residents	0	0	0	0	0	0	0	..
2.4	Shares and other equity	0	0	108	87	70	12	3	..
2.4.1	Shares issued by residents	0	0	69	83	70	12	3	..
2.4.2	Shares issued by non-residents	0	0	39	4	0	0	0	..
2.5	Other, not elsewhere classified	0	0	0	0	0	0	0	..
	Other mutual funds								
2	Financial assets	166 420	160 657	127 194	139 108	146 829	135 001	145 532	..
2.1	Currency and deposits	6 279	8 923	13 932	10 276	10 042	9 410	8 083	..
2.2	Securities other than shares, except financial derivatives	88 538	80 864	69 429	75 765	75 401	74 199	80 792	..
2.2.1	Short-term securities	301	482	515	633	752	1 052	683	..
2.2.2	Long-term securities	88 237	80 381	68 915	75 132	74 649	73 146	80 109	..
2.2.3	Securities issued by residents	17 062	13 948	14 546	15 453	15 473	16 423	17 451	..
2.2.4	Securities issued by non-residents	71 475	66 916	54 884	60 312	59 928	57 776	63 341	..
2.3	Loans	0	0	0	0	0	0	0	..
2.3.1	Short-term loans	0	0	0	0	0	0	0	..
2.3.2	Long-term loans	0	0	0	0	0	0	0	..
2.3.3	Loans granted to residents	0	0	0	0	0	0	0	..
2.3.4	Loans granted to non-residents	0	0	0	0	0	0	0	..
2.4	Shares and other equity	71 559	70 781	43 708	53 067	61 298	51 304	56 578	..
2.4.1	Shares issued by residents	32 102	31 751	23 180	25 941	27 424	23 735	24 618	..
2.4.2	Shares issued by non-residents	39 456	39 029	20 528	27 126	33 874	27 569	31 960	..
2.5	Other, not elsewhere classified	44	89	125	0	89	89	78	..

Table 2. Financial assets of investment funds *(cont.)*

Million EUR (1999 ATS euro)

		2006	2007	2008	2009	2010	2011	2012	2013
	Closed-end companies								
2	Financial assets	..	..	..	..	..	..	..	..
2.1	Currency and deposits	..	..	..	..	..	..	..	..
2.2	Securities other than shares, except financial derivatives	..	..	..	..	..	..	..	..
2.2.1	Short-term securities	..	..	..	..	..	..	..	..
2.2.2	Long-term securities	..	..	..	..	..	..	..	..
2.2.3	Securities issued by residents	..	..	..	..	..	..	..	..
2.2.4	Securities issued by non-residents	..	..	..	..	..	..	..	..
2.3	Loans	..	..	..	..	..	..	..	..
2.3.1	Short-term loans	..	..	..	..	..	..	..	..
2.3.2	Long-term loans	..	..	..	..	..	..	..	..
2.3.3	Loans granted to residents	..	..	..	..	..	..	..	..
2.3.4	Loans granted to non-residents	..	..	..	..	..	..	..	..
2.4	Shares and other equity	..	..	..	..	..	..	..	..
2.4.1	Shares issued by residents	..	..	..	..	..	..	..	..
2.4.2	Shares issued by non-residents	..	..	..	..	..	..	..	..
2.5	Other, not elsewhere classified	..	..	..	..	..	..	..	..

Note: Detailed metadata at: http://metalinks.oecd.org/instinv/20141203/842c

Table 3. Financial assets of insurance corporations and autonomous pension funds

Million EUR (1999 ATS euro)

		2006	2007	2008	2009	2010	2011	2012	2013
	Insurance corporations and autonomous pension funds								
2	Financial assets	93 291	95 883	94 265	103 516	105 995	105 976	114 256	..
2.1	Currency and deposits	3 008	3 184	5 176	4 078	3 085	4 288	4 262	..
2.2	Securities other than shares, except financial derivatives	32 544	34 298	37 213	40 352	42 597	42 486	46 400	..
2.2.1	Short-term securities	35	191	223	116	178	67	10	..
2.2.2	Long-term securities	32 509	34 106	36 990	40 236	42 420	42 419	46 389	..
2.2.3	Securities issued by residents	11 575	12 168	13 548	15 622	16 091	16 380	18 812	..
2.2.4	Securities issued by non-residents	20 969	22 129	23 665	24 730	26 507	26 106	27 588	..
2.3	Loans	4 830	5 240	5 105	5 168	4 459	3 989	4 027	..
2.3.1	Short-term loans	243	181	87	47	134	222	247	..
2.3.2	Long-term loans	4 587	5 059	5 019	5 121	4 325	3 767	3 780	..
2.3.3	Loans granted to residents	3 814	2 870	2 859	2 959	2 283	2 271	2 379	..
2.3.4	Loans granted to non-residents	1 015	2 370	2 246	2 209	2 176	1 718	1 647	..
2.4	Shares and other equity	48 095	48 185	41 613	48 202	51 902	51 589	56 055	..
2.4.1	Shares issued by residents	40 236	39 680	35 220	40 810	43 681	43 173	46 546	..
2.4.2	Shares issued by non-residents	7 860	8 506	6 394	7 393	8 221	8 415	9 509	..
2.5	Other, not elsewhere classified	4 814	4 975	5 158	5 716	3 951	3 625	3 513	..
	Insurance corporations								
2	Financial assets	86 339	87 865	90 627	97 692	100 812	100 184	104 051	..
2.1	Currency and deposits	2 835	2 902	4 386	3 538	2 663	3 644	3 687	..
2.2	Securities other than shares, except financial derivatives	32 592	34 291	37 334	40 516	43 005	42 849	46 851	..
2.2.1	Short-term securities	35	113	177	82	123	31	4	..
2.2.2	Long-term securities	32 557	34 178	37 156	40 434	42 882	42 817	46 846	..
2.2.3	Securities issued by residents	11 757	12 374	13 863	15 995	16 761	16 957	19 414	..
2.2.4	Securities issued by non-residents	20 835	21 917	23 471	24 522	26 244	25 892	27 437	..
2.3	Loans	6 990	7 362	7 257	7 177	7 313	7 078	7 433	..
2.3.1	Short-term loans	2 379	2 323	2 056	1 862	2 192	2 262	2 829	..
2.3.2	Long-term loans	4 611	5 039	5 201	5 315	5 121	4 816	4 604	..
2.3.3	Loans granted to residents	5 974	4 992	5 011	4 968	5 137	5 360	5 785	..
2.3.4	Loans granted to non-residents	1 015	2 370	2 246	2 209	2 176	1 718	1 647	..
2.4	Shares and other equity	38 641	37 784	35 957	40 265	43 411	42 711	42 072	..
2.4.1	Shares issued by residents	31 953	30 878	30 367	33 902	36 362	35 411	34 297	..
2.4.2	Shares issued by non-residents	6 688	6 907	5 590	6 362	7 050	7 299	7 774	..
2.5	Other, not elsewhere classified	5 282	5 526	5 694	6 195	4 419	3 903	4 009	..
	Life insurance corporations								
2	Financial assets	62 387	64 592	59 990	66 497	73 444	73 536	76 272	..
2.1	Currency and deposits	1 854	1 897	2 981	2 091	1 578	2 159	2 292	..
2.2	Securities other than shares, except financial derivatives	28 388	29 215	31 852	33 985	34 307	34 793	37 698	..
2.2.1	Short-term securities	30	96	151	69	98	25	4	..
2.2.2	Long-term securities	28 358	29 118	31 701	33 916	34 209	34 768	37 694	..
2.2.3	Securities issued by residents	10 240	10 542	11 828	13 416	13 371	13 769	15 621	..
2.2.4	Securities issued by non-residents	18 148	18 673	20 024	20 569	20 936	21 024	22 076	..
2.3	Loans	4 082	5 058	3 801	3 617	5 656	5 308	5 749	..
2.3.1	Short-term loans	1 389	1 596	1 077	938	1 695	1 697	2 188	..
2.3.2	Long-term loans	2 693	3 462	2 724	2 679	3 961	3 612	3 561	..
2.3.3	Loans granted to residents	3 489	3 430	2 625	2 504	3 973	4 020	4 475	..
2.3.4	Loans granted to non-residents	593	1 628	1 176	1 113	1 683	1 288	1 274	..
2.4	Shares and other equity	27 551	27 900	20 360	23 985	30 785	30 289	29 693	..
2.4.1	Shares issued by residents	22 782	22 774	16 594	19 660	25 786	25 112	24 206	..
2.4.2	Shares issued by non-residents	4 769	5 125	3 766	4 325	4 999	5 176	5 487	..
2.5	Other, not elsewhere classified	512	522	996	2 819	1 118	987	841	..
	Non-life insurance corporations								
2	Financial assets	23 952	23 273	30 637	31 195	27 369	26 648	27 778	..
2.1	Currency and deposits	981	1 005	1 405	1 447	1 085	1 485	1 396	..
2.2	Securities other than shares, except financial derivatives	4 204	5 076	5 482	6 531	8 698	8 056	9 153	..
2.2.1	Short-term securities	4	17	26	13	25	6	1	..
2.2.2	Long-term securities	4 200	5 060	5 455	6 518	8 673	8 050	9 152	..
2.2.3	Securities issued by residents	1 517	1 832	2 035	2 579	3 390	3 188	3 793	..
2.2.4	Securities issued by non-residents	2 688	3 244	3 447	3 953	5 308	4 868	5 360	..
2.3	Loans	2 908	2 304	3 456	3 560	1 657	1 769	1 684	..
2.3.1	Short-term loans	990	727	979	924	497	566	641	..
2.3.2	Long-term loans	1 918	1 577	2 477	2 636	1 161	1 204	1 043	..
2.3.3	Loans granted to residents	2 485	1 562	2 386	2 464	1 164	1 340	1 311	..
2.3.4	Loans granted to non-residents	422	742	1 070	1 096	493	429	373	..
2.4	Shares and other equity	11 090	9 884	15 597	16 280	12 626	12 422	12 378	..
2.4.1	Shares issued by residents	9 170	8 104	13 773	14 242	10 576	10 299	10 091	..
2.4.2	Shares issued by non-residents	1 919	1 782	1 824	2 037	2 050	2 123	2 287	..
2.5	Other, not elsewhere classified	4 770	5 004	4 698	3 376	3 302	2 916	3 168	..

Table 3. Financial assets of insurance corporations and autonomous pension funds *(cont.)*

Million EUR (1999 ATS euro)

		2006	2007	2008	2009	2010	2011	2012	2013
	Autonomous pension funds								
2	Financial assets	12 247	12 887	11 614	13 671	15 014	14 808	16 407	..
2.1	Currency and deposits	173	282	790	539	422	644	575	..
2.2	Securities other than shares, except financial derivatives	244	323	286	384	451	452	375	..
2.2.1	Short-term securities	0	78	45	34	55	36	6	..
2.2.2	Long-term securities	244	245	241	350	396	416	369	..
2.2.3	Securities issued by residents	111	111	92	176	188	238	224	..
2.2.4	Securities issued by non-residents	133	212	194	208	263	214	151	..
2.3	Loans	27	21	18	17	12	10	31	..
2.3.1	Short-term loans	0	0	0	0	0	0	0	..
2.3.2	Long-term loans	27	21	18	17	12	10	31	..
2.3.3	Loans granted to residents	27	21	18	17	12	10	31	..
2.3.4	Loans granted to non-residents	0	0	0	0	0	0	0	..
2.4	Shares and other equity	11 755	12 219	10 422	12 678	14 070	13 649	15 373	..
2.4.1	Shares issued by residents	10 584	10 620	9 618	11 647	12 899	12 533	13 639	..
2.4.2	Shares issued by non-residents	1 172	1 599	804	1 030	1 171	1 116	1 734	..
2.5	Other, not elsewhere classified	48	43	98	53	59	53	52	..

Note: Detailed metadata at: http://metalinks.oecd.org/instinv/20141203/842c

Table 4. Portfolio composition by type of investor

Percentage of total financial assets

Per cent

		2006	2007	2008	2009	2010	2011	2012	2013
	Investment funds								
2	Financial assets	100.0	100.0	100.0	100.0	100.0	100.0	100.0	..
2.1	Currency and deposits	4.4	6.5	12.6	8.6	8.0	8.1	6.5	..
2.2	Securities other than shares, except financial derivatives	64.4	61.5	66.3	65.6	61.7	65.1	64.9	..
2.2.1	Short-term securities	0.2	0.4	0.5	0.6	0.6	1.0	0.6	..
2.2.2	Long-term securities	64.2	61.1	65.8	65.1	61.1	64.1	64.4	..
2.2.3	Securities issued by residents	12.3	10.5	13.7	13.5	12.7	14.4	14.0	..
2.2.4	Securities issued by non-residents	52.2	51.0	52.5	52.2	49.0	50.7	50.9	..
2.3	Loans	0.0	0.0	0.0	0.0	0.0	0.0	0.0	..
2.3.1	Short-term loans	0.0	0.0	0.0	0.0	0.0	0.0	0.0	..
2.3.2	Long-term loans	0.0	0.0	0.0	0.0	0.0	0.0	0.0	..
2.3.3	Loans granted to residents	0.0	0.0	0.0	0.0	0.0	0.0	0.0	..
2.3.4	Loans granted to non-residents	0.0	0.0	0.0	0.0	0.0	0.0	0.0	..
2.4	Shares and other equity	31.1	31.9	21.0	25.8	30.2	26.7	28.5	..
2.4.1	Shares issued by residents	3.2	3.5	2.3	3.0	3.3	2.9	3.0	..
2.4.2	Shares issued by non-residents	27.9	28.4	18.7	22.7	26.9	23.8	25.6	..
2.5	Other, not elsewhere classified	0.0	0.1	0.1	0.0	0.1	0.1	0.1	..
	Insurance corporations								
2	Financial assets	100.0	100.0	100.0	100.0	100.0	100.0	100.0	..
2.1	Currency and deposits	3.3	3.3	4.8	3.6	2.6	3.6	3.5	..
2.2	Securities other than shares, except financial derivatives	37.7	39.0	41.2	41.5	42.7	42.8	45.0	..
2.2.1	Short-term securities	0.0	0.1	0.2	0.1	0.1	0.0	0.0	..
2.2.2	Long-term securities	37.7	38.9	41.0	41.4	42.5	42.7	45.0	..
2.2.3	Securities issued by residents	13.6	14.1	15.3	16.4	16.6	16.9	18.7	..
2.2.4	Securities issued by non-residents	24.1	24.9	25.9	25.1	26.0	25.8	26.4	..
2.3	Loans	8.1	8.4	8.0	7.3	7.3	7.1	7.1	..
2.3.1	Short-term loans	2.8	2.6	2.3	1.9	2.2	2.3	2.7	..
2.3.2	Long-term loans	5.3	5.7	5.7	5.4	5.1	4.8	4.4	..
2.3.3	Loans granted to residents	6.9	5.7	5.5	5.1	5.1	5.4	5.6	..
2.3.4	Loans granted to non-residents	1.2	2.7	2.5	2.3	2.2	1.7	1.6	..
2.4	Shares and other equity	44.8	43.0	39.7	41.2	43.1	42.6	40.4	..
2.4.1	Shares issued by residents	37.0	35.1	33.5	34.7	36.1	35.3	33.0	..
2.4.2	Shares issued by non-residents	7.7	7.9	6.2	6.5	7.0	7.3	7.5	..
2.5	Other, not elsewhere classified	6.1	6.3	6.3	6.3	4.4	3.9	3.9	..
	Autonomous pension funds								
2	Financial assets	100.0	100.0	100.0	100.0	100.0	100.0	100.0	..
2.1	Currency and deposits	1.4	2.2	6.8	3.9	2.8	4.3	3.5	..
2.2	Securities other than shares, except financial derivatives	2.0	2.5	2.5	2.8	3.0	3.1	2.3	..
2.2.1	Short-term securities	0.0	0.6	0.4	0.2	0.4	0.2	0.0	..
2.2.2	Long-term securities	2.0	1.9	2.1	2.6	2.6	2.8	2.2	..
2.2.3	Securities issued by residents	0.9	0.9	0.8	1.3	1.3	1.6	1.4	..
2.2.4	Securities issued by non-residents	1.1	1.6	1.7	1.5	1.8	1.4	0.9	..
2.3	Loans	0.2	0.2	0.2	0.1	0.1	0.1	0.2	..
2.3.1	Short-term loans	0.0	0.0	0.0	0.0	0.0	0.0	0.0	..
2.3.2	Long-term loans	0.2	0.2	0.2	0.1	0.1	0.1	0.2	..
2.3.3	Loans granted to residents	0.2	0.2	0.2	0.1	0.1	0.1	0.2	..
2.3.4	Loans granted to non-residents	0.0	0.0	0.0	0.0	0.0	0.0	0.0	..
2.4	Shares and other equity	96.0	94.8	89.7	92.7	93.7	92.2	93.7	..
2.4.1	Shares issued by residents	86.4	82.4	82.8	85.2	85.9	84.6	83.1	..
2.4.2	Shares issued by non-residents	9.6	12.4	6.9	7.5	7.8	7.5	10.6	..
2.5	Other, not elsewhere classified	0.4	0.3	0.8	0.4	0.4	0.4	0.3	..

Note: Detailed metadata at: http://metalinks.oecd.org/instinv/20141203/f729

Table 1. Financial assets of institutional investors, 2012

Million EUR (1999 BEF euro)

		Investment funds				
		Total	Open-end companies (mutual funds)			Closed-end companies
			Total	Money market funds	Other mutual funds	Total
2	Financial assets	77 710	87 180	999	86 181	..
2.1	Currency and deposits	7 804	7 804	147	7 656	..
2.2	Securities other than shares, except financial derivatives	25 492	25 492	829	24 662	..
2.2.1	Short-term securities	1 627	1 627	373	1 254	..
2.2.2	Long-term securities	23 865	23 865	457	23 408	..
2.2.3	Securities issued by residents	1 641	1 641	274	1 366	..
2.2.4	Securities issued by non-residents	23 851	23 851	555	23 296	..
2.3	Loans	0	0	0	0	..
2.3.1	Short-term loans	0	0	0	0	..
2.3.2	Long-term loans	0	0	0	0	..
2.3.3	Loans granted to residents	0	0	0	0	..
2.3.4	Loans granted to non-residents	0	0	0	0	..
2.4	Shares and other equity	39 930	49 400	5	49 395	..
2.4.1	Shares issued by residents	4 646	14 116	0	14 116	..
2.4.2	Shares issued by non-residents	35 284	35 284	5	35 279	..
2.5	Other, not elsewhere classified	4 484	4 484	17	4 467	..

		Insurance corporations and autonomous pension funds				
		Total	Insurance corporations			Autonomous pension funds
			Total	Life insurance corporations	Non-life insurance corporations	Total
2	Financial assets	292 464	283 940	..	..	13 602
2.1	Currency and deposits	9 373	9 049	..	..	324
2.2	Securities other than shares, except financial derivatives	198 769	197 032	..	..	1 737
2.2.1	Short-term securities	1 024	1 024	..	..	0
2.2.2	Long-term securities	197 745	196 008	..	..	1 737
2.2.3	Securities issued by residents	83 169	82 610	..	..	559
2.2.4	Securities issued by non-residents	115 600	114 422	..	..	1 178
2.3	Loans	16 830	17 903	..	..	124
2.3.1	Short-term loans	4 739	4 914	..	..	0
2.3.2	Long-term loans	12 090	12 989	..	..	124
2.3.3	Loans granted to residents	16 794	17 868	..	..	124
2.3.4	Loans granted to non-residents	35	35	..	..	0
2.4	Shares and other equity	55 232	44 189	..	..	11 117
2.4.1	Shares issued by residents	22 725	18 899	..	..	3 900
2.4.2	Shares issued by non-residents	32 507	25 290	..	..	7 216
2.5	Other, not elsewhere classified	12 260	15 767	..	..	300

Note: Detailed metadata at: http://metalinks.oecd.org/instinv/20141203/e857

BELGIUM

Table 2. Financial assets of investment funds

Million EUR (1999 BEF euro)

		2006	2007	2008	2009	2010	2011	2012	2013
	Investment funds								
2	Financial assets	115 206	115 785	86 188	91 388	87 826	75 225	77 710	..
2.1	Currency and deposits	29 580	22 961	19 468	15 672	11 588	9 936	7 804	..
2.2	Securities other than shares, except financial derivatives	26 846	35 597	34 174	32 446	31 617	30 112	25 492	..
2.2.1	Short-term securities	2 344	3 117	3 550	3 220	2 173	2 947	1 627	..
2.2.2	Long-term securities	24 502	32 481	30 624	29 227	29 444	27 165	23 865	..
2.2.3	Securities issued by residents	4 008	5 920	5 651	4 629	3 617	3 230	1 641	..
2.2.4	Securities issued by non-residents	22 839	29 677	28 524	27 818	28 001	26 881	23 851	..
2.3	Loans	0	0	0	0	0	0	0	..
2.3.1	Short-term loans	0	0	0	0	0	0	0	..
2.3.2	Long-term loans	0	0	0	0	0	0	0	..
2.3.3	Loans granted to residents	0	0	0	0	0	0	0	..
2.3.4	Loans granted to non-residents	0	0	0	0	0	0	0	..
2.4	Shares and other equity	50 604	47 160	26 236	37 320	39 131	30 508	39 930	..
2.4.1	Shares issued by residents	8 206	7 725	4 372	4 907	4 878	3 612	4 646	..
2.4.2	Shares issued by non-residents	42 398	39 436	21 864	32 412	34 252	26 896	35 284	..
2.5	Other, not elsewhere classified	8 176	10 067	6 311	5 950	5 490	4 668	4 484	..
	Open-end companies (mutual funds)								
2	Financial assets	124 167	124 377	90 147	97 260	96 132	83 427	87 180	..
2.1	Currency and deposits	29 580	22 961	19 468	15 672	11 588	9 936	7 804	..
2.2	Securities other than shares, except financial derivatives	26 846	35 597	34 174	32 446	31 617	30 112	25 492	..
2.2.1	Short-term securities	2 344	3 117	3 550	3 220	2 173	2 947	1 627	..
2.2.2	Long-term securities	24 502	32 481	30 624	29 227	29 444	27 165	23 865	..
2.2.3	Securities issued by residents	4 008	5 920	5 651	4 629	3 617	3 230	1 641	..
2.2.4	Securities issued by non-residents	22 839	29 677	28 524	27 818	28 001	26 881	23 851	..
2.3	Loans	0	0	0	0	0	0	0	..
2.3.1	Short-term loans	0	0	0	0	0	0	0	..
2.3.2	Long-term loans	0	0	0	0	0	0	0	..
2.3.3	Loans granted to residents	0	0	0	0	0	0	0	..
2.3.4	Loans granted to non-residents	0	0	0	0	0	0	0	..
2.4	Shares and other equity	59 565	55 753	30 194	43 192	47 438	38 711	49 400	..
2.4.1	Shares issued by residents	17 167	16 317	8 330	10 779	13 185	11 815	14 116	..
2.4.2	Shares issued by non-residents	42 398	39 436	21 864	32 412	34 252	26 896	35 284	..
2.5	Other, not elsewhere classified	8 176	10 067	6 311	5 950	5 490	4 668	4 484	..
	Money market funds								
2	Financial assets	3 217	6 271	5 535	1 945	1 920	4 376	999	..
2.1	Currency and deposits	527	1 166	812	287	250	535	147	..
2.2	Securities other than shares, except financial derivatives	2 565	4 696	4 539	1 594	1 627	3 755	829	..
2.2.1	Short-term securities	1 273	1 452	2 187	1 101	709	1 106	373	..
2.2.2	Long-term securities	1 292	3 244	2 353	493	919	2 649	457	..
2.2.3	Securities issued by residents	825	2 202	2 188	596	607	1 226	274	..
2.2.4	Securities issued by non-residents	1 740	2 494	2 351	998	1 020	2 529	555	..
2.3	Loans	0	0	0	0	0	0	0	..
2.3.1	Short-term loans	0	0	0	0	0	0	0	..
2.3.2	Long-term loans	0	0	0	0	0	0	0	..
2.3.3	Loans granted to residents	0	0	0	0	0	0	0	..
2.3.4	Loans granted to non-residents	0	0	0	0	0	0	0	..
2.4	Shares and other equity	2	97	0	29	21	0	5	..
2.4.1	Shares issued by residents	1	59	0	15	6	0	0	..
2.4.2	Shares issued by non-residents	1	38	0	14	15	0	5	..
2.5	Other, not elsewhere classified	124	312	184	35	22	86	17	..
	Other mutual funds								
2	Financial assets	120 950	118 106	84 612	95 315	94 212	79 052	86 181	..
2.1	Currency and deposits	29 053	21 795	18 656	15 385	11 338	9 402	7 656	..
2.2	Securities other than shares, except financial derivatives	24 282	30 901	29 635	30 852	29 990	26 356	24 662	..
2.2.1	Short-term securities	1 071	1 664	1 363	2 119	1 464	1 841	1 254	..
2.2.2	Long-term securities	23 210	29 237	28 272	28 734	28 525	24 516	23 408	..
2.2.3	Securities issued by residents	3 183	3 718	3 462	4 032	3 009	2 004	1 366	..
2.2.4	Securities issued by non-residents	21 098	27 183	26 173	26 820	26 981	24 352	23 296	..
2.3	Loans	0	0	0	0	0	0	0	..
2.3.1	Short-term loans	0	0	0	0	0	0	0	..
2.3.2	Long-term loans	0	0	0	0	0	0	0	..
2.3.3	Loans granted to residents	0	0	0	0	0	0	0	..
2.3.4	Loans granted to non-residents	0	0	0	0	0	0	0	..
2.4	Shares and other equity	59 563	55 656	30 194	43 162	47 417	38 711	49 395	..
2.4.1	Shares issued by residents	17 166	16 258	8 330	10 764	13 179	11 815	14 116	..
2.4.2	Shares issued by non-residents	42 397	39 398	21 864	32 398	34 238	26 896	35 279	..
2.5	Other, not elsewhere classified	8 053	9 754	6 126	5 915	5 468	4 583	4 467	..

Table 2. Financial assets of investment funds *(cont.)*

Million EUR (1999 BEF euro)

		2006	2007	2008	2009	2010	2011	2012	2013
	Closed-end companies								
2	Financial assets	..	..	..	..	..	..	..	..
2.1	Currency and deposits	..	..	..	..	..	..	..	..
2.2	Securities other than shares, except financial derivatives	..	..	..	..	..	..	..	..
2.2.1	Short-term securities	..	..	..	..	..	..	..	..
2.2.2	Long-term securities	..	..	..	..	..	..	..	..
2.2.3	Securities issued by residents	..	..	..	..	..	..	..	..
2.2.4	Securities issued by non-residents	..	..	..	..	..	..	..	..
2.3	Loans	..	..	..	..	..	..	..	..
2.3.1	Short-term loans	..	..	..	..	..	..	..	..
2.3.2	Long-term loans	..	..	..	..	..	..	..	..
2.3.3	Loans granted to residents	..	..	..	..	..	..	..	..
2.3.4	Loans granted to non-residents	..	..	..	..	..	..	..	..
2.4	Shares and other equity	..	..	..	..	..	..	..	..
2.4.1	Shares issued by residents	..	..	..	..	..	..	..	..
2.4.2	Shares issued by non-residents	..	..	..	..	..	..	..	..
2.5	Other, not elsewhere classified	..	..	..	..	..	..	..	..

Note: Detailed metadata at: http://metalinks.oecd.org/instinv/20141203/e857

Table 3. Financial assets of insurance corporations and autonomous pension funds

Million EUR (1999 BEF euro)

		2006	2007	2008	2009	2010	2011	2012	2013
	Insurance corporations and autonomous pension funds								
2	Financial assets	216 486	231 031	222 746	244 700	257 103	263 732	292 464	..
2.1	Currency and deposits	11 559	10 669	12 733	9 557	8 490	11 163	9 373	..
2.2	Securities other than shares, except financial derivatives	113 652	132 250	139 524	158 422	170 901	177 817	198 769	..
2.2.1	Short-term securities	899	483	1 251	1 130	958	818	1 024	..
2.2.2	Long-term securities	112 752	131 767	138 273	157 292	169 943	177 000	197 745	..
2.2.3	Securities issued by residents	27 735	25 769	30 721	37 105	43 194	65 977	83 169	..
2.2.4	Securities issued by non-residents	85 917	106 480	108 803	121 317	127 707	111 841	115 600	..
2.3	Loans	10 294	10 470	11 759	11 705	11 890	12 384	16 830	..
2.3.1	Short-term loans	2 837	3 132	3 599	3 646	3 611	3 598	4 739	..
2.3.2	Long-term loans	7 457	7 339	8 161	8 059	8 279	8 785	12 090	..
2.3.3	Loans granted to residents	10 264	10 430	11 696	11 636	11 833	12 355	16 794	..
2.3.4	Loans granted to non-residents	30	40	64	70	57	28	35	..
2.4	Shares and other equity	73 864	68 899	48 426	54 087	54 943	49 561	55 232	..
2.4.1	Shares issued by residents	25 197	19 078	15 387	18 650	17 537	17 293	22 725	..
2.4.2	Shares issued by non-residents	48 667	49 821	33 039	35 437	37 406	32 268	32 507	..
2.5	Other, not elsewhere classified	7 117	8 742	10 303	10 930	10 879	12 807	12 260	..
	Insurance corporations								
2	Financial assets	206 428	219 699	215 356	235 762	248 360	255 545	283 940	..
2.1	Currency and deposits	11 257	10 359	12 235	9 134	7 974	10 845	9 049	..
2.2	Securities other than shares, except financial derivatives	112 964	131 197	138 634	157 371	169 369	176 112	197 032	..
2.2.1	Short-term securities	899	483	1 251	1 130	958	818	1 024	..
2.2.2	Long-term securities	112 064	130 714	137 383	156 241	168 411	175 294	196 008	..
2.2.3	Securities issued by residents	27 280	25 240	30 356	36 688	42 780	65 428	82 610	..
2.2.4	Securities issued by non-residents	85 684	105 957	108 278	120 682	126 589	110 683	114 422	..
2.3	Loans	10 596	10 727	11 832	12 609	13 074	13 543	17 903	..
2.3.1	Short-term loans	2 944	3 234	3 684	3 730	3 750	3 734	4 914	..
2.3.2	Long-term loans	7 652	7 492	8 148	8 879	9 324	9 809	12 989	..
2.3.3	Loans granted to residents	10 566	10 686	11 768	12 539	13 018	13 515	17 868	..
2.3.4	Loans granted to non-residents	30	40	64	70	57	28	35	..
2.4	Shares and other equity	62 664	57 067	40 335	43 753	43 908	38 948	44 189	..
2.4.1	Shares issued by residents	20 271	14 019	12 397	14 639	13 317	13 463	18 899	..
2.4.2	Shares issued by non-residents	42 393	43 048	27 938	29 114	30 591	25 485	25 290	..
2.5	Other, not elsewhere classified	8 947	10 349	12 320	12 896	14 035	16 098	15 767	..
	Life insurance corporations								
2	Financial assets	..	..	..	..	..	..	..	..
2.1	Currency and deposits	..	..	..	..	..	..	..	..
2.2	Securities other than shares, except financial derivatives	..	..	..	..	..	..	..	..
2.2.1	Short-term securities	..	..	..	..	..	..	..	..
2.2.2	Long-term securities	..	..	..	..	..	..	..	..
2.2.3	Securities issued by residents	..	..	..	..	..	..	..	..
2.2.4	Securities issued by non-residents	..	..	..	..	..	..	..	..
2.3	Loans	..	..	..	..	..	..	..	..
2.3.1	Short-term loans	..	..	..	..	..	..	..	..
2.3.2	Long-term loans	..	..	..	..	..	..	..	..
2.3.3	Loans granted to residents	..	..	..	..	..	..	..	..
2.3.4	Loans granted to non-residents	..	..	..	..	..	..	..	..
2.4	Shares and other equity	..	..	..	..	..	..	..	..
2.4.1	Shares issued by residents	..	..	..	..	..	..	..	..
2.4.2	Shares issued by non-residents	..	..	..	..	..	..	..	..
2.5	Other, not elsewhere classified	..	..	..	..	..	..	..	..
	Non-life insurance corporations								
2	Financial assets	..	..	..	..	..	..	..	..
2.1	Currency and deposits	..	..	..	..	..	..	..	..
2.2	Securities other than shares, except financial derivatives	..	..	..	..	..	..	..	..
2.2.1	Short-term securities	..	..	..	..	..	..	..	..
2.2.2	Long-term securities	..	..	..	..	..	..	..	..
2.2.3	Securities issued by residents	..	..	..	..	..	..	..	..
2.2.4	Securities issued by non-residents	..	..	..	..	..	..	..	..
2.3	Loans	..	..	..	..	..	..	..	..
2.3.1	Short-term loans	..	..	..	..	..	..	..	..
2.3.2	Long-term loans	..	..	..	..	..	..	..	..
2.3.3	Loans granted to residents	..	..	..	..	..	..	..	..
2.3.4	Loans granted to non-residents	..	..	..	..	..	..	..	..
2.4	Shares and other equity	..	..	..	..	..	..	..	..
2.4.1	Shares issued by residents	..	..	..	..	..	..	..	..
2.4.2	Shares issued by non-residents	..	..	..	..	..	..	..	..
2.5	Other, not elsewhere classified	..	..	..	..	..	..	..	..

Table 3. Financial assets of insurance corporations and autonomous pension funds *(cont.)*

Million EUR (1999 BEF euro)

		2006	2007	2008	2009	2010	2011	2012	2013
	Autonomous pension funds								
2	Financial assets	12 301	13 338	10 347	12 453	13 854	13 442	13 602	..
2.1	Currency and deposits	302	310	499	423	515	319	324	..
2.2	Securities other than shares, except financial derivatives	688	1 053	890	1 051	1 532	1 706	1 737	..
2.2.1	Short-term securities	0	0	0	0	0	0	0	..
2.2.2	Long-term securities	688	1 053	890	1 051	1 532	1 706	1 737	..
2.2.3	Securities issued by residents	455	530	365	417	415	549	559	..
2.2.4	Securities issued by non-residents	233	523	524	634	1 117	1 157	1 178	..
2.3	Loans	8	4	139	147	111	122	124	..
2.3.1	Short-term loans	0	0	0	0	0	0	0	..
2.3.2	Long-term loans	8	4	139	147	111	122	124	..
2.3.3	Loans granted to residents	8	4	139	147	111	122	124	..
2.3.4	Loans granted to non-residents	0	0	0	0	0	0	0	..
2.4	Shares and other equity	11 200	11 832	8 616	10 726	11 591	11 001	11 117	..
2.4.1	Shares issued by residents	4 926	5 058	3 515	4 402	4 776	4 217	3 900	..
2.4.2	Shares issued by non-residents	6 274	6 773	5 101	6 323	6 815	6 783	7 216	..
2.5	Other, not elsewhere classified	104	140	203	107	104	295	300	..

Note: Detailed metadata at: http://metalinks.oecd.org/instinv/20141203/e857

Table 4. Portfolio composition by type of investor

Percentage of total financial assets

Per cent

		2006	2007	2008	2009	2010	2011	2012	2013
	Investment funds								
2	Financial assets	100.0	100.0	100.0	100.0	100.0	100.0	100.0	..
2.1	Currency and deposits	25.7	19.8	22.6	17.1	13.2	13.2	10.0	..
2.2	Securities other than shares, except financial derivatives	23.3	30.7	39.7	35.5	36.0	40.0	32.8	..
2.2.1	Short-term securities	2.0	2.7	4.1	3.5	2.5	3.9	2.1	..
2.2.2	Long-term securities	21.3	28.1	35.5	32.0	33.5	36.1	30.7	..
2.2.3	Securities issued by residents	3.5	5.1	6.6	5.1	4.1	4.3	2.1	..
2.2.4	Securities issued by non-residents	19.8	25.6	33.1	30.4	31.9	35.7	30.7	..
2.3	Loans	0.0	0.0	0.0	0.0	0.0	0.0	0.0	..
2.3.1	Short-term loans	0.0	0.0	0.0	0.0	0.0	0.0	0.0	..
2.3.2	Long-term loans	0.0	0.0	0.0	0.0	0.0	0.0	0.0	..
2.3.3	Loans granted to residents	0.0	0.0	0.0	0.0	0.0	0.0	0.0	..
2.3.4	Loans granted to non-residents	0.0	0.0	0.0	0.0	0.0	0.0	0.0	..
2.4	Shares and other equity	43.9	40.7	30.4	40.8	44.6	40.6	51.4	..
2.4.1	Shares issued by residents	7.1	6.7	5.1	5.4	5.6	4.8	6.0	..
2.4.2	Shares issued by non-residents	36.8	34.1	25.4	35.5	39.0	35.8	45.4	..
2.5	Other, not elsewhere classified	7.1	8.7	7.3	6.5	6.3	6.2	5.8	..
	Insurance corporations								
2	Financial assets	100.0	100.0	100.0	100.0	100.0	100.0	100.0	..
2.1	Currency and deposits	5.5	4.7	5.7	3.9	3.2	4.2	3.2	..
2.2	Securities other than shares, except financial derivatives	54.7	59.7	64.4	66.7	68.2	68.9	69.4	..
2.2.1	Short-term securities	0.4	0.2	0.6	0.5	0.4	0.3	0.4	..
2.2.2	Long-term securities	54.3	59.5	63.8	66.3	67.8	68.6	69.0	..
2.2.3	Securities issued by residents	13.2	11.5	14.1	15.6	17.2	25.6	29.1	..
2.2.4	Securities issued by non-residents	41.5	48.2	50.3	51.2	51.0	43.3	40.3	..
2.3	Loans	5.1	4.9	5.5	5.3	5.3	5.3	6.3	..
2.3.1	Short-term loans	1.4	1.5	1.7	1.6	1.5	1.5	1.7	..
2.3.2	Long-term loans	3.7	3.4	3.8	3.8	3.8	3.8	4.6	..
2.3.3	Loans granted to residents	5.1	4.9	5.5	5.3	5.2	5.3	6.3	..
2.3.4	Loans granted to non-residents	0.0	0.0	0.0	0.0	0.0	0.0	0.0	..
2.4	Shares and other equity	30.4	26.0	18.7	18.6	17.7	15.2	15.6	..
2.4.1	Shares issued by residents	9.8	6.4	5.8	6.2	5.4	5.3	6.7	..
2.4.2	Shares issued by non-residents	20.5	19.6	13.0	12.3	12.3	10.0	8.9	..
2.5	Other, not elsewhere classified	4.3	4.7	5.7	5.5	5.7	6.3	5.6	..
	Autonomous pension funds								
2	Financial assets	100.0	100.0	100.0	100.0	100.0	100.0	100.0	..
2.1	Currency and deposits	2.5	2.3	4.8	3.4	3.7	2.4	2.4	..
2.2	Securities other than shares, except financial derivatives	5.6	7.9	8.6	8.4	11.1	12.7	12.8	..
2.2.1	Short-term securities	0.0	0.0	0.0	0.0	0.0	0.0	0.0	..
2.2.2	Long-term securities	5.6	7.9	8.6	8.4	11.1	12.7	12.8	..
2.2.3	Securities issued by residents	3.7	4.0	3.5	3.3	3.0	4.1	4.1	..
2.2.4	Securities issued by non-residents	1.9	3.9	5.1	5.1	8.1	8.6	8.7	..
2.3	Loans	0.1	0.0	1.3	1.2	0.8	0.9	0.9	..
2.3.1	Short-term loans	0.0	0.0	0.0	0.0	0.0	0.0	0.0	..
2.3.2	Long-term loans	0.1	0.0	1.3	1.2	0.8	0.9	0.9	..
2.3.3	Loans granted to residents	0.1	0.0	1.3	1.2	0.8	0.9	0.9	..
2.3.4	Loans granted to non-residents	0.0	0.0	0.0	0.0	0.0	0.0	0.0	..
2.4	Shares and other equity	91.0	88.7	83.3	86.1	83.7	81.8	81.7	..
2.4.1	Shares issued by residents	40.0	37.9	34.0	35.3	34.5	31.4	28.7	..
2.4.2	Shares issued by non-residents	51.0	50.8	49.3	50.8	49.2	50.5	53.1	..
2.5	Other, not elsewhere classified	0.8	1.0	2.0	0.9	0.8	2.2	2.2	..

Note: Detailed metadata at: http://metalinks.oecd.org/instinv/20141203/f729

CANADA

Table 1. Financial assets of institutional investors, 2013

Million CAD

		Investment funds				
		Total	Open-end companies (mutual funds)			Closed-end companies
			Total	Money market funds	Other mutual funds	Total
2	Financial assets	1 353 896	1 353 896	30 903	1 322 993	..
2.1	Currency and deposits	14 216	14 216	4 186	10 030	..
2.2	Securities other than shares, except financial derivatives	343 022	343 022	26 279	316 743	..
2.2.1	Short-term securities	43 261	43 261	21 336	21 925	..
2.2.2	Long-term securities	299 761	299 761	4 943	294 818	..
2.2.3	Securities issued by residents	265 880	265 880	25 534	240 346	..
2.2.4	Securities issued by non-residents	77 142	77 142	745	76 397	..
2.3	Loans	7 180	7 180	0	7 180	..
2.3.1	Short-term loans	..	..	..	..	..
2.3.2	Long-term loans	..	..	..	..	..
2.3.3	Loans granted to residents	..	..	..	..	..
2.3.4	Loans granted to non-residents	..	..	..	..	..
2.4	Shares and other equity	918 295	918 295	313	917 982	..
2.4.1	Shares issued by residents	638 900	638 900	307	638 593	..
2.4.2	Shares issued by non-residents	279 395	279 395	6	279 389	..
2.5	Other, not elsewhere classified	71 183	71 183	125	71 058	..

		Insurance corporations and autonomous pension funds				
		Total	Insurance corporations			Autonomous pension funds
			Total	Life insurance corporations	Non-life insurance corporations	Total
2	Financial assets	2 063 427	745 534	604 101	141 433	1 317 893
2.1	Currency and deposits	37 719	9 158	5 163	3 995	28 561
2.2	Securities other than shares, except financial derivatives	707 204	268 011	192 991	75 020	439 193
2.2.1	Short-term securities	31 092	17 590	14 659	2 931	13 502
2.2.2	Long-term securities	676 112	250 421	178 332	72 089	425 691
2.2.3	Securities issued by residents	648 692	264 538	190 854	73 684	384 154
2.2.4	Securities issued by non-residents	58 512	3 473	2 137	1 336	55 039
2.3	Loans	120 610	72 366	71 176	1 190	48 244
2.3.1	Short-term loans	..	..	..	..	..
2.3.2	Long-term loans	..	..	..	..	..
2.3.3	Loans granted to residents	..	..	..	..	..
2.3.4	Loans granted to non-residents	..	..	..	..	..
2.4	Shares and other equity	993 388	276 014	252 836	23 178	717 374
2.4.1	Shares issued by residents	629 503	251 162	230 500	20 662	378 341
2.4.2	Shares issued by non-residents	363 885	24 852	22 336	2 516	339 033
2.5	Other, not elsewhere classified	204 506	119 985	81 935	38 050	84 521

Note: Detailed metadata at: http://metalinks.oecd.org/instinv/20141203/14ca

Table 2. Financial assets of investment funds

Million CAD

		2006	2007	2008	2009	2010	2011	2012	2013
	Investment funds								
2	Financial assets	783 598	860 858	715 081	857 592	964 804	1 001 353	1 133 091	1 353 896
2.1	Currency and deposits	8 047	8 968	5 229	11 413	8 898	10 953	14 218	14 216
2.2	Securities other than shares, except financial derivatives	188 783	214 991	232 787	241 936	257 502	300 545	320 051	343 022
2.2.1	Short-term securities	52 022	61 319	81 531	53 569	40 086	45 618	40 356	43 261
2.2.2	Long-term securities	136 761	153 672	151 256	188 367	217 416	254 927	279 695	299 761
2.2.3	Securities issued by residents	157 790	183 111	207 360	206 173	214 866	245 817	259 604	265 880
2.2.4	Securities issued by non-residents	30 993	31 880	25 427	35 763	42 636	54 728	60 447	77 142
2.3	Loans	4 640	3 371	3 136	4 184	4 897	6 177	6 739	7 180
2.3.1	Short-term loans	..	..	..	..	..	..	..	..
2.3.2	Long-term loans	..	..	..	..	..	..	..	..
2.3.3	Loans granted to residents	..	..	..	..	..	..	..	..
2.3.4	Loans granted to non-residents	..	..	..	..	..	..	..	..
2.4	Shares and other equity	552 507	613 481	436 496	572 424	666 145	650 065	733 938	918 295
2.4.1	Shares issued by residents	364 074	399 582	301 462	411 531	484 116	481 220	534 978	638 900
2.4.2	Shares issued by non-residents	188 433	213 899	135 034	160 893	182 029	168 845	198 960	279 395
2.5	Other, not elsewhere classified	29 621	20 047	37 433	27 635	27 362	33 613	58 145	71 183
	Open-end companies (mutual funds)								
2	Financial assets	783 598	860 858	715 081	857 592	964 804	1 001 353	1 133 091	1 353 896
2.1	Currency and deposits	8 047	8 968	5 229	11 413	8 898	10 953	14 218	14 216
2.2	Securities other than shares, except financial derivatives	188 783	214 991	232 787	241 936	257 502	300 545	320 051	343 022
2.2.1	Short-term securities	52 022	61 319	81 531	53 569	40 086	45 618	40 356	43 261
2.2.2	Long-term securities	136 761	153 672	151 256	188 367	217 416	254 927	279 695	299 761
2.2.3	Securities issued by residents	157 790	183 111	207 360	206 173	214 866	245 817	259 604	265 880
2.2.4	Securities issued by non-residents	30 993	31 880	25 427	35 763	42 636	54 728	60 447	77 142
2.3	Loans	4 640	3 371	3 136	4 184	4 897	6 177	6 739	7 180
2.3.1	Short-term loans	..	..	..	..	..	..	..	..
2.3.2	Long-term loans	..	..	..	..	..	..	..	..
2.3.3	Loans granted to residents	..	..	..	..	..	..	..	..
2.3.4	Loans granted to non-residents	..	..	..	..	..	..	..	..
2.4	Shares and other equity	552 507	613 481	436 496	572 424	666 145	650 065	733 938	918 295
2.4.1	Shares issued by residents	364 074	399 582	301 462	411 531	484 116	481 220	534 978	638 900
2.4.2	Shares issued by non-residents	188 433	213 899	135 034	160 893	182 029	168 845	198 960	279 395
2.5	Other, not elsewhere classified	29 621	20 047	37 433	27 635	27 362	33 613	58 145	71 183
	Money market funds								
2	Financial assets	48 489	58 011	78 172	61 424	42 241	39 591	33 337	30 903
2.1	Currency and deposits	3 633	3 715	1 757	6 556	4 950	4 509	4 388	4 186
2.2	Securities other than shares, except financial derivatives	43 981	53 092	73 869	50 938	34 459	32 879	28 357	26 279
2.2.1	Short-term securities	33 776	41 949	62 796	38 373	25 228	24 526	22 232	21 336
2.2.2	Long-term securities	10 205	11 143	11 073	12 565	9 231	8 353	6 125	4 943
2.2.3	Securities issued by residents	38 325	49 881	73 396	49 571	33 714	32 365	28 176	25 534
2.2.4	Securities issued by non-residents	5 656	3 211	473	1 367	745	514	181	745
2.3	Loans	0	0	0	0	0	0	0	0
2.3.1	Short-term loans	..	..	..	..	..	..	..	..
2.3.2	Long-term loans	..	..	..	..	..	..	..	..
2.3.3	Loans granted to residents	..	..	..	..	..	..	..	..
2.3.4	Loans granted to non-residents	..	..	..	..	..	..	..	..
2.4	Shares and other equity	350	860	1 339	583	397	332	383	313
2.4.1	Shares issued by residents	350	847	1 311	556	376	332	383	307
2.4.2	Shares issued by non-residents	0	13	28	27	21	0	0	6
2.5	Other, not elsewhere classified	525	344	1 207	3 347	2 435	1 871	209	125
	Other mutual funds								
2	Financial assets	735 109	802 847	636 909	796 168	922 563	961 762	1 099 754	1 322 993
2.1	Currency and deposits	4 414	5 253	3 472	4 857	3 948	6 444	9 830	10 030
2.2	Securities other than shares, except financial derivatives	144 802	161 899	158 918	190 998	223 043	267 666	291 694	316 743
2.2.1	Short-term securities	18 246	19 370	18 735	15 196	14 858	21 092	18 124	21 925
2.2.2	Long-term securities	126 556	142 529	140 183	175 802	208 185	246 574	273 570	294 818
2.2.3	Securities issued by residents	119 465	133 230	133 964	156 602	181 152	213 452	231 428	240 346
2.2.4	Securities issued by non-residents	25 337	28 669	24 954	34 396	41 891	54 214	60 266	76 397
2.3	Loans	4 640	3 371	3 136	4 184	4 897	6 177	6 739	7 180
2.3.1	Short-term loans	..	..	..	..	..	..	..	..
2.3.2	Long-term loans	..	..	..	..	..	..	..	..
2.3.3	Loans granted to residents	..	..	..	..	..	..	..	..
2.3.4	Loans granted to non-residents	..	..	..	..	..	..	..	..
2.4	Shares and other equity	552 157	612 621	435 157	571 841	665 748	649 733	733 555	917 982
2.4.1	Shares issued by residents	363 724	398 735	300 151	410 975	483 740	480 888	534 595	638 593
2.4.2	Shares issued by non-residents	188 433	213 886	135 006	160 866	182 008	168 845	198 960	279 389
2.5	Other, not elsewhere classified	29 096	19 703	36 226	24 288	24 927	31 742	57 936	71 058

Table 2. Financial assets of investment funds *(cont.)*

Million CAD

		2006	2007	2008	2009	2010	2011	2012	2013
	Closed-end companies								
2	Financial assets	..	..	..	..	..	..	..	..
2.1	Currency and deposits	..	..	..	..	..	..	..	..
2.2	Securities other than shares, except financial derivatives	..	..	..	..	..	..	..	..
2.2.1	Short-term securities	..	..	..	..	..	..	..	..
2.2.2	Long-term securities	..	..	..	..	..	..	..	..
2.2.3	Securities issued by residents	..	..	..	..	..	..	..	..
2.2.4	Securities issued by non-residents	..	..	..	..	..	..	..	..
2.3	Loans	..	..	..	..	..	..	..	..
2.3.1	Short-term loans	..	..	..	..	..	..	..	..
2.3.2	Long-term loans	..	..	..	..	..	..	..	..
2.3.3	Loans granted to residents	..	..	..	..	..	..	..	..
2.3.4	Loans granted to non-residents	..	..	..	..	..	..	..	..
2.4	Shares and other equity	..	..	..	..	..	..	..	..
2.4.1	Shares issued by residents	..	..	..	..	..	..	..	..
2.4.2	Shares issued by non-residents	..	..	..	..	..	..	..	..
2.5	Other, not elsewhere classified	..	..	..	..	..	..	..	..

Note: Detailed metadata at: http://metalinks.oecd.org/instinv/20141203/14ca

CANADA

Table 3. Financial assets of insurance corporations and autonomous pension funds

Million CAD

		2006	2007	2008	2009	2010	2011	2012	2013
	Insurance corporations and autonomous pension funds								
2	Financial assets	1 458 778	1 506 761	1 346 370	1 488 057	1 667 546	1 760 960	1 905 174	2 063 427
2.1	Currency and deposits	14 189	15 001	16 443	25 129	27 040	31 457	34 295	37 719
2.2	Securities other than shares, except financial derivatives	518 108	554 925	530 395	580 432	619 752	704 533	693 550	707 204
2.2.1	Short-term securities	38 346	40 535	39 653	34 192	27 639	26 534	27 907	31 092
2.2.2	Long-term securities	479 762	514 390	490 742	546 240	592 113	677 999	665 643	676 112
2.2.3	Securities issued by residents	470 363	494 910	474 185	532 268	569 152	648 702	642 266	648 692
2.2.4	Securities issued by non-residents	47 745	60 015	56 210	48 164	50 600	55 831	51 284	58 512
2.3	Loans	88 782	93 627	107 175	112 182	114 673	112 618	115 474	120 610
2.3.1	Short-term loans	..	..	..	..	..	..	..	..
2.3.2	Long-term loans	..	..	..	..	..	..	..	..
2.3.3	Loans granted to residents	..	..	..	..	..	..	..	..
2.3.4	Loans granted to non-residents	..	..	..	..	..	..	..	..
2.4	Shares and other equity	705 675	726 551	554 539	669 731	781 354	775 593	859 276	993 388
2.4.1	Shares issued by residents	488 574	503 208	384 969	476 486	548 247	530 460	584 703	629 503
2.4.2	Shares issued by non-residents	217 101	223 343	169 570	193 245	233 107	245 133	274 573	363 885
2.5	Other, not elsewhere classified	132 024	116 657	137 818	100 583	124 727	136 759	202 579	204 506
	Insurance corporations								
2	Financial assets	539 808	554 714	519 324	574 072	624 441	673 116	715 393	745 534
2.1	Currency and deposits	5 777	5 590	10 130	7 390	7 285	7 796	9 215	9 158
2.2	Securities other than shares, except financial derivatives	224 674	214 001	208 209	231 138	242 643	263 011	265 933	268 011
2.2.1	Short-term securities	18 767	17 220	15 939	18 755	16 985	17 521	17 300	17 590
2.2.2	Long-term securities	205 907	196 781	192 270	212 383	225 658	245 490	248 633	250 421
2.2.3	Securities issued by residents	222 011	212 581	205 951	229 069	240 663	261 467	263 087	264 538
2.2.4	Securities issued by non-residents	2 663	1 420	2 258	2 069	1 980	1 544	2 846	3 473
2.3	Loans	58 167	63 050	64 823	67 659	70 209	72 718	72 019	72 366
2.3.1	Short-term loans	..	..	..	..	..	..	..	..
2.3.2	Long-term loans	..	..	..	..	..	..	..	..
2.3.3	Loans granted to residents	..	..	..	..	..	..	..	..
2.3.4	Loans granted to non-residents	..	..	..	..	..	..	..	..
2.4	Shares and other equity	197 619	212 383	164 541	206 741	233 926	230 990	258 056	276 014
2.4.1	Shares issued by residents	185 287	189 748	145 477	184 741	211 167	212 646	235 811	251 162
2.4.2	Shares issued by non-residents	12 332	22 635	19 064	22 000	22 759	18 344	22 245	24 852
2.5	Other, not elsewhere classified	53 571	59 690	71 621	61 144	70 378	98 601	110 170	119 985
	Life insurance corporations								
2	Financial assets	417 476	435 646	400 447	454 705	498 976	545 137	580 022	604 101
2.1	Currency and deposits	2 799	2 943	4 763	4 146	4 163	4 882	5 681	5 163
2.2	Securities other than shares, except financial derivatives	162 396	154 070	146 568	165 507	175 063	193 950	193 253	192 991
2.2.1	Short-term securities	15 291	13 032	12 722	15 122	13 312	14 977	14 437	14 659
2.2.2	Long-term securities	147 105	141 038	133 846	150 385	161 751	178 973	178 816	178 332
2.2.3	Securities issued by residents	159 974	152 799	144 626	163 793	173 442	192 735	191 554	190 854
2.2.4	Securities issued by non-residents	2 422	1 271	1 942	1 714	1 621	1 215	1 699	2 137
2.3	Loans	57 483	62 392	64 174	66 971	69 570	72 009	71 089	71 176
2.3.1	Short-term loans	..	..	..	..	..	..	..	..
2.3.2	Long-term loans	..	..	..	..	..	..	..	..
2.3.3	Loans granted to residents	..	..	..	..	..	..	..	..
2.3.4	Loans granted to non-residents	..	..	..	..	..	..	..	..
2.4	Shares and other equity	170 063	186 871	143 460	186 645	211 395	210 357	235 370	252 836
2.4.1	Shares issued by residents	159 322	165 903	126 313	167 173	191 227	194 480	215 486	230 500
2.4.2	Shares issued by non-residents	10 741	20 968	17 147	19 472	20 168	15 877	19 884	22 336
2.5	Other, not elsewhere classified	24 735	29 370	41 482	31 436	38 785	63 939	74 629	81 935
	Non-life insurance corporations								
2	Financial assets	122 332	119 068	118 877	119 367	125 465	127 979	135 371	141 433
2.1	Currency and deposits	2 978	2 647	5 367	3 244	3 122	2 914	3 534	3 995
2.2	Securities other than shares, except financial derivatives	62 278	59 931	61 641	65 631	67 580	69 061	72 680	75 020
2.2.1	Short-term securities	3 476	4 188	3 217	3 633	3 673	2 544	2 863	2 931
2.2.2	Long-term securities	58 802	55 743	58 424	61 998	63 907	66 517	69 817	72 089
2.2.3	Securities issued by residents	62 037	59 782	61 325	65 276	67 221	68 732	71 533	73 684
2.2.4	Securities issued by non-residents	241	149	316	355	359	329	1 147	1 336
2.3	Loans	684	658	649	688	639	709	930	1 190
2.3.1	Short-term loans	..	..	..	..	..	..	..	..
2.3.2	Long-term loans	..	..	..	..	..	..	..	..
2.3.3	Loans granted to residents	..	..	..	..	..	..	..	..
2.3.4	Loans granted to non-residents	..	..	..	..	..	..	..	..
2.4	Shares and other equity	27 556	25 512	21 081	20 096	22 531	20 633	22 686	23 178
2.4.1	Shares issued by residents	25 965	23 845	19 164	17 568	19 940	18 166	20 325	20 662
2.4.2	Shares issued by non-residents	1 591	1 667	1 917	2 528	2 591	2 467	2 361	2 516
2.5	Other, not elsewhere classified	28 836	30 320	30 139	29 708	31 593	34 662	35 541	38 050

Table 3. Financial assets of insurance corporations and autonomous pension funds *(cont.)*

Million CAD

		2006	2007	2008	2009	2010	2011	2012	2013
	Autonomous pension funds								
2	Financial assets	918 970	952 047	827 046	913 985	1 043 105	1 087 844	1 189 781	1 317 893
2.1	Currency and deposits	8 412	9 411	6 313	17 739	19 755	23 661	25 080	28 561
2.2	Securities other than shares, except financial derivatives	293 434	340 924	322 186	349 294	377 109	441 522	427 617	439 193
2.2.1	Short-term securities	19 579	23 315	23 714	15 437	10 654	9 013	10 607	13 502
2.2.2	Long-term securities	273 855	317 609	298 472	333 857	366 455	432 509	417 010	425 691
2.2.3	Securities issued by residents	248 352	282 329	268 234	303 199	328 489	387 235	379 179	384 154
2.2.4	Securities issued by non-residents	45 082	58 595	53 952	46 095	48 620	54 287	48 438	55 039
2.3	Loans	30 615	30 577	42 352	44 523	44 464	39 900	43 455	48 244
2.3.1	Short-term loans	..	..	..	..	..	..	..	..
2.3.2	Long-term loans	..	..	..	..	..	..	..	..
2.3.3	Loans granted to residents	..	..	..	..	..	..	..	..
2.3.4	Loans granted to non-residents	..	..	..	..	..	..	..	..
2.4	Shares and other equity	508 056	514 168	389 998	462 990	547 428	544 603	601 220	717 374
2.4.1	Shares issued by residents	303 287	313 460	239 492	291 745	337 080	317 814	348 892	378 341
2.4.2	Shares issued by non-residents	204 769	200 708	150 506	171 245	210 348	226 789	252 328	339 033
2.5	Other, not elsewhere classified	78 453	56 967	66 197	39 439	54 349	38 158	92 409	84 521

Note: Detailed metadata at: http://metalinks.oecd.org/instinv/20141203/14ca

Table 4. Portfolio composition by type of investor

Percentage of total financial assets

Per cent

		2006	2007	2008	2009	2010	2011	2012	2013
	Investment funds								
2	Financial assets	100.0	100.0	100.0	100.0	100.0	100.0	100.0	100.0
2.1	Currency and deposits	1.0	1.0	0.7	1.3	0.9	1.1	1.3	1.1
2.2	Securities other than shares, except financial derivatives	24.1	25.0	32.6	28.2	26.7	30.0	28.2	25.3
2.2.1	Short-term securities	6.6	7.1	11.4	6.2	4.2	4.6	3.6	3.2
2.2.2	Long-term securities	17.5	17.9	21.2	22.0	22.5	25.5	24.7	22.1
2.2.3	Securities issued by residents	20.1	21.3	29.0	24.0	22.3	24.5	22.9	19.6
2.2.4	Securities issued by non-residents	4.0	3.7	3.6	4.2	4.4	5.5	5.3	5.7
2.3	Loans	0.6	0.4	0.4	0.5	0.5	0.6	0.6	0.5
2.3.1	Short-term loans	..	..	..	..	..	..	..	..
2.3.2	Long-term loans	..	..	..	..	..	..	..	..
2.3.3	Loans granted to residents	..	..	..	..	..	..	..	..
2.3.4	Loans granted to non-residents	..	..	..	..	..	..	..	..
2.4	Shares and other equity	70.5	71.3	61.0	66.7	69.0	64.9	64.8	67.8
2.4.1	Shares issued by residents	46.5	46.4	42.2	48.0	50.2	48.1	47.2	47.2
2.4.2	Shares issued by non-residents	24.0	24.8	18.9	18.8	18.9	16.9	17.6	20.6
2.5	Other, not elsewhere classified	3.8	2.3	5.2	3.2	2.8	3.4	5.1	5.3
	Insurance corporations								
2	Financial assets	100.0	100.0	100.0	100.0	100.0	100.0	100.0	100.0
2.1	Currency and deposits	1.1	1.0	2.0	1.3	1.2	1.2	1.3	1.2
2.2	Securities other than shares, except financial derivatives	41.6	38.6	40.1	40.3	38.9	39.1	37.2	35.9
2.2.1	Short-term securities	3.5	3.1	3.1	3.3	2.7	2.6	2.4	2.4
2.2.2	Long-term securities	38.1	35.5	37.0	37.0	36.1	36.5	34.8	33.6
2.2.3	Securities issued by residents	41.1	38.3	39.7	39.9	38.5	38.8	36.8	35.5
2.2.4	Securities issued by non-residents	0.5	0.3	0.4	0.4	0.3	0.2	0.4	0.5
2.3	Loans	10.8	11.4	12.5	11.8	11.2	10.8	10.1	9.7
2.3.1	Short-term loans	..	..	..	..	..	..	..	..
2.3.2	Long-term loans	..	..	..	..	..	..	..	..
2.3.3	Loans granted to residents	..	..	..	..	..	..	..	..
2.3.4	Loans granted to non-residents	..	..	..	..	..	..	..	..
2.4	Shares and other equity	36.6	38.3	31.7	36.0	37.5	34.3	36.1	37.0
2.4.1	Shares issued by residents	34.3	34.2	28.0	32.2	33.8	31.6	33.0	33.7
2.4.2	Shares issued by non-residents	2.3	4.1	3.7	3.8	3.6	2.7	3.1	3.3
2.5	Other, not elsewhere classified	9.9	10.8	13.8	10.7	11.3	14.6	15.4	16.1
	Autonomous pension funds								
2	Financial assets	100.0	100.0	100.0	100.0	100.0	100.0	100.0	100.0
2.1	Currency and deposits	0.9	1.0	0.8	1.9	1.9	2.2	2.1	2.2
2.2	Securities other than shares, except financial derivatives	31.9	35.8	39.0	38.2	36.2	40.6	35.9	33.3
2.2.1	Short-term securities	2.1	2.4	2.9	1.7	1.0	0.8	0.9	1.0
2.2.2	Long-term securities	29.8	33.4	36.1	36.5	35.1	39.8	35.0	32.3
2.2.3	Securities issued by residents	27.0	29.7	32.4	33.2	31.5	35.6	31.9	29.1
2.2.4	Securities issued by non-residents	4.9	6.2	6.5	5.0	4.7	5.0	4.1	4.2
2.3	Loans	3.3	3.2	5.1	4.9	4.3	3.7	3.7	3.7
2.3.1	Short-term loans	..	..	..	..	..	..	..	..
2.3.2	Long-term loans	..	..	..	..	..	..	..	..
2.3.3	Loans granted to residents	..	..	..	..	..	..	..	..
2.3.4	Loans granted to non-residents	..	..	..	..	..	..	..	..
2.4	Shares and other equity	55.3	54.0	47.2	50.7	52.5	50.1	50.5	54.4
2.4.1	Shares issued by residents	33.0	32.9	29.0	31.9	32.3	29.2	29.3	28.7
2.4.2	Shares issued by non-residents	22.3	21.1	18.2	18.7	20.2	20.8	21.2	25.7
2.5	Other, not elsewhere classified	8.5	6.0	8.0	4.3	5.2	3.5	7.8	6.4

Note: Detailed metadata at: http://metalinks.oecd.org/instinv/20141203/f729

Table 1. Financial assets of institutional investors, 2013

Million CLP

		Total	Investment funds			
			Open-end companies (mutual funds)			Closed-end companies
			Total	Money market funds	Other mutual funds	Total
2	Financial assets	25 836 936	20 515 448	10 398 893	10 116 555	5 321 488
2.1	Currency and deposits	..	..	..	..	..
2.2	Securities other than shares, except financial derivatives	19 205 035	17 714 961	10 177 132	7 537 829	1 490 074
2.2.1	Short-term securities	..	..	..	..	..
2.2.2	Long-term securities	..	..	..	..	..
2.2.3	Securities issued by residents	..	..	..	..	..
2.2.4	Securities issued by non-residents	..	..	..	..	..
2.3	Loans	..	..	..	..	..
2.3.1	Short-term loans	..	..	..	..	..
2.3.2	Long-term loans	..	..	..	..	..
2.3.3	Loans granted to residents	..	..	..	..	..
2.3.4	Loans granted to non-residents	..	..	..	..	..
2.4	Shares and other equity	5 451 362	2 530 912	0	2 530 912	2 920 450
2.4.1	Shares issued by residents	..	..	..	..	..
2.4.2	Shares issued by non-residents	..	..	..	..	..
2.5	Other, not elsewhere classified	1 180 539	269 576	221 761	47 815	910 963

		Total	Insurance corporations and autonomous pension funds			
			Insurance corporations			Autonomous pension funds
			Total	Life insurance corporations	Non-life insurance corporations	Total
2	Financial assets	109 816 623	24 450 038	23 258 761	1 191 277	85 366 585
2.1	Currency and deposits	5 419 912	357 889	202 488	155 401	5 062 023
2.2	Securities other than shares, except financial derivatives	52 142 676	17 152 340	16 324 277	828 062	34 990 336
2.2.1	Short-term securities	2 248 840	753 938	571 764	182 174	1 494 902
2.2.2	Long-term securities	49 893 836	16 398 402	15 752 513	645 888	33 495 434
2.2.3	Securities issued by residents	..	..	14 148 434	..	34 391 712
2.2.4	Securities issued by non-residents	..	..	2 175 844	..	598 624
2.3	Loans	2 667 290	2 667 290	2 665 091	2 199	..
2.3.1	Short-term loans	388 357	388 357	388 357	0	..
2.3.2	Long-term loans	2 278 934	2 278 934	2 276 734	2 199	..
2.3.3	Loans granted to residents	..	..	..	..	..
2.3.4	Loans granted to non-residents	..	..	..	..	..
2.4	Shares and other equity	47 822 325	2 440 729	2 392 136	48 593	45 381 596
2.4.1	Shares issued by residents	11 574 903	1 690 581	1 650 335	40 246	9 884 322
2.4.2	Shares issued by non-residents	36 247 422	750 148	741 801	8 347	35 497 274
2.5	Other, not elsewhere classified	1 764 420	1 831 789	1 674 770	157 020	-67 369

Note: Detailed metadata at: http://metalinks.oecd.org/instinv/20141203/b6e2

Table 2. Financial assets of investment funds

Million CLP

		2006	2007	2008	2009	2010	2011	2012	2013
	Investment funds								
2	Financial assets	11 489 841	15 242 562	13 782 415	20 489 273	22 512 685	22 096 629	23 366 367	25 836 936
2.1	Currency and deposits	106 899	184 979	137 286	288 819	262 554	..	..	..
2.2	Securities other than shares, except financial derivatives	7 919 696	9 435 678	10 478 630	14 604 327	14 053 242	15 345 176	16 508 495	19 205 035
2.2.1	Short-term securities	..	..	..	..	..	..	..	..
2.2.2	Long-term securities	..	..	..	..	..	..	..	..
2.2.3	Securities issued by residents	..	..	..	..	..	..	..	..
2.2.4	Securities issued by non-residents	..	..	..	..	..	..	..	..
2.3	Loans	0	0	0	0	0	0	0	..
2.3.1	Short-term loans	..	..	..	..	..	..	..	..
2.3.2	Long-term loans	..	..	..	..	..	..	..	..
2.3.3	Loans granted to residents	..	..	..	..	..	..	..	..
2.3.4	Loans granted to non-residents	..	..	..	..	..	..	..	..
2.4	Shares and other equity	3 129 962	5 124 862	2 676 113	4 989 292	7 537 014	5 737 988	5 744 570	5 451 362
2.4.1	Shares issued by residents	..	..	..	..	..	..	..	..
2.4.2	Shares issued by non-residents	..	..	..	..	..	..	..	..
2.5	Other, not elsewhere classified	333 284	497 043	490 387	606 834	659 875	1 013 465	1 113 303	1 180 539
	Open-end companies (mutual funds)								
2	Financial assets	9 590 827	12 232 738	11 359 569	17 555 443	18 094 999	17 176 539	18 021 428	20 515 448
2.1	Currency and deposits	81 847	103 175	99 779	253 435	223 140	..	..	..
2.2	Securities other than shares, except financial derivatives	7 631 657	9 081 359	9 823 942	13 950 420	13 137 155	14 214 771	15 184 363	17 714 961
2.2.1	Short-term securities	6 069 323	7 029 457	7 779 180	11 413 764	9 929 964	..	..	..
2.2.2	Long-term securities	1 562 334	2 051 901	2 044 762	2 536 656	3 207 191	..	..	..
2.2.3	Securities issued by residents	..	..	..	..	..	..	..	..
2.2.4	Securities issued by non-residents	..	..	..	..	..	..	..	..
2.3	Loans	0	0	0	0	0	0	0	..
2.3.1	Short-term loans	..	..	..	..	..	..	..	..
2.3.2	Long-term loans	..	..	..	..	..	..	..	..
2.3.3	Loans granted to residents	..	..	..	..	..	..	..	..
2.3.4	Loans granted to non-residents	..	..	..	..	..	..	..	..
2.4	Shares and other equity	1 761 265	2 952 608	1 269 919	3 071 388	4 505 197	2 722 059	2 543 098	2 530 912
2.4.1	Shares issued by residents	..	..	..	..	..	..	..	..
2.4.2	Shares issued by non-residents	..	..	..	..	..	..	..	..
2.5	Other, not elsewhere classified	116 058	95 596	165 928	280 200	229 508	239 709	293 967	269 576
	Money market funds								
2	Financial assets	4 557 886	5 656 012	6 718 856	10 119 755	8 823 306	9 293 721	9 792 196	10 398 893
2.1	Currency and deposits	24 085	20 604	47 670	158 729	109 225	..	..	..
2.2	Securities other than shares, except financial derivatives	4 506 199	5 610 098	6 559 860	9 739 614	8 559 454	9 103 393	9 531 394	10 177 132
2.2.1	Short-term securities	4 490 511	5 598 015	6 480 058	9 563 211	8 549 196	..	..	..
2.2.2	Long-term securities	15 688	12 083	79 802	176 403	10 258	..	..	..
2.2.3	Securities issued by residents	..	..	..	..	..	..	..	..
2.2.4	Securities issued by non-residents	..	..	..	..	..	..	..	..
2.3	Loans	0	0	0	0	0	0	0	..
2.3.1	Short-term loans	..	..	..	..	..	..	..	..
2.3.2	Long-term loans	..	..	..	..	..	..	..	..
2.3.3	Loans granted to residents	..	..	..	..	..	..	..	..
2.3.4	Loans granted to non-residents	..	..	..	..	..	..	..	..
2.4	Shares and other equity	0	0	0	0	0	0	0	0
2.4.1	Shares issued by residents	..	..	..	..	..	..	..	..
2.4.2	Shares issued by non-residents	..	..	..	..	..	..	..	..
2.5	Other, not elsewhere classified	27 603	25 310	111 326	221 412	154 627	190 328	260 801	221 761
	Other mutual funds								
2	Financial assets	5 032 941	6 576 725	4 640 713	7 435 689	9 271 693	7 882 818	8 229 232	10 116 555
2.1	Currency and deposits	57 762	82 571	52 110	94 706	113 915	..	..	..
2.2	Securities other than shares, except financial derivatives	3 125 458	3 471 260	3 264 082	4 210 806	4 577 701	5 111 377	5 652 969	7 537 829
2.2.1	Short-term securities	1 578 812	1 431 442	1 299 122	1 850 553	1 380 768	..	..	..
2.2.2	Long-term securities	1 546 646	2 039 818	1 964 960	2 360 253	3 196 932	..	..	..
2.2.3	Securities issued by residents	..	..	..	..	..	..	..	..
2.2.4	Securities issued by non-residents	..	..	..	..	..	..	..	..
2.3	Loans	0	0	0	0	0	0	0	..
2.3.1	Short-term loans	..	..	..	..	..	..	..	..
2.3.2	Long-term loans	..	..	..	..	..	..	..	..
2.3.3	Loans granted to residents	..	..	..	..	..	..	..	..
2.3.4	Loans granted to non-residents	..	..	..	..	..	..	..	..
2.4	Shares and other equity	1 761 265	2 952 608	1 269 919	3 071 388	4 505 197	2 722 059	2 543 098	2 530 912
2.4.1	Shares issued by residents	..	..	..	..	..	..	..	..
2.4.2	Shares issued by non-residents	..	..	..	..	..	..	..	..
2.5	Other, not elsewhere classified	88 455	70 286	54 601	58 789	74 880	49 382	33 166	47 815

Table 2. Financial assets of investment funds *(cont.)*

Million CLP

		2006	2007	2008	2009	2010	2011	2012	2013
	Closed-end companies								
2	Financial assets	1 899 014	3 009 824	2 422 847	2 933 830	4 417 686	4 920 089	5 344 940	5 321 488
2.1	Currency and deposits	25 052	81 803	37 506	35 384	39 414	..	..	..
2.2	Securities other than shares, except financial derivatives	288 039	354 319	654 687	653 907	916 087	1 130 406	1 324 132	1 490 074
2.2.1	Short-term securities	..	..	..	..	..	..	..	..
2.2.2	Long-term securities	..	..	..	..	..	..	..	..
2.2.3	Securities issued by residents	..	..	..	..	..	..	..	..
2.2.4	Securities issued by non-residents	..	..	..	..	..	..	..	..
2.3	Loans	0	0	0	0	0	0	0	..
2.3.1	Short-term loans	..	..	..	..	..	..	..	..
2.3.2	Long-term loans	..	..	..	..	..	..	..	..
2.3.3	Loans granted to residents	..	..	..	..	..	..	..	..
2.3.4	Loans granted to non-residents	..	..	..	..	..	..	..	..
2.4	Shares and other equity	1 368 696	2 172 254	1 406 194	1 917 904	3 031 817	3 015 928	3 201 472	2 920 450
2.4.1	Shares issued by residents	..	..	..	..	..	..	..	..
2.4.2	Shares issued by non-residents	..	..	..	..	..	..	..	..
2.5	Other, not elsewhere classified	217 226	401 447	324 459	326 634	430 367	773 756	819 336	910 963

Note: Detailed metadata at: http://metalinks.oecd.org/instinv/20141203/b6e2

CHILE

Table 3. Financial assets of insurance corporations and autonomous pension funds

Million CLP

		2006	2007	2008	2009	2010	2011	2012	2013
	Insurance corporations and autonomous pension funds								
2	Financial assets	60 246 614	69 895 713	63 639 593	77 165 524	88 432 500	90 877 847	100 200 407	109 816 623
2.1	Currency and deposits	8 369 662	10 291 265	9 812 344	4 540 265	3 459 297	4 636 104	5 257 952	5 419 912
2.2	Securities other than shares, except financial derivatives	23 546 139	25 436 313	30 815 561	30 831 302	34 480 168	43 879 415	47 544 941	52 142 676
2.2.1	Short-term securities	1 550 959	1 298 704	1 529 322	1 541 816	1 444 613	1 637 471	1 569 942	2 248 840
2.2.2	Long-term securities	21 995 180	24 137 609	29 286 240	29 289 487	33 035 555	42 241 944	45 975 000	49 893 836
2.2.3	Securities issued by residents	..	..	..	..	..	..	..	..
2.2.4	Securities issued by non-residents	..	..	..	..	..	..	..	..
2.3	Loans	1 400 774	1 650 179	2 289 874	2 291 632	2 179 307	2 235 578	2 424 619	2 667 290
2.3.1	Short-term loans	49 705	56 888	301 245	341 269	304 748	330 516	363 942	388 357
2.3.2	Long-term loans	1 351 069	1 593 291	1 988 629	1 950 363	1 874 559	1 905 062	2 060 677	2 278 934
2.3.3	Loans granted to residents	..	..	..	..	..	..	..	..
2.3.4	Loans granted to non-residents	..	..	..	..	..	..	..	..
2.4	Shares and other equity	25 641 274	30 645 085	20 416 001	36 891 979	45 252 181	37 795 891	43 165 752	47 822 325
2.4.1	Shares issued by residents	10 332 507	11 260 679	8 431 075	10 617 815	13 976 198	12 380 242	13 091 646	11 574 903
2.4.2	Shares issued by non-residents	15 308 768	19 384 406	11 984 926	26 274 165	31 275 983	25 415 648	30 074 105	36 247 422
2.5	Other, not elsewhere classified	1 288 765	1 872 870	305 812	2 610 345	3 061 548	2 330 859	1 807 143	1 764 420
	Insurance corporations								
2	Financial assets	13 059 939	14 722 561	16 888 706	17 380 187	18 909 047	20 500 428	22 657 166	24 450 038
2.1	Currency and deposits	53 833	77 527	93 922	72 012	182 537	139 679	303 521	357 889
2.2	Securities other than shares, except financial derivatives	9 283 827	10 222 547	11 757 146	11 737 513	12 655 624	14 032 726	15 978 528	17 152 340
2.2.1	Short-term securities	468 488	414 336	546 238	411 848	555 337	650 585	625 880	753 938
2.2.2	Long-term securities	8 815 339	9 808 210	11 210 908	11 325 665	12 100 287	13 382 140	15 352 648	16 398 402
2.2.3	Securities issued by residents	..	..	..	..	..	..	..	..
2.2.4	Securities issued by non-residents	..	..	..	..	..	..	..	..
2.3	Loans	1 400 774	1 650 179	2 289 874	2 291 632	2 179 307	2 235 578	2 424 619	2 667 290
2.3.1	Short-term loans	49 705	56 888	301 245	341 269	304 748	330 516	363 942	388 357
2.3.2	Long-term loans	1 351 069	1 593 291	1 988 629	1 950 363	1 874 559	1 905 062	2 060 677	2 278 934
2.3.3	Loans granted to residents	..	..	..	..	..	..	..	..
2.3.4	Loans granted to non-residents	..	..	..	..	..	..	..	..
2.4	Shares and other equity	1 032 994	1 128 860	867 114	1 162 583	1 480 123	1 428 731	2 238 374	2 440 729
2.4.1	Shares issued by residents	795 989	888 509	703 382	913 448	1 072 976	1 155 013	1 642 334	1 690 581
2.4.2	Shares issued by non-residents	237 005	240 351	163 732	249 135	407 147	273 718	596 040	750 148
2.5	Other, not elsewhere classified	1 288 511	1 643 447	1 880 650	2 116 447	2 411 456	2 663 714	1 712 124	1 831 789
	Life insurance corporations								
2	Financial assets	12 714 064	14 291 642	16 363 381	16 804 682	18 206 364	19 715 047	21 535 538	23 258 761
2.1	Currency and deposits	26 874	41 748	47 880	34 009	50 094	54 069	140 224	202 488
2.2	Securities other than shares, except financial derivatives	9 017 302	9 866 327	11 314 516	11 266 092	12 175 496	13 445 474	15 249 156	16 324 277
2.2.1	Short-term securities	388 646	309 048	406 123	303 485	471 470	526 032	484 362	571 764
2.2.2	Long-term securities	8 628 656	9 557 279	10 908 394	10 962 607	11 704 026	12 919 442	14 764 794	15 752 513
2.2.3	Securities issued by residents	8 560 034	9 176 167	10 497 261	10 559 278	11 210 404	12 029 151	13 592 133	14 148 434
2.2.4	Securities issued by non-residents	457 268	690 160	817 255	706 814	965 092	1 416 323	1 657 023	2 175 844
2.3	Loans	1 400 774	1 650 179	2 289 791	2 291 605	2 179 302	2 235 578	2 422 143	2 665 091
2.3.1	Short-term loans	49 705	56 888	301 245	341 269	304 748	330 516	363 942	388 357
2.3.2	Long-term loans	1 351 069	1 593 291	1 988 545	1 950 336	1 874 554	1 905 062	2 058 200	2 276 734
2.3.3	Loans granted to residents	..	..	..	..	..	..	..	..
2.3.4	Loans granted to non-residents	..	..	..	..	..	..	..	..
2.4	Shares and other equity	980 603	1 091 941	833 797	1 099 536	1 392 914	1 318 904	2 162 789	2 392 136
2.4.1	Shares issued by residents	748 254	862 668	672 147	857 306	992 727	1 050 586	1 571 023	1 650 335
2.4.2	Shares issued by non-residents	232 349	229 273	161 649	242 230	400 187	268 318	591 766	741 801
2.5	Other, not elsewhere classified	1 288 511	1 641 446	1 877 397	2 113 441	2 408 559	2 661 022	1 561 227	1 674 770
	Non-life insurance corporations								
2	Financial assets	345 875	430 919	525 325	575 505	702 683	785 381	1 121 628	1 191 277
2.1	Currency and deposits	26 959	35 779	46 041	38 003	132 443	85 609	163 297	155 401
2.2	Securities other than shares, except financial derivatives	266 525	356 220	442 629	471 421	480 128	587 252	729 372	828 062
2.2.1	Short-term securities	79 842	105 288	140 115	108 364	83 866	124 554	141 518	182 174
2.2.2	Long-term securities	186 683	250 931	302 514	363 057	396 262	462 698	587 853	645 888
2.2.3	Securities issued by residents	..	..	..	..	..	..	..	..
2.2.4	Securities issued by non-residents	..	..	..	..	..	..	..	..
2.3	Loans	0	0	83	27	5	0	2 477	2 199
2.3.1	Short-term loans	0	0	0	0	0	0	0	0
2.3.2	Long-term loans	0	0	83	27	5	0	2 477	2 199
2.3.3	Loans granted to residents	0	0	..	..	..	..	..	..
2.3.4	Loans granted to non-residents	0	0	..	..	..	..	..	..
2.4	Shares and other equity	52 391	36 919	33 318	63 047	87 210	109 827	75 586	48 593
2.4.1	Shares issued by residents	47 736	25 842	31 235	56 142	80 249	104 427	71 312	40 246
2.4.2	Shares issued by non-residents	4 656	11 078	2 083	6 906	6 960	5 400	4 274	8 347
2.5	Other, not elsewhere classified	0	2 001	3 253	3 007	2 897	2 692	150 897	157 020

Table 3. Financial assets of insurance corporations and autonomous pension funds *(cont.)*

Million CLP

		2006	2007	2008	2009	2010	2011	2012	2013
	Autonomous pension funds								
2	Financial assets	47 186 675	55 173 152	46 750 887	59 785 337	69 523 453	70 377 419	77 543 241	85 366 585
2.1	Currency and deposits	8 315 829	10 213 738	9 718 423	4 468 254	3 276 760	4 496 426	4 954 431	5 062 023
2.2	Securities other than shares, except financial derivatives	14 262 312	15 213 767	19 058 416	19 093 790	21 824 543	29 846 689	31 566 413	34 990 336
2.2.1	Short-term securities	1 082 471	884 368	983 084	1 129 967	889 276	986 886	944 061	1 494 902
2.2.2	Long-term securities	13 179 842	14 329 399	18 075 332	17 963 822	20 935 268	28 859 804	30 622 352	33 495 434
2.2.3	Securities issued by residents	14 051 176	14 713 692	17 804 018	19 001 942	21 432 752	29 452 996	31 393 051	34 391 712
2.2.4	Securities issued by non-residents	211 136	500 075	1 254 398	91 847	391 792	393 693	173 362	598 624
2.3	Loans	0	0	0	0	0	0	0	..
2.3.1	Short-term loans	..	..	..	..	..	..	..	..
2.3.2	Long-term loans	..	..	..	..	..	..	..	..
2.3.3	Loans granted to residents	..	..	..	..	..	..	..	..
2.3.4	Loans granted to non-residents	..	..	..	..	..	..	..	..
2.4	Shares and other equity	24 608 280	29 516 225	19 548 887	35 729 396	43 772 057	36 367 159	40 927 377	45 381 596
2.4.1	Shares issued by residents	9 536 518	10 372 169	7 727 693	9 704 367	12 903 222	11 225 229	11 449 312	9 884 322
2.4.2	Shares issued by non-residents	15 071 763	19 144 055	11 821 194	26 025 030	30 868 836	25 141 930	29 478 066	35 497 274
2.5	Other, not elsewhere classified	254	229 422	-1 574 838	493 897	650 092	-332 855	95 019	-67 369

Note: Detailed metadata at: http://metalinks.oecd.org/instinv/20141203/b6e2

Table 4. Portfolio composition by type of investor

Percentage of total financial assets

Per cent

		2006	2007	2008	2009	2010	2011	2012	2013
	Investment funds								
2	Financial assets	100.0	100.0	100.0	100.0	100.0	100.0	100.0	100.0
2.1	Currency and deposits	0.9	1.2	1.0	1.4	1.2	..	..	..
2.2	Securities other than shares, except financial derivatives	68.9	61.9	76.0	71.3	62.4	69.4	70.7	74.3
2.2.1	Short-term securities	..	..	..	..	..	..	..	..
2.2.2	Long-term securities	..	..	..	..	..	..	..	..
2.2.3	Securities issued by residents	..	..	..	..	..	..	..	..
2.2.4	Securities issued by non-residents	..	..	..	..	..	..	..	..
2.3	Loans	0.0	0.0	0.0	0.0	0.0	0.0	0.0	..
2.3.1	Short-term loans	..	..	..	..	..	..	..	..
2.3.2	Long-term loans	..	..	..	..	..	..	..	..
2.3.3	Loans granted to residents	..	..	..	..	..	..	..	..
2.3.4	Loans granted to non-residents	..	..	..	..	..	..	..	..
2.4	Shares and other equity	27.2	33.6	19.4	24.4	33.5	26.0	24.6	21.1
2.4.1	Shares issued by residents	..	..	..	..	..	..	..	..
2.4.2	Shares issued by non-residents	..	..	..	..	..	..	..	..
2.5	Other, not elsewhere classified	2.9	3.3	3.6	3.0	2.9	4.6	4.8	4.6
	Insurance corporations								
2	Financial assets	100.0	100.0	100.0	100.0	100.0	100.0	100.0	100.0
2.1	Currency and deposits	0.4	0.5	0.6	0.4	1.0	0.7	1.3	1.5
2.2	Securities other than shares, except financial derivatives	71.1	69.4	69.6	67.5	66.9	68.5	70.5	70.2
2.2.1	Short-term securities	3.6	2.8	3.2	2.4	2.9	3.2	2.8	3.1
2.2.2	Long-term securities	67.5	66.6	66.4	65.2	64.0	65.3	67.8	67.1
2.2.3	Securities issued by residents	..	..	..	..	..	..	..	..
2.2.4	Securities issued by non-residents	..	..	..	..	..	..	..	..
2.3	Loans	10.7	11.2	13.6	13.2	11.5	10.9	10.7	10.9
2.3.1	Short-term loans	0.4	0.4	1.8	2.0	1.6	1.6	1.6	1.6
2.3.2	Long-term loans	10.3	10.8	11.8	11.2	9.9	9.3	9.1	9.3
2.3.3	Loans granted to residents	..	..	..	..	..	..	..	..
2.3.4	Loans granted to non-residents	..	..	..	..	..	..	..	..
2.4	Shares and other equity	7.9	7.7	5.1	6.7	7.8	7.0	9.9	10.0
2.4.1	Shares issued by residents	6.1	6.0	4.2	5.3	5.7	5.6	7.2	6.9
2.4.2	Shares issued by non-residents	1.8	1.6	1.0	1.4	2.2	1.3	2.6	3.1
2.5	Other, not elsewhere classified	9.9	11.2	11.1	12.2	12.8	13.0	7.6	7.5
	Autonomous pension funds								
2	Financial assets	100.0	100.0	100.0	100.0	100.0	100.0	100.0	100.0
2.1	Currency and deposits	17.6	18.5	20.8	7.5	4.7	6.4	6.4	5.9
2.2	Securities other than shares, except financial derivatives	30.2	27.6	40.8	31.9	31.4	42.4	40.7	41.0
2.2.1	Short-term securities	2.3	1.6	2.1	1.9	1.3	1.4	1.2	1.8
2.2.2	Long-term securities	27.9	26.0	38.7	30.0	30.1	41.0	39.5	39.2
2.2.3	Securities issued by residents	29.8	26.7	38.1	31.8	30.8	41.9	40.5	40.3
2.2.4	Securities issued by non-residents	0.4	0.9	2.7	0.2	0.6	0.6	0.2	0.7
2.3	Loans	0.0	0.0	0.0	0.0	0.0	0.0	0.0	..
2.3.1	Short-term loans	..	..	..	..	..	..	..	..
2.3.2	Long-term loans	..	..	..	..	..	..	..	..
2.3.3	Loans granted to residents	..	..	..	..	..	..	..	..
2.3.4	Loans granted to non-residents	..	..	..	..	..	..	..	..
2.4	Shares and other equity	52.2	53.5	41.8	59.8	63.0	51.7	52.8	53.2
2.4.1	Shares issued by residents	20.2	18.8	16.5	16.2	18.6	16.0	14.8	11.6
2.4.2	Shares issued by non-residents	31.9	34.7	25.3	43.5	44.4	35.7	38.0	41.6
2.5	Other, not elsewhere classified	0.0	0.4	-3.4	0.8	0.9	-0.5	0.1	-0.1

Note: Detailed metadata at: http://metalinks.oecd.org/instinv/20141203/f729

CZECH REPUBLIC

Table 1. Financial assets of institutional investors, 2012

Million CZK

		Total	Investment funds			
			Open-end companies (mutual funds)			Closed-end companies
			Total	Money market funds	Other mutual funds	Total
2	Financial assets	164 852	..	2 790	..	..
2.1	Currency and deposits	34 391	..	1 566	..	..
2.2	Securities other than shares, except financial derivatives	63 593	..	1 223	..	..
2.2.1	Short-term securities	3 904	..	505	..	..
2.2.2	Long-term securities	59 689	..	718	..	..
2.2.3	Securities issued by residents	..	..	..	..	..
2.2.4	Securities issued by non-residents	..	..	..	..	..
2.3	Loans	4 479	..	0	..	..
2.3.1	Short-term loans	542	..	0	..	..
2.3.2	Long-term loans	3 937	..	0	..	..
2.3.3	Loans granted to residents	..	..	..	..	..
2.3.4	Loans granted to non-residents	..	..	..	..	..
2.4	Shares and other equity	57 334	..	0	..	..
2.4.1	Shares issued by residents	..	..	..	..	..
2.4.2	Shares issued by non-residents	..	..	..	..	..
2.5	Other, not elsewhere classified	5 055	..	1	..	..

		Total	Insurance corporations and autonomous pension funds			
			Insurance corporations			Autonomous pension funds
			Total	Life insurance corporations	Non-life insurance corporations	Total
2	Financial assets	750 664	481 826	..	..	268 838
2.1	Currency and deposits	61 084	34 422	..	..	26 662
2.2	Securities other than shares, except financial derivatives	497 511	261 609	..	..	235 902
2.2.1	Short-term securities	12 528	5 094	..	..	7 434
2.2.2	Long-term securities	484 983	256 515	..	..	228 468
2.2.3	Securities issued by residents	400 828	..	..	..	..
2.2.4	Securities issued by non-residents	96 683	..	..	..	..
2.3	Loans	3 454	3 454	..	..	0
2.3.1	Short-term loans	0	0	..	..	0
2.3.2	Long-term loans	3 454	3 454	..	..	0
2.3.3	Loans granted to residents	3 454	..	..	..	..
2.3.4	Loans granted to non-residents	0	..	..	..	..
2.4	Shares and other equity	107 747	103 799	..	..	3 948
2.4.1	Shares issued by residents	45 324	..	..	..	..
2.4.2	Shares issued by non-residents	62 423	..	..	..	..
2.5	Other, not elsewhere classified	80 868	78 542	..	..	2 326

Note: Detailed metadata at: http://metalinks.oecd.org/instinv/20141203/90c3

CZECH REPUBLIC

Table 2. Financial assets of investment funds

Million CZK

		2006	2007	2008	2009	2010	2011	2012	2013
	Investment funds								
2	Financial assets	158 781	192 575	147 597	154 407	172 532	167 801	164 852	..
2.1	Currency and deposits	21 838	33 837	23 114	25 479	25 107	29 648	34 391	..
2.2	Securities other than shares, except financial derivatives	94 924	101 168	87 053	76 215	80 383	72 215	63 593	..
2.2.1	Short-term securities	18 716	15 959	6 853	17 607	24 015	18 929	3 904	..
2.2.2	Long-term securities	76 208	85 209	80 200	58 608	56 368	53 286	59 689	..
2.2.3	Securities issued by residents	..	..	..	..	..	..	..	..
2.2.4	Securities issued by non-residents	..	..	..	..	..	..	..	..
2.3	Loans	17	639	3 413	964	2 456	5 366	4 479	..
2.3.1	Short-term loans	0	71	2 444	95	742	1 028	542	..
2.3.2	Long-term loans	17	568	969	869	1 714	4 338	3 937	..
2.3.3	Loans granted to residents	..	..	..	..	..	..	..	..
2.3.4	Loans granted to non-residents	..	..	..	..	..	..	..	..
2.4	Shares and other equity	40 353	54 542	31 613	49 172	61 739	54 890	57 334	..
2.4.1	Shares issued by residents	..	..	..	..	..	..	..	..
2.4.2	Shares issued by non-residents	..	..	..	..	..	..	..	..
2.5	Other, not elsewhere classified	1 649	2 389	2 404	2 577	2 847	5 682	5 055	..
	Open-end companies (mutual funds)								
2	Financial assets	..	..	..	..	..	..	..	..
2.1	Currency and deposits	..	..	..	..	..	..	..	..
2.2	Securities other than shares, except financial derivatives	..	..	..	..	..	..	..	..
2.2.1	Short-term securities	..	..	..	..	..	..	..	..
2.2.2	Long-term securities	..	..	..	..	..	..	..	..
2.2.3	Securities issued by residents	..	..	..	..	..	..	..	..
2.2.4	Securities issued by non-residents	..	..	..	..	..	..	..	..
2.3	Loans	..	..	..	..	..	..	..	..
2.3.1	Short-term loans	..	..	..	..	..	..	..	..
2.3.2	Long-term loans	..	..	..	..	..	..	..	..
2.3.3	Loans granted to residents	..	..	..	..	..	..	..	..
2.3.4	Loans granted to non-residents	..	..	..	..	..	..	..	..
2.4	Shares and other equity	..	..	..	..	..	..	..	..
2.4.1	Shares issued by residents	..	..	..	..	..	..	..	..
2.4.2	Shares issued by non-residents	..	..	..	..	..	..	..	..
2.5	Other, not elsewhere classified	..	..	..	..	..	..	..	..
	Money market funds								
2	Financial assets	77 868	77 380	56 185	47 233	43 698	12 480	2 790	..
2.1	Currency and deposits	14 241	15 764	11 594	13 007	13 716	3 813	1 566	..
2.2	Securities other than shares, except financial derivatives	60 682	58 393	42 102	33 838	29 548	8 667	1 223	..
2.2.1	Short-term securities	10 204	46 343	33 770	23 095	11 268	3 637	505	..
2.2.2	Long-term securities	50 478	12 050	8 332	10 743	18 280	5 030	718	..
2.2.3	Securities issued by residents	..	..	..	..	..	..	..	..
2.2.4	Securities issued by non-residents	..	..	..	..	..	..	..	..
2.3	Loans	0	9	2 043	0	0	0	0	..
2.3.1	Short-term loans	0	9	2 043	0	0	0	0	..
2.3.2	Long-term loans	0	0	0	0	0	0	0	..
2.3.3	Loans granted to residents	..	..	..	..	..	..	..	..
2.3.4	Loans granted to non-residents	..	..	..	..	..	..	..	..
2.4	Shares and other equity	2 657	2 862	216	315	313	0	0	..
2.4.1	Shares issued by residents	..	..	..	..	..	..	..	..
2.4.2	Shares issued by non-residents	..	..	..	..	..	..	..	..
2.5	Other, not elsewhere classified	288	352	230	73	121	0	1	..
	Other mutual funds								
2	Financial assets	..	..	..	..	..	..	..	..
2.1	Currency and deposits	..	..	..	..	..	..	..	..
2.2	Securities other than shares, except financial derivatives	..	..	..	..	..	..	..	..
2.2.1	Short-term securities	..	..	..	..	..	..	..	..
2.2.2	Long-term securities	..	..	..	..	..	..	..	..
2.2.3	Securities issued by residents	..	..	..	..	..	..	..	..
2.2.4	Securities issued by non-residents	..	..	..	..	..	..	..	..
2.3	Loans	..	..	..	..	..	..	..	..
2.3.1	Short-term loans	..	..	..	..	..	..	..	..
2.3.2	Long-term loans	..	..	..	..	..	..	..	..
2.3.3	Loans granted to residents	..	..	..	..	..	..	..	..
2.3.4	Loans granted to non-residents	..	..	..	..	..	..	..	..
2.4	Shares and other equity	..	..	..	..	..	..	..	..
2.4.1	Shares issued by residents	..	..	..	..	..	..	..	..
2.4.2	Shares issued by non-residents	..	..	..	..	..	..	..	..
2.5	Other, not elsewhere classified	..	..	..	..	..	..	..	..

Table 2. Financial assets of investment funds (*cont.*)

Million CZK

		2006	2007	2008	2009	2010	2011	2012	2013
	Closed-end companies								
2	Financial assets	..	..	..	..	..	..	..	..
2.1	Currency and deposits	..	..	..	..	..	..	..	..
2.2	Securities other than shares, except financial derivatives	..	..	..	..	..	..	..	..
2.2.1	Short-term securities	..	..	..	..	..	..	..	..
2.2.2	Long-term securities	..	..	..	..	..	..	..	..
2.2.3	Securities issued by residents	..	..	..	..	..	..	..	..
2.2.4	Securities issued by non-residents	..	..	..	..	..	..	..	..
2.3	Loans	..	..	..	..	..	..	..	..
2.3.1	Short-term loans	..	..	..	..	..	..	..	..
2.3.2	Long-term loans	..	..	..	..	..	..	..	..
2.3.3	Loans granted to residents	..	..	..	..	..	..	..	..
2.3.4	Loans granted to non-residents	..	..	..	..	..	..	..	..
2.4	Shares and other equity	..	..	..	..	..	..	..	..
2.4.1	Shares issued by residents	..	..	..	..	..	..	..	..
2.4.2	Shares issued by non-residents	..	..	..	..	..	..	..	..
2.5	Other, not elsewhere classified	..	..	..	..	..	..	..	..

Note: Detailed metadata at: http://metalinks.oecd.org/instinv/20141203/90c3

Table 3. Financial assets of insurance corporations and autonomous pension funds

Million CZK

		2006	2007	2008	2009	2010	2011	2012	2013
	Insurance corporations and autonomous pension funds								
2	Financial assets	478 317	537 093	586 416	642 271	693 854	693 156	750 664	..
2.1	Currency and deposits	41 399	54 149	55 004	58 020	50 883	49 063	61 084	..
2.2	Securities other than shares, except financial derivatives	313 848	336 142	383 396	436 360	469 880	473 881	497 511	..
2.2.1	Short-term securities	9 767	9 687	7 387	3 995	3 390	1 551	12 528	..
2.2.2	Long-term securities	304 081	326 455	376 009	432 365	466 490	472 330	484 983	..
2.2.3	Securities issued by residents	251 706	270 524	310 559	356 589	382 542	377 154	400 828	..
2.2.4	Securities issued by non-residents	62 142	65 618	72 837	79 771	87 338	96 727	96 683	..
2.3	Loans	2 058	6 706	2 995	922	805	2 698	3 454	..
2.3.1	Short-term loans	0	0	0	0	0	0	0	..
2.3.2	Long-term loans	2 058	6 706	2 995	922	805	2 698	3 454	..
2.3.3	Loans granted to residents	2 058	6 706	2 995	922	805	2 698	3 454	..
2.3.4	Loans granted to non-residents	0	0	0	0	0	0	0	..
2.4	Shares and other equity	73 542	80 012	74 809	75 605	91 302	91 110	107 747	..
2.4.1	Shares issued by residents	12 178	15 608	16 627	28 778	34 630	33 215	45 324	..
2.4.2	Shares issued by non-residents	61 364	64 404	58 182	46 827	56 672	57 895	62 423	..
2.5	Other, not elsewhere classified	47 470	60 084	70 212	71 364	80 984	76 404	80 868	..
	Insurance corporations								
2	Financial assets	341 626	374 006	402 088	432 504	466 848	450 326	481 826	..
2.1	Currency and deposits	32 064	38 079	37 434	34 284	33 154	29 692	34 422	..
2.2	Securities other than shares, except financial derivatives	198 056	209 356	232 150	264 313	275 945	263 012	261 609	..
2.2.1	Short-term securities	3 035	3 017	1 689	2 660	1 135	518	5 094	..
2.2.2	Long-term securities	195 021	206 339	230 461	261 653	274 810	262 494	256 515	..
2.2.3	Securities issued by residents	..	..	..	..	..	..	..	..
2.2.4	Securities issued by non-residents	..	..	..	..	..	..	..	..
2.3	Loans	2 058	6 706	2 995	922	805	2 698	3 454	..
2.3.1	Short-term loans	0	0	0	0	0	0	0	..
2.3.2	Long-term loans	2 058	6 706	2 995	922	805	2 698	3 454	..
2.3.3	Loans granted to residents	..	..	..	..	..	..	..	..
2.3.4	Loans granted to non-residents	..	..	..	..	..	..	..	..
2.4	Shares and other equity	63 926	62 628	62 916	65 198	80 737	83 919	103 799	..
2.4.1	Shares issued by residents	..	..	..	..	..	..	..	..
2.4.2	Shares issued by non-residents	..	..	..	..	..	..	..	..
2.5	Other, not elsewhere classified	45 522	57 237	66 593	67 787	76 207	71 005	78 542	..
	Life insurance corporations								
2	Financial assets	..	..	..	..	..	..	..	..
2.1	Currency and deposits	..	..	..	..	..	..	..	..
2.2	Securities other than shares, except financial derivatives	..	..	..	..	..	..	..	..
2.2.1	Short-term securities	..	..	..	..	..	..	..	..
2.2.2	Long-term securities	..	..	..	..	..	..	..	..
2.2.3	Securities issued by residents	..	..	..	..	..	..	..	..
2.2.4	Securities issued by non-residents	..	..	..	..	..	..	..	..
2.3	Loans	..	..	..	..	..	..	..	..
2.3.1	Short-term loans	..	..	..	..	..	..	..	..
2.3.2	Long-term loans	..	..	..	..	..	..	..	..
2.3.3	Loans granted to residents	..	..	..	..	..	..	..	..
2.3.4	Loans granted to non-residents	..	..	..	..	..	..	..	..
2.4	Shares and other equity	..	..	..	..	..	..	..	..
2.4.1	Shares issued by residents	..	..	..	..	..	..	..	..
2.4.2	Shares issued by non-residents	..	..	..	..	..	..	..	..
2.5	Other, not elsewhere classified	..	..	..	..	..	..	..	..
	Non-life insurance corporations								
2	Financial assets	..	..	..	..	..	..	..	..
2.1	Currency and deposits	..	..	..	..	..	..	..	..
2.2	Securities other than shares, except financial derivatives	..	..	..	..	..	..	..	..
2.2.1	Short-term securities	..	..	..	..	..	..	..	..
2.2.2	Long-term securities	..	..	..	..	..	..	..	..
2.2.3	Securities issued by residents	..	..	..	..	..	..	..	..
2.2.4	Securities issued by non-residents	..	..	..	..	..	..	..	..
2.3	Loans	..	..	..	..	..	..	..	..
2.3.1	Short-term loans	..	..	..	..	..	..	..	..
2.3.2	Long-term loans	..	..	..	..	..	..	..	..
2.3.3	Loans granted to residents	..	..	..	..	..	..	..	..
2.3.4	Loans granted to non-residents	..	..	..	..	..	..	..	..
2.4	Shares and other equity	..	..	..	..	..	..	..	..
2.4.1	Shares issued by residents	..	..	..	..	..	..	..	..
2.4.2	Shares issued by non-residents	..	..	..	..	..	..	..	..
2.5	Other, not elsewhere classified	..	..	..	..	..	..	..	..

Table 3. Financial assets of insurance corporations and autonomous pension funds *(cont.)*

Million CZK

		2006	2007	2008	2009	2010	2011	2012	2013
	Autonomous pension funds								
2	Financial assets	136 691	163 087	184 328	209 767	227 006	242 830	268 838	..
2.1	Currency and deposits	9 335	16 070	17 570	23 736	17 729	19 371	26 662	..
2.2	Securities other than shares, except financial derivatives	115 792	126 786	151 246	172 047	193 935	210 869	235 902	..
2.2.1	Short-term securities	6 732	6 670	5 698	1 335	2 255	1 033	7 434	..
2.2.2	Long-term securities	109 060	120 116	145 548	170 712	191 680	209 836	228 468	..
2.2.3	Securities issued by residents	..	..	..	..	..	..	..	..
2.2.4	Securities issued by non-residents	..	..	..	..	..	..	..	..
2.3	Loans	0	0	0	0	0	0	0	..
2.3.1	Short-term loans	0	0	0	0	0	0	0	..
2.3.2	Long-term loans	0	0	0	0	0	0	0	..
2.3.3	Loans granted to residents	..	..	..	..	..	..	..	..
2.3.4	Loans granted to non-residents	..	..	..	..	..	..	..	..
2.4	Shares and other equity	9 616	17 384	11 893	10 407	10 565	7 191	3 948	..
2.4.1	Shares issued by residents	..	..	..	..	..	..	..	..
2.4.2	Shares issued by non-residents	..	..	..	..	..	..	..	..
2.5	Other, not elsewhere classified	1 948	2 847	3 619	3 577	4 777	5 399	2 326	..

Note: Detailed metadata at: http://metalinks.oecd.org/instinv/20141203/90c3

CZECH REPUBLIC

Table 4. Portfolio composition by type of investor

Percentage of total financial assets

Per cent

		2006	2007	2008	2009	2010	2011	2012	2013
	Investment funds								
2	Financial assets	100.0	100.0	100.0	100.0	100.0	100.0	100.0	..
2.1	Currency and deposits	13.8	17.6	15.7	16.5	14.6	17.7	20.9	..
2.2	Securities other than shares, except financial derivatives	59.8	52.5	59.0	49.4	46.6	43.0	38.6	..
2.2.1	Short-term securities	11.8	8.3	4.6	11.4	13.9	11.3	2.4	..
2.2.2	Long-term securities	48.0	44.2	54.3	38.0	32.7	31.8	36.2	..
2.2.3	Securities issued by residents	..	..	..	..	..	..	..	..
2.2.4	Securities issued by non-residents	..	..	..	..	..	..	..	..
2.3	Loans	0.0	0.3	2.3	0.6	1.4	3.2	2.7	..
2.3.1	Short-term loans	0.0	0.0	1.7	0.1	0.4	0.6	0.3	..
2.3.2	Long-term loans	0.0	0.3	0.7	0.6	1.0	2.6	2.4	..
2.3.3	Loans granted to residents	..	..	..	..	..	..	..	..
2.3.4	Loans granted to non-residents	..	..	..	..	..	..	..	..
2.4	Shares and other equity	25.4	28.3	21.4	31.8	35.8	32.7	34.8	..
2.4.1	Shares issued by residents	..	..	..	..	..	..	..	..
2.4.2	Shares issued by non-residents	..	..	..	..	..	..	..	..
2.5	Other, not elsewhere classified	1.0	1.2	1.6	1.7	1.7	3.4	3.1	..
	Insurance corporations								
2	Financial assets	100.0	100.0	100.0	100.0	100.0	100.0	100.0	..
2.1	Currency and deposits	9.4	10.2	9.3	7.9	7.1	6.6	7.1	..
2.2	Securities other than shares, except financial derivatives	58.0	56.0	57.7	61.1	59.1	58.4	54.3	..
2.2.1	Short-term securities	0.9	0.8	0.4	0.6	0.2	0.1	1.1	..
2.2.2	Long-term securities	57.1	55.2	57.3	60.5	58.9	58.3	53.2	..
2.2.3	Securities issued by residents	..	..	..	..	..	..	..	..
2.2.4	Securities issued by non-residents	..	..	..	..	..	..	..	..
2.3	Loans	0.6	1.8	0.7	0.2	0.2	0.6	0.7	..
2.3.1	Short-term loans	0.0	0.0	0.0	0.0	0.0	0.0	0.0	..
2.3.2	Long-term loans	0.6	1.8	0.7	0.2	0.2	0.6	0.7	..
2.3.3	Loans granted to residents	..	..	..	..	..	..	..	..
2.3.4	Loans granted to non-residents	..	..	..	..	..	..	..	..
2.4	Shares and other equity	18.7	16.7	15.6	15.1	17.3	18.6	21.5	..
2.4.1	Shares issued by residents	..	..	..	..	..	..	..	..
2.4.2	Shares issued by non-residents	..	..	..	..	..	..	..	..
2.5	Other, not elsewhere classified	13.3	15.3	16.6	15.7	16.3	15.8	16.3	..
	Autonomous pension funds								
2	Financial assets	100.0	100.0	100.0	100.0	100.0	100.0	100.0	..
2.1	Currency and deposits	6.8	9.9	9.5	11.3	7.8	8.0	9.9	..
2.2	Securities other than shares, except financial derivatives	84.7	77.7	82.1	82.0	85.4	86.8	87.7	..
2.2.1	Short-term securities	4.9	4.1	3.1	0.6	1.0	0.4	2.8	..
2.2.2	Long-term securities	79.8	73.7	79.0	81.4	84.4	86.4	85.0	..
2.2.3	Securities issued by residents	..	..	..	..	..	..	..	..
2.2.4	Securities issued by non-residents	..	..	..	..	..	..	..	..
2.3	Loans	0.0	0.0	0.0	0.0	0.0	0.0	0.0	..
2.3.1	Short-term loans	0.0	0.0	0.0	0.0	0.0	0.0	0.0	..
2.3.2	Long-term loans	0.0	0.0	0.0	0.0	0.0	0.0	0.0	..
2.3.3	Loans granted to residents	..	..	..	..	..	..	..	..
2.3.4	Loans granted to non-residents	..	..	..	..	..	..	..	..
2.4	Shares and other equity	7.0	10.7	6.5	5.0	4.7	3.0	1.5	..
2.4.1	Shares issued by residents	..	..	..	..	..	..	..	..
2.4.2	Shares issued by non-residents	..	..	..	..	..	..	..	..
2.5	Other, not elsewhere classified	1.4	1.7	2.0	1.7	2.1	2.2	0.9	..

Note: Detailed metadata at: http://metalinks.oecd.org/instinv/20141203/f729

DENMARK

Table 1. Financial assets of institutional investors, 2013

Million DKK

		Total	Investment funds			
			Open-end companies (mutual funds)			Closed-end companies
			Total	Money market funds	Other mutual funds	Total
2	Financial assets	1 896 500	1 896 500	..	..	..
2.1	Currency and deposits	60 600	60 600	..	..	..
2.2	Securities other than shares, except financial derivatives	1 051 300	1 051 300	..	..	..
2.2.1	Short-term securities	..	..	..	..	..
2.2.2	Long-term securities	..	..	..	..	..
2.2.3	Securities issued by residents	..	..	..	..	..
2.2.4	Securities issued by non-residents	..	..	..	..	..
2.3	Loans	0	0	..	..	..
2.3.1	Short-term loans	0	0	..	..	..
2.3.2	Long-term loans	0	0	..	..	..
2.3.3	Loans granted to residents	..	..	..	..	..
2.3.4	Loans granted to non-residents	..	..	..	..	..
2.4	Shares and other equity	749 800	749 800	..	..	..
2.4.1	Shares issued by residents	..	..	..	..	..
2.4.2	Shares issued by non-residents	..	..	..	..	..
2.5	Other, not elsewhere classified	34 800	34 800	..	..	..

		Total	Insurance corporations and autonomous pension funds			
			Insurance corporations			Autonomous pension funds
			Total	Life insurance corporations	Non-life insurance corporations	Total
2	Financial assets	3 194 079	1 888 541	1 726 591	161 951	1 305 674
2.1	Currency and deposits	50 844	44 223	38 749	5 474	6 622
2.2	Securities other than shares, except financial derivatives	1 238 627	598 321	518 481	79 840	640 308
2.2.1	Short-term securities	4 358	2 104	1 823	280	2 255
2.2.2	Long-term securities	1 234 268	596 217	516 657	79 560	638 053
2.2.3	Securities issued by residents	..	..	..	..	..
2.2.4	Securities issued by non-residents	..	..	..	..	..
2.3	Loans	76 370	8 104	5 876	2 228	68 266
2.3.1	Short-term loans	75 293	8 097	5 876	2 221	67 197
2.3.2	Long-term loans	1 077	8	0	8	1 069
2.3.3	Loans granted to residents	..	..	..	..	..
2.3.4	Loans granted to non-residents	..	..	..	..	..
2.4	Shares and other equity	1 611 304	1 122 593	1 070 449	52 144	488 712
2.4.1	Shares issued by residents	..	..	..	..	..
2.4.2	Shares issued by non-residents	..	..	..	..	..
2.5	Other, not elsewhere classified	216 934	115 301	93 036	22 264	101 767

Note: Detailed metadata at: http://metalinks.oecd.org/instinv/20141203/f0e9

Table 2. Financial assets of investment funds

Million DKK

		2006	2007	2008	2009	2010	2011	2012	2013
	Investment funds								
2	Financial assets	924 800	1 020 800	772 200	865 500	1 286 900	1 426 900	1 675 600	1 896 500
2.1	Currency and deposits	23 900	29 800	40 800	32 300	34 300	50 500	48 500	60 600
2.2	Securities other than shares, except financial derivatives	431 800	477 900	424 400	487 500	765 200	877 900	995 200	1 051 300
2.2.1	Short-term securities	..	..	..	..	..	..	..	..
2.2.2	Long-term securities	..	..	..	..	..	..	..	..
2.2.3	Securities issued by residents	..	..	..	..	..	..	..	..
2.2.4	Securities issued by non-residents	..	..	..	..	..	..	..	..
2.3	Loans	0	0	0	0	0	0	0	0
2.3.1	Short-term loans	0	0	0	0	0	0	0	0
2.3.2	Long-term loans	0	0	0	0	0	0	0	0
2.3.3	Loans granted to residents	..	..	..	..	..	..	..	..
2.3.4	Loans granted to non-residents	..	..	..	..	..	..	..	..
2.4	Shares and other equity	458 200	499 300	288 600	331 000	438 500	481 400	580 100	749 800
2.4.1	Shares issued by residents	..	..	..	..	..	..	..	..
2.4.2	Shares issued by non-residents	..	..	..	..	..	..	..	..
2.5	Other, not elsewhere classified	10 900	13 800	18 400	14 700	48 900	17 100	51 800	34 800
	Open-end companies (mutual funds)								
2	Financial assets	924 800	1 020 800	772 200	865 500	1 286 900	1 426 900	1 675 600	1 896 500
2.1	Currency and deposits	23 900	29 800	40 800	32 300	34 300	50 500	48 500	60 600
2.2	Securities other than shares, except financial derivatives	431 800	477 900	424 400	487 500	765 200	877 900	995 200	1 051 300
2.2.1	Short-term securities	..	..	..	..	..	..	..	..
2.2.2	Long-term securities	..	..	..	..	..	..	..	..
2.2.3	Securities issued by residents	..	..	..	..	..	..	..	..
2.2.4	Securities issued by non-residents	..	..	..	..	..	..	..	..
2.3	Loans	0	0	0	0	0	0	0	0
2.3.1	Short-term loans	0	0	0	0	0	0	0	0
2.3.2	Long-term loans	0	0	0	0	0	0	0	0
2.3.3	Loans granted to residents	..	..	..	..	..	..	..	..
2.3.4	Loans granted to non-residents	..	..	..	..	..	..	..	..
2.4	Shares and other equity	458 200	499 300	288 600	331 000	438 500	481 400	580 100	749 800
2.4.1	Shares issued by residents	..	..	..	..	..	..	..	..
2.4.2	Shares issued by non-residents	..	..	..	..	..	..	..	..
2.5	Other, not elsewhere classified	10 900	13 800	18 400	14 700	48 900	17 100	51 800	34 800
	Money market funds								
2	Financial assets	..	..	..	..	..	..	..	..
2.1	Currency and deposits	..	..	..	..	..	..	..	..
2.2	Securities other than shares, except financial derivatives	..	..	..	..	..	..	..	..
2.2.1	Short-term securities	..	..	..	..	..	..	..	..
2.2.2	Long-term securities	..	..	..	..	..	..	..	..
2.2.3	Securities issued by residents	..	..	..	..	..	..	..	..
2.2.4	Securities issued by non-residents	..	..	..	..	..	..	..	..
2.3	Loans	..	..	..	..	..	..	..	..
2.3.1	Short-term loans	..	..	..	..	..	..	..	..
2.3.2	Long-term loans	..	..	..	..	..	..	..	..
2.3.3	Loans granted to residents	..	..	..	..	..	..	..	..
2.3.4	Loans granted to non-residents	..	..	..	..	..	..	..	..
2.4	Shares and other equity	..	..	..	..	..	..	..	..
2.4.1	Shares issued by residents	..	..	..	..	..	..	..	..
2.4.2	Shares issued by non-residents	..	..	..	..	..	..	..	..
2.5	Other, not elsewhere classified	..	..	..	..	..	..	..	..
	Other mutual funds								
2	Financial assets	..	..	..	..	..	..	..	..
2.1	Currency and deposits	..	..	..	..	..	..	..	..
2.2	Securities other than shares, except financial derivatives	..	..	..	..	..	..	..	..
2.2.1	Short-term securities	..	..	..	..	..	..	..	..
2.2.2	Long-term securities	..	..	..	..	..	..	..	..
2.2.3	Securities issued by residents	..	..	..	..	..	..	..	..
2.2.4	Securities issued by non-residents	..	..	..	..	..	..	..	..
2.3	Loans	..	..	..	..	..	..	..	..
2.3.1	Short-term loans	..	..	..	..	..	..	..	..
2.3.2	Long-term loans	..	..	..	..	..	..	..	..
2.3.3	Loans granted to residents	..	..	..	..	..	..	..	..
2.3.4	Loans granted to non-residents	..	..	..	..	..	..	..	..
2.4	Shares and other equity	..	..	..	..	..	..	..	..
2.4.1	Shares issued by residents	..	..	..	..	..	..	..	..
2.4.2	Shares issued by non-residents	..	..	..	..	..	..	..	..
2.5	Other, not elsewhere classified	..	..	..	..	..	..	..	..

Table 2. Financial assets of investment funds *(cont.)*

Million DKK

		2006	2007	2008	2009	2010	2011	2012	2013
	Closed-end companies								
2	Financial assets	..	..	..	..	..	..	..	..
2.1	Currency and deposits	..	..	..	..	..	..	..	..
2.2	Securities other than shares, except financial derivatives	..	..	..	..	..	..	..	..
2.2.1	Short-term securities	..	..	..	..	..	..	..	..
2.2.2	Long-term securities	..	..	..	..	..	..	..	..
2.2.3	Securities issued by residents	..	..	..	..	..	..	..	..
2.2.4	Securities issued by non-residents	..	..	..	..	..	..	..	..
2.3	Loans	..	..	..	..	..	..	..	..
2.3.1	Short-term loans	..	..	..	..	..	..	..	..
2.3.2	Long-term loans	..	..	..	..	..	..	..	..
2.3.3	Loans granted to residents	..	..	..	..	..	..	..	..
2.3.4	Loans granted to non-residents	..	..	..	..	..	..	..	..
2.4	Shares and other equity	..	..	..	..	..	..	..	..
2.4.1	Shares issued by residents	..	..	..	..	..	..	..	..
2.4.2	Shares issued by non-residents	..	..	..	..	..	..	..	..
2.5	Other, not elsewhere classified	..	..	..	..	..	..	..	..

Note: Detailed metadata at: http://metalinks.oecd.org/instinv/20141203/f0e9

DENMARK

Table 3. Financial assets of insurance corporations and autonomous pension funds

Million DKK

		2006	2007	2008	2009	2010	2011	2012	2013
	Insurance corporations and autonomous pension funds								
2	Financial assets	1 971 675	2 040 627	2 248 995	2 444 049	2 782 233	3 029 668	3 242 707	3 194 079
2.1	Currency and deposits	23 121	34 087	63 736	62 282	33 274	49 547	51 650	50 844
2.2	Securities other than shares, except financial derivatives	1 015 755	1 011 807	1 287 667	1 395 737	1 340 888	1 347 388	1 383 213	1 238 627
2.2.1	Short-term securities	1 761	3 371	3 871	1 455	3 797	6 293	1 500	4 358
2.2.2	Long-term securities	1 013 994	1 008 435	1 283 796	1 394 283	1 337 090	1 341 096	1 381 713	1 234 268
2.2.3	Securities issued by residents	..	..	..	..	..	..	..	..
2.2.4	Securities issued by non-residents	..	..	..	..	..	..	..	..
2.3	Loans	8 603	6 519	19 309	13 935	61 296	74 479	62 509	76 370
2.3.1	Short-term loans	8 382	6 332	7 259	12 326	60 621	74 022	61 988	75 293
2.3.2	Long-term loans	221	187	12 050	1 609	675	456	521	1 077
2.3.3	Loans granted to residents	..	..	..	..	..	..	..	..
2.3.4	Loans granted to non-residents	..	..	..	..	..	..	..	..
2.4	Shares and other equity	829 485	896 227	666 442	824 024	1 193 998	1 262 103	1 448 257	1 611 304
2.4.1	Shares issued by residents	..	..	..	..	..	..	..	..
2.4.2	Shares issued by non-residents	..	..	..	..	..	..	..	..
2.5	Other, not elsewhere classified	94 711	91 987	211 841	148 071	152 777	296 151	297 078	216 934
	Insurance corporations								
2	Financial assets	1 157 421	1 200 721	1 253 941	1 356 567	1 497 500	1 652 949	1 833 536	1 888 541
2.1	Currency and deposits	16 972	24 215	41 825	45 121	24 368	42 167	43 304	44 223
2.2	Securities other than shares, except financial derivatives	629 076	625 638	728 216	753 773	621 432	627 238	646 634	598 321
2.2.1	Short-term securities	1 091	2 084	2 189	785	1 759	2 929	701	2 104
2.2.2	Long-term securities	627 985	623 553	726 027	752 987	619 672	624 309	645 933	596 217
2.2.3	Securities issued by residents	..	..	..	..	..	..	..	..
2.2.4	Securities issued by non-residents	..	..	..	..	..	..	..	..
2.3	Loans	7 582	5 409	5 085	7 786	5 360	8 122	7 282	8 104
2.3.1	Short-term loans	7 543	5 384	5 062	7 763	5 347	8 111	7 272	8 097
2.3.2	Long-term loans	39	24	23	23	14	11	10	8
2.3.3	Loans granted to residents	..	..	..	..	..	..	..	..
2.3.4	Loans granted to non-residents	..	..	..	..	..	..	..	..
2.4	Shares and other equity	439 721	480 180	373 970	475 681	767 839	847 088	998 457	1 122 593
2.4.1	Shares issued by residents	..	..	..	..	..	..	..	..
2.4.2	Shares issued by non-residents	..	..	..	..	..	..	..	..
2.5	Other, not elsewhere classified	64 071	65 279	104 846	74 206	78 501	128 335	137 859	115 301
	Life insurance corporations								
2	Financial assets	1 007 571	1 051 276	1 113 129	1 208 874	1 340 903	1 488 300	1 669 605	1 726 591
2.1	Currency and deposits	11 422	16 650	31 112	34 202	18 038	36 743	38 476	38 749
2.2	Securities other than shares, except financial derivatives	549 890	549 188	652 601	679 515	535 040	536 902	557 694	518 481
2.2.1	Short-term securities	953	1 830	1 962	708	1 515	2 508	605	1 823
2.2.2	Long-term securities	548 937	547 359	650 639	678 807	533 525	534 394	557 089	516 657
2.2.3	Securities issued by residents	..	..	..	..	..	..	..	..
2.2.4	Securities issued by non-residents	..	..	..	..	..	..	..	..
2.3	Loans	5 932	3 878	2 883	5 671	3 372	6 307	5 346	5 876
2.3.1	Short-term loans	5 932	3 878	2 883	5 671	3 372	6 307	5 346	5 876
2.3.2	Long-term loans	0	0	0	0	0	0	0	0
2.3.3	Loans granted to residents	..	..	..	..	..	..	..	..
2.3.4	Loans granted to non-residents	..	..	..	..	..	..	..	..
2.4	Shares and other equity	392 168	433 603	334 538	429 251	721 915	801 511	949 197	1 070 449
2.4.1	Shares issued by residents	..	..	..	..	..	..	..	..
2.4.2	Shares issued by non-residents	..	..	..	..	..	..	..	..
2.5	Other, not elsewhere classified	48 159	47 955	91 995	60 235	62 537	106 837	118 892	93 036
	Non-life insurance corporations								
2	Financial assets	149 851	149 445	140 812	147 693	156 596	164 650	163 931	161 951
2.1	Currency and deposits	5 550	7 565	10 712	10 920	6 330	5 424	4 828	5 474
2.2	Securities other than shares, except financial derivatives	79 185	76 449	75 616	74 257	86 391	90 336	88 940	79 840
2.2.1	Short-term securities	137	255	227	77	244	421	96	280
2.2.2	Long-term securities	79 048	76 194	75 388	74 180	86 147	89 915	88 844	79 560
2.2.3	Securities issued by residents	..	..	..	..	..	..	..	..
2.2.4	Securities issued by non-residents	..	..	..	..	..	..	..	..
2.3	Loans	1 649	1 530	2 201	2 115	1 988	1 815	1 936	2 228
2.3.1	Short-term loans	1 610	1 506	2 179	2 092	1 974	1 804	1 927	2 221
2.3.2	Long-term loans	39	24	23	23	14	11	10	8
2.3.3	Loans granted to residents	..	..	..	..	..	..	..	..
2.3.4	Loans granted to non-residents	..	..	..	..	..	..	..	..
2.4	Shares and other equity	47 553	46 577	39 432	46 429	45 923	45 577	49 260	52 144
2.4.1	Shares issued by residents	..	..	..	..	..	..	..	..
2.4.2	Shares issued by non-residents	..	..	..	..	..	..	..	..
2.5	Other, not elsewhere classified	15 912	17 324	12 850	13 972	15 964	21 499	18 967	22 264

Table 3. Financial assets of insurance corporations and autonomous pension funds *(cont.)*

Million DKK

		2006	2007	2008	2009	2010	2011	2012	2013
	Autonomous pension funds								
2	Financial assets	815 967	841 151	996 484	1 087 926	1 285 523	1 382 556	1 409 474	1 305 674
2.1	Currency and deposits	6 149	9 872	21 911	17 160	8 906	7 381	8 345	6 622
2.2	Securities other than shares, except financial derivatives	386 688	386 178	559 461	641 974	719 458	720 150	736 579	640 308
2.2.1	Short-term securities	671	1 287	1 682	669	2 038	3 364	799	2 255
2.2.2	Long-term securities	386 018	384 891	557 778	641 304	717 420	716 786	735 780	638 053
2.2.3	Securities issued by residents	..	..	..	..	..	..	..	..
2.2.4	Securities issued by non-residents	..	..	..	..	..	..	..	..
2.3	Loans	1 021	1 110	14 225	6 149	55 936	66 357	55 227	68 266
2.3.1	Short-term loans	839	947	2 198	4 563	55 275	65 912	54 715	67 197
2.3.2	Long-term loans	182	163	12 027	1 586	661	445	512	1 069
2.3.3	Loans granted to residents	..	..	..	..	..	..	..	..
2.3.4	Loans granted to non-residents	..	..	..	..	..	..	..	..
2.4	Shares and other equity	389 764	416 046	292 472	348 344	426 160	415 015	449 800	488 712
2.4.1	Shares issued by residents	..	..	..	..	..	..	..	..
2.4.2	Shares issued by non-residents	..	..	..	..	..	..	..	..
2.5	Other, not elsewhere classified	32 345	27 945	108 415	74 300	75 063	173 654	159 523	101 767

Note: Detailed metadata at: http://metalinks.oecd.org/instinv/20141203/f0e9

Table 4. Portfolio composition by type of investor

Percentage of total financial assets

Per cent

		2006	2007	2008	2009	2010	2011	2012	2013
	Investment funds								
2	Financial assets	100.0	100.0	100.0	100.0	100.0	100.0	100.0	100.0
2.1	Currency and deposits	2.6	2.9	5.3	3.7	2.7	3.5	2.9	3.2
2.2	Securities other than shares, except financial derivatives	46.7	46.8	55.0	56.3	59.5	61.5	59.4	55.4
2.2.1	Short-term securities	..	..	..	..	..	..	..	..
2.2.2	Long-term securities	..	..	..	..	..	..	..	..
2.2.3	Securities issued by residents	..	..	..	..	..	..	..	..
2.2.4	Securities issued by non-residents	..	..	..	..	..	..	..	..
2.3	Loans	0.0	0.0	0.0	0.0	0.0	0.0	0.0	0.0
2.3.1	Short-term loans	0.0	0.0	0.0	0.0	0.0	0.0	0.0	0.0
2.3.2	Long-term loans	0.0	0.0	0.0	0.0	0.0	0.0	0.0	0.0
2.3.3	Loans granted to residents	..	..	..	..	..	..	..	..
2.3.4	Loans granted to non-residents	..	..	..	..	..	..	..	..
2.4	Shares and other equity	49.5	48.9	37.4	38.2	34.1	33.7	34.6	39.5
2.4.1	Shares issued by residents	..	..	..	..	..	..	..	..
2.4.2	Shares issued by non-residents	..	..	..	..	..	..	..	..
2.5	Other, not elsewhere classified	1.2	1.4	2.4	1.7	3.8	1.2	3.1	1.8
	Insurance corporations								
2	Financial assets	100.0	100.0	100.0	100.0	100.0	100.0	100.0	100.0
2.1	Currency and deposits	1.5	2.0	3.3	3.3	1.6	2.6	2.4	2.3
2.2	Securities other than shares, except financial derivatives	54.4	52.1	58.1	55.6	41.5	37.9	35.3	31.7
2.2.1	Short-term securities	0.1	0.2	0.2	0.1	0.1	0.2	0.0	0.1
2.2.2	Long-term securities	54.3	51.9	57.9	55.5	41.4	37.8	35.2	31.6
2.2.3	Securities issued by residents	..	..	..	..	..	..	..	..
2.2.4	Securities issued by non-residents	..	..	..	..	..	..	..	..
2.3	Loans	0.7	0.5	0.4	0.6	0.4	0.5	0.4	0.4
2.3.1	Short-term loans	0.7	0.4	0.4	0.6	0.4	0.5	0.4	0.4
2.3.2	Long-term loans	0.0	0.0	0.0	0.0	0.0	0.0	0.0	0.0
2.3.3	Loans granted to residents	..	..	..	..	..	..	..	..
2.3.4	Loans granted to non-residents	..	..	..	..	..	..	..	..
2.4	Shares and other equity	38.0	40.0	29.8	35.1	51.3	51.2	54.5	59.4
2.4.1	Shares issued by residents	..	..	..	..	..	..	..	..
2.4.2	Shares issued by non-residents	..	..	..	..	..	..	..	..
2.5	Other, not elsewhere classified	5.5	5.4	8.4	5.5	5.2	7.8	7.5	6.1
	Autonomous pension funds								
2	Financial assets	100.0	100.0	100.0	100.0	100.0	100.0	100.0	100.0
2.1	Currency and deposits	0.8	1.2	2.2	1.6	0.7	0.5	0.6	0.5
2.2	Securities other than shares, except financial derivatives	47.4	45.9	56.1	59.0	56.0	52.1	52.3	49.0
2.2.1	Short-term securities	0.1	0.2	0.2	0.1	0.2	0.2	0.1	0.2
2.2.2	Long-term securities	47.3	45.8	56.0	58.9	55.8	51.8	52.2	48.9
2.2.3	Securities issued by residents	..	..	..	..	..	..	..	..
2.2.4	Securities issued by non-residents	..	..	..	..	..	..	..	..
2.3	Loans	0.1	0.1	1.4	0.6	4.4	4.8	3.9	5.2
2.3.1	Short-term loans	0.1	0.1	0.2	0.4	4.3	4.8	3.9	5.1
2.3.2	Long-term loans	0.0	0.0	1.2	0.1	0.1	0.0	0.0	0.1
2.3.3	Loans granted to residents	..	..	..	..	..	..	..	..
2.3.4	Loans granted to non-residents	..	..	..	..	..	..	..	..
2.4	Shares and other equity	47.8	49.5	29.4	32.0	33.2	30.0	31.9	37.4
2.4.1	Shares issued by residents	..	..	..	..	..	..	..	..
2.4.2	Shares issued by non-residents	..	..	..	..	..	..	..	..
2.5	Other, not elsewhere classified	4.0	3.3	10.9	6.8	5.8	12.6	11.3	7.8

Note: Detailed metadata at: http://metalinks.oecd.org/instinv/20141203/f729

Table 1. Financial assets of institutional investors, 2013

Million EUR (2011 EEK euro)

		Total	Investment funds			
			Open-end companies (mutual funds)			Closed-end companies
			Total	Money market funds	Other mutual funds	Total
2	Financial assets	619	439	..	439	180
2.1	Currency and deposits	56	21	..	21	35
2.2	Securities other than shares, except financial derivatives	70	69	..	69	1
2.2.1	Short-term securities	0	0	..	0	0
2.2.2	Long-term securities	70	69	..	69	1
2.2.3	Securities issued by residents	2	0	..	0	2
2.2.4	Securities issued by non-residents	68	69	..	69	-1
2.3	Loans	32	0	..	0	32
2.3.1	Short-term loans	7	0	..	0	7
2.3.2	Long-term loans	25	0	..	0	25
2.3.3	Loans granted to residents	28	0	..	0	28
2.3.4	Loans granted to non-residents	4	0	..	0	4
2.4	Shares and other equity	448	344	..	344	104
2.4.1	Shares issued by residents	89	5	..	5	84
2.4.2	Shares issued by non-residents	359	339	..	339	20
2.5	Other, not elsewhere classified	14	5	..	5	9

		Total	Insurance corporations and autonomous pension funds			
			Insurance corporations			Autonomous pension funds
			Total	Life insurance corporations	Non-life insurance corporations	Total
2	Financial assets	2 883	1 007	..	..	1 876
2.1	Currency and deposits	555	238	..	..	317
2.2	Securities other than shares, except financial derivatives	776	390	..	..	386
2.2.1	Short-term securities	1	0	..	..	1
2.2.2	Long-term securities	775	390	..	..	385
2.2.3	Securities issued by residents	57	0	..	..	57
2.2.4	Securities issued by non-residents	719	390	..	..	329
2.3	Loans	0	0	..	..	0
2.3.1	Short-term loans	0	0	..	..	0
2.3.2	Long-term loans	0	0	..	..	0
2.3.3	Loans granted to residents	0	0	..	..	0
2.3.4	Loans granted to non-residents	0	0	..	..	0
2.4	Shares and other equity	1 476	305	..	..	1 171
2.4.1	Shares issued by residents	279	167	..	..	112
2.4.2	Shares issued by non-residents	1 197	138	..	..	1 059
2.5	Other, not elsewhere classified	77	75	..	..	2

Note: Detailed metadata at: http://metalinks.oecd.org/instinv/20141203/eccf

ESTONIA

Table 2. Financial assets of investment funds

Million EUR (2011 EEK euro)

		2006	2007	2008	2009	2010	2011	2012	2013
	Investment funds								
2	Financial assets	..	..	..	..	580	442	502	619
2.1	Currency and deposits	..	..	..	..	27	22	48	56
2.2	Securities other than shares, except financial derivatives	..	..	..	..	67	67	75	70
2.2.1	Short-term securities	..	..	..	..	0	1	0	0
2.2.2	Long-term securities	..	..	..	..	67	65	75	70
2.2.3	Securities issued by residents	..	..	..	..	3	5	3	2
2.2.4	Securities issued by non-residents	..	..	..	..	64	62	72	68
2.3	Loans	..	..	..	..	20	18	14	32
2.3.1	Short-term loans	..	..	..	..	19	7	2	7
2.3.2	Long-term loans	..	..	..	..	1	11	12	25
2.3.3	Loans granted to residents	..	..	..	..	0	10	11	28
2.3.4	Loans granted to non-residents	..	..	..	..	20	8	3	4
2.4	Shares and other equity	..	..	..	..	457	333	357	448
2.4.1	Shares issued by residents	..	..	..	..	28	37	53	89
2.4.2	Shares issued by non-residents	..	..	..	..	429	296	304	359
2.5	Other, not elsewhere classified	..	..	..	..	9	2	7	14
	Open-end companies (mutual funds)								
2	Financial assets	..	..	..	..	486	362	384	439
2.1	Currency and deposits	..	..	..	..	19	13	12	21
2.2	Securities other than shares, except financial derivatives	..	..	..	..	58	59	73	69
2.2.1	Short-term securities	..	..	..	..	0	0	0	0
2.2.2	Long-term securities	..	..	..	..	58	59	73	69
2.2.3	Securities issued by residents	..	..	..	..	2	0	0	0
2.2.4	Securities issued by non-residents	..	..	..	..	56	59	73	69
2.3	Loans	..	..	..	..	0	0	0	0
2.3.1	Short-term loans	..	..	..	..	0	0	0	0
2.3.2	Long-term loans	..	..	..	..	0	0	0	0
2.3.3	Loans granted to residents	..	..	..	..	0	0	0	0
2.3.4	Loans granted to non-residents	..	..	..	..	0	0	0	0
2.4	Shares and other equity	..	..	..	..	404	288	297	344
2.4.1	Shares issued by residents	..	..	..	..	8	8	9	5
2.4.2	Shares issued by non-residents	..	..	..	..	396	281	288	339
2.5	Other, not elsewhere classified	..	..	..	..	5	2	3	5
	Money market funds								
2	Financial assets	..	..	..	..	..	..	..	..
2.1	Currency and deposits	..	..	..	..	..	..	..	..
2.2	Securities other than shares, except financial derivatives	..	..	..	..	..	..	..	..
2.2.1	Short-term securities	..	..	..	..	..	..	..	..
2.2.2	Long-term securities	..	..	..	..	..	..	..	..
2.2.3	Securities issued by residents	..	..	..	..	..	..	..	..
2.2.4	Securities issued by non-residents	..	..	..	..	..	..	..	..
2.3	Loans	..	..	..	..	..	..	..	..
2.3.1	Short-term loans	..	..	..	..	..	..	..	..
2.3.2	Long-term loans	..	..	..	..	..	..	..	..
2.3.3	Loans granted to residents	..	..	..	..	..	..	..	..
2.3.4	Loans granted to non-residents	..	..	..	..	..	..	..	..
2.4	Shares and other equity	..	..	..	..	..	..	..	..
2.4.1	Shares issued by residents	..	..	..	..	..	..	..	..
2.4.2	Shares issued by non-residents	..	..	..	..	..	..	..	..
2.5	Other, not elsewhere classified	..	..	..	..	..	..	..	..
	Other mutual funds								
2	Financial assets	..	..	..	..	486	362	384	439
2.1	Currency and deposits	..	..	..	..	19	13	12	21
2.2	Securities other than shares, except financial derivatives	..	..	..	..	58	59	73	69
2.2.1	Short-term securities	..	..	..	..	0	0	0	0
2.2.2	Long-term securities	..	..	..	..	58	59	73	69
2.2.3	Securities issued by residents	..	..	..	..	2	0	0	0
2.2.4	Securities issued by non-residents	..	..	..	..	56	59	73	69
2.3	Loans	..	..	..	..	0	0	0	0
2.3.1	Short-term loans	..	..	..	..	0	0	0	0
2.3.2	Long-term loans	..	..	..	..	0	0	0	0
2.3.3	Loans granted to residents	..	..	..	..	0	0	0	0
2.3.4	Loans granted to non-residents	..	..	..	..	0	0	0	0
2.4	Shares and other equity	..	..	..	..	404	288	297	344
2.4.1	Shares issued by residents	..	..	..	..	8	8	9	5
2.4.2	Shares issued by non-residents	..	..	..	..	396	281	288	339
2.5	Other, not elsewhere classified	..	..	..	..	5	2	3	5

Table 2. Financial assets of investment funds *(cont.)*

Million EUR (2011 EEK euro)

		2006	2007	2008	2009	2010	2011	2012	2013
	Closed-end companies								
2	Financial assets	..	..	..	..	94	80	118	180
2.1	Currency and deposits	..	..	..	..	8	9	36	35
2.2	Securities other than shares, except financial derivatives	..	..	..	..	9	8	2	1
2.2.1	Short-term securities	..	..	..	..	0	1	0	0
2.2.2	Long-term securities	..	..	..	..	9	6	2	1
2.2.3	Securities issued by residents	..	..	..	..	1	5	3	2
2.2.4	Securities issued by non-residents	..	..	..	..	8	3	-1	-1
2.3	Loans	..	..	..	..	20	18	14	32
2.3.1	Short-term loans	..	..	..	..	19	7	2	7
2.3.2	Long-term loans	..	..	..	..	1	11	12	25
2.3.3	Loans granted to residents	..	..	..	..	0	10	11	28
2.3.4	Loans granted to non-residents	..	..	..	..	20	8	3	4
2.4	Shares and other equity	..	..	..	..	53	45	61	104
2.4.1	Shares issued by residents	..	..	..	..	20	29	44	84
2.4.2	Shares issued by non-residents	..	..	..	..	33	16	16	20
2.5	Other, not elsewhere classified	..	..	..	..	4	0	5	9

Note: Detailed metadata at: http://metalinks.oecd.org/instinv/20141203/eccf

Table 3. Financial assets of insurance corporations and autonomous pension funds

Million EUR (2011 EEK euro)

		2006	2007	2008	2009	2010	2011	2012	2013
	Insurance corporations and autonomous pension funds								
2	Financial assets	..	..	..	..	2 221	2 201	2 584	2 883
2.1	Currency and deposits	..	..	..	..	382	435	527	555
2.2	Securities other than shares, except financial derivatives	..	..	..	..	532	708	770	776
2.2.1	Short-term securities	..	..	..	..	1	2	2	1
2.2.2	Long-term securities	..	..	..	..	531	706	768	775
2.2.3	Securities issued by residents	..	..	..	..	23	30	51	57
2.2.4	Securities issued by non-residents	..	..	..	..	508	679	719	719
2.3	Loans	..	..	..	..	2	16	0	0
2.3.1	Short-term loans	..	..	..	..	0	0	0	0
2.3.2	Long-term loans	..	..	..	..	2	16	0	0
2.3.3	Loans granted to residents	..	..	..	..	2	16	0	0
2.3.4	Loans granted to non-residents	..	..	..	..	0	0	0	0
2.4	Shares and other equity	..	..	..	..	1 216	968	1 214	1 476
2.4.1	Shares issued by residents	..	..	..	..	134	137	157	279
2.4.2	Shares issued by non-residents	..	..	..	..	1 082	832	1 057	1 197
2.5	Other, not elsewhere classified	..	..	..	..	90	75	72	77
	Insurance corporations								
2	Financial assets	..	..	..	..	1 062	982	1 008	1 007
2.1	Currency and deposits	..	..	..	..	275	241	276	238
2.2	Securities other than shares, except financial derivatives	..	..	..	..	335	403	377	390
2.2.1	Short-term securities	..	..	..	..	0	0	0	0
2.2.2	Long-term securities	..	..	..	..	335	403	377	390
2.2.3	Securities issued by residents	..	..	..	..	0	0	0	0
2.2.4	Securities issued by non-residents	..	..	..	..	335	403	377	390
2.3	Loans	..	..	..	..	2	16	0	0
2.3.1	Short-term loans	..	..	..	..	0	0	0	0
2.3.2	Long-term loans	..	..	..	..	2	16	0	0
2.3.3	Loans granted to residents	..	..	..	..	2	16	0	0
2.3.4	Loans granted to non-residents	..	..	..	..	0	0	0	0
2.4	Shares and other equity	..	..	..	..	404	255	284	305
2.4.1	Shares issued by residents	..	..	..	..	82	78	68	167
2.4.2	Shares issued by non-residents	..	..	..	..	322	177	216	138
2.5	Other, not elsewhere classified	..	..	..	..	46	67	71	75
	Life insurance corporations								
2	Financial assets	..	..	..	..	..	..	..	..
2.1	Currency and deposits	..	..	..	..	..	..	..	..
2.2	Securities other than shares, except financial derivatives	..	..	..	..	..	..	..	..
2.2.1	Short-term securities	..	..	..	..	..	..	..	..
2.2.2	Long-term securities	..	..	..	..	..	..	..	..
2.2.3	Securities issued by residents	..	..	..	..	..	..	..	..
2.2.4	Securities issued by non-residents	..	..	..	..	..	..	..	..
2.3	Loans	..	..	..	..	..	..	..	..
2.3.1	Short-term loans	..	..	..	..	..	..	..	..
2.3.2	Long-term loans	..	..	..	..	..	..	..	..
2.3.3	Loans granted to residents	..	..	..	..	..	..	..	..
2.3.4	Loans granted to non-residents	..	..	..	..	..	..	..	..
2.4	Shares and other equity	..	..	..	..	..	..	..	..
2.4.1	Shares issued by residents	..	..	..	..	..	..	..	..
2.4.2	Shares issued by non-residents	..	..	..	..	..	..	..	..
2.5	Other, not elsewhere classified	..	..	..	..	..	..	..	..
	Non-life insurance corporations								
2	Financial assets	..	..	..	..	..	..	..	..
2.1	Currency and deposits	..	..	..	..	..	..	..	..
2.2	Securities other than shares, except financial derivatives	..	..	..	..	..	..	..	..
2.2.1	Short-term securities	..	..	..	..	..	..	..	..
2.2.2	Long-term securities	..	..	..	..	..	..	..	..
2.2.3	Securities issued by residents	..	..	..	..	..	..	..	..
2.2.4	Securities issued by non-residents	..	..	..	..	..	..	..	..
2.3	Loans	..	..	..	..	..	..	..	..
2.3.1	Short-term loans	..	..	..	..	..	..	..	..
2.3.2	Long-term loans	..	..	..	..	..	..	..	..
2.3.3	Loans granted to residents	..	..	..	..	..	..	..	..
2.3.4	Loans granted to non-residents	..	..	..	..	..	..	..	..
2.4	Shares and other equity	..	..	..	..	..	..	..	..
2.4.1	Shares issued by residents	..	..	..	..	..	..	..	..
2.4.2	Shares issued by non-residents	..	..	..	..	..	..	..	..
2.5	Other, not elsewhere classified	..	..	..	..	..	..	..	..

Table 3. Financial assets of insurance corporations and autonomous pension funds *(cont.)*

Million EUR (2011 EEK euro)

		2006	2007	2008	2009	2010	2011	2012	2013
	Autonomous pension funds								
2	Financial assets	..	..	..	..	1 159	1 220	1 576	1 876
2.1	Currency and deposits	..	..	..	..	106	194	252	317
2.2	Securities other than shares, except financial derivatives	..	..	..	..	197	305	393	386
2.2.1	Short-term securities	..	..	..	..	1	2	2	1
2.2.2	Long-term securities	..	..	..	..	196	303	391	385
2.2.3	Securities issued by residents	..	..	..	..	23	30	51	57
2.2.4	Securities issued by non-residents	..	..	..	..	174	276	342	329
2.3	Loans	..	..	..	..	0	0	0	0
2.3.1	Short-term loans	..	..	..	..	0	0	0	0
2.3.2	Long-term loans	..	..	..	..	0	0	0	0
2.3.3	Loans granted to residents	..	..	..	..	0	0	0	0
2.3.4	Loans granted to non-residents	..	..	..	..	0	0	0	0
2.4	Shares and other equity	..	..	..	..	812	713	931	1 171
2.4.1	Shares issued by residents	..	..	..	..	52	58	89	112
2.4.2	Shares issued by non-residents	..	..	..	..	760	655	841	1 059
2.5	Other, not elsewhere classified	..	..	..	..	44	8	1	2

Note: Detailed metadata at: http://metalinks.oecd.org/instinv/20141203/eccf

Table 4. Portfolio composition by type of investor

Percentage of total financial assets

Per cent

		2006	2007	2008	2009	2010	2011	2012	2013
	Investment funds								
2	Financial assets	..	..	..	..	100.0	100.0	100.0	100.0
2.1	Currency and deposits	..	..	..	..	4.7	5.1	9.6	9.0
2.2	Securities other than shares, except financial derivatives	..	..	..	..	11.5	15.1	15.0	11.3
2.2.1	Short-term securities	..	..	..	..	0.0	0.3	0.0	0.0
2.2.2	Long-term securities	..	..	..	..	11.5	14.8	15.0	11.3
2.2.3	Securities issued by residents	..	..	..	..	0.5	1.1	0.6	0.3
2.2.4	Securities issued by non-residents	..	..	..	..	11.0	14.0	14.4	11.0
2.3	Loans	..	..	..	..	3.5	4.1	2.8	5.1
2.3.1	Short-term loans	..	..	..	..	3.3	1.6	0.4	1.1
2.3.2	Long-term loans	..	..	..	..	0.2	2.5	2.4	4.0
2.3.3	Loans granted to residents	..	..	..	..	0.0	2.3	2.1	4.5
2.3.4	Loans granted to non-residents	..	..	..	..	3.5	1.8	0.6	0.6
2.4	Shares and other equity	..	..	..	..	78.7	75.2	71.2	72.4
2.4.1	Shares issued by residents	..	..	..	..	4.8	8.3	10.6	14.4
2.4.2	Shares issued by non-residents	..	..	..	..	73.9	66.9	60.6	58.1
2.5	Other, not elsewhere classified	..	..	..	..	1.5	0.5	1.5	2.2
	Insurance corporations								
2	Financial assets	..	..	..	..	100.0	100.0	100.0	100.0
2.1	Currency and deposits	..	..	..	..	25.9	24.5	27.3	23.6
2.2	Securities other than shares, except financial derivatives	..	..	..	..	31.5	41.1	37.4	38.7
2.2.1	Short-term securities	..	..	..	..	0.0	0.0	0.0	0.0
2.2.2	Long-term securities	..	..	..	..	31.5	41.1	37.4	38.7
2.2.3	Securities issued by residents	..	..	..	..	0.0	0.0	0.0	0.0
2.2.4	Securities issued by non-residents	..	..	..	..	31.5	41.1	37.4	38.7
2.3	Loans	..	..	..	..	0.2	1.6	0.0	0.0
2.3.1	Short-term loans	..	..	..	..	0.0	0.0	0.0	0.0
2.3.2	Long-term loans	..	..	..	..	0.2	1.6	0.0	0.0
2.3.3	Loans granted to residents	..	..	..	..	0.2	1.6	0.0	0.0
2.3.4	Loans granted to non-residents	..	..	..	..	0.0	0.0	0.0	0.0
2.4	Shares and other equity	..	..	..	..	38.0	26.0	28.2	30.3
2.4.1	Shares issued by residents	..	..	..	..	7.7	8.0	6.7	16.6
2.4.2	Shares issued by non-residents	..	..	..	..	30.3	18.0	21.4	13.7
2.5	Other, not elsewhere classified	..	..	..	..	4.3	6.8	7.1	7.4
	Autonomous pension funds								
2	Financial assets	..	..	..	..	100.0	100.0	100.0	100.0
2.1	Currency and deposits	..	..	..	..	9.2	15.9	16.0	16.9
2.2	Securities other than shares, except financial derivatives	..	..	..	..	17.0	25.0	24.9	20.6
2.2.1	Short-term securities	..	..	..	..	0.1	0.2	0.1	0.0
2.2.2	Long-term securities	..	..	..	..	16.9	24.8	24.8	20.5
2.2.3	Securities issued by residents	..	..	..	..	2.0	2.4	3.2	3.0
2.2.4	Securities issued by non-residents	..	..	..	..	15.0	22.6	21.7	17.6
2.3	Loans	..	..	..	..	0.0	0.0	0.0	0.0
2.3.1	Short-term loans	..	..	..	..	0.0	0.0	0.0	0.0
2.3.2	Long-term loans	..	..	..	..	0.0	0.0	0.0	0.0
2.3.3	Loans granted to residents	..	..	..	..	0.0	0.0	0.0	0.0
2.3.4	Loans granted to non-residents	..	..	..	..	0.0	0.0	0.0	0.0
2.4	Shares and other equity	..	..	..	..	70.0	58.5	59.0	62.4
2.4.1	Shares issued by residents	..	..	..	..	4.5	4.8	5.7	6.0
2.4.2	Shares issued by non-residents	..	..	..	..	65.5	53.7	53.4	56.5
2.5	Other, not elsewhere classified	..	..	..	..	3.8	0.7	0.1	0.1

Note: Detailed metadata at: http://metalinks.oecd.org/instinv/20141203/f729

Table 1. Financial assets of institutional investors, 2012

Million EUR (1999 FIM euro)

		Total	Investment funds			
			Open-end companies (mutual funds)			Closed-end companies
			Total	Money market funds	Other mutual funds	Total
2	Financial assets	..	68 831	3 174	65 657	..
2.1	Currency and deposits	..	2 905	293	2 612	..
2.2	Securities other than shares, except financial derivatives	..	28 865	2 844	26 021	..
2.2.1	Short-term securities	..	2 728	1 015	1 713	..
2.2.2	Long-term securities	..	26 137	1 829	24 308	..
2.2.3	Securities issued by residents	..	4 473	981	3 492	..
2.2.4	Securities issued by non-residents	..	24 392	1 863	22 529	..
2.3	Loans	..	0	0	0	..
2.3.1	Short-term loans	..	0	0	0	..
2.3.2	Long-term loans	..	0	0	0	..
2.3.3	Loans granted to residents	..	0	0	0	..
2.3.4	Loans granted to non-residents	..	0	0	0	..
2.4	Shares and other equity	..	36 013	12	36 001	..
2.4.1	Shares issued by residents	..	11 622	2	11 620	..
2.4.2	Shares issued by non-residents	..	24 391	10	24 381	..
2.5	Other, not elsewhere classified	..	1 048	25	1 023	..

		Total	Insurance corporations and autonomous pension funds			
			Insurance corporations			Autonomous pension funds
			Total	Life insurance corporations	Non-life insurance corporations	Total
2	Financial assets	..	55 467	..	..	3 480
2.1	Currency and deposits	..	2 345	..	..	152
2.2	Securities other than shares, except financial derivatives	..	21 980	..	..	798
2.2.1	Short-term securities	..	2 991	..	..	51
2.2.2	Long-term securities	..	18 989	..	..	747
2.2.3	Securities issued by residents	..	9 090	..	..	348
2.2.4	Securities issued by non-residents	..	12 890	..	..	450
2.3	Loans	..	1 428	..	..	252
2.3.1	Short-term loans	..	0	..	..	0
2.3.2	Long-term loans	..	1 428	..	..	252
2.3.3	Loans granted to residents	..	1 419	..	..	244
2.3.4	Loans granted to non-residents	..	9	..	..	8
2.4	Shares and other equity	..	29 406	..	..	2 276
2.4.1	Shares issued by residents	..	18 228	..	..	1 514
2.4.2	Shares issued by non-residents	..	11 178	..	..	762
2.5	Other, not elsewhere classified	..	308	..	..	2

Note: Detailed metadata at: http://metalinks.oecd.org/instinv/20141203/21aa

Table 2. Financial assets of investment funds

Million EUR (1999 FIM euro)

		2006	2007	2008	2009	2010	2011	2012	2013
	Investment funds								
2	Financial assets	..	..	..	..	..	..	..	..
2.1	Currency and deposits	..	..	..	..	..	..	..	..
2.2	Securities other than shares, except financial derivatives	..	..	..	..	..	..	..	..
2.2.1	Short-term securities	..	..	..	..	..	..	..	..
2.2.2	Long-term securities	..	..	..	..	..	..	..	..
2.2.3	Securities issued by residents	..	..	..	..	..	..	..	..
2.2.4	Securities issued by non-residents	..	..	..	..	..	..	..	..
2.3	Loans	..	..	..	..	..	..	..	..
2.3.1	Short-term loans	..	..	..	..	..	..	..	..
2.3.2	Long-term loans	..	..	..	..	..	..	..	..
2.3.3	Loans granted to residents	..	..	..	..	..	..	..	..
2.3.4	Loans granted to non-residents	..	..	..	..	..	..	..	..
2.4	Shares and other equity	..	..	..	..	..	..	..	..
2.4.1	Shares issued by residents	..	..	..	..	..	..	..	..
2.4.2	Shares issued by non-residents	..	..	..	..	..	..	..	..
2.5	Other, not elsewhere classified	..	..	..	..	..	..	..	..
	Open-end companies (mutual funds)								
2	Financial assets	61 816	67 730	42 294	55 064	63 029	56 785	68 831	..
2.1	Currency and deposits	1 877	2 420	2 032	2 002	2 154	2 383	2 905	..
2.2	Securities other than shares, except financial derivatives	28 616	32 930	24 088	26 023	25 271	25 683	28 865	..
2.2.1	Short-term securities	6 101	7 462	4 994	2 802	2 719	3 837	2 728	..
2.2.2	Long-term securities	22 515	25 468	19 094	23 221	22 552	21 846	26 137	..
2.2.3	Securities issued by residents	6 814	8 277	4 740	4 158	3 926	4 727	4 473	..
2.2.4	Securities issued by non-residents	21 802	24 653	19 348	21 865	21 345	20 956	24 392	..
2.3	Loans	0	0	0	0	0	0	0	..
2.3.1	Short-term loans	0	0	0	0	0	0	0	..
2.3.2	Long-term loans	0	0	0	0	0	0	0	..
2.3.3	Loans granted to residents	0	0	0	0	0	0	0	..
2.3.4	Loans granted to non-residents	0	0	0	0	0	0	0	..
2.4	Shares and other equity	31 281	32 200	15 810	27 014	35 217	28 004	36 013	..
2.4.1	Shares issued by residents	11 614	12 219	6 718	9 331	11 437	9 403	11 622	..
2.4.2	Shares issued by non-residents	19 667	19 981	9 092	17 683	23 780	18 601	24 391	..
2.5	Other, not elsewhere classified	42	180	364	25	387	715	1 048	..
	Money market funds								
2	Financial assets	16 551	18 782	12 200	11 964	10 448	11 264	3 174	..
2.1	Currency and deposits	317	568	490	328	331	401	293	..
2.2	Securities other than shares, except financial derivatives	16 209	18 197	11 709	11 427	9 932	10 849	2 844	..
2.2.1	Short-term securities	5 479	6 377	3 962	2 325	2 141	3 537	1 015	..
2.2.2	Long-term securities	10 730	11 820	7 747	9 102	7 791	7 312	1 829	..
2.2.3	Securities issued by residents	5 304	6 197	2 757	2 541	2 567	3 417	981	..
2.2.4	Securities issued by non-residents	10 905	12 000	8 952	8 886	7 365	7 432	1 863	..
2.3	Loans	0	0	0	0	0	0	0	..
2.3.1	Short-term loans	0	0	0	0	0	0	0	..
2.3.2	Long-term loans	0	0	0	0	0	0	0	..
2.3.3	Loans granted to residents	0	0	0	0	0	0	0	..
2.3.4	Loans granted to non-residents	0	0	0	0	0	0	0	..
2.4	Shares and other equity	22	10	0	209	185	14	12	..
2.4.1	Shares issued by residents	19	10	0	209	185	0	2	..
2.4.2	Shares issued by non-residents	3	0	0	0	0	14	10	..
2.5	Other, not elsewhere classified	3	7	1	0	0	0	25	..
	Other mutual funds								
2	Financial assets	45 265	48 948	30 094	43 100	52 581	45 521	65 657	..
2.1	Currency and deposits	1 560	1 852	1 542	1 674	1 823	1 982	2 612	..
2.2	Securities other than shares, except financial derivatives	12 407	14 733	12 379	14 596	15 339	14 834	26 021	..
2.2.1	Short-term securities	622	1 085	1 032	477	578	300	1 713	..
2.2.2	Long-term securities	11 785	13 648	11 347	14 119	14 761	14 534	24 308	..
2.2.3	Securities issued by residents	1 510	2 080	1 983	1 617	1 359	1 310	3 492	..
2.2.4	Securities issued by non-residents	10 897	12 653	10 396	12 979	13 980	13 524	22 529	..
2.3	Loans	0	0	0	0	0	0	0	..
2.3.1	Short-term loans	0	0	0	0	0	0	0	..
2.3.2	Long-term loans	0	0	0	0	0	0	0	..
2.3.3	Loans granted to residents	0	0	0	0	0	0	0	..
2.3.4	Loans granted to non-residents	0	0	0	0	0	0	0	..
2.4	Shares and other equity	31 259	32 190	15 810	26 805	35 032	27 990	36 001	..
2.4.1	Shares issued by residents	11 595	12 209	6 718	9 122	11 252	9 403	11 620	..
2.4.2	Shares issued by non-residents	19 664	19 981	9 092	17 683	23 780	18 587	24 381	..
2.5	Other, not elsewhere classified	39	173	363	25	387	715	1 023	..

Table 2. Financial assets of investment funds *(cont.)*

Million EUR (1999 FIM euro)

		2006	2007	2008	2009	2010	2011	2012	2013
	Closed-end companies								
2	Financial assets	1 809	2 208	2 300	2 500	2 687	2 935	..	..
2.1	Currency and deposits	0	0	0	0	0	0	..	..
2.2	Securities other than shares, except financial derivatives	0	0	0	0	0	0	..	..
2.2.1	Short-term securities	..	..	..	..	..	..	..	..
2.2.2	Long-term securities	..	..	..	..	..	..	..	..
2.2.3	Securities issued by residents	..	..	..	..	..	..	..	..
2.2.4	Securities issued by non-residents	..	..	..	..	..	..	..	..
2.3	Loans	819	1 053	1 150	1 250	1 250	1 363	..	..
2.3.1	Short-term loans	0	0	0	0	0	0	..	..
2.3.2	Long-term loans	819	1 053	1 150	1 250	1 250	1 363	..	..
2.3.3	Loans granted to residents	819	979	1 150	1 250	1 250	1 363	..	..
2.3.4	Loans granted to non-residents	0	74	0	0	0	0	..	..
2.4	Shares and other equity	990	1 155	1 150	1 250	1 437	1 572	..	..
2.4.1	Shares issued by residents	990	1 084	1 150	1 250	1 437	1 572	..	..
2.4.2	Shares issued by non-residents	0	71	0	0	0	0	..	..
2.5	Other, not elsewhere classified	0	0	0	0	0	0	..	..

Note: Detailed metadata at: http://metalinks.oecd.org/instinv/20141203/21aa

Table 3. Financial assets of insurance corporations and autonomous pension funds

Million EUR (1999 FIM euro)

		2006	2007	2008	2009	2010	2011	2012	2013
	Insurance corporations and autonomous pension funds								
2	Financial assets	..	..	..	..	..	..	..	..
2.1	Currency and deposits	..	..	..	..	..	..	..	..
2.2	Securities other than shares, except financial derivatives	..	..	..	..	..	..	..	..
2.2.1	Short-term securities	..	..	..	..	..	..	..	..
2.2.2	Long-term securities	..	..	..	..	..	..	..	..
2.2.3	Securities issued by residents	..	..	..	..	..	..	..	..
2.2.4	Securities issued by non-residents	..	..	..	..	..	..	..	..
2.3	Loans	..	..	..	..	..	..	..	..
2.3.1	Short-term loans	..	..	..	..	..	..	..	..
2.3.2	Long-term loans	..	..	..	..	..	..	..	..
2.3.3	Loans granted to residents	..	..	..	..	..	..	..	..
2.3.4	Loans granted to non-residents	..	..	..	..	..	..	..	..
2.4	Shares and other equity	..	..	..	..	..	..	..	..
2.4.1	Shares issued by residents	..	..	..	..	..	..	..	..
2.4.2	Shares issued by non-residents	..	..	..	..	..	..	..	..
2.5	Other, not elsewhere classified	..	..	..	..	..	..	..	..
	Insurance corporations								
2	Financial assets	46 287	46 297	41 966	46 602	50 741	47 768	55 467	..
2.1	Currency and deposits	768	762	1 003	757	1 393	1 788	2 345	..
2.2	Securities other than shares, except financial derivatives	19 964	19 240	20 267	19 395	20 820	18 066	21 980	..
2.2.1	Short-term securities	4 223	5 168	3 479	2 002	2 766	3 077	2 991	..
2.2.2	Long-term securities	15 741	14 072	16 788	17 393	18 054	14 989	18 989	..
2.2.3	Securities issued by residents	5 345	5 387	6 253	5 779	6 047	6 011	9 090	..
2.2.4	Securities issued by non-residents	14 619	13 853	14 014	13 616	14 773	12 055	12 890	..
2.3	Loans	1 406	1 620	1 079	1 256	1 518	1 514	1 428	..
2.3.1	Short-term loans	0	0	0	0	0	0	0	..
2.3.2	Long-term loans	1 406	1 620	1 079	1 256	1 518	1 514	1 428	..
2.3.3	Loans granted to residents	1 389	1 598	1 065	1 241	1 504	1 500	1 419	..
2.3.4	Loans granted to non-residents	17	22	14	15	14	14	9	..
2.4	Shares and other equity	24 125	24 649	19 235	25 128	26 837	26 124	29 406	..
2.4.1	Shares issued by residents	16 261	17 022	13 903	16 666	17 434	14 589	18 228	..
2.4.2	Shares issued by non-residents	7 864	7 627	5 332	8 462	9 403	11 535	11 178	..
2.5	Other, not elsewhere classified	24	26	382	66	173	276	308	..
	Life insurance corporations								
2	Financial assets	..	..	..	..	..	..	..	..
2.1	Currency and deposits	..	..	..	..	..	..	..	..
2.2	Securities other than shares, except financial derivatives	..	..	..	..	..	..	..	..
2.2.1	Short-term securities	..	..	..	..	..	..	..	..
2.2.2	Long-term securities	..	..	..	..	..	..	..	..
2.2.3	Securities issued by residents	..	..	..	..	..	..	..	..
2.2.4	Securities issued by non-residents	..	..	..	..	..	..	..	..
2.3	Loans	..	..	..	..	..	..	..	..
2.3.1	Short-term loans	..	..	..	..	..	..	..	..
2.3.2	Long-term loans	..	..	..	..	..	..	..	..
2.3.3	Loans granted to residents	..	..	..	..	..	..	..	..
2.3.4	Loans granted to non-residents	..	..	..	..	..	..	..	..
2.4	Shares and other equity	..	..	..	..	..	..	..	..
2.4.1	Shares issued by residents	..	..	..	..	..	..	..	..
2.4.2	Shares issued by non-residents	..	..	..	..	..	..	..	..
2.5	Other, not elsewhere classified	..	..	..	..	..	..	..	..
	Non-life insurance corporations								
2	Financial assets	..	..	..	..	..	..	..	..
2.1	Currency and deposits	..	..	..	..	..	..	..	..
2.2	Securities other than shares, except financial derivatives	..	..	..	..	..	..	..	..
2.2.1	Short-term securities	..	..	..	..	..	..	..	..
2.2.2	Long-term securities	..	..	..	..	..	..	..	..
2.2.3	Securities issued by residents	..	..	..	..	..	..	..	..
2.2.4	Securities issued by non-residents	..	..	..	..	..	..	..	..
2.3	Loans	..	..	..	..	..	..	..	..
2.3.1	Short-term loans	..	..	..	..	..	..	..	..
2.3.2	Long-term loans	..	..	..	..	..	..	..	..
2.3.3	Loans granted to residents	..	..	..	..	..	..	..	..
2.3.4	Loans granted to non-residents	..	..	..	..	..	..	..	..
2.4	Shares and other equity	..	..	..	..	..	..	..	..
2.4.1	Shares issued by residents	..	..	..	..	..	..	..	..
2.4.2	Shares issued by non-residents	..	..	..	..	..	..	..	..
2.5	Other, not elsewhere classified	..	..	..	..	..	..	..	..

Table 3. Financial assets of insurance corporations and autonomous pension funds *(cont.)*

Million EUR (1999 FIM euro)

		2006	2007	2008	2009	2010	2011	2012	2013
	Autonomous pension funds								
2	Financial assets	5 257	5 544	4 429	5 062	4 091	5 790	3 480	..
2.1	Currency and deposits	107	141	184	487	96	378	152	..
2.2	Securities other than shares, except financial derivatives	942	964	1 228	1 042	842	1 243	798	..
2.2.1	Short-term securities	82	114	242	69	67	138	51	..
2.2.2	Long-term securities	860	850	986	973	775	1 105	747	..
2.2.3	Securities issued by residents	338	410	627	431	337	510	348	..
2.2.4	Securities issued by non-residents	604	554	601	611	505	733	450	..
2.3	Loans	719	548	464	601	298	310	252	..
2.3.1	Short-term loans	0	0	0	0	0	0	0	..
2.3.2	Long-term loans	719	548	464	601	298	310	252	..
2.3.3	Loans granted to residents	719	548	464	601	298	301	244	..
2.3.4	Loans granted to non-residents	0	0	0	0	0	9	8	..
2.4	Shares and other equity	3 489	3 891	2 552	2 932	2 855	3 859	2 276	..
2.4.1	Shares issued by residents	2 584	3 003	1 963	2 192	2 130	2 642	1 514	..
2.4.2	Shares issued by non-residents	905	888	589	740	725	1 217	762	..
2.5	Other, not elsewhere classified	0	0	1	0	0	0	2	..

Note: Detailed metadata at: http://metalinks.oecd.org/instinv/20141203/21aa

FINLAND

Table 4. Portfolio composition by type of investor

Percentage of total financial assets

Per cent

		2006	2007	2008	2009	2010	2011	2012	2013
	Investment funds								
2	Financial assets	..	..	..	..	..	..	..	..
2.1	Currency and deposits	..	..	..	..	..	..	..	..
2.2	Securities other than shares, except financial derivatives	..	..	..	..	..	..	..	..
2.2.1	Short-term securities	..	..	..	..	..	..	..	..
2.2.2	Long-term securities	..	..	..	..	..	..	..	..
2.2.3	Securities issued by residents	..	..	..	..	..	..	..	..
2.2.4	Securities issued by non-residents	..	..	..	..	..	..	..	..
2.3	Loans	..	..	..	..	..	..	..	..
2.3.1	Short-term loans	..	..	..	..	..	..	..	..
2.3.2	Long-term loans	..	..	..	..	..	..	..	..
2.3.3	Loans granted to residents	..	..	..	..	..	..	..	..
2.3.4	Loans granted to non-residents	..	..	..	..	..	..	..	..
2.4	Shares and other equity	..	..	..	..	..	..	..	..
2.4.1	Shares issued by residents	..	..	..	..	..	..	..	..
2.4.2	Shares issued by non-residents	..	..	..	..	..	..	..	..
2.5	Other, not elsewhere classified	..	..	..	..	..	..	..	..
	Insurance corporations								
2	Financial assets	100.0	100.0	100.0	100.0	100.0	100.0	100.0	..
2.1	Currency and deposits	1.7	1.6	2.4	1.6	2.7	3.7	4.2	..
2.2	Securities other than shares, except financial derivatives	43.1	41.6	48.3	41.6	41.0	37.8	39.6	..
2.2.1	Short-term securities	9.1	11.2	8.3	4.3	5.5	6.4	5.4	..
2.2.2	Long-term securities	34.0	30.4	40.0	37.3	35.6	31.4	34.2	..
2.2.3	Securities issued by residents	11.5	11.6	14.9	12.4	11.9	12.6	16.4	..
2.2.4	Securities issued by non-residents	31.6	29.9	33.4	29.2	29.1	25.2	23.2	..
2.3	Loans	3.0	3.5	2.6	2.7	3.0	3.2	2.6	..
2.3.1	Short-term loans	0.0	0.0	0.0	0.0	0.0	0.0	0.0	..
2.3.2	Long-term loans	3.0	3.5	2.6	2.7	3.0	3.2	2.6	..
2.3.3	Loans granted to residents	3.0	3.5	2.5	2.7	3.0	3.1	2.6	..
2.3.4	Loans granted to non-residents	0.0	0.0	0.0	0.0	0.0	0.0	0.0	..
2.4	Shares and other equity	52.1	53.2	45.8	53.9	52.9	54.7	53.0	..
2.4.1	Shares issued by residents	35.1	36.8	33.1	35.8	34.4	30.5	32.9	..
2.4.2	Shares issued by non-residents	17.0	16.5	12.7	18.2	18.5	24.1	20.2	..
2.5	Other, not elsewhere classified	0.1	0.1	0.9	0.1	0.3	0.6	0.6	..
	Autonomous pension funds								
2	Financial assets	100.0	100.0	100.0	100.0	100.0	100.0	100.0	..
2.1	Currency and deposits	2.0	2.5	4.2	9.6	2.3	6.5	4.4	..
2.2	Securities other than shares, except financial derivatives	17.9	17.4	27.7	20.6	20.6	21.5	22.9	..
2.2.1	Short-term securities	1.6	2.1	5.5	1.4	1.6	2.4	1.5	..
2.2.2	Long-term securities	16.4	15.3	22.3	19.2	18.9	19.1	21.5	..
2.2.3	Securities issued by residents	6.4	7.4	14.2	8.5	8.2	8.8	10.0	..
2.2.4	Securities issued by non-residents	11.5	10.0	13.6	12.1	12.3	12.7	12.9	..
2.3	Loans	13.7	9.9	10.5	11.9	7.3	5.4	7.2	..
2.3.1	Short-term loans	0.0	0.0	0.0	0.0	0.0	0.0	0.0	..
2.3.2	Long-term loans	13.7	9.9	10.5	11.9	7.3	5.4	7.2	..
2.3.3	Loans granted to residents	13.7	9.9	10.5	11.9	7.3	5.2	7.0	..
2.3.4	Loans granted to non-residents	0.0	0.0	0.0	0.0	0.0	0.2	0.2	..
2.4	Shares and other equity	66.4	70.2	57.6	57.9	69.8	66.6	65.4	..
2.4.1	Shares issued by residents	49.2	54.2	44.3	43.3	52.1	45.6	43.5	..
2.4.2	Shares issued by non-residents	17.2	16.0	13.3	14.6	17.7	21.0	21.9	..
2.5	Other, not elsewhere classified	0.0	0.0	0.0	0.0	0.0	0.0	0.1	..

Note: Detailed metadata at: http://metalinks.oecd.org/instinv/20141203/f729

FRANCE

Table 1. Financial assets of institutional investors, 2013

Million EUR (1999 FRF euro)

		Total	Investment funds			
			Open-end companies (mutual funds)			Closed-end companies
			Total	Money market funds	Other mutual funds	Total
2	Financial assets	1 200 064	1 397 516	324 242	1 073 274	1 775
2.1	Currency and deposits	84 225	84 203	46 812	37 391	22
2.2	Securities other than shares, except financial derivatives	553 059	553 059	237 610	315 449	0
2.2.1	Short-term securities	199 879	199 879	177 802	22 077	0
2.2.2	Long-term securities	353 180	353 180	59 808	293 372	0
2.2.3	Securities issued by residents	252 165	252 165	143 878	108 287	0
2.2.4	Securities issued by non-residents	300 894	300 894	93 732	207 162	0
2.3	Loans	1 696	1 696	795	901	0
2.3.1	Short-term loans	1 696	1 696	795	901	0
2.3.2	Long-term loans	0	0	0	0	0
2.3.3	Loans granted to residents	1 685	1 685	795	890	0
2.3.4	Loans granted to non-residents	11	11	0	11	0
2.4	Shares and other equity	441 164	638 941	35 596	603 345	1 450
2.4.1	Shares issued by residents	170 957	367 458	34 004	333 454	1 450
2.4.2	Shares issued by non-residents	270 207	271 483	1 592	269 891	0
2.5	Other, not elsewhere classified	119 920	119 617	3 429	116 188	303

		Total	Insurance corporations and autonomous pension funds			
			Insurance corporations			Autonomous pension funds
			Total	Life insurance corporations	Non-life insurance corporations	Total
2	Financial assets	2 050 027	2 180 895	1 834 232	346 664	..
2.1	Currency and deposits	29 545	29 545	23 842	5 703	..
2.2	Securities other than shares, except financial derivatives	1 317 115	1 318 722	1 158 328	160 394	..
2.2.1	Short-term securities	25 403	25 403	24 297	1 107	..
2.2.2	Long-term securities	1 291 712	1 293 319	1 134 031	159 287	..
2.2.3	Securities issued by residents	..	710 811	616 929	93 881	..
2.2.4	Securities issued by non-residents	..	607 911	541 398	66 513	..
2.3	Loans	18 368	36 247	29 251	6 996	..
2.3.1	Short-term loans	9 673	10 747	8 673	2 074	..
2.3.2	Long-term loans	8 697	25 500	20 578	4 922	..
2.3.3	Loans granted to residents	17 288	34 531	27 866	6 665	..
2.3.4	Loans granted to non-residents	1 080	1 716	1 385	331	..
2.4	Shares and other equity	683 037	683 704	531 882	151 822	..
2.4.1	Shares issued by residents	..	599 485	458 531	140 955	..
2.4.2	Shares issued by non-residents	..	84 219	73 351	10 868	..
2.5	Other, not elsewhere classified	1 962	112 678	90 929	21 748	..

Note: Detailed metadata at: http://metalinks.oecd.org/instinv/20141203/01bd

Table 2. Financial assets of investment funds

Million EUR (1999 FRF euro)

		2006	2007	2008	2009	2010	2011	2012	2013
	Investment funds								
2	Financial assets	..	..	1 120 295	1 263 577	1 260 893	1 132 799	1 192 496	1 200 064
2.1	Currency and deposits	..	..	105 401	91 351	83 370	84 029	87 060	84 225
2.2	Securities other than shares, except financial derivatives	..	..	584 474	632 198	595 774	558 799	590 318	553 059
2.2.1	Short-term securities	..	..	278 573	303 749	262 527	260 737	267 195	199 879
2.2.2	Long-term securities	..	..	305 901	328 449	333 247	298 062	323 123	353 180
2.2.3	Securities issued by residents	..	..	291 372	289 663	271 543	289 385	291 369	252 165
2.2.4	Securities issued by non-residents	..	..	293 102	342 535	324 231	269 414	298 949	300 894
2.3	Loans	..	..	4 763	3 557	4 694	1 292	716	1 696
2.3.1	Short-term loans	..	..	4 763	3 557	4 694	1 292	716	1 696
2.3.2	Long-term loans	..	..	0	0	0	0	0	0
2.3.3	Loans granted to residents	..	..	4 758	3 557	4 693	1 263	704	1 685
2.3.4	Loans granted to non-residents	..	..	5	0	1	29	12	11
2.4	Shares and other equity	..	..	312 998	409 402	438 471	363 137	389 148	441 164
2.4.1	Shares issued by residents	..	..	148 301	179 582	173 370	143 816	153 516	170 957
2.4.2	Shares issued by non-residents	..	..	164 697	229 820	265 101	219 321	235 632	270 207
2.5	Other, not elsewhere classified	..	..	112 659	127 069	138 584	125 542	125 254	119 920
	Open-end companies (mutual funds)								
2	Financial assets	..	..	1 344 131	1 491 972	1 478 132	1 324 368	1 397 361	1 397 516
2.1	Currency and deposits	..	..	105 379	91 329	83 348	84 007	87 038	84 203
2.2	Securities other than shares, except financial derivatives	..	..	583 390	631 114	594 690	558 799	590 318	553 059
2.2.1	Short-term securities	..	..	277 489	302 665	261 443	260 737	267 195	199 879
2.2.2	Long-term securities	..	..	305 901	328 449	333 247	298 062	323 123	353 180
2.2.3	Securities issued by residents	..	..	290 288	288 579	270 459	289 385	291 369	252 165
2.2.4	Securities issued by non-residents	..	..	293 102	342 535	324 231	269 414	298 949	300 894
2.3	Loans	..	..	6 066	4 621	5 736	1 587	1 249	1 696
2.3.1	Short-term loans	..	..	6 066	4 621	5 736	1 587	1 249	1 696
2.3.2	Long-term loans	..	..	0	0	0	0	0	0
2.3.3	Loans granted to residents	..	..	6 061	4 621	5 735	1 558	1 237	1 685
2.3.4	Loans granted to non-residents	..	..	5	0	1	29	12	11
2.4	Shares and other equity	..	..	536 897	638 142	656 077	554 736	593 805	638 941
2.4.1	Shares issued by residents	..	..	372 200	408 322	388 477	332 554	356 480	367 458
2.4.2	Shares issued by non-residents	..	..	164 697	229 820	267 600	222 182	237 325	271 483
2.5	Other, not elsewhere classified	..	..	112 399	126 766	138 281	125 239	124 951	119 617
	Money market funds								
2	Financial assets	..	..	485 434	501 281	413 573	369 345	370 218	324 242
2.1	Currency and deposits	..	..	73 806	56 673	47 050	41 235	40 832	46 812
2.2	Securities other than shares, except financial derivatives	..	..	323 672	348 276	295 507	274 042	277 539	237 610
2.2.1	Short-term securities	..	..	238 921	275 822	234 549	223 728	236 189	177 802
2.2.2	Long-term securities	..	..	84 751	72 454	60 958	50 314	41 350	59 808
2.2.3	Securities issued by residents	..	..	177 628	179 040	158 216	172 865	173 473	143 878
2.2.4	Securities issued by non-residents	..	..	146 044	169 236	137 291	101 177	104 066	93 732
2.3	Loans	..	..	3 084	2 022	1 048	487	758	795
2.3.1	Short-term loans	..	..	3 084	2 022	1 048	487	758	795
2.3.2	Long-term loans	..	..	0	0	0	0	0	0
2.3.3	Loans granted to residents	..	..	3 079	2 022	1 047	487	758	795
2.3.4	Loans granted to non-residents	..	..	5	0	1	0	0	0
2.4	Shares and other equity	..	..	82 507	72 531	53 388	38 224	48 547	35 596
2.4.1	Shares issued by residents	..	..	80 940	69 007	47 673	34 426	46 489	34 004
2.4.2	Shares issued by non-residents	..	..	1 567	3 524	5 715	3 798	2 058	1 592
2.5	Other, not elsewhere classified	..	..	2 365	21 779	16 580	15 357	2 542	3 429
	Other mutual funds								
2	Financial assets	..	..	858 697	990 691	1 064 559	955 023	1 027 143	1 073 274
2.1	Currency and deposits	..	..	31 573	34 656	36 298	42 772	46 206	37 391
2.2	Securities other than shares, except financial derivatives	..	..	259 718	282 838	299 183	284 757	312 779	315 449
2.2.1	Short-term securities	..	..	38 568	26 843	26 894	37 009	31 006	22 077
2.2.2	Long-term securities	..	..	221 150	255 995	272 289	247 748	281 773	293 372
2.2.3	Securities issued by residents	..	..	112 660	109 539	112 243	116 520	117 896	108 287
2.2.4	Securities issued by non-residents	..	..	147 058	173 299	186 940	168 237	194 883	207 162
2.3	Loans	..	..	2 982	2 599	4 688	1 100	491	901
2.3.1	Short-term loans	..	..	2 982	2 599	4 688	1 100	491	901
2.3.2	Long-term loans	..	..	0	0	0	0	0	0
2.3.3	Loans granted to residents	..	..	2 982	2 599	4 688	1 071	479	890
2.3.4	Loans granted to non-residents	..	..	0	0	0	29	12	11
2.4	Shares and other equity	..	..	454 390	565 611	602 689	516 512	545 258	603 345
2.4.1	Shares issued by residents	..	..	291 260	339 315	340 804	298 128	309 991	333 454
2.4.2	Shares issued by non-residents	..	..	163 130	226 296	261 885	218 384	235 267	269 891
2.5	Other, not elsewhere classified	..	..	110 034	104 987	121 701	109 882	122 409	116 188

Table 2. Financial assets of investment funds *(cont.)*

Million EUR (1999 FRF euro)

		2006	2007	2008	2009	2010	2011	2012	2013
	Closed-end companies								
2	Financial assets	..	..	1 366	1 409	1 409	1 775	1 775	1 775
2.1	Currency and deposits	..	..	22	22	22	22	22	22
2.2	Securities other than shares, except financial derivatives	..	..	1 084	1 084	1 084	0	0	0
2.2.1	Short-term securities	..	..	1 084	1 084	1 084	0	0	0
2.2.2	Long-term securities	..	..	0	0	0	0	0	0
2.2.3	Securities issued by residents	..	..	1 084	1 084	1 084	0	0	0
2.2.4	Securities issued by non-residents	..	..	0	0	0	0	0	0
2.3	Loans	..	..	0	0	0	0	0	0
2.3.1	Short-term loans	..	..	0	0	0	0	0	0
2.3.2	Long-term loans	..	..	0	0	0	0	0	0
2.3.3	Loans granted to residents	..	..	0	0	0	0	0	0
2.3.4	Loans granted to non-residents	..	..	0	0	0	0	0	0
2.4	Shares and other equity	..	..	0	0	0	1 450	1 450	1 450
2.4.1	Shares issued by residents	..	..	0	0	0	1 450	1 450	1 450
2.4.2	Shares issued by non-residents	..	..	0	0	0	0	0	0
2.5	Other, not elsewhere classified	..	..	260	303	303	303	303	303

Note: Detailed metadata at: http://metalinks.oecd.org/instinv/20141203/01bd

Table 3. Financial assets of insurance corporations and autonomous pension funds

Million EUR (1999 FRF euro)

		2006	2007	2008	2009	2010	2011	2012	2013
	Insurance corporations and autonomous pension funds								
2	Financial assets	1 464 961	1 562 018	1 492 908	1 665 646	1 796 326	1 766 687	1 965 190	2 050 027
2.1	Currency and deposits	17 524	15 193	16 972	15 624	17 526	19 301	25 409	29 545
2.2	Securities other than shares, except financial derivatives	807 573	857 609	917 403	1 016 865	1 145 256	1 138 162	1 274 476	1 317 115
2.2.1	Short-term securities	15 985	22 009	22 469	11 111	17 684	36 164	29 890	25 403
2.2.2	Long-term securities	791 588	835 600	894 934	1 005 754	1 127 572	1 101 998	1 244 586	1 291 712
2.2.3	Securities issued by residents	..	..	..	..	..	..	..	..
2.2.4	Securities issued by non-residents	..	..	..	..	..	..	..	..
2.3	Loans	12 929	14 792	15 065	19 529	19 430	17 860	18 568	18 368
2.3.1	Short-term loans	6 404	7 336	7 500	11 825	11 413	9 648	10 094	9 673
2.3.2	Long-term loans	6 525	7 456	7 565	7 704	8 017	8 212	8 474	8 697
2.3.3	Loans granted to residents	12 929	14 792	15 054	15 333	15 944	16 353	16 841	17 288
2.3.4	Loans granted to non-residents	0	0	11	4 196	3 487	1 507	1 729	1 080
2.4	Shares and other equity	624 743	670 847	536 907	608 944	609 351	583 231	641 146	683 037
2.4.1	Shares issued by residents	..	..	..	..	..	..	..	..
2.4.2	Shares issued by non-residents	..	..	..	..	..	..	..	..
2.5	Other, not elsewhere classified	2 192	3 577	6 561	4 684	4 763	8 133	5 591	1 962
	Insurance corporations								
2	Financial assets	1 548 381	1 664 855	1 590 785	1 760 267	1 893 927	1 875 416	2 076 859	2 180 895
2.1	Currency and deposits	17 604	15 193	19 578	17 511	17 526	19 301	25 409	29 545
2.2	Securities other than shares, except financial derivatives	809 866	860 213	919 586	1 018 877	1 147 206	1 139 217	1 275 546	1 318 722
2.2.1	Short-term securities	15 988	22 013	22 470	11 111	17 685	36 164	29 890	25 403
2.2.2	Long-term securities	793 879	838 200	897 116	1 007 766	1 129 520	1 103 053	1 245 655	1 293 319
2.2.3	Securities issued by residents	368 193	393 651	405 161	428 292	525 822	584 616	682 298	710 811
2.2.4	Securities issued by non-residents	441 673	466 561	514 425	590 585	621 384	554 601	593 247	607 911
2.3	Loans	31 916	35 178	37 399	32 597	33 893	37 900	35 524	36 247
2.3.1	Short-term loans	11 327	12 343	12 020	9 953	10 646	13 952	10 800	10 747
2.3.2	Long-term loans	20 589	22 835	25 379	22 644	23 247	23 949	24 724	25 500
2.3.3	Loans granted to residents	26 920	30 753	30 428	30 790	32 069	36 006	33 606	34 531
2.3.4	Loans granted to non-residents	4 996	4 425	6 971	1 807	1 824	1 894	1 918	1 716
2.4	Shares and other equity	626 537	685 787	538 918	612 297	610 464	584 383	642 191	683 704
2.4.1	Shares issued by residents	565 478	622 273	498 417	557 081	551 729	530 027	575 628	599 485
2.4.2	Shares issued by non-residents	61 059	63 515	40 501	55 217	58 734	54 355	66 563	84 219
2.5	Other, not elsewhere classified	62 458	68 485	75 304	78 985	84 839	94 615	98 191	112 678
	Life insurance corporations								
2	Financial assets	1 270 236	1 367 343	1 303 590	1 452 820	1 573 946	1 561 760	1 745 846	1 834 232
2.1	Currency and deposits	13 788	11 900	15 487	13 835	14 178	15 576	20 505	23 842
2.2	Securities other than shares, except financial derivatives	704 872	750 357	795 397	887 773	996 868	992 581	1 115 211	1 158 328
2.2.1	Short-term securities	13 470	19 269	20 257	9 261	16 079	34 111	28 212	24 297
2.2.2	Long-term securities	691 402	731 088	775 139	878 512	980 789	958 470	1 087 000	1 134 031
2.2.3	Securities issued by residents	307 532	329 403	335 183	359 364	444 329	499 992	586 105	616 929
2.2.4	Securities issued by non-residents	397 340	420 955	460 214	528 410	552 539	492 589	529 107	541 398
2.3	Loans	24 998	27 553	29 583	25 755	27 419	30 585	28 667	29 251
2.3.1	Short-term loans	8 872	9 668	9 508	7 864	8 612	11 259	8 715	8 673
2.3.2	Long-term loans	16 126	17 885	20 075	17 891	18 807	19 326	19 952	20 578
2.3.3	Loans granted to residents	21 085	24 087	24 069	24 327	25 944	29 057	27 119	27 866
2.3.4	Loans granted to non-residents	3 913	3 466	5 514	1 428	1 476	1 528	1 548	1 385
2.4	Shares and other equity	477 658	523 893	403 557	463 050	466 846	446 665	502 224	531 882
2.4.1	Shares issued by residents	427 888	471 846	370 726	416 751	415 386	399 116	444 439	458 531
2.4.2	Shares issued by non-residents	49 770	52 046	32 832	46 300	51 459	47 548	57 785	73 351
2.5	Other, not elsewhere classified	48 920	53 640	59 566	62 406	68 635	76 353	79 239	90 929
	Non-life insurance corporations								
2	Financial assets	278 144	297 512	287 195	307 447	319 980	313 656	331 014	346 664
2.1	Currency and deposits	3 816	3 293	4 092	3 675	3 347	3 725	4 904	5 703
2.2	Securities other than shares, except financial derivatives	104 994	109 855	124 189	131 103	150 337	146 635	160 334	160 394
2.2.1	Short-term securities	2 518	2 744	2 213	1 850	1 606	2 052	1 678	1 107
2.2.2	Long-term securities	102 477	107 112	121 977	129 254	148 731	144 583	158 656	159 287
2.2.3	Securities issued by residents	60 661	64 248	69 978	68 928	81 493	84 623	96 193	93 881
2.2.4	Securities issued by non-residents	44 333	45 607	54 212	62 175	68 845	62 012	64 141	66 513
2.3	Loans	6 918	7 625	7 816	6 842	6 474	7 315	6 857	6 996
2.3.1	Short-term loans	2 455	2 675	2 512	2 089	2 033	2 693	2 085	2 074
2.3.2	Long-term loans	4 463	4 949	5 304	4 753	4 440	4 622	4 772	4 922
2.3.3	Loans granted to residents	5 835	6 666	6 359	6 463	6 125	6 950	6 486	6 665
2.3.4	Loans granted to non-residents	1 083	959	1 457	379	348	366	370	331
2.4	Shares and other equity	148 879	161 895	135 361	149 247	143 618	137 718	139 967	151 822
2.4.1	Shares issued by residents	137 589	150 427	127 691	140 330	136 343	130 911	131 189	140 955
2.4.2	Shares issued by non-residents	11 289	11 468	7 669	8 917	7 275	6 807	8 778	10 868
2.5	Other, not elsewhere classified	13 538	14 844	15 738	16 579	16 204	18 262	18 952	21 748

Table 3. Financial assets of insurance corporations and autonomous pension funds *(cont.)*

Million EUR (1999 FRF euro)

		2006	2007	2008	2009	2010	2011	2012	2013
	Autonomous pension funds								
2	Financial assets	..	..	..	..	..	..	..	..
2.1	Currency and deposits	..	..	..	..	..	..	..	..
2.2	Securities other than shares, except financial derivatives	..	..	..	..	..	..	..	..
2.2.1	Short-term securities	..	..	..	..	..	..	..	..
2.2.2	Long-term securities	..	..	..	..	..	..	..	..
2.2.3	Securities issued by residents	..	..	..	..	..	..	..	..
2.2.4	Securities issued by non-residents	..	..	..	..	..	..	..	..
2.3	Loans	..	..	..	..	..	..	..	..
2.3.1	Short-term loans	..	..	..	..	..	..	..	..
2.3.2	Long-term loans	..	..	..	..	..	..	..	..
2.3.3	Loans granted to residents	..	..	..	..	..	..	..	..
2.3.4	Loans granted to non-residents	..	..	..	..	..	..	..	..
2.4	Shares and other equity	..	..	..	..	..	..	..	..
2.4.1	Shares issued by residents	..	..	..	..	..	..	..	..
2.4.2	Shares issued by non-residents	..	..	..	..	..	..	..	..
2.5	Other, not elsewhere classified	..	..	..	..	..	..	..	..

Note: Detailed metadata at: http://metalinks.oecd.org/instinv/20141203/01bd

Table 4. Portfolio composition by type of investor

Percentage of total financial assets

Per cent

		2006	2007	2008	2009	2010	2011	2012	2013
	Investment funds								
2	Financial assets	..	..	100.0	100.0	100.0	100.0	100.0	100.0
2.1	Currency and deposits	..	..	9.4	7.2	6.6	7.4	7.3	7.0
2.2	Securities other than shares, except financial derivatives	..	..	52.2	50.0	47.3	49.3	49.5	46.1
2.2.1	Short-term securities	..	..	24.9	24.0	20.8	23.0	22.4	16.7
2.2.2	Long-term securities	..	..	27.3	26.0	26.4	26.3	27.1	29.4
2.2.3	Securities issued by residents	..	..	26.0	22.9	21.5	25.5	24.4	21.0
2.2.4	Securities issued by non-residents	..	..	26.2	27.1	25.7	23.8	25.1	25.1
2.3	Loans	..	..	0.4	0.3	0.4	0.1	0.1	0.1
2.3.1	Short-term loans	..	..	0.4	0.3	0.4	0.1	0.1	0.1
2.3.2	Long-term loans	..	..	0.0	0.0	0.0	0.0	0.0	0.0
2.3.3	Loans granted to residents	..	..	0.4	0.3	0.4	0.1	0.1	0.1
2.3.4	Loans granted to non-residents	..	..	0.0	0.0	0.0	0.0	0.0	0.0
2.4	Shares and other equity	..	..	27.9	32.4	34.8	32.1	32.6	36.8
2.4.1	Shares issued by residents	..	..	13.2	14.2	13.7	12.7	12.9	14.2
2.4.2	Shares issued by non-residents	..	..	14.7	18.2	21.0	19.4	19.8	22.5
2.5	Other, not elsewhere classified	..	..	10.1	10.1	11.0	11.1	10.5	10.0
	Insurance corporations								
2	Financial assets	100.0	100.0	100.0	100.0	100.0	100.0	100.0	100.0
2.1	Currency and deposits	1.1	0.9	1.2	1.0	0.9	1.0	1.2	1.4
2.2	Securities other than shares, except financial derivatives	52.3	51.7	57.8	57.9	60.6	60.7	61.4	60.5
2.2.1	Short-term securities	1.0	1.3	1.4	0.6	0.9	1.9	1.4	1.2
2.2.2	Long-term securities	51.3	50.3	56.4	57.3	59.6	58.8	60.0	59.3
2.2.3	Securities issued by residents	23.8	23.6	25.5	24.3	27.8	31.2	32.9	32.6
2.2.4	Securities issued by non-residents	28.5	28.0	32.3	33.6	32.8	29.6	28.6	27.9
2.3	Loans	2.1	2.1	2.4	1.9	1.8	2.0	1.7	1.7
2.3.1	Short-term loans	0.7	0.7	0.8	0.6	0.6	0.7	0.5	0.5
2.3.2	Long-term loans	1.3	1.4	1.6	1.3	1.2	1.3	1.2	1.2
2.3.3	Loans granted to residents	1.7	1.8	1.9	1.7	1.7	1.9	1.6	1.6
2.3.4	Loans granted to non-residents	0.3	0.3	0.4	0.1	0.1	0.1	0.1	0.1
2.4	Shares and other equity	40.5	41.2	33.9	34.8	32.2	31.2	30.9	31.3
2.4.1	Shares issued by residents	36.5	37.4	31.3	31.6	29.1	28.3	27.7	27.5
2.4.2	Shares issued by non-residents	3.9	3.8	2.5	3.1	3.1	2.9	3.2	3.9
2.5	Other, not elsewhere classified	4.0	4.1	4.7	4.5	4.5	5.0	4.7	5.2
	Autonomous pension funds								
2	Financial assets	..	..	..	..	..	..	..	..
2.1	Currency and deposits	..	..	..	..	..	..	..	..
2.2	Securities other than shares, except financial derivatives	..	..	..	..	..	..	..	..
2.2.1	Short-term securities	..	..	..	..	..	..	..	..
2.2.2	Long-term securities	..	..	..	..	..	..	..	..
2.2.3	Securities issued by residents	..	..	..	..	..	..	..	..
2.2.4	Securities issued by non-residents	..	..	..	..	..	..	..	..
2.3	Loans	..	..	..	..	..	..	..	..
2.3.1	Short-term loans	..	..	..	..	..	..	..	..
2.3.2	Long-term loans	..	..	..	..	..	..	..	..
2.3.3	Loans granted to residents	..	..	..	..	..	..	..	..
2.3.4	Loans granted to non-residents	..	..	..	..	..	..	..	..
2.4	Shares and other equity	..	..	..	..	..	..	..	..
2.4.1	Shares issued by residents	..	..	..	..	..	..	..	..
2.4.2	Shares issued by non-residents	..	..	..	..	..	..	..	..
2.5	Other, not elsewhere classified	..	..	..	..	..	..	..	..

Note: Detailed metadata at: http://metalinks.oecd.org/instinv/20141203/f729

GERMANY

Table 1. Financial assets of institutional investors, 2012

Million EUR (1999 DEM euro)

			Investment funds			
		Total	Open-end companies (mutual funds)			Closed-end companies
			Total	Money market funds	Other mutual funds	Total
2	Financial assets	..	1 339 052	7 824	1 331 228	..
2.1	Currency and deposits	..	128 625	360	128 265	..
2.2	Securities other than shares, except financial derivatives	..	692 974	7 440	685 534	..
2.2.1	Short-term securities	..	4 331	670	3 661	..
2.2.2	Long-term securities	..	686 617	4 744	681 873	..
2.2.3	Securities issued by residents	..	154 919	4 726	150 193	..
2.2.4	Securities issued by non-residents	..	538 055	2 714	535 341	..
2.3	Loans	..	3 070	24	3 046	..
2.3.1	Short-term loans	..	24	24	0	..
2.3.2	Long-term loans	..	3 046	0	3 046	..
2.3.3	Loans granted to residents	..	2 111	24	2 087	..
2.3.4	Loans granted to non-residents	..	959	0	959	..
2.4	Shares and other equity	..	514 383	0	514 383	..
2.4.1	Shares issued by residents	..	303 347	..	303 347	..
2.4.2	Shares issued by non-residents	..	211 036	..	211 036	..
2.5	Other, not elsewhere classified	..	0	0	0	..

			Insurance corporations and autonomous pension funds			
		Total	Insurance corporations			Autonomous pension funds
			Total	Life insurance corporations	Non-life insurance corporations	Total
2	Financial assets	1 950 234	1 670 744	919 476	751 268	402 370
2.1	Currency and deposits	560 302	416 665	265 321	151 344	143 637
2.2	Securities other than shares, except financial derivatives	286 283	241 003	122 625	118 378	45 280
2.2.1	Short-term securities	3 110	2 618	1 332	1 286	492
2.2.2	Long-term securities	283 173	238 385	121 293	117 092	44 788
2.2.3	Securities issued by residents	54 131	45 569	22 094	23 475	8 562
2.2.4	Securities issued by non-residents	232 152	195 434	100 531	94 903	36 718
2.3	Loans	243 927	264 944	153 582	111 362	25 352
2.3.1	Short-term loans	33 836	56 680	9 564	47 116	984
2.3.2	Long-term loans	210 091	208 264	144 017	64 247	24 368
2.3.3	Loans granted to residents	190 961	214 094	138 645	75 449	23 236
2.3.4	Loans granted to non-residents	52 966	50 850	14 936	35 914	2 116
2.4	Shares and other equity	806 903	632 043	339 383	292 660	174 860
2.4.1	Shares issued by residents	..	..	..	..	..
2.4.2	Shares issued by non-residents	..	..	..	..	..
2.5	Other, not elsewhere classified	52 819	116 089	38 565	77 523	13 241

Note: Detailed metadata at: http://metalinks.oecd.org/instinv/20141203/04e4

GERMANY

Table 2. Financial assets of investment funds

Million EUR (1999 DEM euro)

		2006	2007	2008	2009	2010	2011	2012	2013
	Investment funds								
2	Financial assets	..	..	..	..	..	..	..	..
2.1	Currency and deposits	..	..	..	..	..	..	..	..
2.2	Securities other than shares, except financial derivatives	..	..	..	..	..	..	..	..
2.2.1	Short-term securities	..	..	..	..	..	..	..	..
2.2.2	Long-term securities	..	..	..	..	..	..	..	..
2.2.3	Securities issued by residents	..	..	..	..	..	..	..	..
2.2.4	Securities issued by non-residents	..	..	..	..	..	..	..	..
2.3	Loans	..	..	..	..	..	..	..	..
2.3.1	Short-term loans	..	..	..	..	..	..	..	..
2.3.2	Long-term loans	..	..	..	..	..	..	..	..
2.3.3	Loans granted to residents	..	..	..	..	..	..	..	..
2.3.4	Loans granted to non-residents	..	..	..	..	..	..	..	..
2.4	Shares and other equity	..	..	..	..	..	..	..	..
2.4.1	Shares issued by residents	..	..	..	..	..	..	..	..
2.4.2	Shares issued by non-residents	..	..	..	..	..	..	..	..
2.5	Other, not elsewhere classified	..	..	..	..	..	..	..	..
	Open-end companies (mutual funds)								
2	Financial assets	1 061 990	1 083 338	951 696	1 072 021	1 176 610	1 172 077	1 339 052	..
2.1	Currency and deposits	77 082	105 459	142 121	118 227	113 726	131 649	128 625	..
2.2	Securities other than shares, except financial derivatives	502 497	499 011	475 185	562 066	602 568	604 956	692 974	..
2.2.1	Short-term securities	5 651	12 082	5 579	4 557	6 111	6 686	4 331	..
2.2.2	Long-term securities	496 846	486 929	469 605	557 420	596 313	598 197	686 617	..
2.2.3	Securities issued by residents	185 640	178 260	168 253	162 712	170 870	168 965	154 919	..
2.2.4	Securities issued by non-residents	316 857	320 751	306 932	399 354	431 698	435 991	538 055	..
2.3	Loans	727	721	1 081	1 793	2 028	2 120	3 070	..
2.3.1	Short-term loans	20	25	20	0	0	0	24	..
2.3.2	Long-term loans	707	696	1 061	1 793	2 028	2 120	3 046	..
2.3.3	Loans granted to residents	540	466	861	1 728	1 811	1 855	2 111	..
2.3.4	Loans granted to non-residents	187	255	220	65	217	265	959	..
2.4	Shares and other equity	481 684	478 147	333 309	389 935	458 288	433 352	514 383	..
2.4.1	Shares issued by residents	195 688	214 763	187 803	203 132	242 135	243 159	303 347	..
2.4.2	Shares issued by non-residents	285 996	263 384	145 506	186 803	216 153	190 193	211 036	..
2.5	Other, not elsewhere classified	0	0	0	0	0	0	0	..
	Money market funds								
2	Financial assets	33 349	29 776	17 175	12 260	10 376	6 622	7 824	..
2.1	Currency and deposits	3 260	3 874	4 651	2 805	2 352	622	360	..
2.2	Securities other than shares, except financial derivatives	30 069	25 877	12 504	9 455	8 024	6 000	7 440	..
2.2.1	Short-term securities	3 963	5 663	1 461	1 031	787	879	670	..
2.2.2	Long-term securities	26 106	20 214	11 043	8 336	7 093	5 048	4 744	..
2.2.3	Securities issued by residents	6 818	4 909	2 991	3 190	3 386	3 203	4 726	..
2.2.4	Securities issued by non-residents	23 251	20 968	9 513	6 265	4 638	2 797	2 714	..
2.3	Loans	20	25	20	0	0	0	24	..
2.3.1	Short-term loans	20	25	20	0	0	0	24	..
2.3.2	Long-term loans	0	0	0	0	0	0	0	..
2.3.3	Loans granted to residents	20	25	20	0	0	0	24	..
2.3.4	Loans granted to non-residents	0	0	0	0	0	0	0	..
2.4	Shares and other equity	0	0	0	0	0	0	0	..
2.4.1	Shares issued by residents	..	..	..	..	..	..	..	..
2.4.2	Shares issued by non-residents	..	..	..	..	..	..	..	..
2.5	Other, not elsewhere classified	0	0	0	0	0	0	0	..
	Other mutual funds								
2	Financial assets	1 028 641	1 053 562	934 521	1 059 761	1 166 234	1 165 455	1 331 228	..
2.1	Currency and deposits	73 822	101 585	137 470	115 422	111 374	131 027	128 265	..
2.2	Securities other than shares, except financial derivatives	472 428	473 134	462 681	552 611	594 544	598 956	685 534	..
2.2.1	Short-term securities	1 688	6 419	4 118	3 526	5 324	5 807	3 661	..
2.2.2	Long-term securities	470 740	466 715	458 562	549 084	589 220	593 149	681 873	..
2.2.3	Securities issued by residents	178 822	173 351	165 262	159 522	167 484	165 762	150 193	..
2.2.4	Securities issued by non-residents	293 606	299 783	297 419	393 089	427 060	433 194	535 341	..
2.3	Loans	707	696	1 061	1 793	2 028	2 120	3 046	..
2.3.1	Short-term loans	0	0	0	0	0	0	0	..
2.3.2	Long-term loans	707	696	1 061	1 793	2 028	2 120	3 046	..
2.3.3	Loans granted to residents	520	441	841	1 728	1 811	1 855	2 087	..
2.3.4	Loans granted to non-residents	187	255	220	65	217	265	959	..
2.4	Shares and other equity	481 684	478 147	333 309	389 935	458 288	433 352	514 383	..
2.4.1	Shares issued by residents	195 688	214 763	187 803	203 132	242 135	243 159	303 347	..
2.4.2	Shares issued by non-residents	285 996	263 384	145 506	186 803	216 153	190 193	211 036	..
2.5	Other, not elsewhere classified	0	0	0	0	0	0	0	..

Table 2. Financial assets of investment funds *(cont.)*

Million EUR (1999 DEM euro)

		2006	2007	2008	2009	2010	2011	2012	2013
	Closed-end companies								
2	Financial assets	..	..	..	..	..	..	..	..
2.1	Currency and deposits	..	..	..	..	..	..	..	..
2.2	Securities other than shares, except financial derivatives	..	..	..	..	..	..	..	..
2.2.1	Short-term securities	..	..	..	..	..	..	..	..
2.2.2	Long-term securities	..	..	..	..	..	..	..	..
2.2.3	Securities issued by residents	..	..	..	..	..	..	..	..
2.2.4	Securities issued by non-residents	..	..	..	..	..	..	..	..
2.3	Loans	..	..	..	..	..	..	..	..
2.3.1	Short-term loans	..	..	..	..	..	..	..	..
2.3.2	Long-term loans	..	..	..	..	..	..	..	..
2.3.3	Loans granted to residents	..	..	..	..	..	..	..	..
2.3.4	Loans granted to non-residents	..	..	..	..	..	..	..	..
2.4	Shares and other equity	..	..	..	..	..	..	..	..
2.4.1	Shares issued by residents	..	..	..	..	..	..	..	..
2.4.2	Shares issued by non-residents	..	..	..	..	..	..	..	..
2.5	Other, not elsewhere classified	..	..	..	..	..	..	..	..

Note: Detailed metadata at: http://metalinks.oecd.org/instinv/20141203/04e4

Table 3. Financial assets of insurance corporations and autonomous pension funds

Million EUR (1999 DEM euro)

		2006	2007	2008	2009	2010	2011	2012	2013
	Insurance corporations and autonomous pension funds								
2	Financial assets	1 532 824	1 589 374	1 559 591	1 630 867	1 729 027	1 779 131	1 950 234	..
2.1	Currency and deposits	520 096	558 720	574 664	588 867	570 834	576 221	560 302	..
2.2	Securities other than shares, except financial derivatives	164 276	168 227	175 250	180 179	203 221	219 632	286 283	..
2.2.1	Short-term securities	1 238	1 942	2 563	1 802	2 626	1 897	3 110	..
2.2.2	Long-term securities	163 038	166 285	172 687	178 377	200 595	217 735	283 173	..
2.2.3	Securities issued by residents	64 194	66 114	59 005	53 807	50 868	52 886	54 131	..
2.2.4	Securities issued by non-residents	100 082	102 113	116 245	126 372	152 353	166 746	232 152	..
2.3	Loans	209 404	200 910	200 515	221 287	233 273	237 295	243 927	..
2.3.1	Short-term loans	42 199	25 430	23 848	24 595	27 688	30 043	33 836	..
2.3.2	Long-term loans	167 205	175 480	176 667	196 692	205 585	207 252	210 091	..
2.3.3	Loans granted to residents	156 801	164 354	164 320	182 273	190 583	191 314	190 961	..
2.3.4	Loans granted to non-residents	52 603	36 556	36 195	39 014	42 690	45 981	52 966	..
2.4	Shares and other equity	571 262	608 180	555 002	587 617	667 283	694 573	806 903	..
2.4.1	Shares issued by residents	..	..	..	..	..	..	..	..
2.4.2	Shares issued by non-residents	..	..	..	..	..	..	..	..
2.5	Other, not elsewhere classified	67 786	53 337	54 160	52 917	54 416	51 410	52 819	..
	Insurance corporations								
2	Financial assets	1 403 561	1 428 599	1 382 165	1 414 503	1 485 537	1 516 310	1 670 744	..
2.1	Currency and deposits	405 993	432 542	434 728	438 963	419 945	418 992	416 665	..
2.2	Securities other than shares, except financial derivatives	140 299	143 053	148 136	152 124	173 798	185 029	241 003	..
2.2.1	Short-term securities	1 057	1 651	2 166	1 521	2 246	1 598	2 618	..
2.2.2	Long-term securities	139 242	141 402	145 970	150 603	171 552	183 431	238 385	..
2.2.3	Securities issued by residents	54 825	56 220	49 876	45 429	43 503	44 554	45 569	..
2.2.4	Securities issued by non-residents	85 474	86 833	98 260	106 695	130 295	140 475	195 434	..
2.3	Loans	240 866	232 432	227 296	242 428	251 725	255 637	264 944	..
2.3.1	Short-term loans	69 351	51 202	48 202	47 049	50 365	52 036	56 680	..
2.3.2	Long-term loans	171 515	181 230	179 094	195 379	201 360	203 601	208 264	..
2.3.3	Loans granted to residents	190 558	197 093	192 475	204 977	210 889	211 730	214 094	..
2.3.4	Loans granted to non-residents	50 308	35 339	34 821	37 451	40 836	43 907	50 850	..
2.4	Shares and other equity	475 328	498 341	456 025	474 389	530 231	547 342	632 043	..
2.4.1	Shares issued by residents	..	..	..	..	..	..	..	..
2.4.2	Shares issued by non-residents	..	..	..	..	..	..	..	..
2.5	Other, not elsewhere classified	141 075	122 231	115 980	106 599	109 837	109 310	116 089	..
	Life insurance corporations								
2	Financial assets	761 320	787 080	751 787	789 545	835 702	838 096	919 476	..
2.1	Currency and deposits	272 581	287 971	285 709	286 343	274 310	267 613	265 321	..
2.2	Securities other than shares, except financial derivatives	67 055	70 729	72 163	74 461	84 332	93 273	122 625	..
2.2.1	Short-term securities	505	816	1 055	745	1 090	806	1 332	..
2.2.2	Long-term securities	66 550	69 913	71 108	73 716	83 242	92 467	121 293	..
2.2.3	Securities issued by residents	25 893	27 295	23 586	21 709	20 281	21 843	22 094	..
2.2.4	Securities issued by non-residents	41 162	43 434	48 577	52 752	64 051	71 430	100 531	..
2.3	Loans	142 021	135 013	134 578	146 955	153 372	151 894	153 582	..
2.3.1	Short-term loans	12 881	5 549	6 252	6 568	8 530	9 148	9 564	..
2.3.2	Long-term loans	129 140	129 464	128 327	140 387	144 842	142 745	144 017	..
2.3.3	Loans granted to residents	125 168	125 404	124 488	135 305	139 369	138 568	138 645	..
2.3.4	Loans granted to non-residents	16 853	9 609	10 090	11 650	14 003	13 326	14 936	..
2.4	Shares and other equity	236 052	252 524	220 064	243 784	284 858	287 995	339 383	..
2.4.1	Shares issued by residents	..	..	..	..	..	..	..	..
2.4.2	Shares issued by non-residents	..	..	..	..	..	..	..	..
2.5	Other, not elsewhere classified	43 611	40 844	39 274	38 001	38 830	37 321	38 565	..
	Non-life insurance corporations								
2	Financial assets	642 241	641 519	630 378	624 958	649 835	678 214	751 268	..
2.1	Currency and deposits	133 412	144 571	149 019	152 620	145 635	151 379	151 344	..
2.2	Securities other than shares, except financial derivatives	73 244	72 324	75 973	77 663	89 466	91 756	118 378	..
2.2.1	Short-term securities	552	835	1 111	776	1 156	792	1 286	..
2.2.2	Long-term securities	72 692	71 489	74 862	76 887	88 310	90 964	117 092	..
2.2.3	Securities issued by residents	28 932	28 925	26 290	23 720	23 222	22 711	23 475	..
2.2.4	Securities issued by non-residents	44 312	43 399	49 683	53 943	66 244	69 045	94 903	..
2.3	Loans	98 845	97 419	92 718	95 473	98 353	103 743	111 362	..
2.3.1	Short-term loans	56 470	45 653	41 950	40 481	41 835	42 887	47 116	..
2.3.2	Long-term loans	42 375	51 766	50 768	54 992	56 518	60 856	64 247	..
2.3.3	Loans granted to residents	65 390	71 689	67 987	69 672	71 520	73 163	75 449	..
2.3.4	Loans granted to non-residents	33 455	25 730	24 730	25 802	26 833	30 581	35 914	..
2.4	Shares and other equity	239 276	245 817	235 961	230 604	245 374	259 347	292 660	..
2.4.1	Shares issued by residents	..	..	..	..	..	..	..	..
2.4.2	Shares issued by non-residents	..	..	..	..	..	..	..	..
2.5	Other, not elsewhere classified	97 465	81 387	76 706	68 597	71 007	71 989	77 523	..

Table 3. Financial assets of insurance corporations and autonomous pension funds *(cont.)*

Million EUR (1999 DEM euro)

		2006	2007	2008	2009	2010	2011	2012	2013
	Autonomous pension funds								
2	Financial assets	263 351	291 496	298 124	325 580	353 494	377 030	402 370	..
2.1	Currency and deposits	114 103	126 178	139 936	149 904	150 889	157 229	143 637	..
2.2	Securities other than shares, except financial derivatives	23 977	25 174	27 114	28 055	29 423	34 603	45 280	..
2.2.1	Short-term securities	181	291	397	281	380	299	492	..
2.2.2	Long-term securities	23 796	24 883	26 717	27 774	29 043	34 304	44 788	..
2.2.3	Securities issued by residents	9 369	9 894	9 129	8 378	7 365	8 332	8 562	..
2.2.4	Securities issued by non-residents	14 608	15 280	17 985	19 677	22 058	26 271	36 718	..
2.3	Loans	21 191	21 808	21 548	23 395	24 365	25 475	25 352	..
2.3.1	Short-term loans	1 650	522	577	576	840	946	984	..
2.3.2	Long-term loans	19 541	21 286	20 971	22 819	23 525	24 529	24 368	..
2.3.3	Loans granted to residents	18 896	20 591	20 174	21 832	22 511	23 401	23 236	..
2.3.4	Loans granted to non-residents	2 295	1 217	1 374	1 563	1 854	2 074	2 116	..
2.4	Shares and other equity	95 934	109 839	98 977	113 228	137 052	147 231	174 860	..
2.4.1	Shares issued by residents	..	..	..	..	..	..	..	..
2.4.2	Shares issued by non-residents	..	..	..	..	..	..	..	..
2.5	Other, not elsewhere classified	8 146	8 497	10 549	10 998	11 766	12 492	13 241	..

Note: Detailed metadata at: http://metalinks.oecd.org/instinv/20141203/04e4

GERMANY

Table 4. Portfolio composition by type of investor

Percentage of total financial assets

Per cent

		2006	2007	2008	2009	2010	2011	2012	2013
	Investment funds								
2	Financial assets	..	..	..	..	..	..	..	..
2.1	Currency and deposits	..	..	..	..	..	..	..	..
2.2	Securities other than shares, except financial derivatives	..	..	..	..	..	..	..	..
2.2.1	Short-term securities	..	..	..	..	..	..	..	..
2.2.2	Long-term securities	..	..	..	..	..	..	..	..
2.2.3	Securities issued by residents	..	..	..	..	..	..	..	..
2.2.4	Securities issued by non-residents	..	..	..	..	..	..	..	..
2.3	Loans	..	..	..	..	..	..	..	..
2.3.1	Short-term loans	..	..	..	..	..	..	..	..
2.3.2	Long-term loans	..	..	..	..	..	..	..	..
2.3.3	Loans granted to residents	..	..	..	..	..	..	..	..
2.3.4	Loans granted to non-residents	..	..	..	..	..	..	..	..
2.4	Shares and other equity	..	..	..	..	..	..	..	..
2.4.1	Shares issued by residents	..	..	..	..	..	..	..	..
2.4.2	Shares issued by non-residents	..	..	..	..	..	..	..	..
2.5	Other, not elsewhere classified	..	..	..	..	..	..	..	..
	Insurance corporations								
2	Financial assets	100.0	100.0	100.0	100.0	100.0	100.0	100.0	..
2.1	Currency and deposits	28.9	30.3	31.5	31.0	28.3	27.6	24.9	..
2.2	Securities other than shares, except financial derivatives	10.0	10.0	10.7	10.8	11.7	12.2	14.4	..
2.2.1	Short-term securities	0.1	0.1	0.2	0.1	0.2	0.1	0.2	..
2.2.2	Long-term securities	9.9	9.9	10.6	10.6	11.5	12.1	14.3	..
2.2.3	Securities issued by residents	3.9	3.9	3.6	3.2	2.9	2.9	2.7	..
2.2.4	Securities issued by non-residents	6.1	6.1	7.1	7.5	8.8	9.3	11.7	..
2.3	Loans	17.2	16.3	16.4	17.1	16.9	16.9	15.9	..
2.3.1	Short-term loans	4.9	3.6	3.5	3.3	3.4	3.4	3.4	..
2.3.2	Long-term loans	12.2	12.7	13.0	13.8	13.6	13.4	12.5	..
2.3.3	Loans granted to residents	13.6	13.8	13.9	14.5	14.2	14.0	12.8	..
2.3.4	Loans granted to non-residents	3.6	2.5	2.5	2.6	2.7	2.9	3.0	..
2.4	Shares and other equity	33.9	34.9	33.0	33.5	35.7	36.1	37.8	..
2.4.1	Shares issued by residents	..	..	..	..	..	..	..	..
2.4.2	Shares issued by non-residents	..	..	..	..	..	..	..	..
2.5	Other, not elsewhere classified	10.1	8.6	8.4	7.5	7.4	7.2	6.9	..
	Autonomous pension funds								
2	Financial assets	100.0	100.0	100.0	100.0	100.0	100.0	100.0	..
2.1	Currency and deposits	43.3	43.3	46.9	46.0	42.7	41.7	35.7	..
2.2	Securities other than shares, except financial derivatives	9.1	8.6	9.1	8.6	8.3	9.2	11.3	..
2.2.1	Short-term securities	0.1	0.1	0.1	0.1	0.1	0.1	0.1	..
2.2.2	Long-term securities	9.0	8.5	9.0	8.5	8.2	9.1	11.1	..
2.2.3	Securities issued by residents	3.6	3.4	3.1	2.6	2.1	2.2	2.1	..
2.2.4	Securities issued by non-residents	5.5	5.2	6.0	6.0	6.2	7.0	9.1	..
2.3	Loans	8.0	7.5	7.2	7.2	6.9	6.8	6.3	..
2.3.1	Short-term loans	0.6	0.2	0.2	0.2	0.2	0.3	0.2	..
2.3.2	Long-term loans	7.4	7.3	7.0	7.0	6.7	6.5	6.1	..
2.3.3	Loans granted to residents	7.2	7.1	6.8	6.7	6.4	6.2	5.8	..
2.3.4	Loans granted to non-residents	0.9	0.4	0.5	0.5	0.5	0.6	0.5	..
2.4	Shares and other equity	36.4	37.7	33.2	34.8	38.8	39.1	43.5	..
2.4.1	Shares issued by residents	..	..	..	..	..	..	..	..
2.4.2	Shares issued by non-residents	..	..	..	..	..	..	..	..
2.5	Other, not elsewhere classified	3.1	2.9	3.5	3.4	3.3	3.3	3.3	..

Note: Detailed metadata at: http://metalinks.oecd.org/instinv/20141203/f729

Table 1. Financial assets of institutional investors, 2013

Million EUR (2001 GRD euro)

		Total	Investment funds: Open-end companies (mutual funds): Total	Money market funds	Other mutual funds	Closed-end companies: Total
2	Financial assets	5 132	4 519	720	3 798	613
2.1	Currency and deposits	1 099	729	366	363	371
2.2	Securities other than shares, except financial derivatives	1 770	1 767	347	1 421	2
2.2.1	Short-term securities	555	555	329	226	0
2.2.2	Long-term securities	1 214	1 212	18	1 194	2
2.2.3	Securities issued by residents	1 054	1 052	329	724	2
2.2.4	Securities issued by non-residents	716	715	18	697	1
2.3	Loans	0	0	0	0	0
2.3.1	Short-term loans	0	0	0	0	0
2.3.2	Long-term loans	0	0	0	0	0
2.3.3	Loans granted to residents	0	0	0	0	0
2.3.4	Loans granted to non-residents	0	0	0	0	0
2.4	Shares and other equity	2 097	1 892	2	1 890	205
2.4.1	Shares issued by residents	1 307	1 235	0	1 235	73
2.4.2	Shares issued by non-residents	790	657	2	655	133
2.5	Other, not elsewhere classified	166	130	6	125	35

		Total	Insurance corporations and autonomous pension funds: Insurance corporations: Total	Life insurance corporations	Non-life insurance corporations	Autonomous pension funds: Total
2	Financial assets	14 921	14 921	10 009	4 912	..
2.1	Currency and deposits	3 772	3 772	2 530	1 242	..
2.2	Securities other than shares, except financial derivatives	6 713	6 713	4 503	2 210	..
2.2.1	Short-term securities	860	860	577	283	..
2.2.2	Long-term securities	5 854	5 854	3 927	1 927	..
2.2.3	Securities issued by residents	1 207	1 207	810	397	..
2.2.4	Securities issued by non-residents	5 506	5 506	3 694	1 813	..
2.3	Loans	132	132	88	43	..
2.3.1	Short-term loans	8	8	5	3	..
2.3.2	Long-term loans	124	124	83	41	..
2.3.3	Loans granted to residents	130	130	87	43	..
2.3.4	Loans granted to non-residents	2	2	1	0	..
2.4	Shares and other equity	2 628	2 628	1 763	865	..
2.4.1	Shares issued by residents	1 331	1 331	893	438	..
2.4.2	Shares issued by non-residents	1 297	1 297	870	427	..
2.5	Other, not elsewhere classified	1 676	1 676	1 125	552	..

Note: Detailed metadata at: http://metalinks.oecd.org/instinv/20141203/323a

Table 2. Financial assets of investment funds

Million EUR (2001 GRD euro)

		2006	2007	2008	2009	2010	2011	2012	2013
	Investment funds								
2	Financial assets	23 942	22 029	9 038	8 778	6 958	4 397	4 876	5 132
2.1	Currency and deposits	5 533	3 789	3 087	2 442	1 743	1 302	1 537	1 099
2.2	Securities other than shares, except financial derivatives	7 608	9 601	3 129	2 777	2 297	1 484	1 466	1 770
2.2.1	Short-term securities	126	2 947	149	6	121	91	45	555
2.2.2	Long-term securities	7 483	6 654	2 979	2 771	2 176	1 394	1 421	1 214
2.2.3	Securities issued by residents	1 864	1 106	720	973	820	383	500	1 054
2.2.4	Securities issued by non-residents	5 744	8 495	2 408	1 804	1 477	1 101	966	716
2.3	Loans	0	0	0	0	0	0	0	0
2.3.1	Short-term loans	0	0	0	0	0	0	0	0
2.3.2	Long-term loans	0	0	0	0	0	0	0	0
2.3.3	Loans granted to residents	0	0	0	0	0	0	0	0
2.3.4	Loans granted to non-residents	0	0	0	0	0	0	0	0
2.4	Shares and other equity	9 891	7 117	2 447	3 291	2 576	1 445	1 708	2 097
2.4.1	Shares issued by residents	6 297	5 043	1 760	2 284	1 424	709	987	1 307
2.4.2	Shares issued by non-residents	3 595	2 074	687	1 007	1 152	735	721	790
2.5	Other, not elsewhere classified	909	1 522	375	269	342	165	165	166
	Open-end companies (mutual funds)								
2	Financial assets	23 367	21 195	8 522	8 230	6 372	4 009	4 413	4 519
2.1	Currency and deposits	5 391	3 442	2 736	2 183	1 491	1 019	1 178	729
2.2	Securities other than shares, except financial derivatives	7 588	9 572	3 108	2 758	2 279	1 475	1 465	1 767
2.2.1	Short-term securities	126	2 947	144	6	115	90	45	555
2.2.2	Long-term securities	7 462	6 625	2 963	2 753	2 164	1 385	1 420	1 212
2.2.3	Securities issued by residents	1 863	1 104	714	966	810	383	500	1 052
2.2.4	Securities issued by non-residents	5 725	8 469	2 393	1 792	1 469	1 093	965	715
2.3	Loans	0	0	0	0	0	0	0	0
2.3.1	Short-term loans	0	0	0	0	0	0	0	0
2.3.2	Long-term loans	0	0	0	0	0	0	0	0
2.3.3	Loans granted to residents	0	0	0	0	0	0	0	0
2.3.4	Loans granted to non-residents	0	0	0	0	0	0	0	0
2.4	Shares and other equity	9 580	6 794	2 330	3 040	2 354	1 376	1 638	1 892
2.4.1	Shares issued by residents	6 093	4 840	1 689	2 182	1 360	694	969	1 235
2.4.2	Shares issued by non-residents	3 487	1 954	641	859	994	682	669	657
2.5	Other, not elsewhere classified	808	1 387	348	248	249	139	133	130
	Money market funds								
2	Financial assets	5 936	8 033	2 543	1 778	1 184	744	841	720
2.1	Currency and deposits	4 225	2 234	1 905	1 611	1 013	627	773	366
2.2	Securities other than shares, except financial derivatives	1 612	5 236	618	162	167	109	61	347
2.2.1	Short-term securities	35	2 862	110	2	91	66	26	329
2.2.2	Long-term securities	1 577	2 374	507	160	76	43	35	18
2.2.3	Securities issued by residents	51	32	13	21	92	60	21	329
2.2.4	Securities issued by non-residents	1 561	5 205	604	141	75	49	40	18
2.3	Loans	0	0	0	0	0	0	0	0
2.3.1	Short-term loans	0	0	0	0	0	0	0	0
2.3.2	Long-term loans	0	0	0	0	0	0	0	0
2.3.3	Loans granted to residents	0	0	0	0	0	0	0	0
2.3.4	Loans granted to non-residents	0	0	0	0	0	0	0	0
2.4	Shares and other equity	8	11	7	0	0	5	2	2
2.4.1	Shares issued by residents	0	11	7	0	0	0	0	0
2.4.2	Shares issued by non-residents	8	0	0	0	0	5	2	2
2.5	Other, not elsewhere classified	91	551	12	5	3	4	5	6
	Other mutual funds								
2	Financial assets	17 431	13 162	5 979	6 452	5 189	3 265	3 573	3 798
2.1	Currency and deposits	1 166	1 208	831	573	477	392	405	363
2.2	Securities other than shares, except financial derivatives	5 976	4 336	2 490	2 596	2 112	1 366	1 404	1 421
2.2.1	Short-term securities	90	85	34	3	23	24	18	226
2.2.2	Long-term securities	5 885	4 251	2 456	2 593	2 088	1 342	1 385	1 194
2.2.3	Securities issued by residents	1 812	1 072	701	945	718	322	479	724
2.2.4	Securities issued by non-residents	4 164	3 264	1 789	1 651	1 393	1 044	925	697
2.3	Loans	0	0	0	0	0	0	0	0
2.3.1	Short-term loans	0	0	0	0	0	0	0	0
2.3.2	Long-term loans	0	0	0	0	0	0	0	0
2.3.3	Loans granted to residents	0	0	0	0	0	0	0	0
2.3.4	Loans granted to non-residents	0	0	0	0	0	0	0	0
2.4	Shares and other equity	9 572	6 783	2 323	3 040	2 354	1 371	1 636	1 890
2.4.1	Shares issued by residents	6 093	4 828	1 682	2 182	1 360	694	969	1 235
2.4.2	Shares issued by non-residents	3 480	1 954	641	859	994	678	667	655
2.5	Other, not elsewhere classified	717	835	336	243	245	135	128	125

Table 2. Financial assets of investment funds *(cont.)*

Million EUR (2001 GRD euro)

		2006	2007	2008	2009	2010	2011	2012	2013
	Closed-end companies								
2	Financial assets	575	834	516	548	586	388	463	613
2.1	Currency and deposits	142	347	351	259	253	284	359	371
2.2	Securities other than shares, except financial derivatives	20	29	21	18	18	9	1	2
2.2.1	Short-term securities	0	0	5	0	6	1	1	0
2.2.2	Long-term securities	20	29	16	18	12	8	1	2
2.2.3	Securities issued by residents	1	2	6	7	10	0	0	2
2.2.4	Securities issued by non-residents	19	26	15	12	8	9	1	1
2.3	Loans	0	0	0	0	0	0	0	0
2.3.1	Short-term loans	0	0	0	0	0	0	0	0
2.3.2	Long-term loans	0	0	0	0	0	0	0	0
2.3.3	Loans granted to residents	0	0	0	0	0	0	0	0
2.3.4	Loans granted to non-residents	0	0	0	0	0	0	0	0
2.4	Shares and other equity	311	323	117	250	222	69	70	205
2.4.1	Shares issued by residents	204	203	71	102	64	16	18	73
2.4.2	Shares issued by non-residents	107	119	47	148	158	53	52	133
2.5	Other, not elsewhere classified	101	136	27	20	93	26	33	35

Note: Detailed metadata at: http://metalinks.oecd.org/instinv/20141203/323a

Table 3. Financial assets of insurance corporations and autonomous pension funds

Million EUR (2001 GRD euro)

		2006	2007	2008	2009	2010	2011	2012	2013
	Insurance corporations and autonomous pension funds								
2	Financial assets	11 751	13 205	12 987	13 779	14 023	13 270	14 043	14 921
2.1	Currency and deposits	1 453	1 981	1 956	1 988	2 837	2 771	2 800	3 772
2.2	Securities other than shares, except financial derivatives	5 075	5 526	5 837	6 587	6 605	6 256	6 589	6 713
2.2.1	Short-term securities	12	33	8	3	36	1 011	1 268	860
2.2.2	Long-term securities	5 064	5 493	5 829	6 584	6 569	5 244	5 321	5 854
2.2.3	Securities issued by residents	2 798	3 111	3 260	3 680	3 359	2 519	1 022	1 207
2.2.4	Securities issued by non-residents	2 277	2 415	2 577	2 907	3 247	3 737	5 567	5 506
2.3	Loans	106	100	108	102	101	97	145	132
2.3.1	Short-term loans	12	9	10	12	12	8	16	8
2.3.2	Long-term loans	94	91	99	89	89	89	128	124
2.3.3	Loans granted to residents	102	98	106	100	101	97	145	130
2.3.4	Loans granted to non-residents	4	2	3	2	0	0	0	2
2.4	Shares and other equity	3 140	3 629	2 729	2 808	2 331	2 150	2 632	2 628
2.4.1	Shares issued by residents	2 677	2 705	1 855	1 922	1 547	1 153	1 185	1 331
2.4.2	Shares issued by non-residents	463	924	874	887	783	997	1 447	1 297
2.5	Other, not elsewhere classified	1 977	1 968	2 357	2 295	2 149	1 996	1 878	1 676
	Insurance corporations								
2	Financial assets	11 751	13 205	12 987	13 779	14 023	13 270	14 043	14 921
2.1	Currency and deposits	1 453	1 981	1 956	1 988	2 837	2 771	2 800	3 772
2.2	Securities other than shares, except financial derivatives	5 075	5 526	5 837	6 587	6 605	6 256	6 589	6 713
2.2.1	Short-term securities	12	33	8	3	36	1 011	1 268	860
2.2.2	Long-term securities	5 064	5 493	5 829	6 584	6 569	5 244	5 321	5 854
2.2.3	Securities issued by residents	2 798	3 111	3 260	3 680	3 359	2 519	1 022	1 207
2.2.4	Securities issued by non-residents	2 277	2 415	2 577	2 907	3 247	3 737	5 567	5 506
2.3	Loans	106	100	108	102	101	97	145	132
2.3.1	Short-term loans	12	9	10	12	12	8	16	8
2.3.2	Long-term loans	94	91	99	89	89	89	128	124
2.3.3	Loans granted to residents	102	98	106	100	101	97	145	130
2.3.4	Loans granted to non-residents	4	2	3	2	0	0	0	2
2.4	Shares and other equity	3 140	3 629	2 729	2 808	2 331	2 150	2 632	2 628
2.4.1	Shares issued by residents	2 677	2 705	1 855	1 922	1 547	1 153	1 185	1 331
2.4.2	Shares issued by non-residents	463	924	874	887	783	997	1 447	1 297
2.5	Other, not elsewhere classified	1 977	1 968	2 357	2 295	2 149	1 996	1 878	1 676
	Life insurance corporations								
2	Financial assets	8 370	9 395	8 963	9 583	9 702	8 972	9 431	10 009
2.1	Currency and deposits	1 035	1 410	1 350	1 382	1 963	1 874	1 880	2 530
2.2	Securities other than shares, except financial derivatives	3 615	3 932	4 028	4 581	4 570	4 230	4 425	4 503
2.2.1	Short-term securities	8	23	6	2	25	684	851	577
2.2.2	Long-term securities	3 607	3 909	4 023	4 579	4 545	3 546	3 574	3 927
2.2.3	Securities issued by residents	1 993	2 214	2 250	2 560	2 324	1 703	686	810
2.2.4	Securities issued by non-residents	1 622	1 718	1 778	2 021	2 246	2 527	3 739	3 694
2.3	Loans	75	71	75	71	70	66	97	88
2.3.1	Short-term loans	8	6	7	9	8	6	11	5
2.3.2	Long-term loans	67	65	68	62	61	60	86	83
2.3.3	Loans granted to residents	73	70	73	70	70	66	97	87
2.3.4	Loans granted to non-residents	3	1	2	1	0	0	0	1
2.4	Shares and other equity	2 236	2 582	1 883	1 953	1 613	1 454	1 767	1 763
2.4.1	Shares issued by residents	1 906	1 925	1 280	1 337	1 071	779	796	893
2.4.2	Shares issued by non-residents	330	658	603	617	542	674	972	870
2.5	Other, not elsewhere classified	1 408	1 400	1 626	1 596	1 487	1 349	1 261	1 125
	Non-life insurance corporations								
2	Financial assets	3 381	3 810	4 024	4 196	4 320	4 298	4 612	4 912
2.1	Currency and deposits	418	572	606	605	874	898	919	1 242
2.2	Securities other than shares, except financial derivatives	1 460	1 594	1 809	2 006	2 035	2 026	2 164	2 210
2.2.1	Short-term securities	3	9	3	1	11	328	416	283
2.2.2	Long-term securities	1 457	1 585	1 806	2 005	2 024	1 699	1 748	1 927
2.2.3	Securities issued by residents	805	898	1 010	1 121	1 035	816	336	397
2.2.4	Securities issued by non-residents	655	697	798	885	1 000	1 210	1 828	1 813
2.3	Loans	30	29	34	31	31	31	47	43
2.3.1	Short-term loans	3	3	3	4	4	3	5	3
2.3.2	Long-term loans	27	26	31	27	27	29	42	41
2.3.3	Loans granted to residents	29	28	33	30	31	31	47	43
2.3.4	Loans granted to non-residents	1	1	1	1	0	0	0	0
2.4	Shares and other equity	903	1 047	846	855	718	696	864	865
2.4.1	Shares issued by residents	770	780	575	585	477	373	389	438
2.4.2	Shares issued by non-residents	133	267	271	270	241	323	475	427
2.5	Other, not elsewhere classified	569	568	730	699	662	646	617	552

Table 3. Financial assets of insurance corporations and autonomous pension funds *(cont.)*

Million EUR (2001 GRD euro)

		2006	2007	2008	2009	2010	2011	2012	2013
	Autonomous pension funds								
2	Financial assets	..	..	..	..	..	..	..	..
2.1	Currency and deposits	..	..	..	..	..	..	..	..
2.2	Securities other than shares, except financial derivatives	..	..	..	..	..	..	..	..
2.2.1	Short-term securities	..	..	..	..	..	..	..	..
2.2.2	Long-term securities	..	..	..	..	..	..	..	..
2.2.3	Securities issued by residents	..	..	..	..	..	..	..	..
2.2.4	Securities issued by non-residents	..	..	..	..	..	..	..	..
2.3	Loans	..	..	..	..	..	..	..	..
2.3.1	Short-term loans	..	..	..	..	..	..	..	..
2.3.2	Long-term loans	..	..	..	..	..	..	..	..
2.3.3	Loans granted to residents	..	..	..	..	..	..	..	..
2.3.4	Loans granted to non-residents	..	..	..	..	..	..	..	..
2.4	Shares and other equity	..	..	..	..	..	..	..	..
2.4.1	Shares issued by residents	..	..	..	..	..	..	..	..
2.4.2	Shares issued by non-residents	..	..	..	..	..	..	..	..
2.5	Other, not elsewhere classified	..	..	..	..	..	..	..	..

Note: Detailed metadata at: http://metalinks.oecd.org/instinv/20141203/323a

Table 4. Portfolio composition by type of investor

Percentage of total financial assets

Per cent

		2006	2007	2008	2009	2010	2011	2012	2013
	Investment funds								
2	Financial assets	100.0	100.0	100.0	100.0	100.0	100.0	100.0	100.0
2.1	Currency and deposits	23.1	17.2	34.2	27.8	25.1	29.6	31.5	21.4
2.2	Securities other than shares, except financial derivatives	31.8	43.6	34.6	31.6	33.0	33.8	30.1	34.5
2.2.1	Short-term securities	0.5	13.4	1.7	0.1	1.7	2.1	0.9	10.8
2.2.2	Long-term securities	31.3	30.2	33.0	31.6	31.3	31.7	29.1	23.7
2.2.3	Securities issued by residents	7.8	5.0	8.0	11.1	11.8	8.7	10.2	20.5
2.2.4	Securities issued by non-residents	24.0	38.6	26.6	20.6	21.2	25.0	19.8	13.9
2.3	Loans	0.0	0.0	0.0	0.0	0.0	0.0	0.0	0.0
2.3.1	Short-term loans	0.0	0.0	0.0	0.0	0.0	0.0	0.0	0.0
2.3.2	Long-term loans	0.0	0.0	0.0	0.0	0.0	0.0	0.0	0.0
2.3.3	Loans granted to residents	0.0	0.0	0.0	0.0	0.0	0.0	0.0	0.0
2.3.4	Loans granted to non-residents	0.0	0.0	0.0	0.0	0.0	0.0	0.0	0.0
2.4	Shares and other equity	41.3	32.3	27.1	37.5	37.0	32.9	35.0	40.9
2.4.1	Shares issued by residents	26.3	22.9	19.5	26.0	20.5	16.1	20.2	25.5
2.4.2	Shares issued by non-residents	15.0	9.4	7.6	11.5	16.6	16.7	14.8	15.4
2.5	Other, not elsewhere classified	3.8	6.9	4.2	3.1	4.9	3.8	3.4	3.2
	Insurance corporations								
2	Financial assets	100.0	100.0	100.0	100.0	100.0	100.0	100.0	100.0
2.1	Currency and deposits	12.4	15.0	15.1	14.4	20.2	20.9	19.9	25.3
2.2	Securities other than shares, except financial derivatives	43.2	41.9	44.9	47.8	47.1	47.1	46.9	45.0
2.2.1	Short-term securities	0.1	0.2	0.1	0.0	0.3	7.6	9.0	5.8
2.2.2	Long-term securities	43.1	41.6	44.9	47.8	46.8	39.5	37.9	39.2
2.2.3	Securities issued by residents	23.8	23.6	25.1	26.7	24.0	19.0	7.3	8.1
2.2.4	Securities issued by non-residents	19.4	18.3	19.8	21.1	23.2	28.2	39.6	36.9
2.3	Loans	0.9	0.8	0.8	0.7	0.7	0.7	1.0	0.9
2.3.1	Short-term loans	0.1	0.1	0.1	0.1	0.1	0.1	0.1	0.1
2.3.2	Long-term loans	0.8	0.7	0.8	0.6	0.6	0.7	0.9	0.8
2.3.3	Loans granted to residents	0.9	0.7	0.8	0.7	0.7	0.7	1.0	0.9
2.3.4	Loans granted to non-residents	0.0	0.0	0.0	0.0	0.0	0.0	0.0	0.0
2.4	Shares and other equity	26.7	27.5	21.0	20.4	16.6	16.2	18.7	17.6
2.4.1	Shares issued by residents	22.8	20.5	14.3	13.9	11.0	8.7	8.4	8.9
2.4.2	Shares issued by non-residents	3.9	7.0	6.7	6.4	5.6	7.5	10.3	8.7
2.5	Other, not elsewhere classified	16.8	14.9	18.1	16.7	15.3	15.0	13.4	11.2
	Autonomous pension funds								
2	Financial assets	..	..	..	..	..	..	..	..
2.1	Currency and deposits	..	..	..	..	..	..	..	..
2.2	Securities other than shares, except financial derivatives	..	..	..	..	..	..	..	..
2.2.1	Short-term securities	..	..	..	..	..	..	..	..
2.2.2	Long-term securities	..	..	..	..	..	..	..	..
2.2.3	Securities issued by residents	..	..	..	..	..	..	..	..
2.2.4	Securities issued by non-residents	..	..	..	..	..	..	..	..
2.3	Loans	..	..	..	..	..	..	..	..
2.3.1	Short-term loans	..	..	..	..	..	..	..	..
2.3.2	Long-term loans	..	..	..	..	..	..	..	..
2.3.3	Loans granted to residents	..	..	..	..	..	..	..	..
2.3.4	Loans granted to non-residents	..	..	..	..	..	..	..	..
2.4	Shares and other equity	..	..	..	..	..	..	..	..
2.4.1	Shares issued by residents	..	..	..	..	..	..	..	..
2.4.2	Shares issued by non-residents	..	..	..	..	..	..	..	..
2.5	Other, not elsewhere classified	..	..	..	..	..	..	..	..

Note: Detailed metadata at: http://metalinks.oecd.org/instinv/20141203/f729

Table 1. Financial assets of institutional investors, 2013

Million HUF

		Investment funds				
		Total	Open-end companies (mutual funds)			Closed-end companies
			Total	Money market funds	Other mutual funds	Total
2	Financial assets	4 496 169	4 222 799	1 461 994	2 760 805	273 370
2.1	Currency and deposits	1 996 189	1 819 720	1 044 242	775 479	176 469
2.2	Securities other than shares, except financial derivatives	1 440 693	1 381 131	354 337	1 026 794	59 562
2.2.1	Short-term securities	..	..	..	..	..
2.2.2	Long-term securities	..	..	..	..	..
2.2.3	Securities issued by residents	1 364 604	1 305 636	353 552	952 084	58 968
2.2.4	Securities issued by non-residents	76 089	75 495	785	74 710	594
2.3	Loans	0	0	0	0	0
2.3.1	Short-term loans	0	0	0	0	0
2.3.2	Long-term loans	0	0	0	0	0
2.3.3	Loans granted to residents	0	0	0	0	0
2.3.4	Loans granted to non-residents	0	0	0	0	0
2.4	Shares and other equity	776 574	775 690	3 151	772 540	884
2.4.1	Shares issued by residents	352 869	352 849	3 151	349 698	20
2.4.2	Shares issued by non-residents	423 705	422 842	0	422 842	863
2.5	Other, not elsewhere classified	282 713	246 258	60 265	185 993	36 456

		Insurance corporations and autonomous pension funds				
		Total	Insurance corporations			Autonomous pension funds
			Total	Life insurance corporations	Non-life insurance corporations	Total
2	Financial assets	3 729 510	2 501 374	..	..	1 228 136
2.1	Currency and deposits	207 871	119 017	..	..	88 854
2.2	Securities other than shares, except financial derivatives	2 238 054	1 442 501	..	..	795 553
2.2.1	Short-term securities	350 031	148 829	..	..	201 202
2.2.2	Long-term securities	1 888 023	1 293 672	..	..	594 351
2.2.3	Securities issued by residents	2 156 209	1 369 081	..	..	787 128
2.2.4	Securities issued by non-residents	81 845	73 420	..	..	8 425
2.3	Loans	7 755	6 150	..	..	1 605
2.3.1	Short-term loans	955	955	..	..	0
2.3.2	Long-term loans	6 800	5 195	..	..	1 605
2.3.3	Loans granted to residents	6 800	5 195	..	..	1 605
2.3.4	Loans granted to non-residents	955	955	..	..	0
2.4	Shares and other equity	1 127 456	785 362	..	..	342 094
2.4.1	Shares issued by residents	595 598	409 308	..	..	186 290
2.4.2	Shares issued by non-residents	531 858	376 054	..	..	155 804
2.5	Other, not elsewhere classified	148 374	148 344	..	..	30

Note: Detailed metadata at: http://metalinks.oecd.org/instinv/20141203/db48

HUNGARY

Table 2. Financial assets of investment funds

Million HUF

		2006	2007	2008	2009	2010	2011	2012	2013
	Investment funds								
2	Financial assets	2 449 483	3 334 553	2 425 408	3 030 731	3 722 261	3 089 915	3 267 089	4 496 169
2.1	Currency and deposits	1 013 101	1 259 841	1 146 927	1 299 833	1 408 012	1 558 008	1 677 634	1 996 189
2.2	Securities other than shares, except financial derivatives	700 277	932 610	540 833	701 188	1 055 834	762 857	830 843	1 440 693
2.2.1	Short-term securities	..	..	..	..	..	..	..	..
2.2.2	Long-term securities	..	..	..	..	..	..	..	..
2.2.3	Securities issued by residents	659 610	889 089	515 613	662 269	1 005 689	724 320	786 967	1 364 604
2.2.4	Securities issued by non-residents	40 667	43 521	25 220	38 919	50 145	38 537	43 877	76 089
2.3	Loans	0	0	0	0	0	0	0	0
2.3.1	Short-term loans	0	0	0	0	0	0	0	0
2.3.2	Long-term loans	0	0	0	0	0	0	0	0
2.3.3	Loans granted to residents	0	0	0	0	0	0	0	0
2.3.4	Loans granted to non-residents	0	0	0	0	0	0	0	0
2.4	Shares and other equity	633 982	775 328	542 021	827 435	1 158 095	677 087	608 728	776 574
2.4.1	Shares issued by residents	379 628	432 772	198 632	210 205	276 442	203 339	211 188	352 869
2.4.2	Shares issued by non-residents	254 354	342 555	343 389	617 230	881 653	473 748	397 540	423 705
2.5	Other, not elsewhere classified	102 123	366 774	195 627	202 275	100 320	91 963	149 884	282 713
	Open-end companies (mutual funds)								
2	Financial assets	2 190 368	2 916 533	1 946 776	2 728 936	3 472 336	2 858 095	3 017 972	4 222 799
2.1	Currency and deposits	790 990	901 265	710 089	1 049 182	1 204 156	1 366 514	1 494 407	1 819 720
2.2	Securities other than shares, except financial derivatives	694 894	930 319	534 043	696 823	1 052 353	754 119	803 460	1 381 131
2.2.1	Short-term securities	..	..	..	..	..	..	..	..
2.2.2	Long-term securities	..	..	..	..	..	..	..	..
2.2.3	Securities issued by residents	654 227	886 798	508 929	657 904	1 002 312	716 163	760 222	1 305 636
2.2.4	Securities issued by non-residents	40 667	43 521	25 114	38 919	50 041	37 957	43 238	75 495
2.3	Loans	0	0	0	0	0	0	0	0
2.3.1	Short-term loans	0	0	0	0	0	0	0	0
2.3.2	Long-term loans	0	0	0	0	0	0	0	0
2.3.3	Loans granted to residents	0	0	0	0	0	0	0	0
2.3.4	Loans granted to non-residents	0	0	0	0	0	0	0	0
2.4	Shares and other equity	633 982	775 328	540 909	827 435	1 158 095	677 087	608 728	775 690
2.4.1	Shares issued by residents	379 628	432 772	198 094	210 205	276 442	203 339	211 188	352 849
2.4.2	Shares issued by non-residents	254 354	342 555	342 815	617 230	881 653	473 748	397 540	422 842
2.5	Other, not elsewhere classified	70 502	309 622	161 735	155 496	57 732	60 375	111 377	246 258
	Money market funds								
2	Financial assets	774 118	1 173 119	886 052	1 233 867	1 393 036	1 367 054	1 233 618	1 461 994
2.1	Currency and deposits	499 763	669 366	523 312	839 960	863 934	1 025 047	999 039	1 044 242
2.2	Securities other than shares, except financial derivatives	257 859	330 533	235 865	295 077	505 249	318 725	204 113	354 337
2.2.1	Short-term securities	..	..	..	..	..	..	..	..
2.2.2	Long-term securities	..	..	..	..	..	..	..	..
2.2.3	Securities issued by residents	243 255	320 098	234 486	289 942	501 541	316 832	203 476	353 552
2.2.4	Securities issued by non-residents	14 604	10 435	1 379	5 135	3 707	1 893	637	785
2.3	Loans	0	0	0	0	0	0	0	0
2.3.1	Short-term loans	0	0	0	0	0	0	0	0
2.3.2	Long-term loans	0	0	0	0	0	0	0	0
2.3.3	Loans granted to residents	0	0	0	0	0	0	0	0
2.3.4	Loans granted to non-residents	0	0	0	0	0	0	0	0
2.4	Shares and other equity	2 489	1 568	1 327	9 718	7 669	7 342	4 526	3 151
2.4.1	Shares issued by residents	2 489	616	1 327	9 718	7 669	7 342	4 526	3 151
2.4.2	Shares issued by non-residents	0	951	0	0	0	0	0	0
2.5	Other, not elsewhere classified	14 007	171 652	125 548	89 112	16 184	15 940	25 940	60 265
	Other mutual funds								
2	Financial assets	1 416 250	1 743 414	1 060 724	1 495 069	2 079 299	1 491 041	1 784 354	2 760 805
2.1	Currency and deposits	291 227	231 899	186 777	209 222	340 222	341 467	495 369	775 479
2.2	Securities other than shares, except financial derivatives	437 035	599 786	298 178	401 746	547 104	435 395	599 347	1 026 794
2.2.1	Short-term securities	..	..	..	..	..	..	..	..
2.2.2	Long-term securities	..	..	..	..	..	..	..	..
2.2.3	Securities issued by residents	410 972	566 700	274 443	367 962	500 771	399 331	556 747	952 084
2.2.4	Securities issued by non-residents	26 063	33 086	23 735	33 784	46 333	36 064	42 600	74 710
2.3	Loans	0	0	0	0	0	0	0	0
2.3.1	Short-term loans	0	0	0	0	0	0	0	0
2.3.2	Long-term loans	0	0	0	0	0	0	0	0
2.3.3	Loans granted to residents	0	0	0	0	0	0	0	0
2.3.4	Loans granted to non-residents	0	0	0	0	0	0	0	0
2.4	Shares and other equity	631 493	773 760	539 582	817 717	1 150 426	669 745	604 202	772 540
2.4.1	Shares issued by residents	377 139	432 156	196 767	200 487	268 773	195 997	206 662	349 698
2.4.2	Shares issued by non-residents	254 354	341 604	342 815	617 230	881 653	473 748	397 540	422 842
2.5	Other, not elsewhere classified	56 495	137 970	36 187	66 384	41 548	44 434	85 437	185 993

Table 2. Financial assets of investment funds *(cont.)*

Million HUF

		2006	2007	2008	2009	2010	2011	2012	2013
	Closed-end companies								
2	Financial assets	259 115	418 020	478 632	301 795	249 926	231 820	249 117	273 370
2.1	Currency and deposits	222 111	358 576	436 838	250 651	203 856	191 494	183 227	176 469
2.2	Securities other than shares, except financial derivatives	5 383	2 291	6 790	4 365	3 482	8 738	27 383	59 562
2.2.1	Short-term securities	..	..	..	..	..	..	..	..
2.2.2	Long-term securities	..	..	..	..	..	..	..	..
2.2.3	Securities issued by residents	5 383	2 291	6 684	4 365	3 377	8 158	26 744	58 968
2.2.4	Securities issued by non-residents	0	0	106	0	104	580	639	594
2.3	Loans	0	0	0	0	0	0	0	0
2.3.1	Short-term loans	0	0	0	0	0	0	0	0
2.3.2	Long-term loans	0	0	0	0	0	0	0	0
2.3.3	Loans granted to residents	0	0	0	0	0	0	0	0
2.3.4	Loans granted to non-residents	0	0	0	0	0	0	0	0
2.4	Shares and other equity	0	0	1 112	0	0	0	0	884
2.4.1	Shares issued by residents	0	0	538	0	0	0	0	20
2.4.2	Shares issued by non-residents	0	0	574	0	0	0	0	863
2.5	Other, not elsewhere classified	31 621	57 153	33 892	46 779	42 588	31 588	38 507	36 456

Note: Detailed metadata at: http://metalinks.oecd.org/instinv/20141203/db48

HUNGARY

Table 3. Financial assets of insurance corporations and autonomous pension funds

Million HUF

		2006	2007	2008	2009	2010	2011	2012	2013
	Insurance corporations and autonomous pension funds								
2	Financial assets	4 320 208	5 046 511	4 801 487	5 901 728	6 509 645	3 463 129	3 606 072	3 729 510
2.1	Currency and deposits	121 664	176 563	221 631	278 375	239 809	210 811	170 518	207 871
2.2	Securities other than shares, except financial derivatives	3 102 227	3 312 514	3 088 709	3 475 654	3 654 838	2 030 279	2 174 370	2 238 054
2.2.1	Short-term securities	296 700	358 728	172 149	527 005	534 885	296 451	348 786	350 031
2.2.2	Long-term securities	2 805 527	2 953 786	2 916 560	2 948 649	3 119 953	1 733 828	1 825 584	1 888 023
2.2.3	Securities issued by residents	3 064 696	3 246 100	2 918 642	3 280 406	3 505 586	1 928 693	2 080 213	2 156 209
2.2.4	Securities issued by non-residents	37 531	66 414	170 067	195 248	149 252	101 586	94 157	81 845
2.3	Loans	14 492	14 759	31 017	23 977	18 228	16 658	10 449	7 755
2.3.1	Short-term loans	1 179	1 155	222	2 282	5 443	5 719	789	955
2.3.2	Long-term loans	13 313	13 604	30 795	21 695	12 785	10 939	9 660	6 800
2.3.3	Loans granted to residents	12 835	11 918	12 284	12 690	11 936	10 268	9 489	6 800
2.3.4	Loans granted to non-residents	1 657	2 841	18 733	11 287	6 292	6 390	960	955
2.4	Shares and other equity	945 070	1 403 603	1 300 900	1 961 528	2 416 798	1 056 148	1 090 438	1 127 456
2.4.1	Shares issued by residents	611 227	781 735	684 464	1 171 754	1 506 343	574 794	609 167	595 598
2.4.2	Shares issued by non-residents	333 843	621 868	616 436	789 774	910 455	481 354	481 271	531 858
2.5	Other, not elsewhere classified	136 755	139 072	159 230	162 194	179 972	149 233	160 297	148 374
	Insurance corporations								
2	Financial assets	1 989 297	2 278 766	2 154 960	2 354 455	2 435 137	2 350 350	2 448 970	2 501 374
2.1	Currency and deposits	51 578	105 787	124 784	170 151	155 843	147 468	107 862	119 017
2.2	Securities other than shares, except financial derivatives	1 390 688	1 479 988	1 457 252	1 366 811	1 281 553	1 314 391	1 426 933	1 442 501
2.2.1	Short-term securities	166 686	158 135	80 912	174 590	139 010	143 760	184 513	148 829
2.2.2	Long-term securities	1 224 002	1 321 853	1 376 340	1 192 221	1 142 543	1 170 631	1 242 420	1 293 672
2.2.3	Securities issued by residents	1 375 676	1 453 422	1 387 002	1 284 860	1 206 976	1 220 525	1 340 714	1 369 081
2.2.4	Securities issued by non-residents	15 012	26 566	70 250	81 951	74 577	93 866	86 219	73 420
2.3	Loans	13 468	13 521	29 944	22 715	16 571	15 019	8 873	6 150
2.3.1	Short-term loans	1 179	1 155	222	2 282	5 443	5 719	789	955
2.3.2	Long-term loans	12 289	12 366	29 722	20 433	11 128	9 300	8 084	5 195
2.3.3	Loans granted to residents	11 811	10 680	11 211	11 428	10 279	8 629	7 913	5 195
2.3.4	Loans granted to non-residents	1 657	2 841	18 733	11 287	6 292	6 390	960	955
2.4	Shares and other equity	428 070	573 160	415 375	662 229	801 276	724 312	745 043	785 362
2.4.1	Shares issued by residents	254 646	274 884	204 119	375 216	427 264	380 632	412 680	409 308
2.4.2	Shares issued by non-residents	173 424	298 276	211 256	287 013	374 012	343 680	332 363	376 054
2.5	Other, not elsewhere classified	105 493	106 310	127 605	132 549	179 894	149 160	160 259	148 344
	Life insurance corporations								
2	Financial assets	..	..	..	..	..	..	..	..
2.1	Currency and deposits	..	..	..	..	..	..	..	..
2.2	Securities other than shares, except financial derivatives	..	..	..	..	..	..	..	..
2.2.1	Short-term securities	..	..	..	..	..	..	..	..
2.2.2	Long-term securities	..	..	..	..	..	..	..	..
2.2.3	Securities issued by residents	..	..	..	..	..	..	..	..
2.2.4	Securities issued by non-residents	..	..	..	..	..	..	..	..
2.3	Loans	..	..	..	..	..	..	..	..
2.3.1	Short-term loans	..	..	..	..	..	..	..	..
2.3.2	Long-term loans	..	..	..	..	..	..	..	..
2.3.3	Loans granted to residents	..	..	..	..	..	..	..	..
2.3.4	Loans granted to non-residents	..	..	..	..	..	..	..	..
2.4	Shares and other equity	..	..	..	..	..	..	..	..
2.4.1	Shares issued by residents	..	..	..	..	..	..	..	..
2.4.2	Shares issued by non-residents	..	..	..	..	..	..	..	..
2.5	Other, not elsewhere classified	..	..	..	..	..	..	..	..
	Non-life insurance corporations								
2	Financial assets	..	..	..	..	..	..	..	..
2.1	Currency and deposits	..	..	..	..	..	..	..	..
2.2	Securities other than shares, except financial derivatives	..	..	..	..	..	..	..	..
2.2.1	Short-term securities	..	..	..	..	..	..	..	..
2.2.2	Long-term securities	..	..	..	..	..	..	..	..
2.2.3	Securities issued by residents	..	..	..	..	..	..	..	..
2.2.4	Securities issued by non-residents	..	..	..	..	..	..	..	..
2.3	Loans	..	..	..	..	..	..	..	..
2.3.1	Short-term loans	..	..	..	..	..	..	..	..
2.3.2	Long-term loans	..	..	..	..	..	..	..	..
2.3.3	Loans granted to residents	..	..	..	..	..	..	..	..
2.3.4	Loans granted to non-residents	..	..	..	..	..	..	..	..
2.4	Shares and other equity	..	..	..	..	..	..	..	..
2.4.1	Shares issued by residents	..	..	..	..	..	..	..	..
2.4.2	Shares issued by non-residents	..	..	..	..	..	..	..	..
2.5	Other, not elsewhere classified	..	..	..	..	..	..	..	..

Table 3. Financial assets of insurance corporations and autonomous pension funds *(cont.)*

Million HUF

		2006	2007	2008	2009	2010	2011	2012	2013
	Autonomous pension funds								
2	Financial assets	2 330 911	2 767 745	2 646 527	3 547 273	4 074 508	1 112 779	1 157 102	1 228 136
2.1	Currency and deposits	70 086	70 776	96 847	108 224	83 966	63 343	62 656	88 854
2.2	Securities other than shares, except financial derivatives	1 711 539	1 832 526	1 631 457	2 108 843	2 373 285	715 888	747 437	795 553
2.2.1	Short-term securities	130 014	200 593	91 237	352 415	395 875	152 691	164 273	201 202
2.2.2	Long-term securities	1 581 525	1 631 933	1 540 220	1 756 428	1 977 410	563 197	583 164	594 351
2.2.3	Securities issued by residents	1 689 020	1 792 678	1 531 640	1 995 546	2 298 610	708 168	739 499	787 128
2.2.4	Securities issued by non-residents	22 519	39 848	99 817	113 297	74 675	7 720	7 938	8 425
2.3	Loans	1 024	1 238	1 073	1 262	1 657	1 639	1 576	1 605
2.3.1	Short-term loans	0	0	0	0	0	0	0	0
2.3.2	Long-term loans	1 024	1 238	1 073	1 262	1 657	1 639	1 576	1 605
2.3.3	Loans granted to residents	1 024	1 238	1 073	1 262	1 657	1 639	1 576	1 605
2.3.4	Loans granted to non-residents	0	0	0	0	0	0	0	0
2.4	Shares and other equity	517 000	830 443	885 525	1 299 299	1 615 522	331 836	345 395	342 094
2.4.1	Shares issued by residents	356 581	506 851	480 345	796 538	1 079 079	194 162	196 487	186 290
2.4.2	Shares issued by non-residents	160 419	323 592	405 180	502 761	536 443	137 674	148 908	155 804
2.5	Other, not elsewhere classified	31 262	32 762	31 625	29 645	78	73	38	30

Note: Detailed metadata at: http://metalinks.oecd.org/instinv/20141203/db48

Table 4. Portfolio composition by type of investor

Percentage of total financial assets

Per cent

		2006	2007	2008	2009	2010	2011	2012	2013
	Investment funds								
2	Financial assets	100.0	100.0	100.0	100.0	100.0	100.0	100.0	100.0
2.1	Currency and deposits	41.4	37.8	47.3	42.9	37.8	50.4	51.3	44.4
2.2	Securities other than shares, except financial derivatives	28.6	28.0	22.3	23.1	28.4	24.7	25.4	32.0
2.2.1	Short-term securities	..	..	..	..	..	..	..	..
2.2.2	Long-term securities	..	..	..	..	..	..	..	..
2.2.3	Securities issued by residents	26.9	26.7	21.3	21.9	27.0	23.4	24.1	30.4
2.2.4	Securities issued by non-residents	1.7	1.3	1.0	1.3	1.3	1.2	1.3	1.7
2.3	Loans	0.0	0.0	0.0	0.0	0.0	0.0	0.0	0.0
2.3.1	Short-term loans	0.0	0.0	0.0	0.0	0.0	0.0	0.0	0.0
2.3.2	Long-term loans	0.0	0.0	0.0	0.0	0.0	0.0	0.0	0.0
2.3.3	Loans granted to residents	0.0	0.0	0.0	0.0	0.0	0.0	0.0	0.0
2.3.4	Loans granted to non-residents	0.0	0.0	0.0	0.0	0.0	0.0	0.0	0.0
2.4	Shares and other equity	25.9	23.3	22.3	27.3	31.1	21.9	18.6	17.3
2.4.1	Shares issued by residents	15.5	13.0	8.2	6.9	7.4	6.6	6.5	7.8
2.4.2	Shares issued by non-residents	10.4	10.3	14.2	20.4	23.7	15.3	12.2	9.4
2.5	Other, not elsewhere classified	4.2	11.0	8.1	6.7	2.7	3.0	4.6	6.3
	Insurance corporations								
2	Financial assets	100.0	100.0	100.0	100.0	100.0	100.0	100.0	100.0
2.1	Currency and deposits	2.6	4.6	5.8	7.2	6.4	6.3	4.4	4.8
2.2	Securities other than shares, except financial derivatives	69.9	64.9	67.6	58.1	52.6	55.9	58.3	57.7
2.2.1	Short-term securities	8.4	6.9	3.8	7.4	5.7	6.1	7.5	5.9
2.2.2	Long-term securities	61.5	58.0	63.9	50.6	46.9	49.8	50.7	51.7
2.2.3	Securities issued by residents	69.2	63.8	64.4	54.6	49.6	51.9	54.7	54.7
2.2.4	Securities issued by non-residents	0.8	1.2	3.3	3.5	3.1	4.0	3.5	2.9
2.3	Loans	0.7	0.6	1.4	1.0	0.7	0.6	0.4	0.2
2.3.1	Short-term loans	0.1	0.1	0.0	0.1	0.2	0.2	0.0	0.0
2.3.2	Long-term loans	0.6	0.5	1.4	0.9	0.5	0.4	0.3	0.2
2.3.3	Loans granted to residents	0.6	0.5	0.5	0.5	0.4	0.4	0.3	0.2
2.3.4	Loans granted to non-residents	0.1	0.1	0.9	0.5	0.3	0.3	0.0	0.0
2.4	Shares and other equity	21.5	25.2	19.3	28.1	32.9	30.8	30.4	31.4
2.4.1	Shares issued by residents	12.8	12.1	9.5	15.9	17.5	16.2	16.9	16.4
2.4.2	Shares issued by non-residents	8.7	13.1	9.8	12.2	15.4	14.6	13.6	15.0
2.5	Other, not elsewhere classified	5.3	4.7	5.9	5.6	7.4	6.3	6.5	5.9
	Autonomous pension funds								
2	Financial assets	100.0	100.0	100.0	100.0	100.0	100.0	100.0	100.0
2.1	Currency and deposits	3.0	2.6	3.7	3.1	2.1	5.7	5.4	7.2
2.2	Securities other than shares, except financial derivatives	73.4	66.2	61.6	59.4	58.2	64.3	64.6	64.8
2.2.1	Short-term securities	5.6	7.2	3.4	9.9	9.7	13.7	14.2	16.4
2.2.2	Long-term securities	67.9	59.0	58.2	49.5	48.5	50.6	50.4	48.4
2.2.3	Securities issued by residents	72.5	64.8	57.9	56.3	56.4	63.6	63.9	64.1
2.2.4	Securities issued by non-residents	1.0	1.4	3.8	3.2	1.8	0.7	0.7	0.7
2.3	Loans	0.0	0.0	0.0	0.0	0.0	0.1	0.1	0.1
2.3.1	Short-term loans	0.0	0.0	0.0	0.0	0.0	0.0	0.0	0.0
2.3.2	Long-term loans	0.0	0.0	0.0	0.0	0.0	0.1	0.1	0.1
2.3.3	Loans granted to residents	0.0	0.0	0.0	0.0	0.0	0.1	0.1	0.1
2.3.4	Loans granted to non-residents	0.0	0.0	0.0	0.0	0.0	0.0	0.0	0.0
2.4	Shares and other equity	22.2	30.0	33.5	36.6	39.6	29.8	29.9	27.9
2.4.1	Shares issued by residents	15.3	18.3	18.2	22.5	26.5	17.4	17.0	15.2
2.4.2	Shares issued by non-residents	6.9	11.7	15.3	14.2	13.2	12.4	12.9	12.7
2.5	Other, not elsewhere classified	1.3	1.2	1.2	0.8	0.0	0.0	0.0	0.0

Note: Detailed metadata at: http://metalinks.oecd.org/instinv/20141203/f729

Table 1. Financial assets of institutional investors, 2013

Million ISK

		Total	Investment funds			
			Open-end companies (mutual funds)			Closed-end companies
			Total	Money market funds	Other mutual funds	Total
2	Financial assets	617 420	358 150	26 449	..	259 270
2.1	Currency and deposits	96 422	43 260	21 161	..	53 162
2.2	Securities other than shares, except financial derivatives	389 166	221 195	3 798	..	167 971
2.2.1	Short-term securities	..	..	..	..	..
2.2.2	Long-term securities	..	..	..	..	..
2.2.3	Securities issued by residents	381 659	221 195	3 798	..	160 464
2.2.4	Securities issued by non-residents	7 507	0	0	..	7 507
2.3	Loans	..	..	..	..	..
2.3.1	Short-term loans	..	..	..	..	..
2.3.2	Long-term loans	..	..	..	..	..
2.3.3	Loans granted to residents	..	..	..	..	..
2.3.4	Loans granted to non-residents	..	..	..	..	..
2.4	Shares and other equity	129 033	91 383	0	..	37 650
2.4.1	Shares issued by residents	101 355	81 500	..	..	19 855
2.4.2	Shares issued by non-residents	27 678	9 883	..	..	17 796
2.5	Other, not elsewhere classified	2 800	2 312	1 489	..	487

		Total	Insurance corporations and autonomous pension funds			
			Insurance corporations			Autonomous pension funds
			Total	Life insurance corporations	Non-life insurance corporations	Total
2	Financial assets	2 816 217	163 009	..	..	2 653 208
2.1	Currency and deposits	175 522	10 758	..	..	164 764
2.2	Securities other than shares, except financial derivatives	1 438 583	72 049	..	..	1 366 534
2.2.1	Short-term securities	..	199	..	..	..
2.2.2	Long-term securities	..	71 850	..	..	..
2.2.3	Securities issued by residents	1 430 680	68 390	..	..	1 362 289
2.2.4	Securities issued by non-residents	7 903	3 658	..	..	4 245
2.3	Loans	178 839	2 842	..	..	175 997
2.3.1	Short-term loans	..	..	..	..	..
2.3.2	Long-term loans	..	..	..	..	175 997
2.3.3	Loans granted to residents	..	..	..	..	175 997
2.3.4	Loans granted to non-residents	..	..	..	..	..
2.4	Shares and other equity	1 012 003	44 514	..	..	967 489
2.4.1	Shares issued by residents	413 754	37 806	..	..	375 948
2.4.2	Shares issued by non-residents	598 249	6 708	..	..	591 541
2.5	Other, not elsewhere classified	11 270	32 846	..	..	-21 575

Note: Detailed metadata at: http://metalinks.oecd.org/instinv/20141203/a74d

Table 2. Financial assets of investment funds

Million ISK

		2006	2007	2008	2009	2010	2011	2012	2013
	Investment funds								
2	Financial assets	453 903	696 758	212 133	195 242	284 249	513 797	581 586	617 420
2.1	Currency and deposits	46 609	121 115	18 168	18 306	18 087	62 874	87 863	96 422
2.2	Securities other than shares, except financial derivatives	329 368	490 227	178 327	159 973	236 679	383 664	406 596	389 166
2.2.1	Short-term securities	..	..	..	..	..	..	..	..
2.2.2	Long-term securities	..	..	..	..	..	..	..	..
2.2.3	Securities issued by residents	318 213	458 071	178 327	159 973	236 098	380 542	398 705	381 659
2.2.4	Securities issued by non-residents	11 155	32 156	0	0	580	3 122	7 890	7 507
2.3	Loans	..	..	..	..	..	..	..	..
2.3.1	Short-term loans	..	..	..	..	..	..	..	..
2.3.2	Long-term loans	..	..	..	..	..	..	..	..
2.3.3	Loans granted to residents	..	..	..	..	..	..	..	..
2.3.4	Loans granted to non-residents	..	..	..	..	..	..	..	..
2.4	Shares and other equity	75 910	73 411	13 946	16 318	28 234	58 147	85 288	129 033
2.4.1	Shares issued by residents	53 214	55 028	4 390	6 212	19 428	36 938	58 133	101 355
2.4.2	Shares issued by non-residents	22 696	18 383	9 556	10 106	8 806	21 209	27 155	27 678
2.5	Other, not elsewhere classified	2 016	12 006	1 691	646	1 249	9 111	1 840	2 800
	Open-end companies (mutual funds)								
2	Financial assets	453 903	696 758	212 133	195 242	284 249	303 689	328 936	358 150
2.1	Currency and deposits	46 609	121 115	18 168	18 306	18 087	25 990	29 024	43 260
2.2	Securities other than shares, except financial derivatives	329 368	490 227	178 327	159 973	236 679	241 578	246 323	221 195
2.2.1	Short-term securities	..	..	..	..	..	..	..	..
2.2.2	Long-term securities	..	..	..	..	..	..	..	..
2.2.3	Securities issued by residents	318 213	458 071	178 327	159 973	236 098	241 578	246 323	221 195
2.2.4	Securities issued by non-residents	11 155	32 156	0	0	580	0	0	0
2.3	Loans	..	..	..	..	..	..	..	..
2.3.1	Short-term loans	..	..	..	..	..	..	..	..
2.3.2	Long-term loans	..	..	..	..	..	..	..	..
2.3.3	Loans granted to residents	..	..	..	..	..	..	..	..
2.3.4	Loans granted to non-residents	..	..	..	..	..	..	..	..
2.4	Shares and other equity	75 910	73 411	13 946	16 318	28 234	33 465	52 696	91 383
2.4.1	Shares issued by residents	53 214	55 028	4 390	6 212	19 428	25 861	43 700	81 500
2.4.2	Shares issued by non-residents	22 696	18 383	9 556	10 106	8 806	7 604	8 996	9 883
2.5	Other, not elsewhere classified	2 016	12 006	1 691	646	1 249	2 656	893	2 312
	Money market funds								
2	Financial assets	..	..	..	4 731	13 391	18 294	19 624	26 449
2.1	Currency and deposits	..	..	..	2 769	6 138	11 479	14 872	21 161
2.2	Securities other than shares, except financial derivatives	..	..	..	1 960	7 251	6 801	4 715	3 798
2.2.1	Short-term securities	..	..	..	..	..	..	..	..
2.2.2	Long-term securities	..	..	..	..	..	..	..	..
2.2.3	Securities issued by residents	..	..	..	1 960	7 251	6 801	4 715	3 798
2.2.4	Securities issued by non-residents	..	..	..	0	0	0	0	0
2.3	Loans	..	..	..	..	..	..	..	..
2.3.1	Short-term loans	..	..	..	..	..	..	..	..
2.3.2	Long-term loans	..	..	..	..	..	..	..	..
2.3.3	Loans granted to residents	..	..	..	..	..	..	..	..
2.3.4	Loans granted to non-residents	..	..	..	..	..	..	..	..
2.4	Shares and other equity	..	..	..	0	0	0	0	0
2.4.1	Shares issued by residents	..	..	..	..	..	..	..	..
2.4.2	Shares issued by non-residents	..	..	..	..	..	..	..	..
2.5	Other, not elsewhere classified	..	..	..	1	2	13	37	1 489
	Other mutual funds								
2	Financial assets	..	..	..	..	..	..	..	..
2.1	Currency and deposits	..	..	..	..	..	..	..	..
2.2	Securities other than shares, except financial derivatives	..	..	..	..	..	..	..	..
2.2.1	Short-term securities	..	..	..	..	..	..	..	..
2.2.2	Long-term securities	..	..	..	..	..	..	..	..
2.2.3	Securities issued by residents	..	..	..	..	..	..	..	..
2.2.4	Securities issued by non-residents	..	..	..	..	..	..	..	..
2.3	Loans	..	..	..	..	..	..	..	..
2.3.1	Short-term loans	..	..	..	..	..	..	..	..
2.3.2	Long-term loans	..	..	..	..	..	..	..	..
2.3.3	Loans granted to residents	..	..	..	..	..	..	..	..
2.3.4	Loans granted to non-residents	..	..	..	..	..	..	..	..
2.4	Shares and other equity	..	..	..	..	..	..	..	..
2.4.1	Shares issued by residents	..	..	..	..	..	..	..	..
2.4.2	Shares issued by non-residents	..	..	..	..	..	..	..	..
2.5	Other, not elsewhere classified	..	..	..	..	..	..	..	..

Table 2. Financial assets of investment funds *(cont.)*

Million ISK

		2006	2007	2008	2009	2010	2011	2012	2013
	Closed-end companies								
2	Financial assets	..	..	..	..	..	210 108	252 650	259 270
2.1	Currency and deposits	..	..	..	..	..	36 884	58 839	53 162
2.2	Securities other than shares, except financial derivatives	..	..	..	..	..	142 087	160 272	167 971
2.2.1	Short-term securities	..	..	..	..	..	..	..	..
2.2.2	Long-term securities	..	..	..	..	..	..	..	..
2.2.3	Securities issued by residents	..	..	..	..	..	138 965	152 382	160 464
2.2.4	Securities issued by non-residents	..	..	..	..	..	3 122	7 890	7 507
2.3	Loans	..	..	..	..	..	..	..	..
2.3.1	Short-term loans	..	..	..	..	..	..	..	..
2.3.2	Long-term loans	..	..	..	..	..	..	..	..
2.3.3	Loans granted to residents	..	..	..	..	..	..	..	..
2.3.4	Loans granted to non-residents	..	..	..	..	..	..	..	..
2.4	Shares and other equity	..	..	..	..	..	24 682	32 592	37 650
2.4.1	Shares issued by residents	..	..	..	..	..	11 078	14 433	19 855
2.4.2	Shares issued by non-residents	..	..	..	..	..	13 605	18 159	17 796
2.5	Other, not elsewhere classified	..	..	..	..	..	6 455	947	487

Note: Detailed metadata at: http://metalinks.oecd.org/instinv/20141203/a74d

ICELAND

Table 3. Financial assets of insurance corporations and autonomous pension funds

Million ISK

		2006	2007	2008	2009	2010	2011	2012	2013
	Insurance corporations and autonomous pension funds								
2	Financial assets	1 659 091	1 843 425	1 709 585	1 890 036	2 033 436	2 234 707	2 538 283	2 816 217
2.1	Currency and deposits	19 879	51 306	186 114	175 035	168 679	168 815	178 767	175 522
2.2	Securities other than shares, except financial derivatives	587 562	700 556	765 693	923 791	1 094 265	1 208 952	1 333 222	1 438 583
2.2.1	Short-term securities	..	..	..	..	..	..	..	..
2.2.2	Long-term securities	..	..	..	..	..	..	..	..
2.2.3	Securities issued by residents	566 316	673 037	735 910	899 697	1 076 821	1 195 416	1 322 824	1 430 680
2.2.4	Securities issued by non-residents	21 247	27 519	29 782	24 094	17 445	13 536	10 399	7 903
2.3	Loans	122 544	139 586	171 592	181 045	176 800	179 718	178 315	178 839
2.3.1	Short-term loans	..	..	..	..	..	..	..	..
2.3.2	Long-term loans	..	..	..	..	..	..	..	..
2.3.3	Loans granted to residents	..	..	..	..	..	..	..	..
2.3.4	Loans granted to non-residents	..	..	..	..	..	..	..	..
2.4	Shares and other equity	901 290	916 614	615 022	647 969	633 917	710 263	848 331	1 012 003
2.4.1	Shares issued by residents	469 933	471 412	173 355	129 875	168 793	243 298	296 717	413 754
2.4.2	Shares issued by non-residents	431 357	445 202	441 667	518 094	465 125	466 965	551 614	598 249
2.5	Other, not elsewhere classified	27 815	35 363	-28 836	-37 804	-40 226	-33 041	-352	11 270
	Insurance corporations								
2	Financial assets	168 668	157 923	120 871	129 004	136 528	143 748	152 898	163 009
2.1	Currency and deposits	4 843	6 342	17 083	12 505	10 035	11 507	11 128	10 758
2.2	Securities other than shares, except financial derivatives	14 645	21 255	24 131	45 459	54 920	60 754	65 643	72 049
2.2.1	Short-term securities	0	2 281	0	394	862	760	576	199
2.2.2	Long-term securities	14 645	18 974	24 131	45 065	54 058	59 994	65 067	71 850
2.2.3	Securities issued by residents	14 220	18 222	22 675	44 653	52 176	56 355	61 282	68 390
2.2.4	Securities issued by non-residents	425	3 032	1 456	807	2 744	4 399	4 361	3 658
2.3	Loans	13 367	9 878	8 310	6 609	4 911	4 463	3 180	2 842
2.3.1	Short-term loans	..	..	..	..	..	..	..	..
2.3.2	Long-term loans	..	..	..	..	..	..	..	..
2.3.3	Loans granted to residents	..	..	..	..	..	..	..	..
2.3.4	Loans granted to non-residents	..	..	..	..	..	..	..	..
2.4	Shares and other equity	107 998	85 085	43 376	32 540	34 723	39 904	41 358	44 514
2.4.1	Shares issued by residents	98 867	73 655	35 265	21 243	25 869	32 612	34 778	37 806
2.4.2	Shares issued by non-residents	9 132	11 430	8 111	11 297	8 854	7 291	6 580	6 708
2.5	Other, not elsewhere classified	27 815	35 363	27 972	31 890	31 939	27 120	31 589	32 846
	Life insurance corporations								
2	Financial assets	..	..	..	..	..	..	..	..
2.1	Currency and deposits	..	..	..	..	..	..	..	..
2.2	Securities other than shares, except financial derivatives	..	..	..	..	..	..	..	..
2.2.1	Short-term securities	..	..	..	..	..	..	..	..
2.2.2	Long-term securities	..	..	..	..	..	..	..	..
2.2.3	Securities issued by residents	..	..	..	..	..	..	..	..
2.2.4	Securities issued by non-residents	..	..	..	..	..	..	..	..
2.3	Loans	..	..	..	..	..	..	..	..
2.3.1	Short-term loans	..	..	..	..	..	..	..	..
2.3.2	Long-term loans	..	..	..	..	..	..	..	..
2.3.3	Loans granted to residents	..	..	..	..	..	..	..	..
2.3.4	Loans granted to non-residents	..	..	..	..	..	..	..	..
2.4	Shares and other equity	..	..	..	..	..	..	..	..
2.4.1	Shares issued by residents	..	..	..	..	..	..	..	..
2.4.2	Shares issued by non-residents	..	..	..	..	..	..	..	..
2.5	Other, not elsewhere classified	..	..	..	..	..	..	..	..
	Non-life insurance corporations								
2	Financial assets	..	..	..	..	..	..	..	..
2.1	Currency and deposits	..	..	..	..	..	..	..	..
2.2	Securities other than shares, except financial derivatives	..	..	..	..	..	..	..	..
2.2.1	Short-term securities	..	..	..	..	..	..	..	..
2.2.2	Long-term securities	..	..	..	..	..	..	..	..
2.2.3	Securities issued by residents	..	..	..	..	..	..	..	..
2.2.4	Securities issued by non-residents	..	..	..	..	..	..	..	..
2.3	Loans	..	..	..	..	..	..	..	..
2.3.1	Short-term loans	..	..	..	..	..	..	..	..
2.3.2	Long-term loans	..	..	..	..	..	..	..	..
2.3.3	Loans granted to residents	..	..	..	..	..	..	..	..
2.3.4	Loans granted to non-residents	..	..	..	..	..	..	..	..
2.4	Shares and other equity	..	..	..	..	..	..	..	..
2.4.1	Shares issued by residents	..	..	..	..	..	..	..	..
2.4.2	Shares issued by non-residents	..	..	..	..	..	..	..	..
2.5	Other, not elsewhere classified	..	..	..	..	..	..	..	..

Table 3. Financial assets of insurance corporations and autonomous pension funds *(cont.)*

Million ISK

		2006	2007	2008	2009	2010	2011	2012	2013
	Autonomous pension funds								
2	Financial assets	1 490 423	1 685 503	1 588 713	1 761 033	1 896 908	2 090 959	2 385 384	2 653 208
2.1	Currency and deposits	15 037	44 964	169 032	162 529	158 644	157 308	167 638	164 764
2.2	Securities other than shares, except financial derivatives	572 917	679 301	741 561	878 331	1 039 345	1 148 198	1 267 579	1 366 534
2.2.1	Short-term securities	..	..	..	..	..	..	..	..
2.2.2	Long-term securities	..	..	..	..	..	..	..	..
2.2.3	Securities issued by residents	552 095	654 815	713 235	855 045	1 024 644	1 139 061	1 261 542	1 362 289
2.2.4	Securities issued by non-residents	20 822	24 486	28 326	23 287	14 701	9 137	6 037	4 245
2.3	Loans	109 177	129 708	163 282	174 436	171 889	175 255	175 134	175 997
2.3.1	Short-term loans	..	..	..	..	..	..	..	..
2.3.2	Long-term loans	109 177	129 708	163 282	174 436	171 889	175 255	175 134	175 997
2.3.3	Loans granted to residents	109 177	129 708	163 282	174 436	171 889	175 255	175 134	175 997
2.3.4	Loans granted to non-residents	..	..	..	..	..	..	..	..
2.4	Shares and other equity	793 292	831 529	571 646	615 430	599 195	670 360	806 974	967 489
2.4.1	Shares issued by residents	371 066	397 757	138 091	108 633	142 924	210 686	261 940	375 948
2.4.2	Shares issued by non-residents	422 225	433 772	433 556	506 797	456 271	459 674	545 034	591 541
2.5	Other, not elsewhere classified	..	..	-56 808	-69 694	-72 165	-60 162	-31 941	-21 575

Note: Detailed metadata at: http://metalinks.oecd.org/instinv/20141203/a74d

Table 4. Portfolio composition by type of investor

Percentage of total financial assets

Per cent

		2006	2007	2008	2009	2010	2011	2012	2013
	Investment funds								
2	Financial assets	100.0	100.0	100.0	100.0	100.0	100.0	100.0	100.0
2.1	Currency and deposits	10.3	17.4	8.6	9.4	6.4	12.2	15.1	15.6
2.2	Securities other than shares, except financial derivatives	72.6	70.4	84.1	81.9	83.3	74.7	69.9	63.0
2.2.1	Short-term securities	..	..	..	..	..	..	..	..
2.2.2	Long-term securities	..	..	..	..	..	..	..	..
2.2.3	Securities issued by residents	70.1	65.7	84.1	81.9	83.1	74.1	68.6	61.8
2.2.4	Securities issued by non-residents	2.5	4.6	0.0	0.0	0.2	0.6	1.4	1.2
2.3	Loans	..	..	..	..	..	..	..	..
2.3.1	Short-term loans	..	..	..	..	..	..	..	..
2.3.2	Long-term loans	..	..	..	..	..	..	..	..
2.3.3	Loans granted to residents	..	..	..	..	..	..	..	..
2.3.4	Loans granted to non-residents	..	..	..	..	..	..	..	..
2.4	Shares and other equity	16.7	10.5	6.6	8.4	9.9	11.3	14.7	20.9
2.4.1	Shares issued by residents	11.7	7.9	2.1	3.2	6.8	7.2	10.0	16.4
2.4.2	Shares issued by non-residents	5.0	2.6	4.5	5.2	3.1	4.1	4.7	4.5
2.5	Other, not elsewhere classified	0.4	1.7	0.8	0.3	0.4	1.8	0.3	0.5
	Insurance corporations								
2	Financial assets	100.0	100.0	100.0	100.0	100.0	100.0	100.0	100.0
2.1	Currency and deposits	2.9	4.0	14.1	9.7	7.4	8.0	7.3	6.6
2.2	Securities other than shares, except financial derivatives	8.7	13.5	20.0	35.2	40.2	42.3	42.9	44.2
2.2.1	Short-term securities	0.0	1.4	0.0	0.3	0.6	0.5	0.4	0.1
2.2.2	Long-term securities	8.7	12.0	20.0	34.9	39.6	41.7	42.6	44.1
2.2.3	Securities issued by residents	8.4	11.5	18.8	34.6	38.2	39.2	40.1	42.0
2.2.4	Securities issued by non-residents	0.3	1.9	1.2	0.6	2.0	3.1	2.9	2.2
2.3	Loans	7.9	6.3	6.9	5.1	3.6	3.1	2.1	1.7
2.3.1	Short-term loans	..	..	..	..	..	..	..	..
2.3.2	Long-term loans	..	..	..	..	..	..	..	..
2.3.3	Loans granted to residents	..	..	..	..	..	..	..	..
2.3.4	Loans granted to non-residents	..	..	..	..	..	..	..	..
2.4	Shares and other equity	64.0	53.9	35.9	25.2	25.4	27.8	27.0	27.3
2.4.1	Shares issued by residents	58.6	46.6	29.2	16.5	18.9	22.7	22.7	23.2
2.4.2	Shares issued by non-residents	5.4	7.2	6.7	8.8	6.5	5.1	4.3	4.1
2.5	Other, not elsewhere classified	16.5	22.4	23.1	24.7	23.4	18.9	20.7	20.1
	Autonomous pension funds								
2	Financial assets	100.0	100.0	100.0	100.0	100.0	100.0	100.0	100.0
2.1	Currency and deposits	1.0	2.7	10.6	9.2	8.4	7.5	7.0	6.2
2.2	Securities other than shares, except financial derivatives	38.4	40.3	46.7	49.9	54.8	54.9	53.1	51.5
2.2.1	Short-term securities	..	..	..	..	..	..	..	..
2.2.2	Long-term securities	..	..	..	..	..	..	..	..
2.2.3	Securities issued by residents	37.0	38.8	44.9	48.6	54.0	54.5	52.9	51.3
2.2.4	Securities issued by non-residents	1.4	1.5	1.8	1.3	0.8	0.4	0.3	0.2
2.3	Loans	7.3	7.7	10.3	9.9	9.1	8.4	7.3	6.6
2.3.1	Short-term loans	..	..	..	..	..	..	..	..
2.3.2	Long-term loans	7.3	7.7	10.3	9.9	9.1	8.4	7.3	6.6
2.3.3	Loans granted to residents	7.3	7.7	10.3	9.9	9.1	8.4	7.3	6.6
2.3.4	Loans granted to non-residents	..	..	..	..	..	..	..	..
2.4	Shares and other equity	53.2	49.3	36.0	34.9	31.6	32.1	33.8	36.5
2.4.1	Shares issued by residents	24.9	23.6	8.7	6.2	7.5	10.1	11.0	14.2
2.4.2	Shares issued by non-residents	28.3	25.7	27.3	28.8	24.1	22.0	22.8	22.3
2.5	Other, not elsewhere classified	..	..	-3.6	-4.0	-3.8	-2.9	-1.3	-0.8

Note: Detailed metadata at: http://metalinks.oecd.org/instinv/20141203/f729

IRELAND

Table 1. Financial assets of institutional investors, 2013

Million EUR (1999 IEP euro)

		Investment funds				
		Total	Open-end companies (mutual funds)			Closed-end companies
			Total	Money market funds	Other mutual funds	Total
2	Financial assets	..	1 454 758	274 426	1 180 332	..
2.1	Currency and deposits	..	108 139	51 385	56 753	..
2.2	Securities other than shares, except financial derivatives	..	702 321	221 528	480 794	..
2.2.1	Short-term securities	..	276 538	179 917	96 621	..
2.2.2	Long-term securities	..	425 783	41 610	384 173	..
2.2.3	Securities issued by residents	..	..	..	..	..
2.2.4	Securities issued by non-residents	..	..	..	..	..
2.3	Loans	..	14 687	0	14 688	..
2.3.1	Short-term loans	..	5 945	0	5 945	..
2.3.2	Long-term loans	..	8 742	0	8 742	..
2.3.3	Loans granted to residents	..	..	..	..	..
2.3.4	Loans granted to non-residents	..	..	..	..	..
2.4	Shares and other equity	..	537 174	970	536 204	..
2.4.1	Shares issued by residents	..	..	..	..	..
2.4.2	Shares issued by non-residents	..	..	..	..	..
2.5	Other, not elsewhere classified	..	92 436	543	91 893	..

		Insurance corporations and autonomous pension funds				
		Total	Insurance corporations			Autonomous pension funds
			Total	Life insurance corporations	Non-life insurance corporations	Total
2	Financial assets	304 455	..	..	..	..
2.1	Currency and deposits	19 985	..	..	..	..
2.2	Securities other than shares, except financial derivatives	79 811	..	..	..	..
2.2.1	Short-term securities	8 391	..	..	..	..
2.2.2	Long-term securities	71 420	..	..	..	..
2.2.3	Securities issued by residents	..	..	..	..	..
2.2.4	Securities issued by non-residents	..	..	..	..	..
2.3	Loans	1 325	..	..	..	..
2.3.1	Short-term loans	952	..	..	..	..
2.3.2	Long-term loans	373	..	..	..	..
2.3.3	Loans granted to residents	..	..	..	..	..
2.3.4	Loans granted to non-residents	..	..	..	..	..
2.4	Shares and other equity	161 033	..	..	..	..
2.4.1	Shares issued by residents	..	..	..	..	..
2.4.2	Shares issued by non-residents	..	..	..	..	..
2.5	Other, not elsewhere classified	42 301	..	..	..	..

Note: Detailed metadata at: http://metalinks.oecd.org/instinv/20141203/d47b

Table 2. Financial assets of investment funds

Million EUR (1999 IEP euro)

		2006	2007	2008	2009	2010	2011	2012	2013
	Investment funds								
2	Financial assets	..	..	..	..	..	..	..	..
2.1	Currency and deposits	..	..	..	..	..	..	..	..
2.2	Securities other than shares, except financial derivatives	..	..	..	..	..	..	..	..
2.2.1	Short-term securities	..	..	..	..	..	..	..	..
2.2.2	Long-term securities	..	..	..	..	..	..	..	..
2.2.3	Securities issued by residents	..	..	..	..	..	..	..	..
2.2.4	Securities issued by non-residents	..	..	..	..	..	..	..	..
2.3	Loans	..	..	..	..	..	..	..	..
2.3.1	Short-term loans	..	..	..	..	..	..	..	..
2.3.2	Long-term loans	..	..	..	..	..	..	..	..
2.3.3	Loans granted to residents	..	..	..	..	..	..	..	..
2.3.4	Loans granted to non-residents	..	..	..	..	..	..	..	..
2.4	Shares and other equity	..	..	..	..	..	..	..	..
2.4.1	Shares issued by residents	..	..	..	..	..	..	..	..
2.4.2	Shares issued by non-residents	..	..	..	..	..	..	..	..
2.5	Other, not elsewhere classified	..	..	..	..	..	..	..	..
	Open-end companies (mutual funds)								
2	Financial assets	722 862	800 147	667 315	770 586	1 007 268	1 110 901	1 316 685	1 454 758
2.1	Currency and deposits	35 841	62 144	60 335	48 258	71 970	120 405	126 363	108 139
2.2	Securities other than shares, except financial derivatives	384 673	420 279	369 152	430 569	546 222	573 204	676 456	702 321
2.2.1	Short-term securities	249 060	271 781	198 917	204 955	258 779	257 905	275 097	276 538
2.2.2	Long-term securities	135 613	148 497	170 234	225 614	287 442	315 299	401 359	425 783
2.2.3	Securities issued by residents	..	..	..	..	..	..	..	..
2.2.4	Securities issued by non-residents	..	..	..	..	..	..	..	..
2.3	Loans	1 052	335	435	338	314	16 278	16 898	14 687
2.3.1	Short-term loans	51	9	65	61	93	16 240	6 793	5 945
2.3.2	Long-term loans	1 001	326	370	278	221	38	10 105	8 742
2.3.3	Loans granted to residents	..	..	..	..	..	..	..	..
2.3.4	Loans granted to non-residents	..	..	..	..	..	..	..	..
2.4	Shares and other equity	289 545	304 621	209 926	262 903	343 347	346 805	422 293	537 174
2.4.1	Shares issued by residents	..	..	..	..	..	..	..	..
2.4.2	Shares issued by non-residents	..	..	..	..	..	..	..	..
2.5	Other, not elsewhere classified	11 751	12 768	27 467	28 517	45 416	54 209	74 675	92 436
	Money market funds								
2	Financial assets	275 242	326 170	317 008	310 572	359 265	292 253	298 715	274 426
2.1	Currency and deposits	21 342	51 662	43 706	28 146	46 917	75 514	62 269	51 385
2.2	Securities other than shares, except financial derivatives	252 713	272 124	271 377	280 489	311 145	215 823	235 421	221 528
2.2.1	Short-term securities	238 939	263 309	192 544	190 310	247 333	179 293	192 812	179 917
2.2.2	Long-term securities	13 774	8 815	78 832	90 179	63 811	36 530	42 609	41 610
2.2.3	Securities issued by residents	..	..	..	..	..	..	..	..
2.2.4	Securities issued by non-residents	..	..	..	..	..	..	..	..
2.3	Loans	0	0	0	0	0	0	0	0
2.3.1	Short-term loans	0	0	0	0	0	0	0	0
2.3.2	Long-term loans	0	0	0	0	0	0	0	0
2.3.3	Loans granted to residents	..	..	..	..	..	..	..	..
2.3.4	Loans granted to non-residents	..	..	..	..	..	..	..	..
2.4	Shares and other equity	18	965	1 480	1 642	1 005	581	845	970
2.4.1	Shares issued by residents	..	..	..	..	..	..	..	..
2.4.2	Shares issued by non-residents	..	..	..	..	..	..	..	..
2.5	Other, not elsewhere classified	1 169	1 419	445	294	199	335	180	543
	Other mutual funds								
2	Financial assets	447 620	473 977	350 307	460 014	648 003	818 648	1 017 970	1 180 332
2.1	Currency and deposits	14 499	10 482	16 629	20 112	25 053	44 891	64 095	56 753
2.2	Securities other than shares, except financial derivatives	131 960	148 155	97 775	150 080	235 077	357 381	441 035	480 794
2.2.1	Short-term securities	10 121	8 472	6 373	14 645	11 446	78 612	82 285	96 621
2.2.2	Long-term securities	121 839	139 682	91 402	135 435	223 631	278 769	358 750	384 173
2.2.3	Securities issued by residents	..	..	..	..	..	..	..	..
2.2.4	Securities issued by non-residents	..	..	..	..	..	..	..	..
2.3	Loans	1 052	335	435	338	314	16 278	16 898	14 688
2.3.1	Short-term loans	51	9	65	61	93	16 240	6 792	5 945
2.3.2	Long-term loans	1 001	326	370	278	221	38	10 105	8 742
2.3.3	Loans granted to residents	..	..	..	..	..	..	..	..
2.3.4	Loans granted to non-residents	..	..	..	..	..	..	..	..
2.4	Shares and other equity	289 527	303 656	208 446	261 261	342 342	346 224	421 448	536 204
2.4.1	Shares issued by residents	..	..	..	..	..	..	..	..
2.4.2	Shares issued by non-residents	..	..	..	..	..	..	..	..
2.5	Other, not elsewhere classified	10 582	11 349	27 022	28 223	45 217	53 874	74 495	91 893

Table 2. Financial assets of investment funds *(cont.)*

Million EUR (1999 IEP euro)

		2006	2007	2008	2009	2010	2011	2012	2013
	Closed-end companies								
2	Financial assets	..	..	..	..	..	..	..	..
2.1	Currency and deposits	..	..	..	..	..	..	..	..
2.2	Securities other than shares, except financial derivatives	..	..	..	..	..	..	..	..
2.2.1	Short-term securities	..	..	..	..	..	..	..	..
2.2.2	Long-term securities	..	..	..	..	..	..	..	..
2.2.3	Securities issued by residents	..	..	..	..	..	..	..	..
2.2.4	Securities issued by non-residents	..	..	..	..	..	..	..	..
2.3	Loans	..	..	..	..	..	..	..	..
2.3.1	Short-term loans	..	..	..	..	..	..	..	..
2.3.2	Long-term loans	..	..	..	..	..	..	..	..
2.3.3	Loans granted to residents	..	..	..	..	..	..	..	..
2.3.4	Loans granted to non-residents	..	..	..	..	..	..	..	..
2.4	Shares and other equity	..	..	..	..	..	..	..	..
2.4.1	Shares issued by residents	..	..	..	..	..	..	..	..
2.4.2	Shares issued by non-residents	..	..	..	..	..	..	..	..
2.5	Other, not elsewhere classified	..	..	..	..	..	..	..	..

Note: Detailed metadata at: http://metalinks.oecd.org/instinv/20141203/d47b

IRELAND

Table 3. Financial assets of insurance corporations and autonomous pension funds

Million EUR (1999 IEP euro)

		2006	2007	2008	2009	2010	2011	2012	2013
	Insurance corporations and autonomous pension funds								
2	Financial assets	249 771	259 494	240 482	268 357	295 207	280 246	295 811	304 455
2.1	Currency and deposits	16 732	17 889	22 349	22 261	22 928	23 588	22 720	19 985
2.2	Securities other than shares, except financial derivatives	52 411	58 532	64 053	69 182	73 745	80 233	85 055	79 811
2.2.1	Short-term securities	2 695	3 830	6 758	6 458	8 249	7 985	8 873	8 391
2.2.2	Long-term securities	49 716	54 702	57 295	62 724	65 495	72 248	76 182	71 420
2.2.3	Securities issued by residents	..	..	..	..	..	..	..	..
2.2.4	Securities issued by non-residents	..	..	..	..	..	..	..	..
2.3	Loans	3 724	2 749	2 720	3 331	3 504	3 678	2 785	1 325
2.3.1	Short-term loans	1 299	1 012	1 223	1 270	1 091	792	1 138	952
2.3.2	Long-term loans	2 425	1 737	1 497	2 062	2 413	2 886	1 647	373
2.3.3	Loans granted to residents	..	..	..	..	..	..	..	..
2.3.4	Loans granted to non-residents	..	..	..	..	..	..	..	..
2.4	Shares and other equity	136 192	131 579	99 182	120 482	136 193	126 991	140 927	161 033
2.4.1	Shares issued by residents	..	..	..	..	..	..	..	..
2.4.2	Shares issued by non-residents	..	..	..	..	..	..	..	..
2.5	Other, not elsewhere classified	40 712	48 745	52 178	53 102	58 837	45 757	44 324	42 301
	Insurance corporations								
2	Financial assets	..	..	..	..	..	..	..	..
2.1	Currency and deposits	..	..	..	..	..	..	..	..
2.2	Securities other than shares, except financial derivatives	..	..	..	..	..	..	..	..
2.2.1	Short-term securities	..	..	..	..	..	..	..	..
2.2.2	Long-term securities	..	..	..	..	..	..	..	..
2.2.3	Securities issued by residents	..	..	..	..	..	..	..	..
2.2.4	Securities issued by non-residents	..	..	..	..	..	..	..	..
2.3	Loans	..	..	..	..	..	..	..	..
2.3.1	Short-term loans	..	..	..	..	..	..	..	..
2.3.2	Long-term loans	..	..	..	..	..	..	..	..
2.3.3	Loans granted to residents	..	..	..	..	..	..	..	..
2.3.4	Loans granted to non-residents	..	..	..	..	..	..	..	..
2.4	Shares and other equity	..	..	..	..	..	..	..	..
2.4.1	Shares issued by residents	..	..	..	..	..	..	..	..
2.4.2	Shares issued by non-residents	..	..	..	..	..	..	..	..
2.5	Other, not elsewhere classified	..	..	..	..	..	..	..	..
	Life insurance corporations								
2	Financial assets	..	..	..	..	..	..	..	..
2.1	Currency and deposits	..	..	..	..	..	..	..	..
2.2	Securities other than shares, except financial derivatives	..	..	..	..	..	..	..	..
2.2.1	Short-term securities	..	..	..	..	..	..	..	..
2.2.2	Long-term securities	..	..	..	..	..	..	..	..
2.2.3	Securities issued by residents	..	..	..	..	..	..	..	..
2.2.4	Securities issued by non-residents	..	..	..	..	..	..	..	..
2.3	Loans	..	..	..	..	..	..	..	..
2.3.1	Short-term loans	..	..	..	..	..	..	..	..
2.3.2	Long-term loans	..	..	..	..	..	..	..	..
2.3.3	Loans granted to residents	..	..	..	..	..	..	..	..
2.3.4	Loans granted to non-residents	..	..	..	..	..	..	..	..
2.4	Shares and other equity	..	..	..	..	..	..	..	..
2.4.1	Shares issued by residents	..	..	..	..	..	..	..	..
2.4.2	Shares issued by non-residents	..	..	..	..	..	..	..	..
2.5	Other, not elsewhere classified	..	..	..	..	..	..	..	..
	Non-life insurance corporations								
2	Financial assets	..	..	..	..	..	..	..	..
2.1	Currency and deposits	..	..	..	..	..	..	..	..
2.2	Securities other than shares, except financial derivatives	..	..	..	..	..	..	..	..
2.2.1	Short-term securities	..	..	..	..	..	..	..	..
2.2.2	Long-term securities	..	..	..	..	..	..	..	..
2.2.3	Securities issued by residents	..	..	..	..	..	..	..	..
2.2.4	Securities issued by non-residents	..	..	..	..	..	..	..	..
2.3	Loans	..	..	..	..	..	..	..	..
2.3.1	Short-term loans	..	..	..	..	..	..	..	..
2.3.2	Long-term loans	..	..	..	..	..	..	..	..
2.3.3	Loans granted to residents	..	..	..	..	..	..	..	..
2.3.4	Loans granted to non-residents	..	..	..	..	..	..	..	..
2.4	Shares and other equity	..	..	..	..	..	..	..	..
2.4.1	Shares issued by residents	..	..	..	..	..	..	..	..
2.4.2	Shares issued by non-residents	..	..	..	..	..	..	..	..
2.5	Other, not elsewhere classified	..	..	..	..	..	..	..	..

Table 3. Financial assets of insurance corporations and autonomous pension funds *(cont.)*

Million EUR (1999 IEP euro)

		2006	2007	2008	2009	2010	2011	2012	2013
	Autonomous pension funds								
2	Financial assets	..	..	..	..	..	..	..	..
2.1	Currency and deposits	..	..	..	..	..	..	..	..
2.2	Securities other than shares, except financial derivatives	..	..	..	..	..	..	..	..
2.2.1	Short-term securities	..	..	..	..	..	..	..	..
2.2.2	Long-term securities	..	..	..	..	..	..	..	..
2.2.3	Securities issued by residents	..	..	..	..	..	..	..	..
2.2.4	Securities issued by non-residents	..	..	..	..	..	..	..	..
2.3	Loans	..	..	..	..	..	..	..	..
2.3.1	Short-term loans	..	..	..	..	..	..	..	..
2.3.2	Long-term loans	..	..	..	..	..	..	..	..
2.3.3	Loans granted to residents	..	..	..	..	..	..	..	..
2.3.4	Loans granted to non-residents	..	..	..	..	..	..	..	..
2.4	Shares and other equity	..	..	..	..	..	..	..	..
2.4.1	Shares issued by residents	..	..	..	..	..	..	..	..
2.4.2	Shares issued by non-residents	..	..	..	..	..	..	..	..
2.5	Other, not elsewhere classified	..	..	..	..	..	..	..	..

Note: Detailed metadata at: http://metalinks.oecd.org/instinv/20141203/d47b

Data for:

Table 4. Portfolio composition by type of investor

are not available for Ireland.

Table 1. Financial assets of institutional investors, 2012

Million ILS

		Investment funds				
	Total	Open-end companies (mutual funds)				Closed-end companies
		Total	Money market funds	Other mutual funds		Total
2	Financial assets	170 099	170 099	35 688	134 411	0
2.1	Currency and deposits	23 524	23 524	16 635	6 889	0
2.2	Securities other than shares, except financial derivatives	134 541	134 541	19 053	115 488	0
2.2.1	Short-term securities	34 061	34 061	11 695	22 366	0
2.2.2	Long-term securities	100 480	100 480	7 358	93 122	0
2.2.3	Securities issued by residents	128 554	128 554	18 856	109 698	0
2.2.4	Securities issued by non-residents	5 987	5 987	197	5 790	0
2.3	Loans	0	0	0	0	0
2.3.1	Short-term loans	0	0	0	0	0
2.3.2	Long-term loans	0	0	0	0	0
2.3.3	Loans granted to residents	0	0	0	0	0
2.3.4	Loans granted to non-residents	0	0	0	0	0
2.4	Shares and other equity	12 034	12 034	0	12 034	0
2.4.1	Shares issued by residents	7 446	7 446	0	7 446	0
2.4.2	Shares issued by non-residents	4 588	4 588	0	4 588	0
2.5	Other, not elsewhere classified	0	0	0	0	0

		Total	Insurance corporations and autonomous pension funds			
			Insurance corporations			Autonomous pension funds
			Total	Life insurance corporations	Non-life insurance corporations	Total
2	Financial assets	708 642	339 642	..	..	368 999
2.1	Currency and deposits	79 208	25 111	..	..	54 098
2.2	Securities other than shares, except financial derivatives	458 485	200 223	..	..	258 263
2.2.1	Short-term securities	7 070	3 214	..	..	3 857
2.2.2	Long-term securities	451 415	197 009	..	..	254 406
2.2.3	Securities issued by residents	373 012	163 350	..	..	209 661
2.2.4	Securities issued by non-residents	85 474	36 872	..	..	48 602
2.3	Loans	32 272	19 832	..	..	12 440
2.3.1	Short-term loans	..	..	..	..	..
2.3.2	Long-term loans	..	..	..	..	..
2.3.3	Loans granted to residents	32 272	19 832	..	..	12 440
2.3.4	Loans granted to non-residents	0	0	..	..	0
2.4	Shares and other equity	67 792	41 640	..	..	26 152
2.4.1	Shares issued by residents	57 476	36 318	..	..	21 158
2.4.2	Shares issued by non-residents	10 317	5 322	..	..	4 994
2.5	Other, not elsewhere classified	70 884	52 837	..	..	18 047

Note: Detailed metadata at: http://metalinks.oecd.org/instinv/20141203/f0b0
Information on data for Israel: http://oe.cd/israel-disclaimer

Table 2. Financial assets of investment funds

Million ILS

		2006	2007	2008	2009	2010	2011	2012	2013
	Investment funds								
2	Financial assets	111 467	120 321	98 099	133 199	156 582	142 353	170 099	..
2.1	Currency and deposits	6 510	7 185	23 194	13 932	14 925	17 173	23 524	..
2.2	Securities other than shares, except financial derivatives	78 087	88 098	68 676	104 510	121 659	112 700	134 541	..
2.2.1	Short-term securities	16 208	14 012	16 793	23 172	23 611	32 558	34 061	..
2.2.2	Long-term securities	61 879	74 087	51 884	81 337	98 048	80 142	100 480	..
2.2.3	Securities issued by residents	69 482	80 790	64 582	99 606	115 420	108 351	128 554	..
2.2.4	Securities issued by non-residents	8 605	7 308	4 094	4 904	6 238	4 349	5 987	..
2.3	Loans	0	0	0	0	0	0	0	..
2.3.1	Short-term loans	0	0	0	0	0	0	0	..
2.3.2	Long-term loans	0	0	0	0	0	0	0	..
2.3.3	Loans granted to residents	0	0	0	0	0	0	0	..
2.3.4	Loans granted to non-residents	0	0	0	0	0	0	0	..
2.4	Shares and other equity	26 869	25 038	6 228	14 757	19 998	12 480	12 034	..
2.4.1	Shares issued by residents	16 410	16 332	4 152	10 817	14 627	8 432	7 446	..
2.4.2	Shares issued by non-residents	10 459	8 706	2 076	3 940	5 371	4 048	4 588	..
2.5	Other, not elsewhere classified	0	0	0	0	0	0	0	..
	Open-end companies (mutual funds)								
2	Financial assets	111 467	120 321	98 099	133 199	156 582	142 353	170 099	..
2.1	Currency and deposits	6 510	7 185	23 194	13 932	14 925	17 173	23 524	..
2.2	Securities other than shares, except financial derivatives	78 087	88 098	68 676	104 510	121 659	112 700	134 541	..
2.2.1	Short-term securities	16 208	14 012	16 793	23 172	23 611	32 558	34 061	..
2.2.2	Long-term securities	61 879	74 087	51 884	81 337	98 048	80 142	100 480	..
2.2.3	Securities issued by residents	69 482	80 790	64 582	99 606	115 420	108 351	128 554	..
2.2.4	Securities issued by non-residents	8 605	7 308	4 094	4 904	6 238	4 349	5 987	..
2.3	Loans	0	0	0	0	0	0	0	..
2.3.1	Short-term loans	0	0	0	0	0	0	0	..
2.3.2	Long-term loans	0	0	0	0	0	0	0	..
2.3.3	Loans granted to residents	0	0	0	0	0	0	0	..
2.3.4	Loans granted to non-residents	0	0	0	0	0	0	0	..
2.4	Shares and other equity	26 869	25 038	6 228	14 757	19 998	12 480	12 034	..
2.4.1	Shares issued by residents	16 410	16 332	4 152	10 817	14 627	8 432	7 446	..
2.4.2	Shares issued by non-residents	10 459	8 706	2 076	3 940	5 371	4 048	4 588	..
2.5	Other, not elsewhere classified	0	0	0	0	0	0	0	..
	Money market funds								
2	Financial assets	..	..	32 605	17 173	18 092	34 086	35 688	..
2.1	Currency and deposits	..	..	18 008	7 108	7 738	12 934	16 635	..
2.2	Securities other than shares, except financial derivatives	..	..	14 598	10 064	10 350	21 151	19 053	..
2.2.1	Short-term securities	..	..	8 764	6 615	7 076	12 249	11 695	..
2.2.2	Long-term securities	..	..	5 834	3 449	3 274	8 902	7 358	..
2.2.3	Securities issued by residents	..	..	13 389	9 250	9 879	20 714	18 856	..
2.2.4	Securities issued by non-residents	..	..	1 209	815	471	437	197	..
2.3	Loans	..	..	0	0	0	0	0	..
2.3.1	Short-term loans	..	..	0	0	0	0	0	..
2.3.2	Long-term loans	..	..	0	0	0	0	0	..
2.3.3	Loans granted to residents	..	..	0	0	0	0	0	..
2.3.4	Loans granted to non-residents	..	..	0	0	0	0	0	..
2.4	Shares and other equity	..	..	0	0	4	0	0	..
2.4.1	Shares issued by residents	..	..	0	0	4	0	0	..
2.4.2	Shares issued by non-residents	..	..	0	0	0	0	0	..
2.5	Other, not elsewhere classified	..	..	0	0	0	0	0	..
	Other mutual funds								
2	Financial assets	111 467	120 321	65 493	116 027	138 490	108 267	134 411	..
2.1	Currency and deposits	6 510	7 185	5 187	6 824	7 188	4 239	6 889	..
2.2	Securities other than shares, except financial derivatives	78 087	88 098	54 079	94 445	111 308	91 549	115 488	..
2.2.1	Short-term securities	16 208	14 012	8 029	16 557	16 535	20 309	22 366	..
2.2.2	Long-term securities	61 879	74 087	46 050	77 888	94 774	71 240	93 122	..
2.2.3	Securities issued by residents	69 482	80 790	51 194	90 356	105 541	87 637	109 698	..
2.2.4	Securities issued by non-residents	8 605	7 308	2 885	4 089	5 767	3 912	5 790	..
2.3	Loans	0	0	0	0	0	0	0	..
2.3.1	Short-term loans	0	0	0	0	0	0	0	..
2.3.2	Long-term loans	0	0	0	0	0	0	0	..
2.3.3	Loans granted to residents	0	0	0	0	0	0	0	..
2.3.4	Loans granted to non-residents	0	0	0	0	0	0	0	..
2.4	Shares and other equity	26 869	25 038	6 228	14 757	19 994	12 480	12 034	..
2.4.1	Shares issued by residents	16 410	16 332	4 152	10 817	14 623	8 431	7 446	..
2.4.2	Shares issued by non-residents	10 459	8 706	2 076	3 940	5 371	4 048	4 588	..
2.5	Other, not elsewhere classified	0	0	0	0	0	0	0	..

Table 2. Financial assets of investment funds *(cont.)*

Million ILS

		2006	2007	2008	2009	2010	2011	2012	2013
	Closed-end companies								
2	Financial assets	0	0	0	0	0	0	0	..
2.1	Currency and deposits	0	0	0	0	0	0	0	..
2.2	Securities other than shares, except financial derivatives	0	0	0	0	0	0	0	..
2.2.1	Short-term securities	0	0	0	0	0	0	0	..
2.2.2	Long-term securities	0	0	0	0	0	0	0	..
2.2.3	Securities issued by residents	0	0	0	0	0	0	0	..
2.2.4	Securities issued by non-residents	0	0	0	0	0	0	0	..
2.3	Loans	0	0	0	0	0	0	0	..
2.3.1	Short-term loans	0	0	0	0	0	0	0	..
2.3.2	Long-term loans	0	0	0	0	0	0	0	..
2.3.3	Loans granted to residents	0	0	0	0	0	0	0	..
2.3.4	Loans granted to non-residents	0	0	0	0	0	0	0	..
2.4	Shares and other equity	0	0	0	0	0	0	0	..
2.4.1	Shares issued by residents	0	0	0	0	0	0	0	..
2.4.2	Shares issued by non-residents	0	0	0	0	0	0	0	..
2.5	Other, not elsewhere classified	0	0	0	0	0	0	0	..

Note: Detailed metadata at: http://metalinks.oecd.org/instinv/20141203/f0b0
Information on data for Israel: http://oe.cd/israel-disclaimer

Table 3. Financial assets of insurance corporations and autonomous pension funds

Million ILS

		2006	2007	2008	2009	2010	2011	2012	2013
	Insurance corporations and autonomous pension funds								
2	Financial assets	396 069	410 117	440 387	539 651	601 509	625 820	708 642	..
2.1	Currency and deposits	32 632	30 709	32 897	46 123	61 595	60 232	79 208	..
2.2	Securities other than shares, except financial derivatives	278 546	279 110	315 246	374 564	401 705	420 114	458 485	..
2.2.1	Short-term securities	5 992	3 801	1 733	6 333	8 759	9 848	7 070	..
2.2.2	Long-term securities	272 553	275 309	313 513	368 232	392 946	410 266	451 415	..
2.2.3	Securities issued by residents	264 351	259 417	293 581	327 058	339 817	349 413	373 012	..
2.2.4	Securities issued by non-residents	14 194	19 693	21 664	47 506	61 887	70 700	85 474	..
2.3	Loans	13 243	13 602	12 910	16 427	18 843	24 815	32 272	..
2.3.1	Short-term loans	..	..	..	..	..	..	..	..
2.3.2	Long-term loans	..	..	..	..	..	..	..	..
2.3.3	Loans granted to residents	13 243	13 602	12 910	16 427	18 843	24 815	32 272	..
2.3.4	Loans granted to non-residents	0	0	0	0	0	0	0	..
2.4	Shares and other equity	37 002	43 317	26 308	48 608	62 353	55 558	67 792	..
2.4.1	Shares issued by residents	33 072	38 458	24 002	43 375	54 392	46 401	57 476	..
2.4.2	Shares issued by non-residents	3 929	4 859	2 306	5 233	7 961	9 157	10 317	..
2.5	Other, not elsewhere classified	34 647	43 379	53 027	53 929	57 014	65 101	70 884	..
	Insurance corporations								
2	Financial assets	194 909	214 346	209 009	258 765	290 766	302 010	339 642	..
2.1	Currency and deposits	23 248	22 153	21 522	22 041	22 201	24 361	25 111	..
2.2	Securities other than shares, except financial derivatives	103 165	113 438	119 489	152 572	170 934	175 929	200 223	..
2.2.1	Short-term securities	2 754	3 211	1 509	4 927	4 047	3 604	3 214	..
2.2.2	Long-term securities	100 411	110 227	117 979	147 646	166 887	172 325	197 009	..
2.2.3	Securities issued by residents	93 118	102 701	110 830	127 749	139 993	143 927	163 350	..
2.2.4	Securities issued by non-residents	10 047	10 736	8 658	24 823	30 941	32 002	36 872	..
2.3	Loans	10 442	11 270	10 692	12 598	13 503	16 885	19 832	..
2.3.1	Short-term loans	..	..	..	..	..	..	..	..
2.3.2	Long-term loans	..	..	..	..	..	..	..	..
2.3.3	Loans granted to residents	10 442	11 270	10 692	12 598	13 503	16 885	19 832	..
2.3.4	Loans granted to non-residents	0	0	0	0	0	0	0	..
2.4	Shares and other equity	26 478	30 326	17 206	30 170	38 975	34 799	41 640	..
2.4.1	Shares issued by residents	23 544	27 004	15 605	26 813	34 177	29 456	36 318	..
2.4.2	Shares issued by non-residents	2 934	3 321	1 601	3 357	4 798	5 343	5 322	..
2.5	Other, not elsewhere classified	31 576	37 160	40 100	41 384	45 154	50 037	52 837	..
	Life insurance corporations								
2	Financial assets	..	..	..	..	..	..	..	..
2.1	Currency and deposits	..	..	..	..	..	..	..	..
2.2	Securities other than shares, except financial derivatives	..	..	..	..	..	..	..	..
2.2.1	Short-term securities	..	..	..	..	..	..	..	..
2.2.2	Long-term securities	..	..	..	..	..	..	..	..
2.2.3	Securities issued by residents	..	..	..	..	..	..	..	..
2.2.4	Securities issued by non-residents	..	..	..	..	..	..	..	..
2.3	Loans	..	..	..	..	..	..	..	..
2.3.1	Short-term loans	..	..	..	..	..	..	..	..
2.3.2	Long-term loans	..	..	..	..	..	..	..	..
2.3.3	Loans granted to residents	..	..	..	..	..	..	..	..
2.3.4	Loans granted to non-residents	..	..	..	..	..	..	..	..
2.4	Shares and other equity	..	..	..	..	..	..	..	..
2.4.1	Shares issued by residents	..	..	..	..	..	..	..	..
2.4.2	Shares issued by non-residents	..	..	..	..	..	..	..	..
2.5	Other, not elsewhere classified	..	..	..	..	..	..	..	..
	Non-life insurance corporations								
2	Financial assets	..	..	..	..	..	..	..	..
2.1	Currency and deposits	..	..	..	..	..	..	..	..
2.2	Securities other than shares, except financial derivatives	..	..	..	..	..	..	..	..
2.2.1	Short-term securities	..	..	..	..	..	..	..	..
2.2.2	Long-term securities	..	..	..	..	..	..	..	..
2.2.3	Securities issued by residents	..	..	..	..	..	..	..	..
2.2.4	Securities issued by non-residents	..	..	..	..	..	..	..	..
2.3	Loans	..	..	..	..	..	..	..	..
2.3.1	Short-term loans	..	..	..	..	..	..	..	..
2.3.2	Long-term loans	..	..	..	..	..	..	..	..
2.3.3	Loans granted to residents	..	..	..	..	..	..	..	..
2.3.4	Loans granted to non-residents	..	..	..	..	..	..	..	..
2.4	Shares and other equity	..	..	..	..	..	..	..	..
2.4.1	Shares issued by residents	..	..	..	..	..	..	..	..
2.4.2	Shares issued by non-residents	..	..	..	..	..	..	..	..
2.5	Other, not elsewhere classified	..	..	..	..	..	..	..	..

Table 3. Financial assets of insurance corporations and autonomous pension funds *(cont.)*

Million ILS

		2006	2007	2008	2009	2010	2011	2012	2013
	Autonomous pension funds								
2	Financial assets	201 160	195 771	231 378	280 886	310 742	323 810	368 999	..
2.1	Currency and deposits	9 384	8 556	11 375	24 082	39 395	35 871	54 098	..
2.2	Securities other than shares, except financial derivatives	175 380	165 672	195 757	221 992	230 771	244 185	258 263	..
2.2.1	Short-term securities	3 239	590	223	1 406	4 712	6 243	3 857	..
2.2.2	Long-term securities	172 142	165 082	195 533	220 586	226 059	237 941	254 406	..
2.2.3	Securities issued by residents	171 234	156 715	182 751	199 309	199 824	205 486	209 661	..
2.2.4	Securities issued by non-residents	4 147	8 957	13 006	22 683	30 947	38 699	48 602	..
2.3	Loans	2 801	2 332	2 218	3 829	5 339	7 931	12 440	..
2.3.1	Short-term loans	..	..	..	..	..	..	..	..
2.3.2	Long-term loans	..	..	..	..	..	..	..	..
2.3.3	Loans granted to residents	2 801	2 332	2 218	3 829	5 339	7 931	12 440	..
2.3.4	Loans granted to non-residents	0	0	0	0	0	0	0	..
2.4	Shares and other equity	10 523	12 992	9 102	18 438	23 378	20 759	26 152	..
2.4.1	Shares issued by residents	9 528	11 453	8 397	16 562	20 214	16 945	21 158	..
2.4.2	Shares issued by non-residents	995	1 538	705	1 876	3 164	3 814	4 994	..
2.5	Other, not elsewhere classified	3 071	6 220	12 927	12 545	11 860	15 065	18 047	..

Note: Detailed metadata at: http://metalinks.oecd.org/instinv/20141203/f0b0
Information on data for Israel: http://oe.cd/israel-disclaimer

Table 4. Portfolio composition by type of investor

Percentage of total financial assets

Per cent

		2006	2007	2008	2009	2010	2011	2012	2013
	Investment funds								
2	Financial assets	100.0	100.0	100.0	100.0	100.0	100.0	100.0	..
2.1	Currency and deposits	5.8	6.0	23.6	10.5	9.5	12.1	13.8	..
2.2	Securities other than shares, except financial derivatives	70.1	73.2	70.0	78.5	77.7	79.2	79.1	..
2.2.1	Short-term securities	14.5	11.6	17.1	17.4	15.1	22.9	20.0	..
2.2.2	Long-term securities	55.5	61.6	52.9	61.1	62.6	56.3	59.1	..
2.2.3	Securities issued by residents	62.3	67.1	65.8	74.8	73.7	76.1	75.6	..
2.2.4	Securities issued by non-residents	7.7	6.1	4.2	3.7	4.0	3.1	3.5	..
2.3	Loans	0.0	0.0	0.0	0.0	0.0	0.0	0.0	..
2.3.1	Short-term loans	0.0	0.0	0.0	0.0	0.0	0.0	0.0	..
2.3.2	Long-term loans	0.0	0.0	0.0	0.0	0.0	0.0	0.0	..
2.3.3	Loans granted to residents	0.0	0.0	0.0	0.0	0.0	0.0	0.0	..
2.3.4	Loans granted to non-residents	0.0	0.0	0.0	0.0	0.0	0.0	0.0	..
2.4	Shares and other equity	24.1	20.8	6.3	11.1	12.8	8.8	7.1	..
2.4.1	Shares issued by residents	14.7	13.6	4.2	8.1	9.3	5.9	4.4	..
2.4.2	Shares issued by non-residents	9.4	7.2	2.1	3.0	3.4	2.8	2.7	..
2.5	Other, not elsewhere classified	0.0	0.0	0.0	0.0	0.0	0.0	0.0	..
	Insurance corporations								
2	Financial assets	100.0	100.0	100.0	100.0	100.0	100.0	100.0	..
2.1	Currency and deposits	11.9	10.3	10.3	8.5	7.6	8.1	7.4	..
2.2	Securities other than shares, except financial derivatives	52.9	52.9	57.2	59.0	58.8	58.3	59.0	..
2.2.1	Short-term securities	1.4	1.5	0.7	1.9	1.4	1.2	0.9	..
2.2.2	Long-term securities	51.5	51.4	56.4	57.1	57.4	57.1	58.0	..
2.2.3	Securities issued by residents	47.8	47.9	53.0	49.4	48.1	47.7	48.1	..
2.2.4	Securities issued by non-residents	5.2	5.0	4.1	9.6	10.6	10.6	10.9	..
2.3	Loans	5.4	5.3	5.1	4.9	4.6	5.6	5.8	..
2.3.1	Short-term loans	..	..	..	..	..	..	..	..
2.3.2	Long-term loans	..	..	..	..	..	..	..	..
2.3.3	Loans granted to residents	5.4	5.3	5.1	4.9	4.6	5.6	5.8	..
2.3.4	Loans granted to non-residents	0.0	0.0	0.0	0.0	0.0	0.0	0.0	..
2.4	Shares and other equity	13.6	14.1	8.2	11.7	13.4	11.5	12.3	..
2.4.1	Shares issued by residents	12.1	12.6	7.5	10.4	11.8	9.8	10.7	..
2.4.2	Shares issued by non-residents	1.5	1.5	0.8	1.3	1.7	1.8	1.6	..
2.5	Other, not elsewhere classified	16.2	17.3	19.2	16.0	15.5	16.6	15.6	..
	Autonomous pension funds								
2	Financial assets	100.0	100.0	100.0	100.0	100.0	100.0	100.0	..
2.1	Currency and deposits	4.7	4.4	4.9	8.6	12.7	11.1	14.7	..
2.2	Securities other than shares, except financial derivatives	87.2	84.6	84.6	79.0	74.3	75.4	70.0	..
2.2.1	Short-term securities	1.6	0.3	0.1	0.5	1.5	1.9	1.0	..
2.2.2	Long-term securities	85.6	84.3	84.5	78.5	72.7	73.5	68.9	..
2.2.3	Securities issued by residents	85.1	80.1	79.0	71.0	64.3	63.5	56.8	..
2.2.4	Securities issued by non-residents	2.1	4.6	5.6	8.1	10.0	12.0	13.2	..
2.3	Loans	1.4	1.2	1.0	1.4	1.7	2.4	3.4	..
2.3.1	Short-term loans	..	..	..	..	..	..	..	..
2.3.2	Long-term loans	..	..	..	..	..	..	..	..
2.3.3	Loans granted to residents	1.4	1.2	1.0	1.4	1.7	2.4	3.4	..
2.3.4	Loans granted to non-residents	0.0	0.0	0.0	0.0	0.0	0.0	0.0	..
2.4	Shares and other equity	5.2	6.6	3.9	6.6	7.5	6.4	7.1	..
2.4.1	Shares issued by residents	4.7	5.9	3.6	5.9	6.5	5.2	5.7	..
2.4.2	Shares issued by non-residents	0.5	0.8	0.3	0.7	1.0	1.2	1.4	..
2.5	Other, not elsewhere classified	1.5	3.2	5.6	4.5	3.8	4.7	4.9	..

Note: Detailed metadata at: http://metalinks.oecd.org/instinv/20141203/f729
Information on data for Israel: http://oe.cd/israel-disclaimer

Table 1. Financial assets of institutional investors, 2012

Million EUR (1999 ITL euro)

		Investment funds				
		Total	Open-end companies (mutual funds)			Closed-end companies
			Total	Money market funds	Other mutual funds	Total
2	Financial assets	147 677	141 120	9 464	131 656	6 557
2.1	Currency and deposits	17 204	14 764	1 347	13 416	2 440
2.2	Securities other than shares, except financial derivatives	86 372	85 826	7 770	78 055	546
2.2.1	Short-term securities	13 792	13 514	28	13 486	278
2.2.2	Long-term securities	72 580	72 312	7 742	64 570	268
2.2.3	Securities issued by residents	53 405	52 936	6 791	46 145	469
2.2.4	Securities issued by non-residents	32 967	32 890	979	31 910	77
2.3	Loans	0	0	0	0	0
2.3.1	Short-term loans	..	..	..	..	..
2.3.2	Long-term loans	..	..	..	..	..
2.3.3	Loans granted to residents	..	..	..	..	..
2.3.4	Loans granted to non-residents	..	..	..	..	..
2.4	Shares and other equity	43 480	40 220	36	40 184	3 260
2.4.1	Shares issued by residents	6 590	4 791	0	4 791	1 798
2.4.2	Shares issued by non-residents	36 891	35 429	36	35 393	1 462
2.5	Other, not elsewhere classified	621	310	310	0	310

		Insurance corporations and autonomous pension funds				
		Total	Insurance corporations			Autonomous pension funds
			Total	Life insurance corporations	Non-life insurance corporations	Total
2	Financial assets	581 879	548 051	469 602	78 449	33 828
2.1	Currency and deposits	32 457	28 661	22 459	6 202	3 795
2.2	Securities other than shares, except financial derivatives	375 684	363 603	326 057	37 546	12 082
2.2.1	Short-term securities	5 760	4 887	4 382	505	873
2.2.2	Long-term securities	369 924	358 716	321 675	37 041	11 208
2.2.3	Securities issued by residents	260 578	248 497	222 837	25 660	12 082
2.2.4	Securities issued by non-residents	115 106	115 106	103 220	11 886	0
2.3	Loans	13 504	13 504	12 060	1 444	0
2.3.1	Short-term loans	3 290	3 290	2 938	352	..
2.3.2	Long-term loans	10 214	10 214	9 122	1 092	..
2.3.3	Loans granted to residents	10 214	10 214	9 122	1 092	..
2.3.4	Loans granted to non-residents	3 290	3 290	2 938	352	..
2.4	Shares and other equity	155 997	138 046	107 057	30 988	17 951
2.4.1	Shares issued by residents	59 123	41 172	31 930	9 242	17 951
2.4.2	Shares issued by non-residents	96 874	96 874	75 128	21 746	0
2.5	Other, not elsewhere classified	4 237	4 237	1 969	2 269	0

Note: Detailed metadata at: http://metalinks.oecd.org/instinv/20141203/37af

Table 2. Financial assets of investment funds

Million EUR (1999 ITL euro)

		2006	2007	2008	2009	2010	2011	2012	2013
	Investment funds								
2	Financial assets	299 911	245 615	208 903	211 638	192 586	153 408	147 677	..
2.1	Currency and deposits	15 155	9 448	18 272	21 320	14 675	16 044	17 204	..
2.2	Securities other than shares, except financial derivatives	200 939	177 434	134 153	134 710	119 357	91 612	86 372	..
2.2.1	Short-term securities	4 646	4 695	2 135	7 843	5 841	6 299	13 792	..
2.2.2	Long-term securities	196 293	172 739	132 018	126 867	113 516	85 314	72 580	..
2.2.3	Securities issued by residents	114 943	107 148	84 898	84 529	80 368	58 323	53 405	..
2.2.4	Securities issued by non-residents	85 996	70 286	49 256	50 182	38 989	33 289	32 967	..
2.3	Loans	0	0	0	0	0	0	0	..
2.3.1	Short-term loans	..	..	..	..	..	..	..	..
2.3.2	Long-term loans	..	..	..	..	..	..	..	..
2.3.3	Loans granted to residents	..	..	..	..	..	..	..	..
2.3.4	Loans granted to non-residents	..	..	..	..	..	..	..	..
2.4	Shares and other equity	82 409	57 312	53 182	54 552	57 161	44 946	43 480	..
2.4.1	Shares issued by residents	19 275	13 342	10 373	10 115	8 594	6 796	6 590	..
2.4.2	Shares issued by non-residents	63 134	43 970	42 809	44 437	48 568	38 150	36 891	..
2.5	Other, not elsewhere classified	1 408	1 421	3 296	1 057	1 393	806	621	..
	Open-end companies (mutual funds)								
2	Financial assets	299 911	245 615	201 728	204 112	185 224	146 484	141 120	..
2.1	Currency and deposits	15 155	9 448	16 151	18 339	12 023	13 099	14 764	..
2.2	Securities other than shares, except financial derivatives	200 939	177 434	133 506	134 132	118 559	91 127	85 826	..
2.2.1	Short-term securities	4 646	4 695	2 077	7 747	5 507	6 237	13 514	..
2.2.2	Long-term securities	196 293	172 739	131 429	126 385	113 052	84 890	72 312	..
2.2.3	Securities issued by residents	114 943	107 148	84 449	84 151	79 801	58 068	52 936	..
2.2.4	Securities issued by non-residents	85 996	70 286	49 057	49 981	38 758	33 059	32 890	..
2.3	Loans	0	0	0	0	0	0	0	..
2.3.1	Short-term loans	..	..	..	..	..	..	..	..
2.3.2	Long-term loans	..	..	..	..	..	..	..	..
2.3.3	Loans granted to residents	..	..	..	..	..	..	..	..
2.3.4	Loans granted to non-residents	..	..	..	..	..	..	..	..
2.4	Shares and other equity	82 409	57 312	50 422	51 113	53 946	41 854	40 220	..
2.4.1	Shares issued by residents	19 275	13 342	8 927	8 339	6 701	4 783	4 791	..
2.4.2	Shares issued by non-residents	63 134	43 970	41 496	42 774	47 245	37 072	35 429	..
2.5	Other, not elsewhere classified	1 408	1 421	1 648	528	696	403	310	..
	Money market funds								
2	Financial assets	77 259	75 462	59 143	55 749	39 360	27 941	9 464	..
2.1	Currency and deposits	11 533	6 909	7 181	9 648	2 666	2 925	1 347	..
2.2	Securities other than shares, except financial derivatives	64 292	67 082	50 183	45 393	35 878	24 485	7 770	..
2.2.1	Short-term securities	30	0	0	0	0	2	28	..
2.2.2	Long-term securities	64 262	67 082	50 183	45 393	35 878	24 483	7 742	..
2.2.3	Securities issued by residents	51 855	54 124	41 961	37 275	32 518	21 640	6 791	..
2.2.4	Securities issued by non-residents	12 437	12 958	8 222	8 118	3 359	2 845	979	..
2.3	Loans	0	0	0	0	0	0	0	..
2.3.1	Short-term loans	..	..	..	..	..	..	..	..
2.3.2	Long-term loans	..	..	..	..	..	..	..	..
2.3.3	Loans granted to residents	..	..	..	..	..	..	..	..
2.3.4	Loans granted to non-residents	..	..	..	..	..	..	..	..
2.4	Shares and other equity	26	50	131	180	120	127	36	..
2.4.1	Shares issued by residents	0	0	0	0	0	29	0	..
2.4.2	Shares issued by non-residents	26	50	131	180	120	98	36	..
2.5	Other, not elsewhere classified	1 408	1 421	1 648	528	696	403	310	..
	Other mutual funds								
2	Financial assets	222 652	170 153	142 585	148 363	145 864	118 543	131 656	..
2.1	Currency and deposits	3 622	2 539	8 971	8 691	9 356	10 174	13 416	..
2.2	Securities other than shares, except financial derivatives	136 647	110 352	83 323	88 739	82 681	66 642	78 055	..
2.2.1	Short-term securities	4 616	4 695	2 077	7 747	5 507	6 235	13 486	..
2.2.2	Long-term securities	132 031	105 657	81 246	80 992	77 174	60 407	64 570	..
2.2.3	Securities issued by residents	63 088	53 024	42 488	46 876	47 282	36 428	46 145	..
2.2.4	Securities issued by non-residents	73 559	57 328	40 835	41 863	35 399	30 215	31 910	..
2.3	Loans	0	0	0	0	0	0	0	..
2.3.1	Short-term loans	..	..	..	..	..	..	..	..
2.3.2	Long-term loans	..	..	..	..	..	..	..	..
2.3.3	Loans granted to residents	..	..	..	..	..	..	..	..
2.3.4	Loans granted to non-residents	..	..	..	..	..	..	..	..
2.4	Shares and other equity	82 383	57 262	50 291	50 933	53 826	41 727	40 184	..
2.4.1	Shares issued by residents	19 275	13 342	8 927	8 339	6 701	4 753	4 791	..
2.4.2	Shares issued by non-residents	63 108	43 920	41 364	42 594	47 125	36 974	35 393	..
2.5	Other, not elsewhere classified	0	0	0	0	0	0	0	..

Table 2. Financial assets of investment funds *(cont.)*

Million EUR (1999 ITL euro)

		2006	2007	2008	2009	2010	2011	2012	2013
	Closed-end companies								
2	Financial assets	..	..	7 175	7 526	7 362	6 924	6 557	..
2.1	Currency and deposits	..	..	2 121	2 981	2 652	2 944	2 440	..
2.2	Securities other than shares, except financial derivatives	..	..	647	579	798	485	546	..
2.2.1	Short-term securities	..	..	58	96	334	61	278	..
2.2.2	Long-term securities	..	..	589	482	464	424	268	..
2.2.3	Securities issued by residents	..	..	449	378	568	256	469	..
2.2.4	Securities issued by non-residents	..	..	198	201	230	230	77	..
2.3	Loans	..	..	0	0	0	0	0	..
2.3.1	Short-term loans	..	..	..	..	..	..	..	..
2.3.2	Long-term loans	..	..	..	..	..	..	..	..
2.3.3	Loans granted to residents	..	..	..	..	..	..	..	..
2.3.4	Loans granted to non-residents	..	..	..	..	..	..	..	..
2.4	Shares and other equity	..	..	2 760	3 438	3 215	3 092	3 260	..
2.4.1	Shares issued by residents	..	..	1 447	1 775	1 893	2 013	1 798	..
2.4.2	Shares issued by non-residents	..	..	1 313	1 663	1 322	1 079	1 462	..
2.5	Other, not elsewhere classified	..	..	1 648	528	696	403	310	..

Note: Detailed metadata at: http://metalinks.oecd.org/instinv/20141203/37af

Table 3. Financial assets of insurance corporations and autonomous pension funds

Million EUR (1999 ITL euro)

		2006	2007	2008	2009	2010	2011	2012	2013
	Insurance corporations and autonomous pension funds								
2	Financial assets	565 181	530 120	503 806	563 680	549 826	540 461	581 879	..
2.1	Currency and deposits	23 507	23 022	26 959	24 484	23 583	25 413	32 457	..
2.2	Securities other than shares, except financial derivatives	329 453	323 809	316 736	363 809	355 990	350 855	375 684	..
2.2.1	Short-term securities	3 548	2 379	3 167	3 812	4 406	6 294	5 760	..
2.2.2	Long-term securities	325 906	321 430	313 569	359 996	351 583	344 560	369 924	..
2.2.3	Securities issued by residents	191 047	184 666	173 005	204 993	215 087	225 680	260 578	..
2.2.4	Securities issued by non-residents	138 406	139 143	143 731	158 816	140 903	125 174	115 106	..
2.3	Loans	9 658	10 397	13 104	13 500	13 416	13 179	13 504	..
2.3.1	Short-term loans	0	0	2 665	2 881	2 609	3 018	3 290	..
2.3.2	Long-term loans	9 658	10 397	10 439	10 619	10 807	10 161	10 214	..
2.3.3	Loans granted to residents	9 658	10 397	10 439	10 619	10 807	10 161	10 214	..
2.3.4	Loans granted to non-residents	0	0	2 665	2 881	2 609	3 018	3 290	..
2.4	Shares and other equity	197 961	169 556	143 234	158 102	152 728	146 904	155 997	..
2.4.1	Shares issued by residents	99 106	64 104	79 098	78 005	55 590	55 434	59 123	..
2.4.2	Shares issued by non-residents	98 855	105 452	64 136	80 097	97 137	91 470	96 874	..
2.5	Other, not elsewhere classified	4 602	3 337	3 773	3 785	4 108	4 110	4 237	..
	Insurance corporations								
2	Financial assets	545 917	507 202	482 603	537 768	519 614	509 520	548 051	..
2.1	Currency and deposits	20 884	19 524	23 086	21 368	19 036	21 677	28 661	..
2.2	Securities other than shares, except financial derivatives	322 604	315 320	308 563	353 844	345 878	340 131	363 603	..
2.2.1	Short-term securities	3 240	2 020	2 835	3 360	3 768	5 091	4 887	..
2.2.2	Long-term securities	319 364	313 299	305 728	350 485	342 110	335 040	358 716	..
2.2.3	Securities issued by residents	184 198	176 177	164 832	195 029	204 975	214 956	248 497	..
2.2.4	Securities issued by non-residents	138 406	139 143	143 731	158 816	140 903	125 174	115 106	..
2.3	Loans	9 658	10 397	13 104	13 500	13 416	13 179	13 504	..
2.3.1	Short-term loans	0	0	2 665	2 881	2 609	3 018	3 290	..
2.3.2	Long-term loans	9 658	10 397	10 439	10 619	10 807	10 161	10 214	..
2.3.3	Loans granted to residents	9 658	10 397	10 439	10 619	10 807	10 161	10 214	..
2.3.4	Loans granted to non-residents	0	0	2 665	2 881	2 609	3 018	3 290	..
2.4	Shares and other equity	188 169	158 624	134 077	145 271	137 176	130 423	138 046	..
2.4.1	Shares issued by residents	89 314	53 172	69 941	65 174	40 038	38 953	41 172	..
2.4.2	Shares issued by non-residents	98 855	105 452	64 136	80 097	97 137	91 470	96 874	..
2.5	Other, not elsewhere classified	4 602	3 337	3 773	3 785	4 108	4 110	4 237	..
	Life insurance corporations								
2	Financial assets	445 168	418 161	397 948	449 823	443 430	435 162	469 602	..
2.1	Currency and deposits	13 140	13 295	18 562	15 718	13 677	16 340	22 459	..
2.2	Securities other than shares, except financial derivatives	280 538	274 214	269 214	312 616	310 351	305 196	326 057	..
2.2.1	Short-term securities	2 817	1 757	2 474	2 968	3 381	4 568	4 382	..
2.2.2	Long-term securities	277 721	272 457	266 741	309 648	306 970	300 628	321 675	..
2.2.3	Securities issued by residents	160 179	153 210	143 812	172 305	183 921	192 878	222 837	..
2.2.4	Securities issued by non-residents	120 359	121 004	125 402	140 311	126 430	112 318	103 220	..
2.3	Loans	8 396	9 364	11 815	12 239	12 227	11 743	12 060	..
2.3.1	Short-term loans	0	0	2 403	2 612	2 378	2 689	2 938	..
2.3.2	Long-term loans	8 396	9 364	9 412	9 627	9 850	9 054	9 122	..
2.3.3	Loans granted to residents	8 396	9 364	9 412	9 627	9 850	9 054	9 122	..
2.3.4	Loans granted to non-residents	0	0	2 403	2 612	2 378	2 689	2 938	..
2.4	Shares and other equity	140 643	119 696	96 543	107 270	104 868	99 519	107 057	..
2.4.1	Shares issued by residents	66 756	40 123	50 361	48 126	30 609	29 723	31 930	..
2.4.2	Shares issued by non-residents	73 887	79 573	46 182	59 145	74 259	69 796	75 128	..
2.5	Other, not elsewhere classified	2 450	1 592	1 814	1 979	2 307	2 364	1 969	..
	Non-life insurance corporations								
2	Financial assets	100 749	89 040	84 655	87 945	76 185	74 358	78 449	..
2.1	Currency and deposits	7 744	6 229	4 524	5 650	5 359	5 337	6 202	..
2.2	Securities other than shares, except financial derivatives	42 066	41 105	39 349	41 228	35 527	34 935	37 546	..
2.2.1	Short-term securities	422	263	362	391	387	523	505	..
2.2.2	Long-term securities	41 643	40 842	38 987	40 837	35 140	34 412	37 041	..
2.2.3	Securities issued by residents	24 018	22 967	21 020	22 724	21 054	22 078	25 660	..
2.2.4	Securities issued by non-residents	18 047	18 139	18 329	18 504	14 473	12 857	11 886	..
2.3	Loans	1 262	1 033	1 289	1 260	1 189	1 436	1 444	..
2.3.1	Short-term loans	0	0	262	269	231	329	352	..
2.3.2	Long-term loans	1 262	1 033	1 027	991	958	1 107	1 092	..
2.3.3	Loans granted to residents	1 262	1 033	1 027	991	958	1 107	1 092	..
2.3.4	Loans granted to non-residents	0	0	262	269	231	329	352	..
2.4	Shares and other equity	47 526	38 928	37 534	38 000	32 308	30 904	30 988	..
2.4.1	Shares issued by residents	22 558	13 049	19 580	17 049	9 430	9 230	9 242	..
2.4.2	Shares issued by non-residents	24 968	25 879	17 955	20 952	22 878	21 674	21 746	..
2.5	Other, not elsewhere classified	2 152	1 745	1 959	1 806	1 802	1 747	2 269	..

Table 3. Financial assets of insurance corporations and autonomous pension funds *(cont.)*

Million EUR (1999 ITL euro)

		2006	2007	2008	2009	2010	2011	2012	2013
	Autonomous pension funds								
2	Financial assets	19 265	22 919	21 202	25 911	30 211	30 941	33 828	..
2.1	Currency and deposits	2 623	3 498	3 872	3 116	4 547	3 737	3 795	..
2.2	Securities other than shares, except financial derivatives	6 850	8 490	8 173	9 964	10 112	10 724	12 082	..
2.2.1	Short-term securities	308	359	332	453	639	1 203	873	..
2.2.2	Long-term securities	6 542	8 131	7 841	9 512	9 473	9 521	11 208	..
2.2.3	Securities issued by residents	6 849	8 490	8 173	9 964	10 112	10 724	12 082	..
2.2.4	Securities issued by non-residents	0	0	0	0	0	0	0	..
2.3	Loans	0	0	0	0	0	0	0	..
2.3.1	Short-term loans	..	..	..	..	..	..	..	..
2.3.2	Long-term loans	..	..	..	..	..	..	..	..
2.3.3	Loans granted to residents	..	..	..	..	..	..	..	..
2.3.4	Loans granted to non-residents	..	..	..	..	..	..	..	..
2.4	Shares and other equity	9 792	10 932	9 157	12 831	15 552	16 481	17 951	..
2.4.1	Shares issued by residents	9 792	10 932	9 157	12 831	15 552	16 481	17 951	..
2.4.2	Shares issued by non-residents	0	0	0	0	0	0	0	..
2.5	Other, not elsewhere classified	0	0	0	0	0	0	0	..

Note: Detailed metadata at: http://metalinks.oecd.org/instinv/20141203/37af

Table 4. Portfolio composition by type of investor

Percentage of total financial assets

Per cent

		2006	2007	2008	2009	2010	2011	2012	2013
	Investment funds								
2	Financial assets	100.0	100.0	100.0	100.0	100.0	100.0	100.0	..
2.1	Currency and deposits	5.1	3.8	8.7	10.1	7.6	10.5	11.6	..
2.2	Securities other than shares, except financial derivatives	67.0	72.2	64.2	63.7	62.0	59.7	58.5	..
2.2.1	Short-term securities	1.5	1.9	1.0	3.7	3.0	4.1	9.3	..
2.2.2	Long-term securities	65.5	70.3	63.2	59.9	58.9	55.6	49.1	..
2.2.3	Securities issued by residents	38.3	43.6	40.6	39.9	41.7	38.0	36.2	..
2.2.4	Securities issued by non-residents	28.7	28.6	23.6	23.7	20.2	21.7	22.3	..
2.3	Loans	0.0	0.0	0.0	0.0	0.0	0.0	0.0	..
2.3.1	Short-term loans	..	..	..	..	..	..	..	..
2.3.2	Long-term loans	..	..	..	..	..	..	..	..
2.3.3	Loans granted to residents	..	..	..	..	..	..	..	..
2.3.4	Loans granted to non-residents	..	..	..	..	..	..	..	..
2.4	Shares and other equity	27.5	23.3	25.5	25.8	29.7	29.3	29.4	..
2.4.1	Shares issued by residents	6.4	5.4	5.0	4.8	4.5	4.4	4.5	..
2.4.2	Shares issued by non-residents	21.1	17.9	20.5	21.0	25.2	24.9	25.0	..
2.5	Other, not elsewhere classified	0.5	0.6	1.6	0.5	0.7	0.5	0.4	..
	Insurance corporations								
2	Financial assets	100.0	100.0	100.0	100.0	100.0	100.0	100.0	..
2.1	Currency and deposits	3.8	3.8	4.8	4.0	3.7	4.3	5.2	..
2.2	Securities other than shares, except financial derivatives	59.1	62.2	63.9	65.8	66.6	66.8	66.3	..
2.2.1	Short-term securities	0.6	0.4	0.6	0.6	0.7	1.0	0.9	..
2.2.2	Long-term securities	58.5	61.8	63.3	65.2	65.8	65.8	65.5	..
2.2.3	Securities issued by residents	33.7	34.7	34.2	36.3	39.4	42.2	45.3	..
2.2.4	Securities issued by non-residents	25.4	27.4	29.8	29.5	27.1	24.6	21.0	..
2.3	Loans	1.8	2.0	2.7	2.5	2.6	2.6	2.5	..
2.3.1	Short-term loans	0.0	0.0	0.6	0.5	0.5	0.6	0.6	..
2.3.2	Long-term loans	1.8	2.0	2.2	2.0	2.1	2.0	1.9	..
2.3.3	Loans granted to residents	1.8	2.0	2.2	2.0	2.1	2.0	1.9	..
2.3.4	Loans granted to non-residents	0.0	0.0	0.6	0.5	0.5	0.6	0.6	..
2.4	Shares and other equity	34.5	31.3	27.8	27.0	26.4	25.6	25.2	..
2.4.1	Shares issued by residents	16.4	10.5	14.5	12.1	7.7	7.6	7.5	..
2.4.2	Shares issued by non-residents	18.1	20.8	13.3	14.9	18.7	18.0	17.7	..
2.5	Other, not elsewhere classified	0.8	0.7	0.8	0.7	0.8	0.8	0.8	..
	Autonomous pension funds								
2	Financial assets	100.0	100.0	100.0	100.0	100.0	100.0	100.0	..
2.1	Currency and deposits	13.6	15.3	18.3	12.0	15.1	12.1	11.2	..
2.2	Securities other than shares, except financial derivatives	35.6	37.0	38.5	38.5	33.5	34.7	35.7	..
2.2.1	Short-term securities	1.6	1.6	1.6	1.7	2.1	3.9	2.6	..
2.2.2	Long-term securities	34.0	35.5	37.0	36.7	31.4	30.8	33.1	..
2.2.3	Securities issued by residents	35.6	37.0	38.5	38.5	33.5	34.7	35.7	..
2.2.4	Securities issued by non-residents	0.0	0.0	0.0	0.0	0.0	0.0	0.0	..
2.3	Loans	0.0	0.0	0.0	0.0	0.0	0.0	0.0	..
2.3.1	Short-term loans	..	..	..	..	..	..	..	..
2.3.2	Long-term loans	..	..	..	..	..	..	..	..
2.3.3	Loans granted to residents	..	..	..	..	..	..	..	..
2.3.4	Loans granted to non-residents	..	..	..	..	..	..	..	..
2.4	Shares and other equity	50.8	47.7	43.2	49.5	51.5	53.3	53.1	..
2.4.1	Shares issued by residents	50.8	47.7	43.2	49.5	51.5	53.3	53.1	..
2.4.2	Shares issued by non-residents	0.0	0.0	0.0	0.0	0.0	0.0	0.0	..
2.5	Other, not elsewhere classified	0.0	0.0	0.0	0.0	0.0	0.0	0.0	..

Note: Detailed metadata at: http://metalinks.oecd.org/instinv/20141203/f729

Table 1. Financial assets of institutional investors, 2012

Billion JPY

		Total	Investment funds: Open-end companies (mutual funds): Total	Open-end companies (mutual funds): Money market funds	Open-end companies (mutual funds): Other mutual funds	Closed-end companies: Total
2	Financial assets	332 614	..	..	..	..
2.1	Currency and deposits	11 095	..	..	..	..
2.2	Securities other than shares, except financial derivatives	49 727	..	..	..	..
2.2.1	Short-term securities	..	..	..	..	..
2.2.2	Long-term securities	..	..	..	..	..
2.2.3	Securities issued by residents	..	..	..	..	..
2.2.4	Securities issued by non-residents	..	..	..	..	..
2.3	Loans	141 098	..	..	..	..
2.3.1	Short-term loans	..	..	..	..	..
2.3.2	Long-term loans	..	..	..	..	..
2.3.3	Loans granted to residents	..	..	..	..	..
2.3.4	Loans granted to non-residents	..	..	..	..	..
2.4	Shares and other equity	38 208	..	..	..	..
2.4.1	Shares issued by residents	..	..	..	..	..
2.4.2	Shares issued by non-residents	..	..	..	..	..
2.5	Other, not elsewhere classified	92 486	..	..	..	..

		Insurance corporations and autonomous pension funds: Total	Insurance corporations: Total	Insurance corporations: Life insurance corporations	Insurance corporations: Non-life insurance corporations	Autonomous pension funds: Total
2	Financial assets	541 157	416 380	386 433	29 948	124 777
2.1	Currency and deposits	11 984	5 066	4 135	930	6 918
2.2	Securities other than shares, except financial derivatives	314 152	269 398	259 872	9 527	44 753
2.2.1	Short-term securities	..	..	..	..	..
2.2.2	Long-term securities	..	..	..	..	..
2.2.3	Securities issued by residents	..	..	..	..	..
2.2.4	Securities issued by non-residents	..	..	..	..	..
2.3	Loans	53 149	50 470	47 874	2 596	2 679
2.3.1	Short-term loans	..	..	..	..	..
2.3.2	Long-term loans	..	..	..	..	..
2.3.3	Loans granted to residents	..	..	..	..	..
2.3.4	Loans granted to non-residents	..	..	..	..	..
2.4	Shares and other equity	41 387	27 710	17 495	10 214	13 677
2.4.1	Shares issued by residents	..	..	..	..	..
2.4.2	Shares issued by non-residents	..	..	..	..	..
2.5	Other, not elsewhere classified	120 486	63 737	57 057	6 680	56 749

Note: Detailed metadata at: http://metalinks.oecd.org/instinv/20141203/8acc

Table 2. Financial assets of investment funds

Billion JPY

		2006	2007	2008	2009	2010	2011	2012	2013
	Investment funds								
2	Financial assets	368 773	373 833	296 665	313 023	309 051	311 349	332 614	..
2.1	Currency and deposits	8 872	9 166	9 265	9 391	12 936	10 492	11 095	..
2.2	Securities other than shares, except financial derivatives	35 472	51 911	47 054	51 381	50 112	47 761	49 727	..
2.2.1	Short-term securities	..	..	..	..	..	..	..	..
2.2.2	Long-term securities	..	..	..	..	..	..	..	..
2.2.3	Securities issued by residents	..	..	..	..	..	..	..	..
2.2.4	Securities issued by non-residents	..	..	..	..	..	..	..	..
2.3	Loans	187 932	189 244	147 144	146 621	135 676	140 346	141 098	..
2.3.1	Short-term loans	..	..	..	..	..	..	..	..
2.3.2	Long-term loans	..	..	..	..	..	..	..	..
2.3.3	Loans granted to residents	..	..	..	..	..	..	..	..
2.3.4	Loans granted to non-residents	..	..	..	..	..	..	..	..
2.4	Shares and other equity	57 652	38 323	25 064	32 048	30 428	30 811	38 208	..
2.4.1	Shares issued by residents	..	..	..	..	..	..	..	..
2.4.2	Shares issued by non-residents	..	..	..	..	..	..	..	..
2.5	Other, not elsewhere classified	78 844	85 189	68 137	73 582	79 899	81 939	92 486	..
	Open-end companies (mutual funds)								
2	Financial assets	..	..	..	..	..	..	..	..
2.1	Currency and deposits	..	..	..	..	..	..	..	..
2.2	Securities other than shares, except financial derivatives	..	..	..	..	..	..	..	..
2.2.1	Short-term securities	..	..	..	..	..	..	..	..
2.2.2	Long-term securities	..	..	..	..	..	..	..	..
2.2.3	Securities issued by residents	..	..	..	..	..	..	..	..
2.2.4	Securities issued by non-residents	..	..	..	..	..	..	..	..
2.3	Loans	..	..	..	..	..	..	..	..
2.3.1	Short-term loans	..	..	..	..	..	..	..	..
2.3.2	Long-term loans	..	..	..	..	..	..	..	..
2.3.3	Loans granted to residents	..	..	..	..	..	..	..	..
2.3.4	Loans granted to non-residents	..	..	..	..	..	..	..	..
2.4	Shares and other equity	..	..	..	..	..	..	..	..
2.4.1	Shares issued by residents	..	..	..	..	..	..	..	..
2.4.2	Shares issued by non-residents	..	..	..	..	..	..	..	..
2.5	Other, not elsewhere classified	..	..	..	..	..	..	..	..
	Money market funds								
2	Financial assets	..	..	..	..	..	..	..	..
2.1	Currency and deposits	..	..	..	..	..	..	..	..
2.2	Securities other than shares, except financial derivatives	..	..	..	..	..	..	..	..
2.2.1	Short-term securities	..	..	..	..	..	..	..	..
2.2.2	Long-term securities	..	..	..	..	..	..	..	..
2.2.3	Securities issued by residents	..	..	..	..	..	..	..	..
2.2.4	Securities issued by non-residents	..	..	..	..	..	..	..	..
2.3	Loans	..	..	..	..	..	..	..	..
2.3.1	Short-term loans	..	..	..	..	..	..	..	..
2.3.2	Long-term loans	..	..	..	..	..	..	..	..
2.3.3	Loans granted to residents	..	..	..	..	..	..	..	..
2.3.4	Loans granted to non-residents	..	..	..	..	..	..	..	..
2.4	Shares and other equity	..	..	..	..	..	..	..	..
2.4.1	Shares issued by residents	..	..	..	..	..	..	..	..
2.4.2	Shares issued by non-residents	..	..	..	..	..	..	..	..
2.5	Other, not elsewhere classified	..	..	..	..	..	..	..	..
	Other mutual funds								
2	Financial assets	..	..	..	..	..	..	..	..
2.1	Currency and deposits	..	..	..	..	..	..	..	..
2.2	Securities other than shares, except financial derivatives	..	..	..	..	..	..	..	..
2.2.1	Short-term securities	..	..	..	..	..	..	..	..
2.2.2	Long-term securities	..	..	..	..	..	..	..	..
2.2.3	Securities issued by residents	..	..	..	..	..	..	..	..
2.2.4	Securities issued by non-residents	..	..	..	..	..	..	..	..
2.3	Loans	..	..	..	..	..	..	..	..
2.3.1	Short-term loans	..	..	..	..	..	..	..	..
2.3.2	Long-term loans	..	..	..	..	..	..	..	..
2.3.3	Loans granted to residents	..	..	..	..	..	..	..	..
2.3.4	Loans granted to non-residents	..	..	..	..	..	..	..	..
2.4	Shares and other equity	..	..	..	..	..	..	..	..
2.4.1	Shares issued by residents	..	..	..	..	..	..	..	..
2.4.2	Shares issued by non-residents	..	..	..	..	..	..	..	..
2.5	Other, not elsewhere classified	..	..	..	..	..	..	..	..

Table 2. Financial assets of investment funds *(cont.)*

Billion JPY

		2006	2007	2008	2009	2010	2011	2012	2013
	Closed-end companies								
2	Financial assets	..	..	..	..	..	..	..	..
2.1	Currency and deposits	..	..	..	..	..	..	..	..
2.2	Securities other than shares, except financial derivatives	..	..	..	..	..	..	..	..
2.2.1	Short-term securities	..	..	..	..	..	..	..	..
2.2.2	Long-term securities	..	..	..	..	..	..	..	..
2.2.3	Securities issued by residents	..	..	..	..	..	..	..	..
2.2.4	Securities issued by non-residents	..	..	..	..	..	..	..	..
2.3	Loans	..	..	..	..	..	..	..	..
2.3.1	Short-term loans	..	..	..	..	..	..	..	..
2.3.2	Long-term loans	..	..	..	..	..	..	..	..
2.3.3	Loans granted to residents	..	..	..	..	..	..	..	..
2.3.4	Loans granted to non-residents	..	..	..	..	..	..	..	..
2.4	Shares and other equity	..	..	..	..	..	..	..	..
2.4.1	Shares issued by residents	..	..	..	..	..	..	..	..
2.4.2	Shares issued by non-residents	..	..	..	..	..	..	..	..
2.5	Other, not elsewhere classified	..	..	..	..	..	..	..	..

Note: Detailed metadata at: http://metalinks.oecd.org/instinv/20141203/8acc

Table 3. Financial assets of insurance corporations and autonomous pension funds

Billion JPY

		2006	2007	2008	2009	2010	2011	2012	2013
	Insurance corporations and autonomous pension funds								
2	Financial assets	516 183	497 155	470 485	480 567	492 044	503 168	541 157	..
2.1	Currency and deposits	13 129	14 142	12 309	11 711	12 882	11 195	11 984	..
2.2	Securities other than shares, except financial derivatives	248 190	253 550	249 393	258 177	273 891	291 921	314 152	..
2.2.1	Short-term securities	..	..	..	..	..	..	..	..
2.2.2	Long-term securities	..	..	..	..	..	..	..	..
2.2.3	Securities issued by residents	..	..	..	..	..	..	..	..
2.2.4	Securities issued by non-residents	..	..	..	..	..	..	..	..
2.3	Loans	71 199	69 061	64 650	58 832	56 282	54 225	53 149	..
2.3.1	Short-term loans	..	..	..	..	..	..	..	..
2.3.2	Long-term loans	..	..	..	..	..	..	..	..
2.3.3	Loans granted to residents	..	..	..	..	..	..	..	..
2.3.4	Loans granted to non-residents	..	..	..	..	..	..	..	..
2.4	Shares and other equity	77 043	51 109	31 493	41 028	38 175	36 046	41 387	..
2.4.1	Shares issued by residents	..	..	..	..	..	..	..	..
2.4.2	Shares issued by non-residents	..	..	..	..	..	..	..	..
2.5	Other, not elsewhere classified	106 622	109 295	112 640	110 818	110 814	109 783	120 486	..
	Insurance corporations								
2	Financial assets	387 538	375 282	357 047	364 083	377 863	388 348	416 380	..
2.1	Currency and deposits	5 706	6 552	6 467	6 419	7 166	4 962	5 066	..
2.2	Securities other than shares, except financial derivatives	208 890	212 720	212 899	218 282	236 212	251 279	269 398	..
2.2.1	Short-term securities	..	..	..	..	..	..	..	..
2.2.2	Long-term securities	..	..	..	..	..	..	..	..
2.2.3	Securities issued by residents	..	..	..	..	..	..	..	..
2.2.4	Securities issued by non-residents	..	..	..	..	..	..	..	..
2.3	Loans	68 118	66 226	61 984	56 142	53 421	52 155	50 470	..
2.3.1	Short-term loans	..	..	..	..	..	..	..	..
2.3.2	Long-term loans	..	..	..	..	..	..	..	..
2.3.3	Loans granted to residents	..	..	..	..	..	..	..	..
2.3.4	Loans granted to non-residents	..	..	..	..	..	..	..	..
2.4	Shares and other equity	51 881	34 309	21 149	27 711	26 691	24 789	27 710	..
2.4.1	Shares issued by residents	..	..	..	..	..	..	..	..
2.4.2	Shares issued by non-residents	..	..	..	..	..	..	..	..
2.5	Other, not elsewhere classified	52 944	55 476	54 549	55 530	54 373	55 165	63 737	..
	Life insurance corporations								
2	Financial assets	349 545	340 343	327 126	332 263	347 111	359 276	386 433	..
2.1	Currency and deposits	4 760	5 650	5 576	5 484	6 261	4 046	4 135	..
2.2	Securities other than shares, except financial derivatives	197 593	201 197	203 359	207 591	226 457	241 493	259 872	..
2.2.1	Short-term securities	..	..	..	..	..	..	..	..
2.2.2	Long-term securities	..	..	..	..	..	..	..	..
2.2.3	Securities issued by residents	..	..	..	..	..	..	..	..
2.2.4	Securities issued by non-residents	..	..	..	..	..	..	..	..
2.3	Loans	64 800	62 898	58 469	53 221	50 353	49 476	47 874	..
2.3.1	Short-term loans	..	..	..	..	..	..	..	..
2.3.2	Long-term loans	..	..	..	..	..	..	..	..
2.3.3	Loans granted to residents	..	..	..	..	..	..	..	..
2.3.4	Loans granted to non-residents	..	..	..	..	..	..	..	..
2.4	Shares and other equity	35 774	22 432	12 742	17 749	16 883	15 703	17 495	..
2.4.1	Shares issued by residents	..	..	..	..	..	..	..	..
2.4.2	Shares issued by non-residents	..	..	..	..	..	..	..	..
2.5	Other, not elsewhere classified	46 619	48 166	46 981	48 218	47 158	48 557	57 057	..
	Non-life insurance corporations								
2	Financial assets	37 993	34 939	29 921	31 819	30 751	29 073	29 948	..
2.1	Currency and deposits	947	902	891	934	905	916	930	..
2.2	Securities other than shares, except financial derivatives	11 297	11 523	9 540	10 690	9 755	9 786	9 527	..
2.2.1	Short-term securities	..	..	..	..	..	..	..	..
2.2.2	Long-term securities	..	..	..	..	..	..	..	..
2.2.3	Securities issued by residents	..	..	..	..	..	..	..	..
2.2.4	Securities issued by non-residents	..	..	..	..	..	..	..	..
2.3	Loans	3 318	3 327	3 515	2 921	3 068	2 679	2 596	..
2.3.1	Short-term loans	..	..	..	..	..	..	..	..
2.3.2	Long-term loans	..	..	..	..	..	..	..	..
2.3.3	Loans granted to residents	..	..	..	..	..	..	..	..
2.3.4	Loans granted to non-residents	..	..	..	..	..	..	..	..
2.4	Shares and other equity	16 106	11 877	8 407	9 962	9 808	9 086	10 214	..
2.4.1	Shares issued by residents	..	..	..	..	..	..	..	..
2.4.2	Shares issued by non-residents	..	..	..	..	..	..	..	..
2.5	Other, not elsewhere classified	6 325	7 310	7 567	7 312	7 215	6 607	6 680	..

Table 3. Financial assets of insurance corporations and autonomous pension funds *(cont.)*

Billion JPY

		2006	2007	2008	2009	2010	2011	2012	2013
	Autonomous pension funds								
2	Financial assets	128 645	121 873	113 438	116 484	114 182	114 820	124 777	..
2.1	Currency and deposits	7 423	7 590	5 842	5 292	5 717	6 233	6 918	..
2.2	Securities other than shares, except financial derivatives	39 300	40 830	36 494	39 896	37 679	40 642	44 753	..
2.2.1	Short-term securities	..	..	..	..	..	..	..	..
2.2.2	Long-term securities	..	..	..	..	..	..	..	..
2.2.3	Securities issued by residents	..	..	..	..	..	..	..	..
2.2.4	Securities issued by non-residents	..	..	..	..	..	..	..	..
2.3	Loans	3 081	2 835	2 667	2 690	2 861	2 070	2 679	..
2.3.1	Short-term loans	..	..	..	..	..	..	..	..
2.3.2	Long-term loans	..	..	..	..	..	..	..	..
2.3.3	Loans granted to residents	..	..	..	..	..	..	..	..
2.3.4	Loans granted to non-residents	..	..	..	..	..	..	..	..
2.4	Shares and other equity	25 162	16 800	10 345	13 318	11 484	11 257	13 677	..
2.4.1	Shares issued by residents	..	..	..	..	..	..	..	..
2.4.2	Shares issued by non-residents	..	..	..	..	..	..	..	..
2.5	Other, not elsewhere classified	53 679	53 819	58 091	55 289	56 441	54 618	56 749	..

Note: Detailed metadata at: http://metalinks.oecd.org/instinv/20141203/8acc

Table 4. Portfolio composition by type of investor

Percentage of total financial assets

Per cent

		2006	2007	2008	2009	2010	2011	2012	2013
	Investment funds								
2	Financial assets	100.0	100.0	100.0	100.0	100.0	100.0	100.0	..
2.1	Currency and deposits	2.4	2.5	3.1	3.0	4.2	3.4	3.3	..
2.2	Securities other than shares, except financial derivatives	9.6	13.9	15.9	16.4	16.2	15.3	15.0	..
2.2.1	Short-term securities	..	..	..	..	..	..	..	..
2.2.2	Long-term securities	..	..	..	..	..	..	..	..
2.2.3	Securities issued by residents	..	..	..	..	..	..	..	..
2.2.4	Securities issued by non-residents	..	..	..	..	..	..	..	..
2.3	Loans	51.0	50.6	49.6	46.8	43.9	45.1	42.4	..
2.3.1	Short-term loans	..	..	..	..	..	..	..	..
2.3.2	Long-term loans	..	..	..	..	..	..	..	..
2.3.3	Loans granted to residents	..	..	..	..	..	..	..	..
2.3.4	Loans granted to non-residents	..	..	..	..	..	..	..	..
2.4	Shares and other equity	15.6	10.3	8.4	10.2	9.8	9.9	11.5	..
2.4.1	Shares issued by residents	..	..	..	..	..	..	..	..
2.4.2	Shares issued by non-residents	..	..	..	..	..	..	..	..
2.5	Other, not elsewhere classified	21.4	22.8	23.0	23.5	25.9	26.3	27.8	..
	Insurance corporations								
2	Financial assets	100.0	100.0	100.0	100.0	100.0	100.0	100.0	..
2.1	Currency and deposits	1.5	1.7	1.8	1.8	1.9	1.3	1.2	..
2.2	Securities other than shares, except financial derivatives	53.9	56.7	59.6	60.0	62.5	64.7	64.7	..
2.2.1	Short-term securities	..	..	..	..	..	..	..	..
2.2.2	Long-term securities	..	..	..	..	..	..	..	..
2.2.3	Securities issued by residents	..	..	..	..	..	..	..	..
2.2.4	Securities issued by non-residents	..	..	..	..	..	..	..	..
2.3	Loans	17.6	17.6	17.4	15.4	14.1	13.4	12.1	..
2.3.1	Short-term loans	..	..	..	..	..	..	..	..
2.3.2	Long-term loans	..	..	..	..	..	..	..	..
2.3.3	Loans granted to residents	..	..	..	..	..	..	..	..
2.3.4	Loans granted to non-residents	..	..	..	..	..	..	..	..
2.4	Shares and other equity	13.4	9.1	5.9	7.6	7.1	6.4	6.7	..
2.4.1	Shares issued by residents	..	..	..	..	..	..	..	..
2.4.2	Shares issued by non-residents	..	..	..	..	..	..	..	..
2.5	Other, not elsewhere classified	13.7	14.8	15.3	15.3	14.4	14.2	15.3	..
	Autonomous pension funds								
2	Financial assets	100.0	100.0	100.0	100.0	100.0	100.0	100.0	..
2.1	Currency and deposits	5.8	6.2	5.1	4.5	5.0	5.4	5.5	..
2.2	Securities other than shares, except financial derivatives	30.5	33.5	32.2	34.2	33.0	35.4	35.9	..
2.2.1	Short-term securities	..	..	..	..	..	..	..	..
2.2.2	Long-term securities	..	..	..	..	..	..	..	..
2.2.3	Securities issued by residents	..	..	..	..	..	..	..	..
2.2.4	Securities issued by non-residents	..	..	..	..	..	..	..	..
2.3	Loans	2.4	2.3	2.4	2.3	2.5	1.8	2.1	..
2.3.1	Short-term loans	..	..	..	..	..	..	..	..
2.3.2	Long-term loans	..	..	..	..	..	..	..	..
2.3.3	Loans granted to residents	..	..	..	..	..	..	..	..
2.3.4	Loans granted to non-residents	..	..	..	..	..	..	..	..
2.4	Shares and other equity	19.6	13.8	9.1	11.4	10.1	9.8	11.0	..
2.4.1	Shares issued by residents	..	..	..	..	..	..	..	..
2.4.2	Shares issued by non-residents	..	..	..	..	..	..	..	..
2.5	Other, not elsewhere classified	41.7	44.2	51.2	47.5	49.4	47.6	45.5	..

Note: Detailed metadata at: http://metalinks.oecd.org/instinv/20141203/f729

Table 1. Financial assets of institutional investors, 2011

Billion KRW

		Total	Investment funds			
			Open-end companies (mutual funds)			Closed-end companies
			Total	Money market funds	Other mutual funds	Total
2	Financial assets	398 139	..	..	..	..
2.1	Currency and deposits	28 789	..	..	..	..
2.2	Securities other than shares, except financial derivatives	198 431	..	..	..	..
2.2.1	Short-term securities	..	..	..	..	..
2.2.2	Long-term securities	..	..	..	..	..
2.2.3	Securities issued by residents	168 034	..	..	..	..
2.2.4	Securities issued by non-residents	30 397	..	..	..	..
2.3	Loans	14 798	..	..	..	..
2.3.1	Short-term loans	..	..	..	..	..
2.3.2	Long-term loans	..	..	..	..	..
2.3.3	Loans granted to residents	14 798	..	..	..	..
2.3.4	Loans granted to non-residents	..	..	..	..	..
2.4	Shares and other equity	113 382	..	..	..	..
2.4.1	Shares issued by residents	113 382	..	..	..	..
2.4.2	Shares issued by non-residents	..	..	..	..	..
2.5	Other, not elsewhere classified	42 739	..	..	..	..

		Total	Insurance corporations and autonomous pension funds			
			Insurance corporations			Autonomous pension funds
			Total	Life insurance corporations	Non-life insurance corporations	Total
2	Financial assets	655 354	603 381	486 224	117 157	51 973
2.1	Currency and deposits	39 380	35 653	23 565	12 088	3 728
2.2	Securities other than shares, except financial derivatives	394 278	370 689	313 179	57 510	23 589
2.2.1	Short-term securities	..	..	..	..	..
2.2.2	Long-term securities	..	..	..	..	..
2.2.3	Securities issued by residents	381 769	358 181	301 993	56 187	23 589
2.2.4	Securities issued by non-residents	12 509	12 509	11 185	1 323	..
2.3	Loans	117 063	103 077	78 961	24 116	13 986
2.3.1	Short-term loans	..	..	..	..	..
2.3.2	Long-term loans	..	..	..	..	..
2.3.3	Loans granted to residents	117 063	103 077	78 961	24 116	13 986
2.3.4	Loans granted to non-residents	..	..	..	..	..
2.4	Shares and other equity	52 769	44 864	39 409	5 454	7 905
2.4.1	Shares issued by residents	52 769	44 864	39 409	5 454	7 905
2.4.2	Shares issued by non-residents	..	..	..	..	..
2.5	Other, not elsewhere classified	51 864	49 099	31 110	17 989	2 765

Note: Detailed metadata at: http://metalinks.oecd.org/instinv/20141203/f5b8

Table 2. Financial assets of investment funds

Billion KRW

		2006	2007	2008	2009	2010	2011	2012	2013
	Investment funds								
2	Financial assets	296 880	399 577	388 978	420 552	423 432	398 139	..	..
2.1	Currency and deposits	37 506	42 326	69 262	43 004	37 246	28 789	..	..
2.2	Securities other than shares, except financial derivatives	140 099	192 189	161 860	206 600	228 015	198 431	..	..
2.2.1	Short-term securities	..	..	..	..	..	..	..	..
2.2.2	Long-term securities	..	..	..	..	..	..	..	..
2.2.3	Securities issued by residents	123 920	120 693	130 339	157 403	183 810	168 034	..	..
2.2.4	Securities issued by non-residents	16 179	71 496	31 521	49 197	44 205	30 397	..	..
2.3	Loans	8 920	9 868	12 043	2 249	8 567	14 798	..	..
2.3.1	Short-term loans	..	..	..	..	..	..	..	..
2.3.2	Long-term loans	..	..	..	..	..	..	..	..
2.3.3	Loans granted to residents	8 920	9 868	12 043	2 249	8 567	14 798	..	..
2.3.4	Loans granted to non-residents	..	..	..	..	..	..	..	..
2.4	Shares and other equity	75 317	113 684	96 327	108 587	104 804	113 382	..	..
2.4.1	Shares issued by residents	75 317	113 684	96 327	108 587	104 804	113 382	..	..
2.4.2	Shares issued by non-residents	..	..	..	..	..	..	..	..
2.5	Other, not elsewhere classified	35 038	41 511	49 486	60 111	44 800	42 739	..	..
	Open-end companies (mutual funds)								
2	Financial assets	..	..	..	..	..	..	..	..
2.1	Currency and deposits	..	..	..	..	..	..	..	..
2.2	Securities other than shares, except financial derivatives	..	..	..	..	..	..	..	..
2.2.1	Short-term securities	..	..	..	..	..	..	..	..
2.2.2	Long-term securities	..	..	..	..	..	..	..	..
2.2.3	Securities issued by residents	..	..	..	..	..	..	..	..
2.2.4	Securities issued by non-residents	..	..	..	..	..	..	..	..
2.3	Loans	..	..	..	..	..	..	..	..
2.3.1	Short-term loans	..	..	..	..	..	..	..	..
2.3.2	Long-term loans	..	..	..	..	..	..	..	..
2.3.3	Loans granted to residents	..	..	..	..	..	..	..	..
2.3.4	Loans granted to non-residents	..	..	..	..	..	..	..	..
2.4	Shares and other equity	..	..	..	..	..	..	..	..
2.4.1	Shares issued by residents	..	..	..	..	..	..	..	..
2.4.2	Shares issued by non-residents	..	..	..	..	..	..	..	..
2.5	Other, not elsewhere classified	..	..	..	..	..	..	..	..
	Money market funds								
2	Financial assets	..	..	..	..	..	..	..	..
2.1	Currency and deposits	..	..	..	..	..	..	..	..
2.2	Securities other than shares, except financial derivatives	..	..	..	..	..	..	..	..
2.2.1	Short-term securities	..	..	..	..	..	..	..	..
2.2.2	Long-term securities	..	..	..	..	..	..	..	..
2.2.3	Securities issued by residents	..	..	..	..	..	..	..	..
2.2.4	Securities issued by non-residents	..	..	..	..	..	..	..	..
2.3	Loans	..	..	..	..	..	..	..	..
2.3.1	Short-term loans	..	..	..	..	..	..	..	..
2.3.2	Long-term loans	..	..	..	..	..	..	..	..
2.3.3	Loans granted to residents	..	..	..	..	..	..	..	..
2.3.4	Loans granted to non-residents	..	..	..	..	..	..	..	..
2.4	Shares and other equity	..	..	..	..	..	..	..	..
2.4.1	Shares issued by residents	..	..	..	..	..	..	..	..
2.4.2	Shares issued by non-residents	..	..	..	..	..	..	..	..
2.5	Other, not elsewhere classified	..	..	..	..	..	..	..	..
	Other mutual funds								
2	Financial assets	..	..	..	..	..	..	..	..
2.1	Currency and deposits	..	..	..	..	..	..	..	..
2.2	Securities other than shares, except financial derivatives	..	..	..	..	..	..	..	..
2.2.1	Short-term securities	..	..	..	..	..	..	..	..
2.2.2	Long-term securities	..	..	..	..	..	..	..	..
2.2.3	Securities issued by residents	..	..	..	..	..	..	..	..
2.2.4	Securities issued by non-residents	..	..	..	..	..	..	..	..
2.3	Loans	..	..	..	..	..	..	..	..
2.3.1	Short-term loans	..	..	..	..	..	..	..	..
2.3.2	Long-term loans	..	..	..	..	..	..	..	..
2.3.3	Loans granted to residents	..	..	..	..	..	..	..	..
2.3.4	Loans granted to non-residents	..	..	..	..	..	..	..	..
2.4	Shares and other equity	..	..	..	..	..	..	..	..
2.4.1	Shares issued by residents	..	..	..	..	..	..	..	..
2.4.2	Shares issued by non-residents	..	..	..	..	..	..	..	..
2.5	Other, not elsewhere classified	..	..	..	..	..	..	..	..

Table 2. Financial assets of investment funds *(cont.)*

Billion KRW

		2006	2007	2008	2009	2010	2011	2012	2013
	Closed-end companies								
2	Financial assets	..	..	..	..	..	..	..	..
2.1	Currency and deposits	..	..	..	..	..	..	..	..
2.2	Securities other than shares, except financial derivatives	..	..	..	..	..	..	..	..
2.2.1	Short-term securities	..	..	..	..	..	..	..	..
2.2.2	Long-term securities	..	..	..	..	..	..	..	..
2.2.3	Securities issued by residents	..	..	..	..	..	..	..	..
2.2.4	Securities issued by non-residents	..	..	..	..	..	..	..	..
2.3	Loans	..	..	..	..	..	..	..	..
2.3.1	Short-term loans	..	..	..	..	..	..	..	..
2.3.2	Long-term loans	..	..	..	..	..	..	..	..
2.3.3	Loans granted to residents	..	..	..	..	..	..	..	..
2.3.4	Loans granted to non-residents	..	..	..	..	..	..	..	..
2.4	Shares and other equity	..	..	..	..	..	..	..	..
2.4.1	Shares issued by residents	..	..	..	..	..	..	..	..
2.4.2	Shares issued by non-residents	..	..	..	..	..	..	..	..
2.5	Other, not elsewhere classified	..	..	..	..	..	..	..	..

Note: Detailed metadata at: http://metalinks.oecd.org/instinv/20141203/f5b8

Table 3. Financial assets of insurance corporations and autonomous pension funds

Billion KRW

		2006	2007	2008	2009	2010	2011	2012	2013
	Insurance corporations and autonomous pension funds								
2	Financial assets	384 959	433 530	462 192	529 068	596 734	655 354	..	..
2.1	Currency and deposits	21 218	27 480	35 124	32 988	35 298	39 380	..	..
2.2	Securities other than shares, except financial derivatives	218 800	241 167	256 141	296 443	345 531	394 278	..	..
2.2.1	Short-term securities	..	..	..	..	..	..	..	..
2.2.2	Long-term securities	..	..	..	..	..	..	..	..
2.2.3	Securities issued by residents	202 686	222 170	237 355	281 169	333 820	381 769	..	..
2.2.4	Securities issued by non-residents	16 114	18 997	18 785	15 274	11 710	12 509	..	..
2.3	Loans	76 257	86 216	99 846	102 986	107 999	117 063	..	..
2.3.1	Short-term loans	..	..	..	..	..	..	..	..
2.3.2	Long-term loans	..	..	..	..	..	..	..	..
2.3.3	Loans granted to residents	76 257	86 216	99 846	102 986	107 999	117 063	..	..
2.3.4	Loans granted to non-residents	..	..	..	..	..	..	..	..
2.4	Shares and other equity	29 988	37 643	32 014	47 038	55 239	52 769	..	..
2.4.1	Shares issued by residents	29 988	37 643	32 014	47 038	55 239	52 769	..	..
2.4.2	Shares issued by non-residents	..	..	..	..	..	..	..	..
2.5	Other, not elsewhere classified	38 695	41 024	39 067	49 613	52 666	51 864	..	..
	Insurance corporations								
2	Financial assets	349 195	395 260	425 006	485 532	545 893	603 381	..	..
2.1	Currency and deposits	19 576	25 303	33 291	29 806	31 088	35 653	..	..
2.2	Securities other than shares, except financial derivatives	203 744	226 474	241 759	279 614	323 550	370 689	..	..
2.2.1	Short-term securities	..	..	..	..	..	..	..	..
2.2.2	Long-term securities	..	..	..	..	..	..	..	..
2.2.3	Securities issued by residents	187 629	207 476	222 974	264 339	311 839	358 181	..	..
2.2.4	Securities issued by non-residents	16 114	18 997	18 785	15 274	11 710	12 509	..	..
2.3	Loans	65 547	74 494	87 326	90 674	94 345	103 077	..	..
2.3.1	Short-term loans	..	..	..	..	..	..	..	..
2.3.2	Long-term loans	..	..	..	..	..	..	..	..
2.3.3	Loans granted to residents	65 547	74 494	87 326	90 674	94 345	103 077	..	..
2.3.4	Loans granted to non-residents	..	..	..	..	..	..	..	..
2.4	Shares and other equity	23 568	29 992	25 407	37 622	47 020	44 864	..	..
2.4.1	Shares issued by residents	23 568	29 992	25 407	37 622	47 020	44 864	..	..
2.4.2	Shares issued by non-residents	..	..	..	..	..	..	..	..
2.5	Other, not elsewhere classified	36 761	38 997	37 223	47 816	49 890	49 099	..	..
	Life insurance corporations								
2	Financial assets	295 569	332 939	353 662	401 126	446 954	486 224	..	..
2.1	Currency and deposits	13 140	17 147	24 582	21 361	22 267	23 565	..	..
2.2	Securities other than shares, except financial derivatives	179 401	198 880	210 979	240 762	274 680	313 179	..	..
2.2.1	Short-term securities	..	..	..	..	..	..	..	..
2.2.2	Long-term securities	..	..	..	..	..	..	..	..
2.2.3	Securities issued by residents	164 805	181 424	193 212	226 628	264 102	301 993	..	..
2.2.4	Securities issued by non-residents	14 595	17 456	17 768	14 134	10 578	11 185	..	..
2.3	Loans	53 960	61 196	71 304	73 392	74 965	78 961	..	..
2.3.1	Short-term loans	..	..	..	..	..	..	..	..
2.3.2	Long-term loans	..	..	..	..	..	..	..	..
2.3.3	Loans granted to residents	53 960	61 196	71 304	73 392	74 965	78 961	..	..
2.3.4	Loans granted to non-residents	..	..	..	..	..	..	..	..
2.4	Shares and other equity	20 371	26 167	22 128	33 217	41 549	39 409	..	..
2.4.1	Shares issued by residents	20 371	26 167	22 128	33 217	41 549	39 409	..	..
2.4.2	Shares issued by non-residents	..	..	..	..	..	..	..	..
2.5	Other, not elsewhere classified	28 696	29 548	24 669	32 395	33 493	31 110	..	..
	Non-life insurance corporations								
2	Financial assets	53 627	62 321	71 343	84 405	98 939	117 157	..	..
2.1	Currency and deposits	6 436	8 156	8 709	8 444	8 821	12 088	..	..
2.2	Securities other than shares, except financial derivatives	24 343	27 593	30 779	38 852	48 870	57 510	..	..
2.2.1	Short-term securities	..	..	..	..	..	..	..	..
2.2.2	Long-term securities	..	..	..	..	..	..	..	..
2.2.3	Securities issued by residents	22 824	26 052	29 762	37 712	47 737	56 187	..	..
2.2.4	Securities issued by non-residents	1 519	1 542	1 018	1 140	1 133	1 323	..	..
2.3	Loans	11 587	13 298	16 023	17 283	19 380	24 116	..	..
2.3.1	Short-term loans	..	..	..	..	..	..	..	..
2.3.2	Long-term loans	..	..	..	..	..	..	..	..
2.3.3	Loans granted to residents	11 587	13 298	16 023	17 283	19 380	24 116	..	..
2.3.4	Loans granted to non-residents	..	..	..	..	..	..	..	..
2.4	Shares and other equity	3 196	3 825	3 279	4 405	5 471	5 454	..	..
2.4.1	Shares issued by residents	3 196	3 825	3 279	4 405	5 471	5 454	..	..
2.4.2	Shares issued by non-residents	..	..	..	..	..	..	..	..
2.5	Other, not elsewhere classified	8 065	9 449	12 554	15 421	16 397	17 989	..	..

Table 3. Financial assets of insurance corporations and autonomous pension funds *(cont.)*

Billion KRW

		2006	2007	2008	2009	2010	2011	2012	2013
	Autonomous pension funds								
2	Financial assets	35 764	38 270	37 186	43 537	50 841	51 973	..	..
2.1	Currency and deposits	1 642	2 177	1 833	3 183	4 211	3 728	..	..
2.2	Securities other than shares, except financial derivatives	15 057	14 693	14 382	16 830	21 981	23 589	..	..
2.2.1	Short-term securities	..	..	..	..	..	..	..	..
2.2.2	Long-term securities	..	..	..	..	..	..	..	..
2.2.3	Securities issued by residents	15 057	14 693	14 382	16 830	21 981	23 589	..	..
2.2.4	Securities issued by non-residents	0	0	..	..	..	..	..	..
2.3	Loans	10 710	11 721	12 520	12 311	13 654	13 986	..	..
2.3.1	Short-term loans	..	..	..	..	..	..	..	..
2.3.2	Long-term loans	..	..	..	..	..	..	..	..
2.3.3	Loans granted to residents	10 710	11 721	12 520	12 311	13 654	13 986	..	..
2.3.4	Loans granted to non-residents	..	..	..	..	..	..	..	..
2.4	Shares and other equity	6 421	7 651	6 607	9 417	8 219	7 905	..	..
2.4.1	Shares issued by residents	6 421	7 651	6 607	9 417	8 219	7 905	..	..
2.4.2	Shares issued by non-residents	..	..	..	..	..	..	..	..
2.5	Other, not elsewhere classified	1 934	2 027	1 844	1 796	2 776	2 765	..	..

Note: Detailed metadata at: http://metalinks.oecd.org/instinv/20141203/f5b8

Table 4. Portfolio composition by type of investor

Percentage of total financial assets

Per cent

		2006	2007	2008	2009	2010	2011	2012	2013
	Investment funds								
2	Financial assets	100.0	100.0	100.0	100.0	100.0	100.0	..	..
2.1	Currency and deposits	12.6	10.6	17.8	10.2	8.8	7.2	..	..
2.2	Securities other than shares, except financial derivatives	47.2	48.1	41.6	49.1	53.8	49.8	..	..
2.2.1	Short-term securities	..	..	..	..	..	..	..	..
2.2.2	Long-term securities	..	..	..	..	..	..	..	..
2.2.3	Securities issued by residents	41.7	30.2	33.5	37.4	43.4	42.2	..	..
2.2.4	Securities issued by non-residents	5.4	17.9	8.1	11.7	10.4	7.6	..	..
2.3	Loans	3.0	2.5	3.1	0.5	2.0	3.7	..	..
2.3.1	Short-term loans	..	..	..	..	..	..	..	..
2.3.2	Long-term loans	..	..	..	..	..	..	..	..
2.3.3	Loans granted to residents	3.0	2.5	3.1	0.5	2.0	3.7	..	..
2.3.4	Loans granted to non-residents	..	..	..	..	..	..	..	..
2.4	Shares and other equity	25.4	28.5	24.8	25.8	24.8	28.5	..	..
2.4.1	Shares issued by residents	25.4	28.5	24.8	25.8	24.8	28.5	..	..
2.4.2	Shares issued by non-residents	..	..	..	..	..	..	..	..
2.5	Other, not elsewhere classified	11.8	10.4	12.7	14.3	10.6	10.7	..	..
	Insurance corporations								
2	Financial assets	100.0	100.0	100.0	100.0	100.0	100.0	..	..
2.1	Currency and deposits	5.6	6.4	7.8	6.1	5.7	5.9	..	..
2.2	Securities other than shares, except financial derivatives	58.3	57.3	56.9	57.6	59.3	61.4	..	..
2.2.1	Short-term securities	..	..	..	..	..	..	..	..
2.2.2	Long-term securities	..	..	..	..	..	..	..	..
2.2.3	Securities issued by residents	53.7	52.5	52.5	54.4	57.1	59.4	..	..
2.2.4	Securities issued by non-residents	4.6	4.8	4.4	3.1	2.1	2.1	..	..
2.3	Loans	18.8	18.8	20.5	18.7	17.3	17.1	..	..
2.3.1	Short-term loans	..	..	..	..	..	..	..	..
2.3.2	Long-term loans	..	..	..	..	..	..	..	..
2.3.3	Loans granted to residents	18.8	18.8	20.5	18.7	17.3	17.1	..	..
2.3.4	Loans granted to non-residents	..	..	..	..	..	..	..	..
2.4	Shares and other equity	6.7	7.6	6.0	7.7	8.6	7.4	..	..
2.4.1	Shares issued by residents	6.7	7.6	6.0	7.7	8.6	7.4	..	..
2.4.2	Shares issued by non-residents	..	..	..	..	..	..	..	..
2.5	Other, not elsewhere classified	10.5	9.9	8.8	9.8	9.1	8.1	..	..
	Autonomous pension funds								
2	Financial assets	100.0	100.0	100.0	100.0	100.0	100.0	..	..
2.1	Currency and deposits	4.6	5.7	4.9	7.3	8.3	7.2	..	..
2.2	Securities other than shares, except financial derivatives	42.1	38.4	38.7	38.7	43.2	45.4	..	..
2.2.1	Short-term securities	..	..	..	..	..	..	..	..
2.2.2	Long-term securities	..	..	..	..	..	..	..	..
2.2.3	Securities issued by residents	42.1	38.4	38.7	38.7	43.2	45.4	..	..
2.2.4	Securities issued by non-residents	0.0	0.0	..	..	..	..	..	..
2.3	Loans	29.9	30.6	33.7	28.3	26.9	26.9	..	..
2.3.1	Short-term loans	..	..	..	..	..	..	..	..
2.3.2	Long-term loans	..	..	..	..	..	..	..	..
2.3.3	Loans granted to residents	29.9	30.6	33.7	28.3	26.9	26.9	..	..
2.3.4	Loans granted to non-residents	..	..	..	..	..	..	..	..
2.4	Shares and other equity	18.0	20.0	17.8	21.6	16.2	15.2	..	..
2.4.1	Shares issued by residents	18.0	20.0	17.8	21.6	16.2	15.2	..	..
2.4.2	Shares issued by non-residents	..	..	..	..	..	..	..	..
2.5	Other, not elsewhere classified	5.4	5.3	5.0	4.1	5.5	5.3	..	..

Note: Detailed metadata at: http://metalinks.oecd.org/instinv/20141203/f729

Table 1. Financial assets of institutional investors, 2013

Million EUR (1999 LUF euro)

		Investment funds				
	Total	Open-end companies (mutual funds)			Closed-end companies
		Total	Money market funds	Other mutual funds	Total
2	Financial assets	2 916 597	2 901 714	198 793	2 702 921	14 883
2.1	Currency and deposits	228 296	226 008	43 604	182 404	2 288
2.2	Securities other than shares, except financial derivatives	1 203 067	1 201 008	149 345	1 051 664	2 059
2.2.1	Short-term securities	203 143	203 140	118 810	84 330	3
2.2.2	Long-term securities	999 924	997 869	30 535	967 334	2 056
2.2.3	Securities issued by residents	37 982	37 150	2 246	34 904	832
2.2.4	Securities issued by non-residents	1 165 085	1 163 858	147 099	1 016 760	1 226
2.3	Loans	0	0	0	0	0
2.3.1	Short-term loans	0	0	0	0	0
2.3.2	Long-term loans	0	0	0	0	0
2.3.3	Loans granted to residents	0	0	0	0	0
2.3.4	Loans granted to non-residents	0	0	0	0	0
2.4	Shares and other equity	1 196 533	1 187 272	3 555	1 183 716	9 262
2.4.1	Shares issued by residents	208 874	205 222	3 275	201 947	3 652
2.4.2	Shares issued by non-residents	987 659	982 050	280	981 770	5 609
2.5	Other, not elsewhere classified	288 700	287 425	2 289	285 137	1 274

		Insurance corporations and autonomous pension funds				
		Total	Insurance corporations			Autonomous pension funds
			Total	Life insurance corporations	Non-life insurance corporations	Total
2	Financial assets	148 780	147 564	117 599	29 965	1 216
2.1	Currency and deposits	12 885	12 840	9 097	3 742	45
2.2	Securities other than shares, except financial derivatives	40 842	40 261	29 312	10 950	581
2.2.1	Short-term securities	1 535	1 535	1 118	418	0
2.2.2	Long-term securities	39 307	38 726	28 194	10 532	581
2.2.3	Securities issued by residents	2 503	2 466	1 796	671	36
2.2.4	Securities issued by non-residents	38 340	37 795	27 516	10 279	545
2.3	Loans	2 366	2 365	382	1 983	1
2.3.1	Short-term loans	2 232	2 231	300	1 931	1
2.3.2	Long-term loans	135	135	82	52	0
2.3.3	Loans granted to residents	258	257	21	235	1
2.3.4	Loans granted to non-residents	2 108	2 108	361	1 748	0
2.4	Shares and other equity	72 406	71 829	62 636	9 193	577
2.4.1	Shares issued by residents	39 314	38 960	34 426	4 533	354
2.4.2	Shares issued by non-residents	33 092	32 869	28 209	4 660	223
2.5	Other, not elsewhere classified	20 281	20 269	16 173	4 096	12

Note: Detailed metadata at: http://metalinks.oecd.org/instinv/20141203/ec1e

Table 2. Financial assets of investment funds

Million EUR (1999 LUF euro)

		2006	2007	2008	2009	2010	2011	2012	2013
	Investment funds								
2	Financial assets	1 902 939	2 166 791	1 739 109	2 008 110	2 390 288	2 349 456	2 647 832	2 916 597
2.1	Currency and deposits	115 775	162 794	234 491	158 239	179 004	215 449	202 614	228 296
2.2	Securities other than shares, except financial derivatives	747 934	797 718	726 847	867 417	980 459	1 000 657	1 174 758	1 203 067
2.2.1	Short-term securities	147 160	176 945	204 110	244 346	226 757	224 339	209 027	203 143
2.2.2	Long-term securities	600 773	620 773	522 737	623 071	753 702	776 318	965 731	999 924
2.2.3	Securities issued by residents	23 109	28 461	11 833	17 475	20 427	21 379	33 509	37 982
2.2.4	Securities issued by non-residents	724 825	769 257	715 014	849 942	960 031	979 277	1 141 248	1 165 085
2.3	Loans	0	0	0	0	0	0	0	0
2.3.1	Short-term loans	0	0	0	0	0	0	0	0
2.3.2	Long-term loans	0	0	0	0	0	0	0	0
2.3.3	Loans granted to residents	0	0	0	0	0	0	0	0
2.3.4	Loans granted to non-residents	0	0	0	0	0	0	0	0
2.4	Shares and other equity	954 102	1 126 200	594 648	803 638	998 404	867 741	994 214	1 196 533
2.4.1	Shares issued by residents	121 382	153 935	94 171	113 028	143 858	138 018	164 717	208 874
2.4.2	Shares issued by non-residents	832 720	972 264	500 477	690 609	854 546	729 722	829 496	987 659
2.5	Other, not elsewhere classified	85 128	80 079	183 123	178 816	232 421	265 609	276 246	288 700
	Open-end companies (mutual funds)								
2	Financial assets	1 900 559	2 164 835	1 734 415	2 002 041	2 382 742	2 338 142	2 634 247	2 901 714
2.1	Currency and deposits	115 451	162 601	233 696	157 391	178 303	212 210	199 727	226 008
2.2	Securities other than shares, except financial derivatives	747 923	797 717	726 450	866 524	978 168	998 390	1 172 213	1 201 008
2.2.1	Short-term securities	147 160	176 945	204 081	244 322	226 755	224 309	208 514	203 140
2.2.2	Long-term securities	600 762	620 772	522 369	622 202	751 413	774 081	963 700	997 869
2.2.3	Securities issued by residents	23 109	28 461	11 832	17 470	20 110	21 261	32 928	37 150
2.2.4	Securities issued by non-residents	724 814	769 256	714 618	849 055	958 058	977 129	1 139 285	1 163 858
2.3	Loans	0	0	0	0	0	0	0	0
2.3.1	Short-term loans	0	0	0	0	0	0	0	0
2.3.2	Long-term loans	0	0	0	0	0	0	0	0
2.3.3	Loans granted to residents	0	0	0	0	0	0	0	0
2.3.4	Loans granted to non-residents	0	0	0	0	0	0	0	0
2.4	Shares and other equity	952 485	1 124 791	591 678	800 377	994 438	862 291	987 151	1 187 272
2.4.1	Shares issued by residents	..	..	93 901	112 255	142 876	136 728	162 690	205 222
2.4.2	Shares issued by non-residents	..	..	497 777	688 122	851 562	725 563	824 461	982 050
2.5	Other, not elsewhere classified	84 700	79 726	182 591	177 749	231 833	265 251	275 156	287 425
	Money market funds								
2	Financial assets	190 242	253 641	340 223	319 372	284 554	302 696	224 286	198 793
2.1	Currency and deposits	22 628	58 833	105 718	54 891	57 410	75 586	52 086	43 604
2.2	Securities other than shares, except financial derivatives	163 952	187 532	228 513	262 240	221 052	219 965	167 631	149 345
2.2.1	Short-term securities	96 712	117 411	154 710	194 599	160 359	158 932	127 478	118 810
2.2.2	Long-term securities	67 240	70 121	73 803	67 641	60 693	61 033	40 153	30 535
2.2.3	Securities issued by residents	3 523	5 473	2 665	3 094	3 734	3 113	3 686	2 246
2.2.4	Securities issued by non-residents	160 429	182 059	225 848	259 146	217 318	216 852	163 945	147 099
2.3	Loans	0	0	0	0	0	0	0	0
2.3.1	Short-term loans	0	0	0	0	0	0	0	0
2.3.2	Long-term loans	0	0	0	0	0	0	0	0
2.3.3	Loans granted to residents	0	0	0	0	0	0	0	0
2.3.4	Loans granted to non-residents	0	0	0	0	0	0	0	0
2.4	Shares and other equity	189	537	498	459	783	925	647	3 555
2.4.1	Shares issued by residents	188	253	231	210	379	350	211	3 275
2.4.2	Shares issued by non-residents	2	284	267	249	403	574	436	280
2.5	Other, not elsewhere classified	3 473	6 740	5 493	1 783	5 310	6 221	3 922	2 289
	Other mutual funds								
2	Financial assets	1 710 317	1 911 194	1 394 192	1 682 670	2 098 188	2 035 446	2 409 962	2 702 921
2.1	Currency and deposits	92 823	103 769	127 977	102 500	120 893	136 625	147 641	182 404
2.2	Securities other than shares, except financial derivatives	583 971	610 186	497 937	604 285	757 116	778 425	1 004 583	1 051 664
2.2.1	Short-term securities	50 448	59 534	49 371	49 723	66 396	65 378	81 035	84 330
2.2.2	Long-term securities	533 523	550 652	448 566	554 562	690 720	713 047	923 547	967 334
2.2.3	Securities issued by residents	19 586	22 989	9 167	14 376	16 376	18 148	29 242	34 904
2.2.4	Securities issued by non-residents	564 385	587 197	488 770	589 909	740 739	760 277	975 340	1 016 760
2.3	Loans	0	0	0	0	0	0	0	0
2.3.1	Short-term loans	0	0	0	0	0	0	0	0
2.3.2	Long-term loans	0	0	0	0	0	0	0	0
2.3.3	Loans granted to residents	0	0	0	0	0	0	0	0
2.3.4	Loans granted to non-residents	0	0	0	0	0	0	0	0
2.4	Shares and other equity	952 296	1 124 254	591 180	799 919	993 655	861 366	986 504	1 183 716
2.4.1	Shares issued by residents	..	..	93 670	112 045	142 497	136 378	162 479	201 947
2.4.2	Shares issued by non-residents	..	..	497 509	687 873	851 159	724 989	824 025	981 770
2.5	Other, not elsewhere classified	81 227	72 986	177 098	175 966	226 523	259 031	271 234	285 137

Table 2. Financial assets of investment funds *(cont.)*

Million EUR (1999 LUF euro)

		2006	2007	2008	2009	2010	2011	2012	2013
	Closed-end companies								
2	Financial assets	2 380	1 956	4 694	6 069	7 546	11 314	13 584	14 883
2.1	Currency and deposits	324	193	796	848	702	3 239	2 887	2 288
2.2	Securities other than shares, except financial derivatives	11	1	397	893	2 291	2 267	2 544	2 059
2.2.1	Short-term securities	0	0	28	24	2	30	513	3
2.2.2	Long-term securities	11	1	368	868	2 289	2 237	2 031	2 056
2.2.3	Securities issued by residents	0	0	1	6	317	118	581	832
2.2.4	Securities issued by non-residents	11	1	395	887	1 974	2 149	1 963	1 226
2.3	Loans	0	0	0	0	0	0	0	0
2.3.1	Short-term loans	0	0	0	0	0	0	0	0
2.3.2	Long-term loans	0	0	0	0	0	0	0	0
2.3.3	Loans granted to residents	0	0	0	0	0	0	0	0
2.3.4	Loans granted to non-residents	0	0	0	0	0	0	0	0
2.4	Shares and other equity	1 617	1 409	2 970	3 261	3 965	5 450	7 063	9 262
2.4.1	Shares issued by residents	..	..	270	773	982	1 290	2 028	3 652
2.4.2	Shares issued by non-residents	..	..	2 700	2 487	2 984	4 159	5 035	5 609
2.5	Other, not elsewhere classified	428	353	532	1 067	588	358	1 090	1 274

Note: Detailed metadata at: http://metalinks.oecd.org/instinv/20141203/ec1e

Table 3. Financial assets of insurance corporations and autonomous pension funds

Million EUR (1999 LUF euro)

		2006	2007	2008	2009	2010	2011	2012	2013
	Insurance corporations and autonomous pension funds								
2	Financial assets	75 133	82 497	81 724	102 048	121 917	123 153	135 052	148 780
2.1	Currency and deposits	5 996	7 073	8 086	9 457	9 385	10 830	11 748	12 885
2.2	Securities other than shares, except financial derivatives	22 690	24 577	25 447	29 815	36 510	37 256	40 096	40 842
2.2.1	Short-term securities	..	..	720	530	1 424	1 921	2 306	1 535
2.2.2	Long-term securities	..	..	24 727	29 286	35 086	35 335	37 791	39 307
2.2.3	Securities issued by residents	..	..	1 073	1 629	2 270	2 038	2 256	2 503
2.2.4	Securities issued by non-residents	..	..	24 374	28 187	34 240	35 217	37 841	38 340
2.3	Loans	1 042	1 167	1 884	1 504	1 625	1 786	2 076	2 366
2.3.1	Short-term loans	1 005	1 124	1 828	1 470	1 593	1 743	1 987	2 232
2.3.2	Long-term loans	37	44	56	34	31	43	89	135
2.3.3	Loans granted to residents	262	383	356	417	268	353	263	258
2.3.4	Loans granted to non-residents	781	784	1 528	1 086	1 357	1 433	1 813	2 108
2.4	Shares and other equity	36 800	41 088	36 706	47 335	56 215	55 832	62 269	72 406
2.4.1	Shares issued by residents	..	..	20 611	26 957	29 924	30 532	34 616	39 314
2.4.2	Shares issued by non-residents	..	..	16 095	20 378	26 291	25 300	27 652	33 092
2.5	Other, not elsewhere classified	8 604	8 591	9 601	13 937	18 182	17 450	18 864	20 281
	Insurance corporations								
2	Financial assets	74 766	82 119	81 334	101 204	121 020	122 184	133 963	147 564
2.1	Currency and deposits	5 986	7 064	8 040	9 200	9 312	10 789	11 707	12 840
2.2	Securities other than shares, except financial derivatives	22 629	24 510	25 388	29 623	36 057	36 752	39 554	40 261
2.2.1	Short-term securities	..	..	720	530	1 424	1 921	2 306	1 535
2.2.2	Long-term securities	..	..	24 669	29 093	34 633	34 831	37 249	38 726
2.2.3	Securities issued by residents	..	..	1 070	1 618	2 242	2 011	2 225	2 466
2.2.4	Securities issued by non-residents	..	..	24 318	28 004	33 815	34 742	37 330	37 795
2.3	Loans	1 040	1 165	1 880	1 502	1 623	1 784	2 075	2 365
2.3.1	Short-term loans	1 003	1 122	1 824	1 469	1 592	1 741	1 986	2 231
2.3.2	Long-term loans	37	44	56	34	31	43	89	135
2.3.3	Loans granted to residents	259	381	352	416	266	351	262	257
2.3.4	Loans granted to non-residents	781	784	1 528	1 086	1 357	1 433	1 813	2 108
2.4	Shares and other equity	36 510	40 789	36 430	46 947	55 857	55 425	61 776	71 829
2.4.1	Shares issued by residents	..	..	20 442	26 723	29 702	30 275	34 308	38 960
2.4.2	Shares issued by non-residents	..	..	15 988	20 224	26 155	25 150	27 468	32 869
2.5	Other, not elsewhere classified	8 601	8 589	9 596	13 932	18 171	17 434	18 852	20 269
	Life insurance corporations								
2	Financial assets	54 917	60 236	57 090	73 862	93 667	94 606	106 803	117 599
2.1	Currency and deposits	3 493	4 068	5 110	5 961	6 236	7 416	8 198	9 097
2.2	Securities other than shares, except financial derivatives	14 827	15 272	16 429	20 159	25 804	26 468	28 829	29 312
2.2.1	Short-term securities	..	..	466	360	1 019	1 383	1 680	1 118
2.2.2	Long-term securities	..	..	15 964	19 799	24 785	25 085	27 149	28 194
2.2.3	Securities issued by residents	..	..	693	1 101	1 605	1 448	1 622	1 796
2.2.4	Securities issued by non-residents	..	..	15 737	19 058	24 200	25 020	27 208	27 516
2.3	Loans	124	173	173	207	264	319	350	382
2.3.1	Short-term loans	100	144	146	180	240	292	296	300
2.3.2	Long-term loans	25	30	27	27	25	27	55	82
2.3.3	Loans granted to residents	6	9	19	13	16	19	20	21
2.3.4	Loans granted to non-residents	119	165	153	194	248	299	331	361
2.4	Shares and other equity	30 733	35 215	29 182	36 987	46 871	46 544	54 409	62 636
2.4.1	Shares issued by residents	..	..	16 663	20 622	26 173	26 666	30 739	34 426
2.4.2	Shares issued by non-residents	..	..	12 519	16 365	20 697	19 879	23 671	28 209
2.5	Other, not elsewhere classified	5 740	5 507	6 196	10 547	14 491	13 859	15 016	16 173
	Non-life insurance corporations								
2	Financial assets	19 849	21 883	24 244	27 342	27 353	27 578	27 160	29 965
2.1	Currency and deposits	2 492	2 996	2 930	3 239	3 076	3 373	3 509	3 742
2.2	Securities other than shares, except financial derivatives	7 802	9 239	8 959	9 463	10 253	10 284	10 725	10 950
2.2.1	Short-term securities	..	..	254	169	405	538	625	418
2.2.2	Long-term securities	..	..	8 705	9 294	9 848	9 746	10 100	10 532
2.2.3	Securities issued by residents	..	..	378	517	638	563	603	671
2.2.4	Securities issued by non-residents	..	..	8 581	8 946	9 615	9 721	10 122	10 279
2.3	Loans	916	992	1 708	1 295	1 359	1 466	1 725	1 983
2.3.1	Short-term loans	903	978	1 679	1 289	1 352	1 449	1 690	1 931
2.3.2	Long-term loans	13	14	29	6	6	16	34	52
2.3.3	Loans granted to residents	254	373	333	403	250	332	242	235
2.3.4	Loans granted to non-residents	662	619	1 375	892	1 108	1 134	1 483	1 748
2.4	Shares and other equity	5 778	5 575	7 248	9 959	8 986	8 881	7 366	9 193
2.4.1	Shares issued by residents	..	..	3 779	6 101	3 529	3 609	3 569	4 533
2.4.2	Shares issued by non-residents	..	..	3 469	3 859	5 457	5 271	3 797	4 660
2.5	Other, not elsewhere classified	2 861	3 082	3 400	3 385	3 680	3 575	3 836	4 096

Table 3. Financial assets of insurance corporations and autonomous pension funds *(cont.)*

Million EUR (1999 LUF euro)

		2006	2007	2008	2009	2010	2011	2012	2013
	Autonomous pension funds								
2	Financial assets	367	378	390	844	896	969	1 089	1 216
2.1	Currency and deposits	11	9	47	256	73	41	41	45
2.2	Securities other than shares, except financial derivatives	61	66	58	193	453	503	542	581
2.2.1	Short-term securities	0	0	0	0	0	0	0	0
2.2.2	Long-term securities	61	66	58	193	453	503	542	581
2.2.3	Securities issued by residents	..	..	2	10	28	27	31	36
2.2.4	Securities issued by non-residents	..	..	56	182	425	476	511	545
2.3	Loans	2	2	4	2	2	2	1	1
2.3.1	Short-term loans	2	2	4	2	2	2	1	1
2.3.2	Long-term loans	0	0	0	0	0	0	0	0
2.3.3	Loans granted to residents	2	2	4	2	2	2	1	1
2.3.4	Loans granted to non-residents	0	0	0	0	0	0	0	0
2.4	Shares and other equity	289	298	276	388	359	407	493	577
2.4.1	Shares issued by residents	..	..	169	234	222	257	309	354
2.4.2	Shares issued by non-residents	..	..	107	154	137	150	184	223
2.5	Other, not elsewhere classified	3	2	5	5	11	16	12	12

Note: Detailed metadata at: http://metalinks.oecd.org/instinv/20141203/ec1e

Table 4. Portfolio composition by type of investor

Percentage of total financial assets

Per cent

		2006	2007	2008	2009	2010	2011	2012	2013
	Investment funds								
2	Financial assets	100.0	100.0	100.0	100.0	100.0	100.0	100.0	100.0
2.1	Currency and deposits	6.1	7.5	13.5	7.9	7.5	9.2	7.7	7.8
2.2	Securities other than shares, except financial derivatives	39.3	36.8	41.8	43.2	41.0	42.6	44.4	41.2
2.2.1	Short-term securities	7.7	8.2	11.7	12.2	9.5	9.5	7.9	7.0
2.2.2	Long-term securities	31.6	28.6	30.1	31.0	31.5	33.0	36.5	34.3
2.2.3	Securities issued by residents	1.2	1.3	0.7	0.9	0.9	0.9	1.3	1.3
2.2.4	Securities issued by non-residents	38.1	35.5	41.1	42.3	40.2	41.7	43.1	39.9
2.3	Loans	0.0	0.0	0.0	0.0	0.0	0.0	0.0	0.0
2.3.1	Short-term loans	0.0	0.0	0.0	0.0	0.0	0.0	0.0	0.0
2.3.2	Long-term loans	0.0	0.0	0.0	0.0	0.0	0.0	0.0	0.0
2.3.3	Loans granted to residents	0.0	0.0	0.0	0.0	0.0	0.0	0.0	0.0
2.3.4	Loans granted to non-residents	0.0	0.0	0.0	0.0	0.0	0.0	0.0	0.0
2.4	Shares and other equity	50.1	52.0	34.2	40.0	41.8	36.9	37.5	41.0
2.4.1	Shares issued by residents	6.4	7.1	5.4	5.6	6.0	5.9	6.2	7.2
2.4.2	Shares issued by non-residents	43.8	44.9	28.8	34.4	35.8	31.1	31.3	33.9
2.5	Other, not elsewhere classified	4.5	3.7	10.5	8.9	9.7	11.3	10.4	9.9
	Insurance corporations								
2	Financial assets	100.0	100.0	100.0	100.0	100.0	100.0	100.0	100.0
2.1	Currency and deposits	8.0	8.6	9.9	9.1	7.7	8.8	8.7	8.7
2.2	Securities other than shares, except financial derivatives	30.3	29.8	31.2	29.3	29.8	30.1	29.5	27.3
2.2.1	Short-term securities	..	..	0.9	0.5	1.2	1.6	1.7	1.0
2.2.2	Long-term securities	..	..	30.3	28.7	28.6	28.5	27.8	26.2
2.2.3	Securities issued by residents	..	..	1.3	1.6	1.9	1.6	1.7	1.7
2.2.4	Securities issued by non-residents	..	..	29.9	27.7	27.9	28.4	27.9	25.6
2.3	Loans	1.4	1.4	2.3	1.5	1.3	1.5	1.5	1.6
2.3.1	Short-term loans	1.3	1.4	2.2	1.5	1.3	1.4	1.5	1.5
2.3.2	Long-term loans	0.1	0.1	0.1	0.0	0.0	0.0	0.1	0.1
2.3.3	Loans granted to residents	0.3	0.5	0.4	0.4	0.2	0.3	0.2	0.2
2.3.4	Loans granted to non-residents	1.0	1.0	1.9	1.1	1.1	1.2	1.4	1.4
2.4	Shares and other equity	48.8	49.7	44.8	46.4	46.2	45.4	46.1	48.7
2.4.1	Shares issued by residents	..	..	25.1	26.4	24.5	24.8	25.6	26.4
2.4.2	Shares issued by non-residents	..	..	19.7	20.0	21.6	20.6	20.5	22.3
2.5	Other, not elsewhere classified	11.5	10.5	11.8	13.8	15.0	14.3	14.1	13.7
	Autonomous pension funds								
2	Financial assets	100.0	100.0	100.0	100.0	100.0	100.0	100.0	100.0
2.1	Currency and deposits	2.9	2.3	12.0	30.4	8.1	4.2	3.8	3.7
2.2	Securities other than shares, except financial derivatives	16.6	17.6	14.9	22.8	50.5	52.0	49.8	47.8
2.2.1	Short-term securities	0.0	0.0	0.0	0.0	0.0	0.0	0.0	0.0
2.2.2	Long-term securities	16.6	17.6	14.9	22.8	50.5	52.0	49.8	47.8
2.2.3	Securities issued by residents	..	..	0.6	1.2	3.1	2.8	2.8	3.0
2.2.4	Securities issued by non-residents	..	..	14.4	21.6	47.4	49.1	46.9	44.8
2.3	Loans	0.6	0.6	1.0	0.2	0.2	0.2	0.1	0.1
2.3.1	Short-term loans	0.6	0.6	1.0	0.2	0.2	0.2	0.1	0.1
2.3.2	Long-term loans	0.0	0.0	0.0	0.0	0.0	0.0	0.0	0.0
2.3.3	Loans granted to residents	0.6	0.6	1.0	0.2	0.2	0.2	0.1	0.1
2.3.4	Loans granted to non-residents	0.0	0.0	0.0	0.0	0.0	0.0	0.0	0.0
2.4	Shares and other equity	78.9	78.9	70.7	46.0	40.0	42.0	45.3	47.4
2.4.1	Shares issued by residents	..	..	43.4	27.7	24.8	26.5	28.3	29.1
2.4.2	Shares issued by non-residents	..	..	27.4	18.3	15.2	15.5	16.9	18.3
2.5	Other, not elsewhere classified	0.9	0.6	1.3	0.6	1.2	1.6	1.1	1.0

Note: Detailed metadata at: http://metalinks.oecd.org/instinv/20141203/f729

Table 1. Financial assets of institutional investors, 2013

Million MXN

		Total	Investment funds			
			Open-end companies (mutual funds)			Closed-end companies
			Total	Money market funds	Other mutual funds	Total
2	Financial assets	..	..	..	..	..
2.1	Currency and deposits	..	..	..	..	..
2.2	Securities other than shares, except financial derivatives	..	..	..	..	..
2.2.1	Short-term securities	..	..	..	..	..
2.2.2	Long-term securities	..	..	..	..	..
2.2.3	Securities issued by residents	..	..	..	..	..
2.2.4	Securities issued by non-residents	..	..	..	..	..
2.3	Loans	..	..	..	..	..
2.3.1	Short-term loans	..	..	..	..	..
2.3.2	Long-term loans	..	..	..	..	..
2.3.3	Loans granted to residents	..	..	..	..	..
2.3.4	Loans granted to non-residents	..	..	..	..	..
2.4	Shares and other equity	..	..	..	..	..
2.4.1	Shares issued by residents	..	..	..	..	..
2.4.2	Shares issued by non-residents	..	..	..	..	..
2.5	Other, not elsewhere classified	..	..	..	..	..

		Total	Insurance corporations and autonomous pension funds			
			Insurance corporations			Autonomous pension funds
			Total	Life insurance corporations	Non-life insurance corporations	Total
2	Financial assets	..	735 751	..	..	2 370 177
2.1	Currency and deposits	..	2 804	..	..	21 349
2.2	Securities other than shares, except financial derivatives	..	541 542	..	..	1 758 863
2.2.1	Short-term securities	..	..	..	..	..
2.2.2	Long-term securities	..	..	..	..	..
2.2.3	Securities issued by residents	..	..	..	..	..
2.2.4	Securities issued by non-residents	..	..	..	..	..
2.3	Loans	..	24 303	..	..	..
2.3.1	Short-term loans	..	..	..	..	..
2.3.2	Long-term loans	..	..	..	..	..
2.3.3	Loans granted to residents	..	..	..	..	..
2.3.4	Loans granted to non-residents	..	..	..	..	..
2.4	Shares and other equity	..	79 384	..	..	537 081
2.4.1	Shares issued by residents	..	..	..	..	..
2.4.2	Shares issued by non-residents	..	..	..	..	..
2.5	Other, not elsewhere classified	..	87 718	..	..	52 884

Note: Detailed metadata at: http://metalinks.oecd.org/instinv/20141203/9430

Table 2. Financial assets of investment funds

Million MXN

		2006	2007	2008	2009	2010	2011	2012	2013
	Investment funds								
2	Financial assets	700 793	854 872	787 442	948 294	1 228 396	..	..	..
2.1	Currency and deposits	0	0	0	0	0	..	..	..
2.2	Securities other than shares, except financial derivatives	605 526	736 903	706 612	822 654	974 330	..	..	..
2.2.1	Short-term securities	438 535	509 082	508 007	633 261	796 474	..	..	..
2.2.2	Long-term securities	166 991	227 821	198 605	189 393	177 856	..	..	..
2.2.3	Securities issued by residents	..	..	..	..	..	..	..	..
2.2.4	Securities issued by non-residents	..	..	..	..	..	..	..	..
2.3	Loans	0	0	0	0	0	..	..	..
2.3.1	Short-term loans	..	..	..	..	..	..	..	..
2.3.2	Long-term loans	..	..	..	..	..	..	..	..
2.3.3	Loans granted to residents	..	..	..	..	..	..	..	..
2.3.4	Loans granted to non-residents	..	..	..	..	..	..	..	..
2.4	Shares and other equity	95 267	117 969	80 830	125 640	254 066	..	..	..
2.4.1	Shares issued by residents	44 739	83 957	55 515	94 568	222 621	..	..	..
2.4.2	Shares issued by non-residents	50 528	34 012	25 315	31 072	31 445	..	..	..
2.5	Other, not elsewhere classified	0	0	0	0	0	..	..	..
	Open-end companies (mutual funds)								
2	Financial assets	700 793	854 872	787 442	948 294	1 228 396	..	..	..
2.1	Currency and deposits	0	0	0	0	0	..	..	..
2.2	Securities other than shares, except financial derivatives	605 526	736 903	706 612	822 654	974 330	..	..	..
2.2.1	Short-term securities	438 535	509 082	508 007	633 261	796 474	..	..	..
2.2.2	Long-term securities	166 991	227 821	198 605	189 393	177 856	..	..	..
2.2.3	Securities issued by residents	..	..	..	..	..	..	..	..
2.2.4	Securities issued by non-residents	..	..	..	..	..	..	..	..
2.3	Loans	0	0	0	0	0	..	..	..
2.3.1	Short-term loans	..	..	..	..	..	..	..	..
2.3.2	Long-term loans	..	..	..	..	..	..	..	..
2.3.3	Loans granted to residents	..	..	..	..	..	..	..	..
2.3.4	Loans granted to non-residents	..	..	..	..	..	..	..	..
2.4	Shares and other equity	95 267	117 969	80 830	125 640	254 066	..	..	..
2.4.1	Shares issued by residents	44 739	83 957	55 515	94 568	222 621	..	..	..
2.4.2	Shares issued by non-residents	50 528	34 012	25 315	31 072	31 445	..	..	..
2.5	Other, not elsewhere classified	0	0	0	0	0	..	..	..
	Money market funds								
2	Financial assets	10 419	3 748	4 706	4 003	1	..	..	..
2.1	Currency and deposits	0	0	0	0	0	..	..	..
2.2	Securities other than shares, except financial derivatives	10 419	3 748	4 706	4 003	1	..	..	..
2.2.1	Short-term securities	10 419	3 728	4 706	4 003	1	..	..	..
2.2.2	Long-term securities	0	20	0	0	0	..	..	..
2.2.3	Securities issued by residents	..	..	..	..	..	..	..	..
2.2.4	Securities issued by non-residents	..	..	..	..	..	..	..	..
2.3	Loans	0	0	0	0	0	..	..	..
2.3.1	Short-term loans	..	..	..	..	..	..	..	..
2.3.2	Long-term loans	..	..	..	..	..	..	..	..
2.3.3	Loans granted to residents	..	..	..	..	..	..	..	..
2.3.4	Loans granted to non-residents	..	..	..	..	..	..	..	..
2.4	Shares and other equity	0	0	0	0	0	..	..	..
2.4.1	Shares issued by residents	..	..	..	..	..	..	..	..
2.4.2	Shares issued by non-residents	..	..	..	..	..	..	..	..
2.5	Other, not elsewhere classified	0	0	0	0	0	..	..	..
	Other mutual funds								
2	Financial assets	690 374	851 124	782 736	944 291	1 228 395	..	..	..
2.1	Currency and deposits	0	0	0	0	0	..	..	..
2.2	Securities other than shares, except financial derivatives	595 107	733 155	701 906	818 651	974 329	..	..	..
2.2.1	Short-term securities	428 116	505 354	503 301	629 258	796 473	..	..	..
2.2.2	Long-term securities	166 991	227 801	198 605	189 393	177 856	..	..	..
2.2.3	Securities issued by residents	..	..	..	..	..	..	..	..
2.2.4	Securities issued by non-residents	..	..	..	..	..	..	..	..
2.3	Loans	0	0	0	0	0	..	..	..
2.3.1	Short-term loans	..	..	..	..	..	..	..	..
2.3.2	Long-term loans	..	..	..	..	..	..	..	..
2.3.3	Loans granted to residents	..	..	..	..	..	..	..	..
2.3.4	Loans granted to non-residents	..	..	..	..	..	..	..	..
2.4	Shares and other equity	95 267	117 969	80 830	125 640	254 066	..	..	..
2.4.1	Shares issued by residents	44 739	83 957	55 515	94 568	222 621	..	..	..
2.4.2	Shares issued by non-residents	50 528	34 012	25 315	31 072	31 445	..	..	..
2.5	Other, not elsewhere classified	0	0	0	0	0	..	..	..

Table 2. Financial assets of investment funds *(cont.)*

Million MXN

		2006	2007	2008	2009	2010	2011	2012	2013
	Closed-end companies								
2	Financial assets	..	..	..	..	..	..	..	..
2.1	Currency and deposits	..	..	..	..	..	..	..	..
2.2	Securities other than shares, except financial derivatives	..	..	..	..	..	..	..	..
2.2.1	Short-term securities	..	..	..	..	..	..	..	..
2.2.2	Long-term securities	..	..	..	..	..	..	..	..
2.2.3	Securities issued by residents	..	..	..	..	..	..	..	..
2.2.4	Securities issued by non-residents	..	..	..	..	..	..	..	..
2.3	Loans	..	..	..	..	..	..	..	..
2.3.1	Short-term loans	..	..	..	..	..	..	..	..
2.3.2	Long-term loans	..	..	..	..	..	..	..	..
2.3.3	Loans granted to residents	..	..	..	..	..	..	..	..
2.3.4	Loans granted to non-residents	..	..	..	..	..	..	..	..
2.4	Shares and other equity	..	..	..	..	..	..	..	..
2.4.1	Shares issued by residents	..	..	..	..	..	..	..	..
2.4.2	Shares issued by non-residents	..	..	..	..	..	..	..	..
2.5	Other, not elsewhere classified	..	..	..	..	..	..	..	..

Note: Detailed metadata at: http://metalinks.oecd.org/instinv/20141203/9430

Table 3. Financial assets of insurance corporations and autonomous pension funds

Million MXN

		2006	2007	2008	2009	2010	2011	2012	2013
	Insurance corporations and autonomous pension funds								
2	Financial assets	1 039 281	1 222 848	1 343 314	1 596 040	1 887 356	..	..	..
2.1	Currency and deposits	1 292	1 788	2 457	17 436	11 686	..	..	..
2.2	Securities other than shares, except financial derivatives	913 588	1 046 882	1 195 214	1 368 106	1 567 423	..	..	..
2.2.1	Short-term securities	..	..	..	..	..	..	..	..
2.2.2	Long-term securities	..	..	..	..	..	..	..	..
2.2.3	Securities issued by residents	..	..	..	..	..	..	..	..
2.2.4	Securities issued by non-residents	..	..	..	..	..	..	..	..
2.3	Loans	4 532	5 231	9 119	12 658	15 120	..	..	..
2.3.1	Short-term loans	..	..	..	..	..	..	..	..
2.3.2	Long-term loans	..	..	..	..	..	..	..	..
2.3.3	Loans granted to residents	..	..	..	..	..	..	..	..
2.3.4	Loans granted to non-residents	..	..	..	..	..	..	..	..
2.4	Shares and other equity	74 180	94 219	90 348	157 883	226 736	..	..	..
2.4.1	Shares issued by residents	..	..	..	..	..	..	..	..
2.4.2	Shares issued by non-residents	..	..	..	..	..	..	..	..
2.5	Other, not elsewhere classified	45 689	74 727	46 176	39 957	66 391	..	..	..
	Insurance corporations								
2	Financial assets	299 104	351 091	407 592	454 222	513 693	597 554	669 872	735 751
2.1	Currency and deposits	1 291	1 757	2 196	2 786	4 025	2 709	2 677	2 804
2.2	Securities other than shares, except financial derivatives	244 340	285 367	330 831	346 943	380 362	443 178	477 539	541 542
2.2.1	Short-term securities	..	..	..	..	..	..	..	..
2.2.2	Long-term securities	..	..	..	..	..	..	..	..
2.2.3	Securities issued by residents	..	..	..	..	..	..	..	..
2.2.4	Securities issued by non-residents	..	..	..	..	..	..	..	..
2.3	Loans	4 532	5 231	9 119	12 658	15 120	21 275	21 390	24 303
2.3.1	Short-term loans	..	..	..	..	..	..	..	..
2.3.2	Long-term loans	..	..	..	..	..	..	..	..
2.3.3	Loans granted to residents	..	..	..	..	..	..	..	..
2.3.4	Loans granted to non-residents	..	..	..	..	..	..	..	..
2.4	Shares and other equity	22 100	26 281	30 138	44 481	54 761	59 252	71 954	79 384
2.4.1	Shares issued by residents	..	..	..	..	..	..	..	..
2.4.2	Shares issued by non-residents	..	..	..	..	..	..	..	..
2.5	Other, not elsewhere classified	26 842	32 455	35 308	47 354	59 424	71 139	96 312	87 718
	Life insurance corporations								
2	Financial assets	..	..	..	..	..	..	..	..
2.1	Currency and deposits	..	..	..	..	..	..	..	..
2.2	Securities other than shares, except financial derivatives	..	..	..	..	..	..	..	..
2.2.1	Short-term securities	..	..	..	..	..	..	..	..
2.2.2	Long-term securities	..	..	..	..	..	..	..	..
2.2.3	Securities issued by residents	..	..	..	..	..	..	..	..
2.2.4	Securities issued by non-residents	..	..	..	..	..	..	..	..
2.3	Loans	..	..	..	..	..	..	..	..
2.3.1	Short-term loans	..	..	..	..	..	..	..	..
2.3.2	Long-term loans	..	..	..	..	..	..	..	..
2.3.3	Loans granted to residents	..	..	..	..	..	..	..	..
2.3.4	Loans granted to non-residents	..	..	..	..	..	..	..	..
2.4	Shares and other equity	..	..	..	..	..	..	..	..
2.4.1	Shares issued by residents	..	..	..	..	..	..	..	..
2.4.2	Shares issued by non-residents	..	..	..	..	..	..	..	..
2.5	Other, not elsewhere classified	..	..	..	..	..	..	..	..
	Non-life insurance corporations								
2	Financial assets	..	..	..	..	..	..	..	..
2.1	Currency and deposits	..	..	..	..	..	..	..	..
2.2	Securities other than shares, except financial derivatives	..	..	..	..	..	..	..	..
2.2.1	Short-term securities	..	..	..	..	..	..	..	..
2.2.2	Long-term securities	..	..	..	..	..	..	..	..
2.2.3	Securities issued by residents	..	..	..	..	..	..	..	..
2.2.4	Securities issued by non-residents	..	..	..	..	..	..	..	..
2.3	Loans	..	..	..	..	..	..	..	..
2.3.1	Short-term loans	..	..	..	..	..	..	..	..
2.3.2	Long-term loans	..	..	..	..	..	..	..	..
2.3.3	Loans granted to residents	..	..	..	..	..	..	..	..
2.3.4	Loans granted to non-residents	..	..	..	..	..	..	..	..
2.4	Shares and other equity	..	..	..	..	..	..	..	..
2.4.1	Shares issued by residents	..	..	..	..	..	..	..	..
2.4.2	Shares issued by non-residents	..	..	..	..	..	..	..	..
2.5	Other, not elsewhere classified	..	..	..	..	..	..	..	..

Table 3. Financial assets of insurance corporations and autonomous pension funds *(cont.)*

Million MXN

		2006	2007	2008	2009	2010	2011	2012	2013
	Autonomous pension funds								
2	Financial assets	740 176	871 757	935 722	1 141 819	1 373 663	..	2 193 025	2 370 177
2.1	Currency and deposits	1	31	262	14 650	7 661	..	13 377	21 349
2.2	Securities other than shares, except financial derivatives	669 248	761 515	864 383	1 021 163	1 187 061	..	1 688 539	1 758 863
2.2.1	Short-term securities	145 241	128 971	152 598	149 316	112 968	..	..	..
2.2.2	Long-term securities	524 007	632 544	711 785	871 847	1 074 093	..	..	..
2.2.3	Securities issued by residents	637 669	715 671	811 311	972 020	1 140 339	..	..	..
2.2.4	Securities issued by non-residents	31 579	45 845	53 072	49 143	46 722	..	..	..
2.3	Loans	0	0	0	0	0	..	..	..
2.3.1	Short-term loans	..	..	..	..	..	..	..	..
2.3.2	Long-term loans	..	..	..	..	..	..	..	..
2.3.3	Loans granted to residents	..	..	..	..	..	..	..	..
2.3.4	Loans granted to non-residents	..	..	..	..	..	..	..	..
2.4	Shares and other equity	52 080	67 938	60 210	113 402	171 975	..	422 698	537 081
2.4.1	Shares issued by residents	14 462	32 091	40 961	83 039	101 416	..	..	..
2.4.2	Shares issued by non-residents	37 619	35 848	19 249	30 364	70 559	..	..	..
2.5	Other, not elsewhere classified	18 847	42 273	10 867	-7 397	6 967	..	68 410	52 884

Note: Detailed metadata at: http://metalinks.oecd.org/instinv/20141203/9430

Table 4. Portfolio composition by type of investor

Percentage of total financial assets

Per cent

		2006	2007	2008	2009	2010	2011	2012	2013
	Investment funds								
2	Financial assets	100.0	100.0	100.0	100.0	100.0	..	..	..
2.1	Currency and deposits	0.0	0.0	0.0	0.0	0.0	..	..	..
2.2	Securities other than shares, except financial derivatives	86.4	86.2	89.7	86.8	79.3	..	..	..
2.2.1	Short-term securities	62.6	59.6	64.5	66.8	64.8	..	..	..
2.2.2	Long-term securities	23.8	26.6	25.2	20.0	14.5	..	..	..
2.2.3	Securities issued by residents	..	..	..	..	..	..	..	..
2.2.4	Securities issued by non-residents	..	..	..	..	..	..	..	..
2.3	Loans	0.0	0.0	0.0	0.0	0.0	..	..	..
2.3.1	Short-term loans	..	..	..	..	..	..	..	..
2.3.2	Long-term loans	..	..	..	..	..	..	..	..
2.3.3	Loans granted to residents	..	..	..	..	..	..	..	..
2.3.4	Loans granted to non-residents	..	..	..	..	..	..	..	..
2.4	Shares and other equity	13.6	13.8	10.3	13.2	20.7	..	..	..
2.4.1	Shares issued by residents	6.4	9.8	7.1	10.0	18.1	..	..	..
2.4.2	Shares issued by non-residents	7.2	4.0	3.2	3.3	2.6	..	..	..
2.5	Other, not elsewhere classified	0.0	0.0	0.0	0.0	0.0	..	..	..
	Insurance corporations								
2	Financial assets	100.0	100.0	100.0	100.0	100.0	100.0	100.0	100.0
2.1	Currency and deposits	0.4	0.5	0.5	0.6	0.8	0.5	0.4	0.4
2.2	Securities other than shares, except financial derivatives	81.7	81.3	81.2	76.4	74.0	74.2	71.3	73.6
2.2.1	Short-term securities	..	..	..	..	..	..	..	..
2.2.2	Long-term securities	..	..	..	..	..	..	..	..
2.2.3	Securities issued by residents	..	..	..	..	..	..	..	..
2.2.4	Securities issued by non-residents	..	..	..	..	..	..	..	..
2.3	Loans	1.5	1.5	2.2	2.8	2.9	3.6	3.2	3.3
2.3.1	Short-term loans	..	..	..	..	..	..	..	..
2.3.2	Long-term loans	..	..	..	..	..	..	..	..
2.3.3	Loans granted to residents	..	..	..	..	..	..	..	..
2.3.4	Loans granted to non-residents	..	..	..	..	..	..	..	..
2.4	Shares and other equity	7.4	7.5	7.4	9.8	10.7	9.9	10.7	10.8
2.4.1	Shares issued by residents	..	..	..	..	..	..	..	..
2.4.2	Shares issued by non-residents	..	..	..	..	..	..	..	..
2.5	Other, not elsewhere classified	9.0	9.2	8.7	10.4	11.6	11.9	14.4	11.9
	Autonomous pension funds								
2	Financial assets	100.0	100.0	100.0	100.0	100.0	..	100.0	100.0
2.1	Currency and deposits	0.0	0.0	0.0	1.3	0.6	..	0.6	0.9
2.2	Securities other than shares, except financial derivatives	90.4	87.4	92.4	89.4	86.4	..	77.0	74.2
2.2.1	Short-term securities	19.6	14.8	16.3	13.1	8.2	..	..	..
2.2.2	Long-term securities	70.8	72.6	76.1	76.4	78.2	..	..	..
2.2.3	Securities issued by residents	86.2	82.1	86.7	85.1	83.0	..	..	..
2.2.4	Securities issued by non-residents	4.3	5.3	5.7	4.3	3.4	..	..	..
2.3	Loans	0.0	0.0	0.0	0.0	0.0	..	..	..
2.3.1	Short-term loans	..	..	..	..	..	..	..	..
2.3.2	Long-term loans	..	..	..	..	..	..	..	..
2.3.3	Loans granted to residents	..	..	..	..	..	..	..	..
2.3.4	Loans granted to non-residents	..	..	..	..	..	..	..	..
2.4	Shares and other equity	7.0	7.8	6.4	9.9	12.5	..	19.3	22.7
2.4.1	Shares issued by residents	2.0	3.7	4.4	7.3	7.4	..	..	..
2.4.2	Shares issued by non-residents	5.1	4.1	2.1	2.7	5.1	..	..	..
2.5	Other, not elsewhere classified	2.5	4.8	1.2	-0.6	0.5	..	3.1	2.2

Note: Detailed metadata at: http://metalinks.oecd.org/instinv/20141203/f729

Table 1. Financial assets of institutional investors, 2013

Million EUR (1999 NLG euro)

		Total	Investment funds			
			Open-end companies (mutual funds)			Closed-end companies
			Total	Money market funds	Other mutual funds	Total
2	Financial assets	455 876	..	..	..	..
2.1	Currency and deposits	4 415	..	..	..	..
2.2	Securities other than shares, except financial derivatives	152 320	..	..	..	..
2.2.1	Short-term securities	611	..	..	..	..
2.2.2	Long-term securities	151 709	..	..	..	..
2.2.3	Securities issued by residents	11 958	..	..	..	..
2.2.4	Securities issued by non-residents	140 362	..	..	..	..
2.3	Loans	36 091	..	..	..	..
2.3.1	Short-term loans	27 479	..	..	..	..
2.3.2	Long-term loans	8 612	..	..	..	..
2.3.3	Loans granted to residents	31 419	..	..	..	..
2.3.4	Loans granted to non-residents	4 672	..	..	..	..
2.4	Shares and other equity	262 446	..	..	..	..
2.4.1	Shares issued by residents	14 332	..	..	..	..
2.4.2	Shares issued by non-residents	248 114	..	..	..	..
2.5	Other, not elsewhere classified	604	..	..	..	..

		Total	Insurance corporations and autonomous pension funds			
			Insurance corporations			Autonomous pension funds
			Total	Life insurance corporations	Non-life insurance corporations	Total
2	Financial assets	1 384 726	425 172	..	..	959 554
2.1	Currency and deposits	39 740	19 581	..	..	20 159
2.2	Securities other than shares, except financial derivatives	448 065	184 651	..	..	263 414
2.2.1	Short-term securities	8 118	1 538	..	..	6 580
2.2.2	Long-term securities	439 947	183 113	..	..	256 834
2.2.3	Securities issued by residents	130 219	68 428	..	..	61 791
2.2.4	Securities issued by non-residents	317 846	116 223	..	..	201 623
2.3	Loans	115 881	79 877	..	..	36 004
2.3.1	Short-term loans	31 115	9 297	..	..	21 818
2.3.2	Long-term loans	84 766	70 580	..	..	14 186
2.3.3	Loans granted to residents	105 744	76 155	..	..	29 589
2.3.4	Loans granted to non-residents	10 137	3 722	..	..	6 415
2.4	Shares and other equity	749 487	133 706	..	..	615 781
2.4.1	Shares issued by residents	464 977	65 376	..	..	399 601
2.4.2	Shares issued by non-residents	284 510	68 330	..	..	216 180
2.5	Other, not elsewhere classified	31 553	7 357	..	..	24 196

Note: Detailed metadata at: http://metalinks.oecd.org/instinv/20141203/bf64

Table 2. Financial assets of investment funds

Million EUR (1999 NLG euro)

		2006	2007	2008	2009	2010	2011	2012	2013
	Investment funds								
2	Financial assets	88 197	82 564	61 094	315 298	344 011	358 374	412 414	455 876
2.1	Currency and deposits	2 246	2 619	2 462	14 752	9 056	6 201	5 061	4 415
2.2	Securities other than shares, except financial derivatives	14 469	12 382	12 261	102 519	102 216	115 443	136 270	152 320
2.2.1	Short-term securities	94	39	127	560	707	977	1 630	611
2.2.2	Long-term securities	14 375	12 343	12 134	101 959	101 509	114 466	134 640	151 709
2.2.3	Securities issued by residents	2 131	1 498	882	7 557	10 104	13 266	12 537	11 958
2.2.4	Securities issued by non-residents	12 338	10 884	11 379	94 962	92 112	102 177	123 733	140 362
2.3	Loans	7 334	7 695	6 948	29 237	22 109	21 011	27 638	36 091
2.3.1	Short-term loans	0	0	250	21 713	10 967	16 815	21 334	27 479
2.3.2	Long-term loans	7 334	7 695	6 698	7 524	11 142	4 196	6 304	8 612
2.3.3	Loans granted to residents	7 326	7 684	6 827	28 470	19 074	18 068	23 533	31 419
2.3.4	Loans granted to non-residents	8	11	121	767	3 035	2 943	4 105	4 672
2.4	Shares and other equity	63 679	59 226	37 917	169 697	211 385	216 155	241 188	262 446
2.4.1	Shares issued by residents	8 830	8 203	5 109	17 439	17 891	14 413	15 748	14 332
2.4.2	Shares issued by non-residents	54 849	51 023	32 808	152 258	193 494	201 742	225 440	248 114
2.5	Other, not elsewhere classified	469	642	1 506	-907	-755	-436	2 257	604
	Open-end companies (mutual funds)								
2	Financial assets	..	..	..	..	..	..	..	..
2.1	Currency and deposits	..	..	..	..	..	..	..	..
2.2	Securities other than shares, except financial derivatives	..	..	..	..	..	..	..	..
2.2.1	Short-term securities	..	..	..	..	..	..	..	..
2.2.2	Long-term securities	..	..	..	..	..	..	..	..
2.2.3	Securities issued by residents	..	..	..	..	..	..	..	..
2.2.4	Securities issued by non-residents	..	..	..	..	..	..	..	..
2.3	Loans	..	..	..	..	..	..	..	..
2.3.1	Short-term loans	..	..	..	..	..	..	..	..
2.3.2	Long-term loans	..	..	..	..	..	..	..	..
2.3.3	Loans granted to residents	..	..	..	..	..	..	..	..
2.3.4	Loans granted to non-residents	..	..	..	..	..	..	..	..
2.4	Shares and other equity	..	..	..	..	..	..	..	..
2.4.1	Shares issued by residents	..	..	..	..	..	..	..	..
2.4.2	Shares issued by non-residents	..	..	..	..	..	..	..	..
2.5	Other, not elsewhere classified	..	..	..	..	..	..	..	..
	Money market funds								
2	Financial assets	..	..	..	..	..	..	..	..
2.1	Currency and deposits	..	..	..	..	..	..	..	..
2.2	Securities other than shares, except financial derivatives	..	..	..	..	..	..	..	..
2.2.1	Short-term securities	..	..	..	..	..	..	..	..
2.2.2	Long-term securities	..	..	..	..	..	..	..	..
2.2.3	Securities issued by residents	..	..	..	..	..	..	..	..
2.2.4	Securities issued by non-residents	..	..	..	..	..	..	..	..
2.3	Loans	..	..	..	..	..	..	..	..
2.3.1	Short-term loans	..	..	..	..	..	..	..	..
2.3.2	Long-term loans	..	..	..	..	..	..	..	..
2.3.3	Loans granted to residents	..	..	..	..	..	..	..	..
2.3.4	Loans granted to non-residents	..	..	..	..	..	..	..	..
2.4	Shares and other equity	..	..	..	..	..	..	..	..
2.4.1	Shares issued by residents	..	..	..	..	..	..	..	..
2.4.2	Shares issued by non-residents	..	..	..	..	..	..	..	..
2.5	Other, not elsewhere classified	..	..	..	..	..	..	..	..
	Other mutual funds								
2	Financial assets	..	..	..	..	..	..	..	..
2.1	Currency and deposits	..	..	..	..	..	..	..	..
2.2	Securities other than shares, except financial derivatives	..	..	..	..	..	..	..	..
2.2.1	Short-term securities	..	..	..	..	..	..	..	..
2.2.2	Long-term securities	..	..	..	..	..	..	..	..
2.2.3	Securities issued by residents	..	..	..	..	..	..	..	..
2.2.4	Securities issued by non-residents	..	..	..	..	..	..	..	..
2.3	Loans	..	..	..	..	..	..	..	..
2.3.1	Short-term loans	..	..	..	..	..	..	..	..
2.3.2	Long-term loans	..	..	..	..	..	..	..	..
2.3.3	Loans granted to residents	..	..	..	..	..	..	..	..
2.3.4	Loans granted to non-residents	..	..	..	..	..	..	..	..
2.4	Shares and other equity	..	..	..	..	..	..	..	..
2.4.1	Shares issued by residents	..	..	..	..	..	..	..	..
2.4.2	Shares issued by non-residents	..	..	..	..	..	..	..	..
2.5	Other, not elsewhere classified	..	..	..	..	..	..	..	..

Table 2. Financial assets of investment funds *(cont.)*

Million EUR (1999 NLG euro)

		2006	2007	2008	2009	2010	2011	2012	2013
	Closed-end companies								
2	Financial assets	..	..	..	..	..	..	..	..
2.1	Currency and deposits	..	..	..	..	..	..	..	..
2.2	Securities other than shares, except financial derivatives	..	..	..	..	..	..	..	..
2.2.1	Short-term securities	..	..	..	..	..	..	..	..
2.2.2	Long-term securities	..	..	..	..	..	..	..	..
2.2.3	Securities issued by residents	..	..	..	..	..	..	..	..
2.2.4	Securities issued by non-residents	..	..	..	..	..	..	..	..
2.3	Loans	..	..	..	..	..	..	..	..
2.3.1	Short-term loans	..	..	..	..	..	..	..	..
2.3.2	Long-term loans	..	..	..	..	..	..	..	..
2.3.3	Loans granted to residents	..	..	..	..	..	..	..	..
2.3.4	Loans granted to non-residents	..	..	..	..	..	..	..	..
2.4	Shares and other equity	..	..	..	..	..	..	..	..
2.4.1	Shares issued by residents	..	..	..	..	..	..	..	..
2.4.2	Shares issued by non-residents	..	..	..	..	..	..	..	..
2.5	Other, not elsewhere classified	..	..	..	..	..	..	..	..

Note: Detailed metadata at: http://metalinks.oecd.org/instinv/20141203/bf64

NETHERLANDS

Table 3. Financial assets of insurance corporations and autonomous pension funds

Million EUR (1999 NLG euro)

		2006	2007	2008	2009	2010	2011	2012	2013
	Insurance corporations and autonomous pension funds								
2	Financial assets	1 026 256	1 050 674	948 343	1 037 701	1 140 306	1 222 755	1 379 526	1 384 726
2.1	Currency and deposits	46 321	48 987	54 709	45 034	43 765	45 287	49 076	39 740
2.2	Securities other than shares, except financial derivatives	413 442	427 497	409 459	360 496	370 754	401 676	460 695	448 065
2.2.1	Short-term securities	3 139	3 207	7 093	7 289	7 228	7 804	12 115	8 118
2.2.2	Long-term securities	410 303	424 290	402 366	353 207	363 526	393 872	448 580	439 947
2.2.3	Securities issued by residents	73 463	78 565	71 401	82 202	95 763	124 096	132 081	130 219
2.2.4	Securities issued by non-residents	339 979	348 932	338 058	278 294	274 991	277 580	328 614	317 846
2.3	Loans	85 023	84 271	102 858	92 079	111 769	116 430	116 610	115 881
2.3.1	Short-term loans	12 053	13 643	35 932	25 647	40 329	40 630	38 125	31 115
2.3.2	Long-term loans	72 970	70 628	66 926	66 432	71 440	75 800	78 485	84 766
2.3.3	Loans granted to residents	75 038	78 296	80 595	77 808	102 371	106 582	106 563	105 744
2.3.4	Loans granted to non-residents	9 985	5 975	22 263	14 271	9 398	9 848	10 047	10 137
2.4	Shares and other equity	473 327	489 214	337 303	527 858	596 833	601 045	686 334	749 487
2.4.1	Shares issued by residents	139 343	116 493	66 964	283 683	332 913	355 048	413 705	464 977
2.4.2	Shares issued by non-residents	333 984	372 721	270 339	244 175	263 920	245 997	272 629	284 510
2.5	Other, not elsewhere classified	8 143	705	44 014	12 234	17 185	58 317	66 811	31 553
	Insurance corporations								
2	Financial assets	335 180	349 431	342 326	355 308	387 759	414 879	439 754	425 172
2.1	Currency and deposits	17 463	16 216	24 154	19 777	22 027	27 028	27 110	19 581
2.2	Securities other than shares, except financial derivatives	135 961	147 146	151 813	165 758	173 685	181 796	204 691	184 651
2.2.1	Short-term securities	1 217	466	1 774	1 567	1 529	1 399	4 230	1 538
2.2.2	Long-term securities	134 744	146 680	150 039	164 191	172 156	180 397	200 461	183 113
2.2.3	Securities issued by residents	39 710	45 999	45 084	54 865	61 206	72 670	73 712	68 428
2.2.4	Securities issued by non-residents	96 251	101 147	106 729	110 893	112 479	109 126	130 979	116 223
2.3	Loans	55 479	55 711	60 562	59 558	66 680	74 888	73 855	79 877
2.3.1	Short-term loans	3 740	8 593	14 653	12 119	13 497	15 039	11 178	9 297
2.3.2	Long-term loans	51 739	47 118	45 909	47 439	53 183	59 849	62 677	70 580
2.3.3	Loans granted to residents	54 380	55 205	59 889	58 654	64 545	71 786	70 488	76 155
2.3.4	Loans granted to non-residents	1 099	506	673	904	2 135	3 102	3 367	3 722
2.4	Shares and other equity	124 269	129 629	97 530	106 044	119 264	117 205	120 373	133 706
2.4.1	Shares issued by residents	87 951	74 810	38 897	39 783	50 506	51 490	54 001	65 376
2.4.2	Shares issued by non-residents	36 318	54 819	58 633	66 261	68 758	65 715	66 372	68 330
2.5	Other, not elsewhere classified	2 008	729	8 267	4 171	6 103	13 962	13 725	7 357
	Life insurance corporations								
2	Financial assets	288 038	303 000	289 881	..	..	..	..	..
2.1	Currency and deposits	14 019	12 935	16 133	..	..	..	..	..
2.2	Securities other than shares, except financial derivatives	110 651	121 566	125 717	..	..	..	..	..
2.2.1	Short-term securities	1 217	466	296	..	..	..	..	..
2.2.2	Long-term securities	109 434	121 100	125 421	..	..	..	..	..
2.2.3	Securities issued by residents	32 153	39 452	37 287	..	..	..	..	..
2.2.4	Securities issued by non-residents	78 498	82 114	88 430	..	..	..	..	..
2.3	Loans	49 083	50 597	52 935	..	..	..	..	..
2.3.1	Short-term loans	2 167	7 066	10 556	..	..	..	..	..
2.3.2	Long-term loans	46 916	43 531	42 379	..	..	..	..	..
2.3.3	Loans granted to residents	48 172	50 219	52 811	..	..	..	..	..
2.3.4	Loans granted to non-residents	911	378	124	..	..	..	..	..
2.4	Shares and other equity	112 311	117 197	87 035	..	..	..	..	..
2.4.1	Shares issued by residents	79 921	67 953	32 477	..	..	..	..	..
2.4.2	Shares issued by non-residents	32 390	49 244	54 558	..	..	..	..	..
2.5	Other, not elsewhere classified	1 974	705	8 061	..	..	..	..	..
	Non-life insurance corporations								
2	Financial assets	47 142	46 431	52 445	..	..	..	..	..
2.1	Currency and deposits	3 444	3 281	8 021	..	..	..	..	..
2.2	Securities other than shares, except financial derivatives	25 310	25 580	26 096	..	..	..	..	..
2.2.1	Short-term securities	0	0	1 478	..	..	..	..	..
2.2.2	Long-term securities	25 310	25 580	24 618	..	..	..	..	..
2.2.3	Securities issued by residents	7 557	6 547	7 797	..	..	..	..	..
2.2.4	Securities issued by non-residents	17 753	19 033	18 299	..	..	..	..	..
2.3	Loans	6 396	5 114	7 627	..	..	..	..	..
2.3.1	Short-term loans	1 573	1 527	4 097	..	..	..	..	..
2.3.2	Long-term loans	4 823	3 587	3 530	..	..	..	..	..
2.3.3	Loans granted to residents	6 208	4 986	7 078	..	..	..	..	..
2.3.4	Loans granted to non-residents	188	128	549	..	..	..	..	..
2.4	Shares and other equity	11 958	12 432	10 495	..	..	..	..	..
2.4.1	Shares issued by residents	8 030	6 857	6 420	..	..	..	..	..
2.4.2	Shares issued by non-residents	3 928	5 575	4 075	..	..	..	..	..
2.5	Other, not elsewhere classified	34	24	206	..	..	..	..	..

Table 3. Financial assets of insurance corporations and autonomous pension funds *(cont.)*

Million EUR (1999 NLG euro)

		2006	2007	2008	2009	2010	2011	2012	2013
	Autonomous pension funds								
2	Financial assets	691 076	701 243	606 017	682 393	752 547	807 876	939 772	959 554
2.1	Currency and deposits	28 858	32 771	30 555	25 257	21 738	18 259	21 966	20 159
2.2	Securities other than shares, except financial derivatives	277 481	280 351	257 646	194 738	197 069	219 880	256 004	263 414
2.2.1	Short-term securities	1 922	2 741	5 319	5 722	5 699	6 405	7 885	6 580
2.2.2	Long-term securities	275 559	277 610	252 327	189 016	191 370	213 475	248 119	256 834
2.2.3	Securities issued by residents	33 753	32 566	26 317	27 337	34 557	51 426	58 369	61 791
2.2.4	Securities issued by non-residents	243 728	247 785	231 329	167 401	162 512	168 454	197 635	201 623
2.3	Loans	29 544	28 560	42 296	32 521	45 089	41 542	42 755	36 004
2.3.1	Short-term loans	8 313	5 050	21 279	13 528	26 832	25 591	26 947	21 818
2.3.2	Long-term loans	21 231	23 510	21 017	18 993	18 257	15 951	15 808	14 186
2.3.3	Loans granted to residents	20 658	23 091	20 706	19 154	37 826	34 796	36 075	29 589
2.3.4	Loans granted to non-residents	8 886	5 469	21 590	13 367	7 263	6 746	6 680	6 415
2.4	Shares and other equity	349 058	359 585	239 773	421 814	477 569	483 840	565 961	615 781
2.4.1	Shares issued by residents	51 392	41 683	28 067	243 900	282 407	303 558	359 704	399 601
2.4.2	Shares issued by non-residents	297 666	317 902	211 706	177 914	195 162	180 282	206 257	216 180
2.5	Other, not elsewhere classified	6 135	-24	35 747	8 063	11 082	44 355	53 086	24 196

Note: Detailed metadata at: http://metalinks.oecd.org/instinv/20141203/bf64

Table 4. Portfolio composition by type of investor

Percentage of total financial assets

Per cent

		2006	2007	2008	2009	2010	2011	2012	2013
	Investment funds								
2	Financial assets	100.0	100.0	100.0	100.0	100.0	100.0	100.0	100.0
2.1	Currency and deposits	2.5	3.2	4.0	4.7	2.6	1.7	1.2	1.0
2.2	Securities other than shares, except financial derivatives	16.4	15.0	20.1	32.5	29.7	32.2	33.0	33.4
2.2.1	Short-term securities	0.1	0.0	0.2	0.2	0.2	0.3	0.4	0.1
2.2.2	Long-term securities	16.3	14.9	19.9	32.3	29.5	31.9	32.6	33.3
2.2.3	Securities issued by residents	2.4	1.8	1.4	2.4	2.9	3.7	3.0	2.6
2.2.4	Securities issued by non-residents	14.0	13.2	18.6	30.1	26.8	28.5	30.0	30.8
2.3	Loans	8.3	9.3	11.4	9.3	6.4	5.9	6.7	7.9
2.3.1	Short-term loans	0.0	0.0	0.4	6.9	3.2	4.7	5.2	6.0
2.3.2	Long-term loans	8.3	9.3	11.0	2.4	3.2	1.2	1.5	1.9
2.3.3	Loans granted to residents	8.3	9.3	11.2	9.0	5.5	5.0	5.7	6.9
2.3.4	Loans granted to non-residents	0.0	0.0	0.2	0.2	0.9	0.8	1.0	1.0
2.4	Shares and other equity	72.2	71.7	62.1	53.8	61.4	60.3	58.5	57.6
2.4.1	Shares issued by residents	10.0	9.9	8.4	5.5	5.2	4.0	3.8	3.1
2.4.2	Shares issued by non-residents	62.2	61.8	53.7	48.3	56.2	56.3	54.7	54.4
2.5	Other, not elsewhere classified	0.5	0.8	2.5	-0.3	-0.2	-0.1	0.5	0.1
	Insurance corporations								
2	Financial assets	100.0	100.0	100.0	100.0	100.0	100.0	100.0	100.0
2.1	Currency and deposits	5.2	4.6	7.1	5.6	5.7	6.5	6.2	4.6
2.2	Securities other than shares, except financial derivatives	40.6	42.1	44.3	46.7	44.8	43.8	46.5	43.4
2.2.1	Short-term securities	0.4	0.1	0.5	0.4	0.4	0.3	1.0	0.4
2.2.2	Long-term securities	40.2	42.0	43.8	46.2	44.4	43.5	45.6	43.1
2.2.3	Securities issued by residents	11.8	13.2	13.2	15.4	15.8	17.5	16.8	16.1
2.2.4	Securities issued by non-residents	28.7	28.9	31.2	31.2	29.0	26.3	29.8	27.3
2.3	Loans	16.6	15.9	17.7	16.8	17.2	18.1	16.8	18.8
2.3.1	Short-term loans	1.1	2.5	4.3	3.4	3.5	3.6	2.5	2.2
2.3.2	Long-term loans	15.4	13.5	13.4	13.4	13.7	14.4	14.3	16.6
2.3.3	Loans granted to residents	16.2	15.8	17.5	16.5	16.6	17.3	16.0	17.9
2.3.4	Loans granted to non-residents	0.3	0.1	0.2	0.3	0.6	0.7	0.8	0.9
2.4	Shares and other equity	37.1	37.1	28.5	29.8	30.8	28.3	27.4	31.4
2.4.1	Shares issued by residents	26.2	21.4	11.4	11.2	13.0	12.4	12.3	15.4
2.4.2	Shares issued by non-residents	10.8	15.7	17.1	18.6	17.7	15.8	15.1	16.1
2.5	Other, not elsewhere classified	0.6	0.2	2.4	1.2	1.6	3.4	3.1	1.7
	Autonomous pension funds								
2	Financial assets	100.0	100.0	100.0	100.0	100.0	100.0	100.0	100.0
2.1	Currency and deposits	4.2	4.7	5.0	3.7	2.9	2.3	2.3	2.1
2.2	Securities other than shares, except financial derivatives	40.2	40.0	42.5	28.5	26.2	27.2	27.2	27.5
2.2.1	Short-term securities	0.3	0.4	0.9	0.8	0.8	0.8	0.8	0.7
2.2.2	Long-term securities	39.9	39.6	41.6	27.7	25.4	26.4	26.4	26.8
2.2.3	Securities issued by residents	4.9	4.6	4.3	4.0	4.6	6.4	6.2	6.4
2.2.4	Securities issued by non-residents	35.3	35.3	38.2	24.5	21.6	20.9	21.0	21.0
2.3	Loans	4.3	4.1	7.0	4.8	6.0	5.1	4.5	3.8
2.3.1	Short-term loans	1.2	0.7	3.5	2.0	3.6	3.2	2.9	2.3
2.3.2	Long-term loans	3.1	3.4	3.5	2.8	2.4	2.0	1.7	1.5
2.3.3	Loans granted to residents	3.0	3.3	3.4	2.8	5.0	4.3	3.8	3.1
2.3.4	Loans granted to non-residents	1.3	0.8	3.6	2.0	1.0	0.8	0.7	0.7
2.4	Shares and other equity	50.5	51.3	39.6	61.8	63.5	59.9	60.2	64.2
2.4.1	Shares issued by residents	7.4	5.9	4.6	35.7	37.5	37.6	38.3	41.6
2.4.2	Shares issued by non-residents	43.1	45.3	34.9	26.1	25.9	22.3	21.9	22.5
2.5	Other, not elsewhere classified	0.9	0.0	5.9	1.2	1.5	5.5	5.6	2.5

Note: Detailed metadata at: http://metalinks.oecd.org/instinv/20141203/f729

Table 1. Financial assets of institutional investors, 2013

Million NOK

			Investment funds			
		Total	Open-end companies (mutual funds)			Closed-end companies
			Total	Money market funds	Other mutual funds	Total
2	Financial assets	..	722 494	92 279	630 215	..
2.1	Currency and deposits	..	32 099	11 014	21 085	..
2.2	Securities other than shares, except financial derivatives	..	245 539	67 280	178 259	..
2.2.1	Short-term securities	..	21 021	12 896	8 125	..
2.2.2	Long-term securities	..	224 518	54 384	170 134	..
2.2.3	Securities issued by residents	..	158 663	59 780	98 883	..
2.2.4	Securities issued by non-residents	..	86 876	7 500	79 376	..
2.3	Loans	..	0	0	0	..
2.3.1	Short-term loans	..	0	0	0	..
2.3.2	Long-term loans	..	0	0	0	..
2.3.3	Loans granted to residents	..	0	0	0	..
2.3.4	Loans granted to non-residents	..	0	0	0	..
2.4	Shares and other equity	..	440 217	13 377	426 840	..
2.4.1	Shares issued by residents	..	168 633	13 377	155 256	..
2.4.2	Shares issued by non-residents	..	271 584	0	271 584	..
2.5	Other, not elsewhere classified	..	4 639	608	4 031	..

			Insurance corporations and autonomous pension funds			
		Total	Insurance corporations			Autonomous pension funds
			Total	Life insurance corporations	Non-life insurance corporations	Total
2	Financial assets	1 526 204	1 288 951	1 083 603	205 348	247 401
2.1	Currency and deposits	54 857	48 033	41 556	6 477	6 824
2.2	Securities other than shares, except financial derivatives	738 135	611 720	524 924	86 796	127 098
2.2.1	Short-term securities	62 765	51 662	39 832	11 830	11 103
2.2.2	Long-term securities	675 370	560 058	485 092	74 966	115 995
2.2.3	Securities issued by residents	453 961	355 329	293 428	61 901	99 315
2.2.4	Securities issued by non-residents	284 174	256 391	231 496	24 895	27 783
2.3	Loans	66 179	61 927	58 848	3 079	4 264
2.3.1	Short-term loans	140	140	140	0	0
2.3.2	Long-term loans	66 039	61 787	58 708	3 079	4 264
2.3.3	Loans granted to residents	57 941	53 689	50 612	3 077	4 264
2.3.4	Loans granted to non-residents	8 238	8 238	8 236	2	0
2.4	Shares and other equity	597 064	493 240	446 953	46 287	105 098
2.4.1	Shares issued by residents	428 168	370 499	346 863	23 636	58 943
2.4.2	Shares issued by non-residents	168 896	122 741	100 090	22 651	46 155
2.5	Other, not elsewhere classified	69 969	74 031	11 322	62 709	4 117

Note: Detailed metadata at: http://metalinks.oecd.org/instinv/20141203/927c

Table 2. Financial assets of investment funds

Million NOK

		2006	2007	2008	2009	2010	2011	2012	2013
	Investment funds								
2	Financial assets	..	..	..	..	..	..	..	..
2.1	Currency and deposits	..	..	..	..	..	..	..	..
2.2	Securities other than shares, except financial derivatives	..	..	..	..	..	..	..	..
2.2.1	Short-term securities	..	..	..	..	..	..	..	..
2.2.2	Long-term securities	..	..	..	..	..	..	..	..
2.2.3	Securities issued by residents	..	..	..	..	..	..	..	..
2.2.4	Securities issued by non-residents	..	..	..	..	..	..	..	..
2.3	Loans	..	..	..	..	..	..	..	..
2.3.1	Short-term loans	..	..	..	..	..	..	..	..
2.3.2	Long-term loans	..	..	..	..	..	..	..	..
2.3.3	Loans granted to residents	..	..	..	..	..	..	..	..
2.3.4	Loans granted to non-residents	..	..	..	..	..	..	..	..
2.4	Shares and other equity	..	..	..	..	..	..	..	..
2.4.1	Shares issued by residents	..	..	..	..	..	..	..	..
2.4.2	Shares issued by non-residents	..	..	..	..	..	..	..	..
2.5	Other, not elsewhere classified	..	..	..	..	..	..	..	..
	Open-end companies (mutual funds)								
2	Financial assets	385 194	459 413	320 796	452 666	544 951	529 659	610 222	722 494
2.1	Currency and deposits	11 928	15 638	11 897	22 667	19 925	21 964	25 625	32 099
2.2	Securities other than shares, except financial derivatives	115 184	156 382	143 004	152 299	175 667	205 375	234 068	245 539
2.2.1	Short-term securities	24 262	37 683	26 834	25 341	31 469	35 997	32 774	21 021
2.2.2	Long-term securities	90 922	118 699	116 170	126 958	144 198	169 378	201 294	224 518
2.2.3	Securities issued by residents	95 426	125 901	110 652	117 904	130 227	145 801	161 839	158 663
2.2.4	Securities issued by non-residents	19 758	30 481	32 352	34 395	45 440	59 574	72 229	86 876
2.3	Loans	0	0	0	0	0	0	0	0
2.3.1	Short-term loans	0	0	0	0	0	0	0	0
2.3.2	Long-term loans	0	0	0	0	0	0	0	0
2.3.3	Loans granted to residents	0	0	0	0	0	0	0	0
2.3.4	Loans granted to non-residents	0	0	0	0	0	0	0	0
2.4	Shares and other equity	255 319	282 824	161 465	273 295	343 117	298 257	345 884	440 217
2.4.1	Shares issued by residents	109 980	120 694	65 916	112 873	139 722	119 123	137 161	168 633
2.4.2	Shares issued by non-residents	145 339	162 130	95 549	160 422	203 395	179 134	208 723	271 584
2.5	Other, not elsewhere classified	2 763	4 569	4 430	4 405	6 242	4 063	4 645	4 639
	Money market funds								
2	Financial assets	87 799	126 300	107 796	111 816	109 163	120 276	96 940	92 279
2.1	Currency and deposits	2 949	6 257	5 117	6 525	6 845	5 494	6 070	11 014
2.2	Securities other than shares, except financial derivatives	72 864	102 093	87 801	89 737	85 875	98 069	76 395	67 280
2.2.1	Short-term securities	22 576	34 580	25 103	23 643	26 223	25 461	20 510	12 896
2.2.2	Long-term securities	50 288	67 513	62 698	66 094	59 652	72 608	55 885	54 384
2.2.3	Securities issued by residents	68 875	94 733	80 990	82 109	79 634	92 650	73 660	59 780
2.2.4	Securities issued by non-residents	3 989	7 360	6 811	7 628	6 241	5 419	2 735	7 500
2.3	Loans	0	0	0	0	0	0	0	0
2.3.1	Short-term loans	0	0	0	0	0	0	0	0
2.3.2	Long-term loans	0	0	0	0	0	0	0	0
2.3.3	Loans granted to residents	0	0	0	0	0	0	0	0
2.3.4	Loans granted to non-residents	0	0	0	0	0	0	0	0
2.4	Shares and other equity	11 226	16 625	13 433	14 694	15 488	16 006	13 866	13 377
2.4.1	Shares issued by residents	11 226	16 625	13 433	14 694	15 488	16 006	13 866	13 377
2.4.2	Shares issued by non-residents	0	0	0	0	0	0	0	0
2.5	Other, not elsewhere classified	760	1 325	1 445	860	955	707	609	608
	Other mutual funds								
2	Financial assets	297 395	333 113	213 000	340 850	435 788	409 383	513 282	630 215
2.1	Currency and deposits	8 979	9 381	6 780	16 142	13 080	16 470	19 555	21 085
2.2	Securities other than shares, except financial derivatives	42 320	54 289	55 203	62 562	89 792	107 306	157 673	178 259
2.2.1	Short-term securities	1 686	3 103	1 731	1 698	5 246	10 536	12 264	8 125
2.2.2	Long-term securities	40 634	51 186	53 472	60 864	84 546	96 770	145 409	170 134
2.2.3	Securities issued by residents	26 551	31 168	29 662	35 795	50 593	53 151	88 179	98 883
2.2.4	Securities issued by non-residents	15 769	23 121	25 541	26 767	39 199	54 155	69 494	79 376
2.3	Loans	0	0	0	0	0	0	0	0
2.3.1	Short-term loans	0	0	0	0	0	0	0	0
2.3.2	Long-term loans	0	0	0	0	0	0	0	0
2.3.3	Loans granted to residents	0	0	0	0	0	0	0	0
2.3.4	Loans granted to non-residents	0	0	0	0	0	0	0	0
2.4	Shares and other equity	244 093	266 199	148 032	258 601	327 629	282 251	332 018	426 840
2.4.1	Shares issued by residents	98 754	104 069	52 483	98 179	124 234	103 117	123 295	155 256
2.4.2	Shares issued by non-residents	145 339	162 130	95 549	160 422	203 395	179 134	208 723	271 584
2.5	Other, not elsewhere classified	2 003	3 244	2 985	3 545	5 287	3 356	4 036	4 031

Table 2. Financial assets of investment funds *(cont.)*

Million NOK

		2006	2007	2008	2009	2010	2011	2012	2013
	Closed-end companies								
2	Financial assets	..	..	..	..	..	..	..	..
2.1	Currency and deposits	..	..	..	..	..	..	..	..
2.2	Securities other than shares, except financial derivatives	..	..	..	..	..	..	..	..
2.2.1	Short-term securities	..	..	..	..	..	..	..	..
2.2.2	Long-term securities	..	..	..	..	..	..	..	..
2.2.3	Securities issued by residents	..	..	..	..	..	..	..	..
2.2.4	Securities issued by non-residents	..	..	..	..	..	..	..	..
2.3	Loans	..	..	..	..	..	..	..	..
2.3.1	Short-term loans	..	..	..	..	..	..	..	..
2.3.2	Long-term loans	..	..	..	..	..	..	..	..
2.3.3	Loans granted to residents	..	..	..	..	..	..	..	..
2.3.4	Loans granted to non-residents	..	..	..	..	..	..	..	..
2.4	Shares and other equity	..	..	..	..	..	..	..	..
2.4.1	Shares issued by residents	..	..	..	..	..	..	..	..
2.4.2	Shares issued by non-residents	..	..	..	..	..	..	..	..
2.5	Other, not elsewhere classified	..	..	..	..	..	..	..	..

Note: Detailed metadata at: http://metalinks.oecd.org/instinv/20141203/927c

Table 3. Financial assets of insurance corporations and autonomous pension funds

Million NOK

		2006	2007	2008	2009	2010	2011	2012	2013
	Insurance corporations and autonomous pension funds								
2	Financial assets	931 205	1 010 838	1 021 189	1 094 036	1 197 725	1 261 112	1 376 910	1 526 204
2.1	Currency and deposits	36 405	48 955	47 061	40 250	39 356	38 605	44 295	54 857
2.2	Securities other than shares, except financial derivatives	452 198	442 065	528 427	542 686	550 195	615 481	657 438	738 135
2.2.1	Short-term securities	32 114	32 402	46 375	36 361	44 224	65 652	60 693	62 765
2.2.2	Long-term securities	420 084	409 663	482 052	506 325	505 971	549 829	596 745	675 370
2.2.3	Securities issued by residents	261 974	244 254	296 868	284 077	302 215	354 026	398 569	453 961
2.2.4	Securities issued by non-residents	190 224	197 811	231 559	258 609	247 980	261 455	258 869	284 174
2.3	Loans	23 637	30 894	50 198	72 405	55 941	52 685	55 500	66 179
2.3.1	Short-term loans	2	2	1 649	734	375	375	373	140
2.3.2	Long-term loans	23 635	30 891	48 549	71 670	55 565	52 310	55 127	66 039
2.3.3	Loans granted to residents	22 668	23 476	39 004	63 272	47 725	44 299	48 668	57 941
2.3.4	Loans granted to non-residents	969	7 418	11 194	9 133	8 216	8 386	6 832	8 238
2.4	Shares and other equity	361 489	418 310	315 165	378 593	484 376	491 368	548 913	597 064
2.4.1	Shares issued by residents	202 952	260 489	210 020	251 841	336 087	351 746	400 821	428 168
2.4.2	Shares issued by non-residents	158 537	157 821	105 145	126 752	148 289	139 622	148 092	168 896
2.5	Other, not elsewhere classified	57 476	70 614	80 338	60 102	67 857	62 973	70 764	69 969
	Insurance corporations								
2	Financial assets	783 637	855 121	875 779	920 168	1 003 419	1 062 144	1 157 801	1 288 951
2.1	Currency and deposits	29 097	43 032	39 789	32 610	33 744	32 731	38 011	48 033
2.2	Securities other than shares, except financial derivatives	379 805	362 485	437 077	447 088	450 946	502 554	542 985	611 720
2.2.1	Short-term securities	28 298	28 197	42 555	29 430	35 604	47 471	50 956	51 662
2.2.2	Long-term securities	351 507	334 288	394 522	417 658	415 342	455 083	492 029	560 058
2.2.3	Securities issued by residents	200 435	187 209	230 309	209 602	223 892	265 047	307 535	355 329
2.2.4	Securities issued by non-residents	179 370	175 276	206 768	237 486	227 054	237 507	235 450	256 391
2.3	Loans	21 088	28 745	47 938	70 277	53 682	48 653	51 241	61 927
2.3.1	Short-term loans	2	2	1 649	734	375	375	373	140
2.3.2	Long-term loans	21 086	28 742	46 289	69 542	53 306	48 278	50 868	61 787
2.3.3	Loans granted to residents	20 119	21 327	36 744	61 144	45 466	40 267	44 409	53 689
2.3.4	Loans granted to non-residents	969	7 418	11 194	9 133	8 216	8 386	6 832	8 238
2.4	Shares and other equity	299 260	345 304	263 921	305 222	395 728	412 240	453 190	493 240
2.4.1	Shares issued by residents	162 552	213 213	176 825	206 768	280 845	304 272	346 882	370 499
2.4.2	Shares issued by non-residents	136 708	132 091	87 096	98 454	114 883	107 968	106 308	122 741
2.5	Other, not elsewhere classified	54 388	75 555	87 053	64 970	69 320	65 966	72 373	74 031
	Life insurance corporations								
2	Financial assets	651 399	700 637	711 289	760 585	836 264	894 669	976 057	1 083 603
2.1	Currency and deposits	23 058	35 466	32 335	26 217	27 368	25 707	31 476	41 556
2.2	Securities other than shares, except financial derivatives	324 940	310 678	374 793	386 538	389 103	437 286	470 596	524 924
2.2.1	Short-term securities	18 012	18 318	30 046	14 128	20 986	33 330	36 224	39 832
2.2.2	Long-term securities	306 928	292 360	344 747	372 410	368 117	403 956	434 372	485 092
2.2.3	Securities issued by residents	163 034	153 234	188 486	174 676	186 023	223 563	259 464	293 428
2.2.4	Securities issued by non-residents	161 906	157 444	186 307	211 862	203 080	213 723	211 132	231 496
2.3	Loans	19 781	27 738	47 097	69 641	53 104	48 110	50 544	58 848
2.3.1	Short-term loans	2	2	1 634	723	373	373	373	140
2.3.2	Long-term loans	19 779	27 736	45 463	68 918	52 730	47 737	50 171	58 708
2.3.3	Loans granted to residents	18 893	20 390	35 903	60 511	44 892	39 727	43 714	50 612
2.3.4	Loans granted to non-residents	888	7 348	11 194	9 130	8 212	8 383	6 830	8 236
2.4	Shares and other equity	265 945	303 790	229 382	267 342	353 905	373 667	412 586	446 953
2.4.1	Shares issued by residents	147 329	192 612	159 112	184 420	255 916	281 284	324 906	346 863
2.4.2	Shares issued by non-residents	118 616	111 178	70 270	82 922	97 989	92 383	87 680	100 090
2.5	Other, not elsewhere classified	17 675	22 966	27 683	10 847	12 785	9 898	10 855	11 322
	Non-life insurance corporations								
2	Financial assets	132 238	154 483	164 489	159 583	167 155	167 475	181 744	205 348
2.1	Currency and deposits	6 038	7 567	7 454	6 394	6 376	7 023	6 535	6 477
2.2	Securities other than shares, except financial derivatives	54 865	51 807	62 284	60 550	61 843	65 268	72 389	86 796
2.2.1	Short-term securities	10 286	9 879	12 509	15 302	14 618	14 141	14 732	11 830
2.2.2	Long-term securities	44 579	41 928	49 775	45 248	47 225	51 127	57 657	74 966
2.2.3	Securities issued by residents	37 401	33 975	41 823	34 926	37 869	41 484	48 071	61 901
2.2.4	Securities issued by non-residents	17 464	17 832	20 461	25 624	23 974	23 784	24 318	24 895
2.3	Loans	1 307	1 007	841	636	578	543	697	3 079
2.3.1	Short-term loans	0	0	15	11	2	2	0	0
2.3.2	Long-term loans	1 307	1 007	826	624	576	541	697	3 079
2.3.3	Loans granted to residents	1 226	937	841	633	574	540	695	3 077
2.3.4	Loans granted to non-residents	81	70	0	3	4	3	2	2
2.4	Shares and other equity	33 314	41 514	34 540	37 881	41 823	38 572	40 604	46 287
2.4.1	Shares issued by residents	15 222	20 601	17 714	22 349	24 929	22 987	21 976	23 636
2.4.2	Shares issued by non-residents	18 092	20 913	16 826	15 532	16 894	15 585	18 628	22 651
2.5	Other, not elsewhere classified	36 713	52 589	59 370	54 123	56 535	56 069	61 519	62 709

Table 3. Financial assets of insurance corporations and autonomous pension funds *(cont.)*

Million NOK

		2006	2007	2008	2009	2010	2011	2012	2013
	Autonomous pension funds								
2	Financial assets	149 746	166 610	157 901	183 878	202 819	207 269	226 844	247 401
2.1	Currency and deposits	7 308	5 923	7 272	7 640	5 612	5 874	6 284	6 824
2.2	Securities other than shares, except financial derivatives	72 471	79 628	91 922	96 405	99 857	113 464	115 153	127 098
2.2.1	Short-term securities	3 816	4 205	3 820	6 931	8 620	18 181	9 737	11 103
2.2.2	Long-term securities	68 655	75 423	88 102	89 474	91 237	95 283	105 416	115 995
2.2.3	Securities issued by residents	61 617	57 093	67 131	75 282	78 931	89 516	91 734	99 315
2.2.4	Securities issued by non-residents	10 854	22 535	24 791	21 123	20 926	23 948	23 419	27 783
2.3	Loans	2 550	2 150	2 260	2 129	2 259	4 032	4 264	4 264
2.3.1	Short-term loans	0	0	0	0	0	0	0	0
2.3.2	Long-term loans	2 550	2 150	2 260	2 129	2 259	4 032	4 264	4 264
2.3.3	Loans granted to residents	2 550	2 150	2 260	2 129	2 259	4 032	4 264	4 264
2.3.4	Loans granted to non-residents	0	0	0	0	0	0	0	0
2.4	Shares and other equity	62 876	73 775	51 955	74 057	89 836	80 024	96 630	105 098
2.4.1	Shares issued by residents	41 047	48 045	33 906	45 759	56 430	48 370	54 846	58 943
2.4.2	Shares issued by non-residents	21 829	25 730	18 049	28 298	33 406	31 654	41 784	46 155
2.5	Other, not elsewhere classified	4 541	5 134	4 492	3 647	5 255	3 875	4 513	4 117

Note: Detailed metadata at: http://metalinks.oecd.org/instinv/20141203/927c

Table 4. Portfolio composition by type of investor

Percentage of total financial assets

Per cent

		2006	2007	2008	2009	2010	2011	2012	2013
	Investment funds								
2	Financial assets	..	..	..	..	..	..	..	..
2.1	Currency and deposits	..	..	..	..	..	..	..	..
2.2	Securities other than shares, except financial derivatives	..	..	..	..	..	..	..	..
2.2.1	Short-term securities	..	..	..	..	..	..	..	..
2.2.2	Long-term securities	..	..	..	..	..	..	..	..
2.2.3	Securities issued by residents	..	..	..	..	..	..	..	..
2.2.4	Securities issued by non-residents	..	..	..	..	..	..	..	..
2.3	Loans	..	..	..	..	..	..	..	..
2.3.1	Short-term loans	..	..	..	..	..	..	..	..
2.3.2	Long-term loans	..	..	..	..	..	..	..	..
2.3.3	Loans granted to residents	..	..	..	..	..	..	..	..
2.3.4	Loans granted to non-residents	..	..	..	..	..	..	..	..
2.4	Shares and other equity	..	..	..	..	..	..	..	..
2.4.1	Shares issued by residents	..	..	..	..	..	..	..	..
2.4.2	Shares issued by non-residents	..	..	..	..	..	..	..	..
2.5	Other, not elsewhere classified	..	..	..	..	..	..	..	..
	Insurance corporations								
2	Financial assets	100.0	100.0	100.0	100.0	100.0	100.0	100.0	100.0
2.1	Currency and deposits	3.7	5.0	4.5	3.5	3.4	3.1	3.3	3.7
2.2	Securities other than shares, except financial derivatives	48.5	42.4	49.9	48.6	44.9	47.3	46.9	47.5
2.2.1	Short-term securities	3.6	3.3	4.9	3.2	3.5	4.5	4.4	4.0
2.2.2	Long-term securities	44.9	39.1	45.0	45.4	41.4	42.8	42.5	43.5
2.2.3	Securities issued by residents	25.6	21.9	26.3	22.8	22.3	25.0	26.6	27.6
2.2.4	Securities issued by non-residents	22.9	20.5	23.6	25.8	22.6	22.4	20.3	19.9
2.3	Loans	2.7	3.4	5.5	7.6	5.3	4.6	4.4	4.8
2.3.1	Short-term loans	0.0	0.0	0.2	0.1	0.0	0.0	0.0	0.0
2.3.2	Long-term loans	2.7	3.4	5.3	7.6	5.3	4.5	4.4	4.8
2.3.3	Loans granted to residents	2.6	2.5	4.2	6.6	4.5	3.8	3.8	4.2
2.3.4	Loans granted to non-residents	0.1	0.9	1.3	1.0	0.8	0.8	0.6	0.6
2.4	Shares and other equity	38.2	40.4	30.1	33.2	39.4	38.8	39.1	38.3
2.4.1	Shares issued by residents	20.7	24.9	20.2	22.5	28.0	28.6	30.0	28.7
2.4.2	Shares issued by non-residents	17.4	15.4	9.9	10.7	11.4	10.2	9.2	9.5
2.5	Other, not elsewhere classified	6.9	8.8	9.9	7.1	6.9	6.2	6.3	5.7
	Autonomous pension funds								
2	Financial assets	100.0	100.0	100.0	100.0	100.0	100.0	100.0	100.0
2.1	Currency and deposits	4.9	3.6	4.6	4.2	2.8	2.8	2.8	2.8
2.2	Securities other than shares, except financial derivatives	48.4	47.8	58.2	52.4	49.2	54.7	50.8	51.4
2.2.1	Short-term securities	2.5	2.5	2.4	3.8	4.3	8.8	4.3	4.5
2.2.2	Long-term securities	45.8	45.3	55.8	48.7	45.0	46.0	46.5	46.9
2.2.3	Securities issued by residents	41.1	34.3	42.5	40.9	38.9	43.2	40.4	40.1
2.2.4	Securities issued by non-residents	7.2	13.5	15.7	11.5	10.3	11.6	10.3	11.2
2.3	Loans	1.7	1.3	1.4	1.2	1.1	1.9	1.9	1.7
2.3.1	Short-term loans	0.0	0.0	0.0	0.0	0.0	0.0	0.0	0.0
2.3.2	Long-term loans	1.7	1.3	1.4	1.2	1.1	1.9	1.9	1.7
2.3.3	Loans granted to residents	1.7	1.3	1.4	1.2	1.1	1.9	1.9	1.7
2.3.4	Loans granted to non-residents	0.0	0.0	0.0	0.0	0.0	0.0	0.0	0.0
2.4	Shares and other equity	42.0	44.3	32.9	40.3	44.3	38.6	42.6	42.5
2.4.1	Shares issued by residents	27.4	28.8	21.5	24.9	27.8	23.3	24.2	23.8
2.4.2	Shares issued by non-residents	14.6	15.4	11.4	15.4	16.5	15.3	18.4	18.7
2.5	Other, not elsewhere classified	3.0	3.1	2.8	2.0	2.6	1.9	2.0	1.7

Note: Detailed metadata at: http://metalinks.oecd.org/instinv/20141203/f729

Table 1. Financial assets of institutional investors, 2013

Million PLN

		Total	Investment funds: Open-end companies (mutual funds): Total	Money market funds	Other mutual funds	Closed-end companies: Total
2	Financial assets	207 369	130 846	2 813	128 033	76 523
2.1	Currency and deposits	19 567	14 492	1 112	13 380	5 075
2.2	Securities other than shares, except financial derivatives	87 777	70 756	1 690	69 066	17 021
2.2.1	Short-term securities	4 173	2 062	300	1 762	2 111
2.2.2	Long-term securities	83 605	68 694	1 391	67 303	14 911
2.2.3	Securities issued by residents	82 702	66 731	1 665	65 066	15 971
2.2.4	Securities issued by non-residents	5 075	4 024	25	3 999	1 051
2.3	Loans	895	2	0	2	893
2.3.1	Short-term loans	174	2	0	2	172
2.3.2	Long-term loans	720	0	0	0	720
2.3.3	Loans granted to residents	672	2	0	2	670
2.3.4	Loans granted to non-residents	223	0	0	0	223
2.4	Shares and other equity	87 714	43 541	0	43 541	44 173
2.4.1	Shares issued by residents	65 481	29 390	0	29 390	36 091
2.4.2	Shares issued by non-residents	22 232	14 151	0	14 151	8 081
2.5	Other, not elsewhere classified	11 416	2 056	11	2 045	9 360

		Insurance corporations and autonomous pension funds: Total	Insurance corporations: Total	Life insurance corporations	Non-life insurance corporations	Autonomous pension funds: Total
2	Financial assets	467 485	164 616	..	..	302 869
2.1	Currency and deposits	29 340	12 994	..	..	16 345
2.2	Securities other than shares, except financial derivatives	222 295	62 892	..	..	159 403
2.2.1	Short-term securities	1 818	13	..	..	1 806
2.2.2	Long-term securities	220 477	62 879	..	..	157 597
2.2.3	Securities issued by residents	219 053	59 775	..	..	159 278
2.2.4	Securities issued by non-residents	3 242	3 118	..	..	125
2.3	Loans	5 115	5 115	..	..	0
2.3.1	Short-term loans	4 432	4 432	..	..	0
2.3.2	Long-term loans	683	683	..	..	0
2.3.3	Loans granted to residents	5 115	5 115	..	..	0
2.3.4	Loans granted to non-residents	0	0	..	..	0
2.4	Shares and other equity	192 442	66 157	..	..	126 285
2.4.1	Shares issued by residents	183 628	61 556	..	..	122 072
2.4.2	Shares issued by non-residents	8 813	4 601	..	..	4 212
2.5	Other, not elsewhere classified	18 293	17 458	..	..	836

Note: Detailed metadata at: http://metalinks.oecd.org/instinv/20141203/d13e

Table 2. Financial assets of investment funds

Million PLN

		2006	2007	2008	2009	2010	2011	2012	2013
	Investment funds								
2	Financial assets	102 628	148 964	84 318	104 930	132 057	121 223	153 741	207 369
2.1	Currency and deposits	10 844	9 605	4 802	6 393	7 433	7 869	10 670	19 567
2.2	Securities other than shares, except financial derivatives	42 678	53 599	39 250	40 895	54 700	53 551	66 734	87 777
2.2.1	Short-term securities	2 704	8 139	3 374	3 743	4 264	3 867	4 050	4 173
2.2.2	Long-term securities	39 974	45 460	35 876	37 152	50 437	49 684	62 683	83 605
2.2.3	Securities issued by residents	..	..	..	..	51 924	50 356	63 136	82 702
2.2.4	Securities issued by non-residents	..	..	..	..	2 776	3 196	3 598	5 075
2.3	Loans	0	0	0	0	317	294	395	895
2.3.1	Short-term loans	0	0	0	0	135	89	120	174
2.3.2	Long-term loans	0	0	0	0	182	205	275	720
2.3.3	Loans granted to residents	0	0	0	0	311	287	386	672
2.3.4	Loans granted to non-residents	0	0	0	0	6	8	9	223
2.4	Shares and other equity	47 251	77 984	36 389	53 873	67 117	55 011	66 742	87 714
2.4.1	Shares issued by residents	..	..	..	..	50 823	43 758	54 332	65 481
2.4.2	Shares issued by non-residents	..	..	..	..	16 294	11 254	12 410	22 232
2.5	Other, not elsewhere classified	1 855	7 776	3 877	3 770	2 489	4 498	9 200	11 416
	Open-end companies (mutual funds)								
2	Financial assets	95 571	132 472	69 711	86 282	107 361	87 561	104 921	130 846
2.1	Currency and deposits	10 491	7 669	3 576	5 317	6 034	5 440	7 598	14 492
2.2	Securities other than shares, except financial derivatives	40 712	49 388	36 618	38 835	51 610	49 258	61 329	70 756
2.2.1	Short-term securities	2 621	7 378	1 627	2 235	3 883	3 209	2 491	2 062
2.2.2	Long-term securities	38 090	42 010	34 991	36 600	47 726	46 049	58 838	68 694
2.2.3	Securities issued by residents	..	..	..	..	49 463	46 821	58 848	66 731
2.2.4	Securities issued by non-residents	..	..	..	..	2 147	2 437	2 481	4 024
2.3	Loans	0	0	0	0	0	0	2	2
2.3.1	Short-term loans	0	0	0	0	0	0	2	2
2.3.2	Long-term loans	0	0	0	0	0	0	0	0
2.3.3	Loans granted to residents	0	0	0	0	0	0	2	2
2.3.4	Loans granted to non-residents	0	0	0	0	0	0	0	0
2.4	Shares and other equity	43 350	68 760	27 319	39 985	48 332	30 948	33 760	43 541
2.4.1	Shares issued by residents	..	..	..	..	34 501	21 659	23 279	29 390
2.4.2	Shares issued by non-residents	..	..	..	..	13 831	9 289	10 481	14 151
2.5	Other, not elsewhere classified	1 019	6 655	2 198	2 145	1 386	1 916	2 232	2 056
	Money market funds								
2	Financial assets	..	..	..	..	874	865	887	2 813
2.1	Currency and deposits	..	..	..	..	300	213	433	1 112
2.2	Securities other than shares, except financial derivatives	..	..	..	..	497	630	449	1 690
2.2.1	Short-term securities	..	..	..	..	106	27	71	300
2.2.2	Long-term securities	..	..	..	..	391	603	378	1 391
2.2.3	Securities issued by residents	..	..	..	..	452	585	424	1 665
2.2.4	Securities issued by non-residents	..	..	..	..	45	45	25	25
2.3	Loans	..	..	..	..	0	0	0	0
2.3.1	Short-term loans	..	..	..	..	0	0	0	0
2.3.2	Long-term loans	..	..	..	..	0	0	0	0
2.3.3	Loans granted to residents	..	..	..	..	0	0	0	0
2.3.4	Loans granted to non-residents	..	..	..	..	0	0	0	0
2.4	Shares and other equity	..	..	..	..	0	0	0	0
2.4.1	Shares issued by residents	..	..	..	..	0	0	0	0
2.4.2	Shares issued by non-residents	..	..	..	..	0	0	0	0
2.5	Other, not elsewhere classified	..	..	..	..	77	22	4	11
	Other mutual funds								
2	Financial assets	..	..	..	..	106 487	86 696	104 034	128 033
2.1	Currency and deposits	..	..	..	..	5 734	5 227	7 165	13 380
2.2	Securities other than shares, except financial derivatives	..	..	..	..	51 113	48 628	60 880	69 066
2.2.1	Short-term securities	..	..	..	..	3 777	3 182	2 420	1 762
2.2.2	Long-term securities	..	..	..	..	47 335	45 446	58 460	67 303
2.2.3	Securities issued by residents	..	..	..	..	49 011	46 236	58 424	65 066
2.2.4	Securities issued by non-residents	..	..	..	..	2 102	2 392	2 456	3 999
2.3	Loans	..	..	..	..	0	0	2	2
2.3.1	Short-term loans	..	..	..	..	0	0	2	2
2.3.2	Long-term loans	..	..	..	..	0	0	0	0
2.3.3	Loans granted to residents	..	..	..	..	0	0	2	2
2.3.4	Loans granted to non-residents	..	..	..	..	0	0	0	0
2.4	Shares and other equity	..	..	..	..	48 332	30 948	33 760	43 541
2.4.1	Shares issued by residents	..	..	..	..	34 501	21 659	23 279	29 390
2.4.2	Shares issued by non-residents	..	..	..	..	13 831	9 289	10 481	14 151
2.5	Other, not elsewhere classified	..	..	..	..	1 309	1 894	2 228	2 045

Table 2. Financial assets of investment funds *(cont.)*

Million PLN

		2006	2007	2008	2009	2010	2011	2012	2013
	Closed-end companies								
2	Financial assets	7 056	16 493	14 607	18 648	24 696	33 662	48 820	76 523
2.1	Currency and deposits	353	1 936	1 226	1 076	1 399	2 429	3 072	5 075
2.2	Securities other than shares, except financial derivatives	1 966	4 211	2 632	2 060	3 090	4 293	5 405	17 021
2.2.1	Short-term securities	83	761	1 747	1 509	381	658	1 559	2 111
2.2.2	Long-term securities	1 884	3 450	886	552	2 711	3 635	3 845	14 911
2.2.3	Securities issued by residents	..	..	..	..	2 461	3 535	4 288	15 971
2.2.4	Securities issued by non-residents	..	..	..	..	629	759	1 117	1 051
2.3	Loans	0	0	0	0	317	294	393	893
2.3.1	Short-term loans	0	0	0	0	135	89	118	172
2.3.2	Long-term loans	0	0	0	0	182	205	275	720
2.3.3	Loans granted to residents	..	..	..	..	311	287	384	670
2.3.4	Loans granted to non-residents	..	..	..	..	6	8	9	223
2.4	Shares and other equity	3 901	9 224	9 070	13 888	18 785	24 063	32 982	44 173
2.4.1	Shares issued by residents	..	..	..	..	16 322	22 099	31 053	36 091
2.4.2	Shares issued by non-residents	..	..	..	..	2 463	1 965	1 929	8 081
2.5	Other, not elsewhere classified	836	1 121	1 679	1 624	1 103	2 582	6 968	9 360

Note: Detailed metadata at: http://metalinks.oecd.org/instinv/20141203/d13e

Table 3. Financial assets of insurance corporations and autonomous pension funds

Million PLN

		2006	2007	2008	2009	2010	2011	2012	2013
	Insurance corporations and autonomous pension funds								
2	Financial assets	223 352	266 902	275 686	318 628	366 818	372 284	434 169	467 485
2.1	Currency and deposits	8 637	11 933	25 867	21 151	24 360	28 402	36 250	29 340
2.2	Securities other than shares, except financial derivatives	131 233	153 143	175 355	189 359	198 804	211 037	223 590	222 295
2.2.1	Short-term securities	4 625	4 233	3 789	4 001	3 179	2 604	4 021	1 818
2.2.2	Long-term securities	126 607	148 910	171 566	185 358	195 625	208 433	219 569	220 477
2.2.3	Securities issued by residents	129 401	150 779	172 775	186 901	196 670	208 510	220 683	219 053
2.2.4	Securities issued by non-residents	1 832	2 364	2 580	2 458	2 135	2 528	2 907	3 242
2.3	Loans	5 896	2 813	1 137	914	2 125	2 107	3 410	5 115
2.3.1	Short-term loans	5 685	2 620	1 057	829	1 968	1 935	3 206	4 432
2.3.2	Long-term loans	211	193	79	85	156	172	204	683
2.3.3	Loans granted to residents	5 890	2 801	1 107	858	2 093	2 016	3 410	5 115
2.3.4	Loans granted to non-residents	6	12	30	56	32	92	0	0
2.4	Shares and other equity	70 526	90 251	62 655	95 243	127 755	115 237	155 137	192 442
2.4.1	Shares issued by residents	67 621	86 515	60 134	91 532	122 901	111 019	148 912	183 628
2.4.2	Shares issued by non-residents	2 905	3 736	2 521	3 711	4 854	4 217	6 225	8 813
2.5	Other, not elsewhere classified	7 060	8 761	10 672	11 961	13 774	15 501	15 781	18 293
	Insurance corporations								
2	Financial assets	106 297	125 215	135 895	136 755	141 985	143 262	159 976	164 616
2.1	Currency and deposits	5 692	8 107	23 582	16 943	15 374	16 103	16 576	12 994
2.2	Securities other than shares, except financial derivatives	57 733	65 617	69 044	68 179	65 929	66 508	66 380	62 892
2.2.1	Short-term securities	1 942	857	2 023	2 899	1 164	764	599	13
2.2.2	Long-term securities	55 792	64 760	67 021	65 280	64 766	65 744	65 780	62 879
2.2.3	Securities issued by residents	56 346	64 060	67 037	66 297	64 409	64 521	63 669	59 775
2.2.4	Securities issued by non-residents	1 388	1 557	2 007	1 882	1 520	1 987	2 711	3 118
2.3	Loans	5 896	2 813	1 137	914	2 125	2 107	3 410	5 115
2.3.1	Short-term loans	5 685	2 620	1 057	829	1 968	1 935	3 206	4 432
2.3.2	Long-term loans	211	193	79	85	156	172	204	683
2.3.3	Loans granted to residents	5 890	2 801	1 107	858	2 093	2 016	3 410	5 115
2.3.4	Loans granted to non-residents	6	12	30	56	32	92	0	0
2.4	Shares and other equity	30 163	40 275	31 648	39 279	45 389	43 821	58 075	66 157
2.4.1	Shares issued by residents	28 221	37 457	29 549	36 431	41 552	40 223	54 002	61 556
2.4.2	Shares issued by non-residents	1 943	2 818	2 099	2 848	3 837	3 598	4 072	4 601
2.5	Other, not elsewhere classified	6 812	8 402	10 484	11 441	13 168	14 723	15 536	17 458
	Life insurance corporations								
2	Financial assets	..	..	..	..	..	..	..	..
2.1	Currency and deposits	..	..	..	..	..	..	..	..
2.2	Securities other than shares, except financial derivatives	..	..	..	..	..	..	..	..
2.2.1	Short-term securities	..	..	..	..	..	..	..	..
2.2.2	Long-term securities	..	..	..	..	..	..	..	..
2.2.3	Securities issued by residents	..	..	..	..	..	..	..	..
2.2.4	Securities issued by non-residents	..	..	..	..	..	..	..	..
2.3	Loans	..	..	..	..	..	..	..	..
2.3.1	Short-term loans	..	..	..	..	..	..	..	..
2.3.2	Long-term loans	..	..	..	..	..	..	..	..
2.3.3	Loans granted to residents	..	..	..	..	..	..	..	..
2.3.4	Loans granted to non-residents	..	..	..	..	..	..	..	..
2.4	Shares and other equity	..	..	..	..	..	..	..	..
2.4.1	Shares issued by residents	..	..	..	..	..	..	..	..
2.4.2	Shares issued by non-residents	..	..	..	..	..	..	..	..
2.5	Other, not elsewhere classified	..	..	..	..	..	..	..	..
	Non-life insurance corporations								
2	Financial assets	..	..	..	..	..	..	..	..
2.1	Currency and deposits	..	..	..	..	..	..	..	..
2.2	Securities other than shares, except financial derivatives	..	..	..	..	..	..	..	..
2.2.1	Short-term securities	..	..	..	..	..	..	..	..
2.2.2	Long-term securities	..	..	..	..	..	..	..	..
2.2.3	Securities issued by residents	..	..	..	..	..	..	..	..
2.2.4	Securities issued by non-residents	..	..	..	..	..	..	..	..
2.3	Loans	..	..	..	..	..	..	..	..
2.3.1	Short-term loans	..	..	..	..	..	..	..	..
2.3.2	Long-term loans	..	..	..	..	..	..	..	..
2.3.3	Loans granted to residents	..	..	..	..	..	..	..	..
2.3.4	Loans granted to non-residents	..	..	..	..	..	..	..	..
2.4	Shares and other equity	..	..	..	..	..	..	..	..
2.4.1	Shares issued by residents	..	..	..	..	..	..	..	..
2.4.2	Shares issued by non-residents	..	..	..	..	..	..	..	..
2.5	Other, not elsewhere classified	..	..	..	..	..	..	..	..

Table 3. Financial assets of insurance corporations and autonomous pension funds *(cont.)*

Million PLN

		2006	2007	2008	2009	2010	2011	2012	2013
	Autonomous pension funds								
2	Financial assets	117 055	141 687	139 792	181 873	224 833	229 022	274 193	302 869
2.1	Currency and deposits	2 945	3 826	2 285	4 209	8 986	12 299	19 674	16 345
2.2	Securities other than shares, except financial derivatives	73 499	87 526	106 311	121 181	132 875	144 529	157 211	159 403
2.2.1	Short-term securities	2 683	3 376	1 765	1 102	2 015	1 840	3 422	1 806
2.2.2	Long-term securities	70 816	84 150	104 545	120 078	130 860	142 689	153 789	157 597
2.2.3	Securities issued by residents	73 055	86 719	105 738	120 604	132 260	143 989	157 014	159 278
2.2.4	Securities issued by non-residents	444	807	573	576	615	540	196	125
2.3	Loans	0	0	0	0	0	0	0	0
2.3.1	Short-term loans	0	0	0	0	0	0	0	0
2.3.2	Long-term loans	0	0	0	0	0	0	0	0
2.3.3	Loans granted to residents	0	0	0	0	0	0	0	0
2.3.4	Loans granted to non-residents	0	0	0	0	0	0	0	0
2.4	Shares and other equity	40 363	49 976	31 007	55 963	82 366	71 416	97 063	126 285
2.4.1	Shares issued by residents	39 400	49 058	30 585	55 101	81 349	70 796	94 909	122 072
2.4.2	Shares issued by non-residents	962	918	422	863	1 017	619	2 153	4 212
2.5	Other, not elsewhere classified	248	359	188	520	606	778	246	836

Note: Detailed metadata at: http://metalinks.oecd.org/instinv/20141203/d13e

Table 4. Portfolio composition by type of investor

Percentage of total financial assets

Per cent

		2006	2007	2008	2009	2010	2011	2012	2013
	Investment funds								
2	Financial assets	100.0	100.0	100.0	100.0	100.0	100.0	100.0	100.0
2.1	Currency and deposits	10.6	6.4	5.7	6.1	5.6	6.5	6.9	9.4
2.2	Securities other than shares, except financial derivatives	41.6	36.0	46.6	39.0	41.4	44.2	43.4	42.3
2.2.1	Short-term securities	2.6	5.5	4.0	3.6	3.2	3.2	2.6	2.0
2.2.2	Long-term securities	39.0	30.5	42.5	35.4	38.2	41.0	40.8	40.3
2.2.3	Securities issued by residents	..	..	..	..	39.3	41.5	41.1	39.9
2.2.4	Securities issued by non-residents	..	..	..	..	2.1	2.6	2.3	2.4
2.3	Loans	0.0	0.0	0.0	0.0	0.2	0.2	0.3	0.4
2.3.1	Short-term loans	0.0	0.0	0.0	0.0	0.1	0.1	0.1	0.1
2.3.2	Long-term loans	0.0	0.0	0.0	0.0	0.1	0.2	0.2	0.3
2.3.3	Loans granted to residents	0.0	0.0	0.0	0.0	0.2	0.2	0.3	0.3
2.3.4	Loans granted to non-residents	0.0	0.0	0.0	0.0	0.0	0.0	0.0	0.1
2.4	Shares and other equity	46.0	52.4	43.2	51.3	50.8	45.4	43.4	42.3
2.4.1	Shares issued by residents	..	..	..	..	38.5	36.1	35.3	31.6
2.4.2	Shares issued by non-residents	..	..	..	..	12.3	9.3	8.1	10.7
2.5	Other, not elsewhere classified	1.8	5.2	4.6	3.6	1.9	3.7	6.0	5.5
	Insurance corporations								
2	Financial assets	100.0	100.0	100.0	100.0	100.0	100.0	100.0	100.0
2.1	Currency and deposits	5.4	6.5	17.4	12.4	10.8	11.2	10.4	7.9
2.2	Securities other than shares, except financial derivatives	54.3	52.4	50.8	49.9	46.4	46.4	41.5	38.2
2.2.1	Short-term securities	1.8	0.7	1.5	2.1	0.8	0.5	0.4	0.0
2.2.2	Long-term securities	52.5	51.7	49.3	47.7	45.6	45.9	41.1	38.2
2.2.3	Securities issued by residents	53.0	51.2	49.3	48.5	45.4	45.0	39.8	36.3
2.2.4	Securities issued by non-residents	1.3	1.2	1.5	1.4	1.1	1.4	1.7	1.9
2.3	Loans	5.5	2.2	0.8	0.7	1.5	1.5	2.1	3.1
2.3.1	Short-term loans	5.3	2.1	0.8	0.6	1.4	1.4	2.0	2.7
2.3.2	Long-term loans	0.2	0.2	0.1	0.1	0.1	0.1	0.1	0.4
2.3.3	Loans granted to residents	5.5	2.2	0.8	0.6	1.5	1.4	2.1	3.1
2.3.4	Loans granted to non-residents	0.0	0.0	0.0	0.0	0.0	0.1	0.0	0.0
2.4	Shares and other equity	28.4	32.2	23.3	28.7	32.0	30.6	36.3	40.2
2.4.1	Shares issued by residents	26.5	29.9	21.7	26.6	29.3	28.1	33.8	37.4
2.4.2	Shares issued by non-residents	1.8	2.3	1.5	2.1	2.7	2.5	2.5	2.8
2.5	Other, not elsewhere classified	6.4	6.7	7.7	8.4	9.3	10.3	9.7	10.6
	Autonomous pension funds								
2	Financial assets	100.0	100.0	100.0	100.0	100.0	100.0	100.0	100.0
2.1	Currency and deposits	2.5	2.7	1.6	2.3	4.0	5.4	7.2	5.4
2.2	Securities other than shares, except financial derivatives	62.8	61.8	76.0	66.6	59.1	63.1	57.3	52.6
2.2.1	Short-term securities	2.3	2.4	1.3	0.6	0.9	0.8	1.2	0.6
2.2.2	Long-term securities	60.5	59.4	74.8	66.0	58.2	62.3	56.1	52.0
2.2.3	Securities issued by residents	62.4	61.2	75.6	66.3	58.8	62.9	57.3	52.6
2.2.4	Securities issued by non-residents	0.4	0.6	0.4	0.3	0.3	0.2	0.1	0.0
2.3	Loans	0.0	0.0	0.0	0.0	0.0	0.0	0.0	0.0
2.3.1	Short-term loans	0.0	0.0	0.0	0.0	0.0	0.0	0.0	0.0
2.3.2	Long-term loans	0.0	0.0	0.0	0.0	0.0	0.0	0.0	0.0
2.3.3	Loans granted to residents	0.0	0.0	0.0	0.0	0.0	0.0	0.0	0.0
2.3.4	Loans granted to non-residents	0.0	0.0	0.0	0.0	0.0	0.0	0.0	0.0
2.4	Shares and other equity	34.5	35.3	22.2	30.8	36.6	31.2	35.4	41.7
2.4.1	Shares issued by residents	33.7	34.6	21.9	30.3	36.2	30.9	34.6	40.3
2.4.2	Shares issued by non-residents	0.8	0.6	0.3	0.5	0.5	0.3	0.8	1.4
2.5	Other, not elsewhere classified	0.2	0.3	0.1	0.3	0.3	0.3	0.1	0.3

Note: Detailed metadata at: http://metalinks.oecd.org/instinv/20141203/f729

Table 1. Financial assets of institutional investors, 2013

Million EUR (1999 PTE euro)

		Investment funds				
		Total	Open-end companies (mutual funds)			Closed-end companies
			Total	Money market funds	Other mutual funds	Total
2	Financial assets	14 477	12 296	2 392	9 904	2 766
2.1	Currency and deposits	4 353	3 413	1 961	1 452	940
2.2	Securities other than shares, except financial derivatives	6 048	5 308	420	4 888	740
2.2.1	Short-term securities	1 348	1 344	289	1 055	4
2.2.2	Long-term securities	4 700	3 964	131	3 833	736
2.2.3	Securities issued by residents	2 616	2 368	295	2 073	247
2.2.4	Securities issued by non-residents	3 432	2 939	125	2 814	493
2.3	Loans	0	0	0	0	0
2.3.1	Short-term loans	0	0	0	0	0
2.3.2	Long-term loans	0	0	0	0	0
2.3.3	Loans granted to residents	0	0	0	0	0
2.3.4	Loans granted to non-residents	0	0	0	0	0
2.4	Shares and other equity	3 100	3 217	0	3 217	467
2.4.1	Shares issued by residents	740	907	0	907	417
2.4.2	Shares issued by non-residents	2 360	2 310	0	2 310	50
2.5	Other, not elsewhere classified	977	358	11	347	619

		Insurance corporations and autonomous pension funds				
		Total	Insurance corporations			Autonomous pension funds
			Total	Life insurance corporations	Non-life insurance corporations	Total
2	Financial assets	73 264	59 514	..	..	14 231
2.1	Currency and deposits	8 343	6 540	..	..	1 803
2.2	Securities other than shares, except financial derivatives	45 968	39 359	..	..	6 717
2.2.1	Short-term securities	1 663	1 455	..	..	209
2.2.2	Long-term securities	44 305	37 904	..	..	6 508
2.2.3	Securities issued by residents	21 349	19 280	..	..	2 176
2.2.4	Securities issued by non-residents	24 619	20 079	..	..	4 541
2.3	Loans	512	512	..	..	0
2.3.1	Short-term loans	18	18	..	..	0
2.3.2	Long-term loans	494	494	..	..	0
2.3.3	Loans granted to residents	92	92	..	..	0
2.3.4	Loans granted to non-residents	421	420	..	..	0
2.4	Shares and other equity	11 613	6 228	..	..	5 424
2.4.1	Shares issued by residents	5 795	3 511	..	..	2 324
2.4.2	Shares issued by non-residents	5 817	2 717	..	..	3 100
2.5	Other, not elsewhere classified	6 828	6 875	..	..	287

Note: Detailed metadata at: http://metalinks.oecd.org/instinv/20141203/42e3

PORTUGAL

Table 2. Financial assets of investment funds

Million EUR (1999 PTE euro)

		2006	2007	2008	2009	2010	2011	2012	2013
	Investment funds								
2	Financial assets	29 603	27 583	15 739	18 855	15 832	12 205	13 815	14 477
2.1	Currency and deposits	3 259	3 702	2 356	3 414	2 469	1 796	3 023	4 353
2.2	Securities other than shares, except financial derivatives	19 777	16 359	9 217	10 583	8 338	6 371	6 851	6 048
2.2.1	Short-term securities	2 320	1 129	840	878	663	1 032	1 722	1 348
2.2.2	Long-term securities	17 457	15 231	8 377	9 705	7 675	5 340	5 129	4 700
2.2.3	Securities issued by residents	2 720	2 969	2 295	3 588	2 858	2 689	2 589	2 616
2.2.4	Securities issued by non-residents	17 057	13 391	6 923	6 996	5 480	3 682	4 262	3 432
2.3	Loans	0	0	0	0	0	0	0	0
2.3.1	Short-term loans	0	0	0	0	0	0	0	0
2.3.2	Long-term loans	0	0	0	0	0	0	0	0
2.3.3	Loans granted to residents	0	0	0	0	0	0	0	0
2.3.4	Loans granted to non-residents	0	0	0	0	0	0	0	0
2.4	Shares and other equity	5 541	6 189	3 173	3 870	4 088	3 037	3 020	3 100
2.4.1	Shares issued by residents	1 413	1 702	804	1 134	892	639	745	740
2.4.2	Shares issued by non-residents	4 128	4 487	2 370	2 736	3 196	2 399	2 275	2 360
2.5	Other, not elsewhere classified	1 025	1 332	993	987	937	1 000	921	977
	Open-end companies (mutual funds)								
2	Financial assets	28 846	25 595	13 936	16 983	13 957	10 921	12 153	12 296
2.1	Currency and deposits	2 779	3 102	1 803	2 814	1 943	1 323	2 542	3 413
2.2	Securities other than shares, except financial derivatives	18 196	14 559	7 939	9 372	7 086	5 693	5 981	5 308
2.2.1	Short-term securities	2 320	1 129	840	877	663	1 032	1 721	1 344
2.2.2	Long-term securities	15 876	13 431	7 099	8 495	6 423	4 662	4 261	3 964
2.2.3	Securities issued by residents	1 920	1 963	1 485	2 757	2 430	2 538	2 325	2 368
2.2.4	Securities issued by non-residents	16 277	12 596	6 454	6 615	4 656	3 155	3 656	2 939
2.3	Loans	0	0	0	0	0	0	0	0
2.3.1	Short-term loans	0	0	0	0	0	0	0	0
2.3.2	Long-term loans	0	0	0	0	0	0	0	0
2.3.3	Loans granted to residents	0	0	0	0	0	0	0	0
2.3.4	Loans granted to non-residents	0	0	0	0	0	0	0	0
2.4	Shares and other equity	7 220	7 238	3 723	4 403	4 521	3 399	3 158	3 217
2.4.1	Shares issued by residents	3 094	2 753	1 358	1 678	1 342	1 014	897	907
2.4.2	Shares issued by non-residents	4 126	4 485	2 365	2 726	3 179	2 385	2 261	2 310
2.5	Other, not elsewhere classified	651	695	471	394	407	506	471	358
	Money market funds								
2	Financial assets	763	385	15	12	46	65	1 309	2 392
2.1	Currency and deposits	10	66	12	10	32	50	1 227	1 961
2.2	Securities other than shares, except financial derivatives	746	320	3	2	14	15	78	420
2.2.1	Short-term securities	257	78	3	2	8	15	76	289
2.2.2	Long-term securities	489	241	0	0	6	0	2	131
2.2.3	Securities issued by residents	27	17	3	2	8	13	55	295
2.2.4	Securities issued by non-residents	719	303	0	0	5	2	24	125
2.3	Loans	0	0	0	0	0	0	0	0
2.3.1	Short-term loans	0	0	0	0	0	0	0	0
2.3.2	Long-term loans	0	0	0	0	0	0	0	0
2.3.3	Loans granted to residents	0	0	0	0	0	0	0	0
2.3.4	Loans granted to non-residents	0	0	0	0	0	0	0	0
2.4	Shares and other equity	1	0	0	0	0	0	0	0
2.4.1	Shares issued by residents	0	0	0	0	0	0	0	0
2.4.2	Shares issued by non-residents	1	0	0	0	0	0	0	0
2.5	Other, not elsewhere classified	6	0	0	0	0	0	4	11
	Other mutual funds								
2	Financial assets	28 083	25 209	13 920	16 971	13 911	10 856	10 843	9 904
2.1	Currency and deposits	2 769	3 036	1 791	2 804	1 910	1 274	1 315	1 452
2.2	Securities other than shares, except financial derivatives	17 450	14 239	7 936	9 370	7 072	5 678	5 903	4 888
2.2.1	Short-term securities	2 063	1 050	837	875	655	1 017	1 644	1 055
2.2.2	Long-term securities	15 387	13 189	7 099	8 495	6 417	4 662	4 258	3 833
2.2.3	Securities issued by residents	1 893	1 947	1 482	2 755	2 422	2 525	2 270	2 073
2.2.4	Securities issued by non-residents	15 558	12 293	6 454	6 615	4 651	3 153	3 633	2 814
2.3	Loans	0	0	0	0	0	0	0	0
2.3.1	Short-term loans	0	0	0	0	0	0	0	0
2.3.2	Long-term loans	0	0	0	0	0	0	0	0
2.3.3	Loans granted to residents	0	0	0	0	0	0	0	0
2.3.4	Loans granted to non-residents	0	0	0	0	0	0	0	0
2.4	Shares and other equity	7 220	7 238	3 723	4 403	4 521	3 399	3 158	3 217
2.4.1	Shares issued by residents	3 094	2 753	1 358	1 678	1 342	1 014	897	907
2.4.2	Shares issued by non-residents	4 126	4 485	2 365	2 726	3 179	2 385	2 261	2 310
2.5	Other, not elsewhere classified	645	695	471	394	407	505	467	347

Table 2. Financial assets of investment funds *(cont.)*

Million EUR (1999 PTE euro)

		2006	2007	2008	2009	2010	2011	2012	2013
	Closed-end companies								
2	Financial assets	2 643	3 296	2 614	2 638	2 561	1 907	2 197	2 766
2.1	Currency and deposits	480	600	553	600	527	473	481	940
2.2	Securities other than shares, except financial derivatives	1 581	1 800	1 278	1 211	1 252	678	870	740
2.2.1	Short-term securities	0	0	0	1	0	0	1	4
2.2.2	Long-term securities	1 581	1 800	1 278	1 210	1 252	678	868	736
2.2.3	Securities issued by residents	801	1 006	810	830	429	151	264	247
2.2.4	Securities issued by non-residents	780	795	469	381	823	527	606	493
2.3	Loans	0	0	0	0	0	0	0	0
2.3.1	Short-term loans	0	0	0	0	0	0	0	0
2.3.2	Long-term loans	0	0	0	0	0	0	0	0
2.3.3	Loans granted to residents	0	0	0	0	0	0	0	0
2.3.4	Loans granted to non-residents	0	0	0	0	0	0	0	0
2.4	Shares and other equity	207	258	261	234	253	262	397	467
2.4.1	Shares issued by residents	205	256	257	223	236	248	383	417
2.4.2	Shares issued by non-residents	2	2	4	11	16	14	14	50
2.5	Other, not elsewhere classified	374	637	522	593	530	495	450	619

Note: Detailed metadata at: http://metalinks.oecd.org/instinv/20141203/42e3

Table 3. Financial assets of insurance corporations and autonomous pension funds

Million EUR (1999 PTE euro)

		2006	2007	2008	2009	2010	2011	2012	2013
	Insurance corporations and autonomous pension funds								
2	Financial assets	69 646	75 839	75 871	83 851	83 956	73 769	72 444	73 264
2.1	Currency and deposits	5 372	4 954	8 173	6 654	8 118	8 082	9 144	8 343
2.2	Securities other than shares, except financial derivatives	44 635	48 965	49 130	56 639	56 024	46 370	46 578	45 968
2.2.1	Short-term securities	856	577	653	520	1 362	1 878	2 210	1 663
2.2.2	Long-term securities	43 779	48 387	48 477	56 119	54 662	44 493	44 368	44 305
2.2.3	Securities issued by residents	9 598	10 556	11 438	13 959	18 521	19 801	21 889	21 349
2.2.4	Securities issued by non-residents	35 037	38 408	37 692	42 680	37 503	26 569	24 689	24 619
2.3	Loans	207	211	357	410	440	467	387	512
2.3.1	Short-term loans	18	18	18	18	18	18	18	18
2.3.2	Long-term loans	188	193	339	392	422	449	368	494
2.3.3	Loans granted to residents	105	115	86	83	82	81	68	92
2.3.4	Loans granted to non-residents	102	96	271	327	358	386	319	421
2.4	Shares and other equity	17 724	18 436	13 426	14 826	13 738	11 433	9 808	11 613
2.4.1	Shares issued by residents	8 488	8 396	7 157	7 986	6 830	6 324	5 249	5 795
2.4.2	Shares issued by non-residents	9 236	10 039	6 269	6 840	6 908	5 109	4 559	5 817
2.5	Other, not elsewhere classified	1 708	3 273	4 785	5 321	5 637	7 416	6 528	6 828
	Insurance corporations								
2	Financial assets	50 129	54 804	56 712	63 261	65 803	59 498	59 177	59 514
2.1	Currency and deposits	4 278	3 788	5 333	5 240	5 648	6 308	6 981	6 540
2.2	Securities other than shares, except financial derivatives	37 236	40 684	39 976	45 616	47 197	39 592	39 781	39 359
2.2.1	Short-term securities	581	530	486	462	1 132	1 334	1 951	1 455
2.2.2	Long-term securities	36 655	40 154	39 490	45 154	46 065	38 258	37 830	37 904
2.2.3	Securities issued by residents	8 274	8 911	9 619	11 608	15 849	17 067	19 655	19 280
2.2.4	Securities issued by non-residents	28 962	31 773	30 357	34 008	31 348	22 525	20 126	20 079
2.3	Loans	206	211	357	410	440	467	386	512
2.3.1	Short-term loans	18	18	18	18	18	18	18	18
2.3.2	Long-term loans	188	193	339	392	422	449	368	494
2.3.3	Loans granted to residents	105	115	86	83	82	81	68	92
2.3.4	Loans granted to non-residents	101	96	271	327	358	386	318	420
2.4	Shares and other equity	6 577	7 062	6 077	6 624	6 727	5 492	5 266	6 228
2.4.1	Shares issued by residents	2 798	3 048	4 002	4 349	3 577	3 430	3 220	3 511
2.4.2	Shares issued by non-residents	3 779	4 014	2 075	2 275	3 150	2 062	2 046	2 717
2.5	Other, not elsewhere classified	1 832	3 059	4 969	5 371	5 791	7 639	6 763	6 875
	Life insurance corporations								
2	Financial assets	..	..	..	..	..	..	..	..
2.1	Currency and deposits	..	..	..	..	..	..	..	..
2.2	Securities other than shares, except financial derivatives	..	..	..	..	..	..	..	..
2.2.1	Short-term securities	..	..	..	..	..	..	..	..
2.2.2	Long-term securities	..	..	..	..	..	..	..	..
2.2.3	Securities issued by residents	..	..	..	..	..	..	..	..
2.2.4	Securities issued by non-residents	..	..	..	..	..	..	..	..
2.3	Loans	..	..	..	..	..	..	..	..
2.3.1	Short-term loans	..	..	..	..	..	..	..	..
2.3.2	Long-term loans	..	..	..	..	..	..	..	..
2.3.3	Loans granted to residents	..	..	..	..	..	..	..	..
2.3.4	Loans granted to non-residents	..	..	..	..	..	..	..	..
2.4	Shares and other equity	..	..	..	..	..	..	..	..
2.4.1	Shares issued by residents	..	..	..	..	..	..	..	..
2.4.2	Shares issued by non-residents	..	..	..	..	..	..	..	..
2.5	Other, not elsewhere classified	..	..	..	..	..	..	..	..
	Non-life insurance corporations								
2	Financial assets	..	..	..	..	..	..	..	..
2.1	Currency and deposits	..	..	..	..	..	..	..	..
2.2	Securities other than shares, except financial derivatives	..	..	..	..	..	..	..	..
2.2.1	Short-term securities	..	..	..	..	..	..	..	..
2.2.2	Long-term securities	..	..	..	..	..	..	..	..
2.2.3	Securities issued by residents	..	..	..	..	..	..	..	..
2.2.4	Securities issued by non-residents	..	..	..	..	..	..	..	..
2.3	Loans	..	..	..	..	..	..	..	..
2.3.1	Short-term loans	..	..	..	..	..	..	..	..
2.3.2	Long-term loans	..	..	..	..	..	..	..	..
2.3.3	Loans granted to residents	..	..	..	..	..	..	..	..
2.3.4	Loans granted to non-residents	..	..	..	..	..	..	..	..
2.4	Shares and other equity	..	..	..	..	..	..	..	..
2.4.1	Shares issued by residents	..	..	..	..	..	..	..	..
2.4.2	Shares issued by non-residents	..	..	..	..	..	..	..	..
2.5	Other, not elsewhere classified	..	..	..	..	..	..	..	..

Table 3. Financial assets of insurance corporations and autonomous pension funds *(cont.)*

Million EUR (1999 PTE euro)

		2006	2007	2008	2009	2010	2011	2012	2013
	Autonomous pension funds								
2	Financial assets	19 849	21 427	19 559	21 051	18 658	14 760	13 751	14 231
2.1	Currency and deposits	1 094	1 167	2 840	1 414	2 469	1 774	2 163	1 803
2.2	Securities other than shares, except financial derivatives	7 417	8 364	9 244	11 136	8 939	6 898	6 904	6 717
2.2.1	Short-term securities	274	47	167	59	230	544	259	209
2.2.2	Long-term securities	7 143	8 317	9 077	11 077	8 709	6 354	6 645	6 508
2.2.3	Securities issued by residents	1 343	1 728	1 910	2 464	2 785	2 853	2 341	2 176
2.2.4	Securities issued by non-residents	6 074	6 636	7 334	8 672	6 154	4 045	4 563	4 541
2.3	Loans	0	0	0	0	0	0	0	0
2.3.1	Short-term loans	0	0	0	0	0	0	0	0
2.3.2	Long-term loans	0	0	0	0	0	0	0	0
2.3.3	Loans granted to residents	0	0	0	0	0	0	0	0
2.3.4	Loans granted to non-residents	0	0	0	0	0	0	0	0
2.4	Shares and other equity	11 162	11 382	7 363	8 215	7 053	5 983	4 585	5 424
2.4.1	Shares issued by residents	5 704	5 358	3 168	3 650	3 294	2 937	2 070	2 324
2.4.2	Shares issued by non-residents	5 458	6 024	4 195	4 565	3 759	3 046	2 515	3 100
2.5	Other, not elsewhere classified	176	514	112	286	197	105	99	287

Note: Detailed metadata at: http://metalinks.oecd.org/instinv/20141203/42e3

PORTUGAL

Table 4. Portfolio composition by type of investor

Percentage of total financial assets

Per cent

		2006	2007	2008	2009	2010	2011	2012	2013
	Investment funds								
2	Financial assets	100.0	100.0	100.0	100.0	100.0	100.0	100.0	100.0
2.1	Currency and deposits	11.0	13.4	15.0	18.1	15.6	14.7	21.9	30.1
2.2	Securities other than shares, except financial derivatives	66.8	59.3	58.6	56.1	52.7	52.2	49.6	41.8
2.2.1	Short-term securities	7.8	4.1	5.3	4.7	4.2	8.5	12.5	9.3
2.2.2	Long-term securities	59.0	55.2	53.2	51.5	48.5	43.8	37.1	32.5
2.2.3	Securities issued by residents	9.2	10.8	14.6	19.0	18.1	22.0	18.7	18.1
2.2.4	Securities issued by non-residents	57.6	48.5	44.0	37.1	34.6	30.2	30.9	23.7
2.3	Loans	0.0	0.0	0.0	0.0	0.0	0.0	0.0	0.0
2.3.1	Short-term loans	0.0	0.0	0.0	0.0	0.0	0.0	0.0	0.0
2.3.2	Long-term loans	0.0	0.0	0.0	0.0	0.0	0.0	0.0	0.0
2.3.3	Loans granted to residents	0.0	0.0	0.0	0.0	0.0	0.0	0.0	0.0
2.3.4	Loans granted to non-residents	0.0	0.0	0.0	0.0	0.0	0.0	0.0	0.0
2.4	Shares and other equity	18.7	22.4	20.2	20.5	25.8	24.9	21.9	21.4
2.4.1	Shares issued by residents	4.8	6.2	5.1	6.0	5.6	5.2	5.4	5.1
2.4.2	Shares issued by non-residents	13.9	16.3	15.1	14.5	20.2	19.7	16.5	16.3
2.5	Other, not elsewhere classified	3.5	4.8	6.3	5.2	5.9	8.2	6.7	6.8
	Insurance corporations								
2	Financial assets	100.0	100.0	100.0	100.0	100.0	100.0	100.0	100.0
2.1	Currency and deposits	8.5	6.9	9.4	8.3	8.6	10.6	11.8	11.0
2.2	Securities other than shares, except financial derivatives	74.3	74.2	70.5	72.1	71.7	66.5	67.2	66.1
2.2.1	Short-term securities	1.2	1.0	0.9	0.7	1.7	2.2	3.3	2.4
2.2.2	Long-term securities	73.1	73.3	69.6	71.4	70.0	64.3	63.9	63.7
2.2.3	Securities issued by residents	16.5	16.3	17.0	18.3	24.1	28.7	33.2	32.4
2.2.4	Securities issued by non-residents	57.8	58.0	53.5	53.8	47.6	37.9	34.0	33.7
2.3	Loans	0.4	0.4	0.6	0.6	0.7	0.8	0.7	0.9
2.3.1	Short-term loans	0.0	0.0	0.0	0.0	0.0	0.0	0.0	0.0
2.3.2	Long-term loans	0.4	0.4	0.6	0.6	0.6	0.8	0.6	0.8
2.3.3	Loans granted to residents	0.2	0.2	0.2	0.1	0.1	0.1	0.1	0.2
2.3.4	Loans granted to non-residents	0.2	0.2	0.5	0.5	0.5	0.6	0.5	0.7
2.4	Shares and other equity	13.1	12.9	10.7	10.5	10.2	9.2	8.9	10.5
2.4.1	Shares issued by residents	5.6	5.6	7.1	6.9	5.4	5.8	5.4	5.9
2.4.2	Shares issued by non-residents	7.5	7.3	3.7	3.6	4.8	3.5	3.5	4.6
2.5	Other, not elsewhere classified	3.7	5.6	8.8	8.5	8.8	12.8	11.4	11.6
	Autonomous pension funds								
2	Financial assets	100.0	100.0	100.0	100.0	100.0	100.0	100.0	100.0
2.1	Currency and deposits	5.5	5.4	14.5	6.7	13.2	12.0	15.7	12.7
2.2	Securities other than shares, except financial derivatives	37.4	39.0	47.3	52.9	47.9	46.7	50.2	47.2
2.2.1	Short-term securities	1.4	0.2	0.9	0.3	1.2	3.7	1.9	1.5
2.2.2	Long-term securities	36.0	38.8	46.4	52.6	46.7	43.0	48.3	45.7
2.2.3	Securities issued by residents	6.8	8.1	9.8	11.7	14.9	19.3	17.0	15.3
2.2.4	Securities issued by non-residents	30.6	31.0	37.5	41.2	33.0	27.4	33.2	31.9
2.3	Loans	0.0	0.0	0.0	0.0	0.0	0.0	0.0	0.0
2.3.1	Short-term loans	0.0	0.0	0.0	0.0	0.0	0.0	0.0	0.0
2.3.2	Long-term loans	0.0	0.0	0.0	0.0	0.0	0.0	0.0	0.0
2.3.3	Loans granted to residents	0.0	0.0	0.0	0.0	0.0	0.0	0.0	0.0
2.3.4	Loans granted to non-residents	0.0	0.0	0.0	0.0	0.0	0.0	0.0	0.0
2.4	Shares and other equity	56.2	53.1	37.6	39.0	37.8	40.5	33.3	38.1
2.4.1	Shares issued by residents	28.7	25.0	16.2	17.3	17.7	19.9	15.1	16.3
2.4.2	Shares issued by non-residents	27.5	28.1	21.4	21.7	20.1	20.6	18.3	21.8
2.5	Other, not elsewhere classified	0.9	2.4	0.6	1.4	1.1	0.7	0.7	2.0

Note: Detailed metadata at: http://metalinks.oecd.org/instinv/20141203/f729

Table 1. Financial assets of institutional investors, 2011

Million EUR (2009 SKK euro)

		Total	Investment funds: Open-end companies (mutual funds): Total	Money market funds	Other mutual funds	Closed-end companies: Total
2	Financial assets	3 247	3 247	384	2 863	..
2.1	Currency and deposits	977	977	197	780	..
2.2	Securities other than shares, except financial derivatives	1 467	1 467	186	1 281	..
2.2.1	Short-term securities	126	126	30	96	..
2.2.2	Long-term securities	1 341	1 341	156	1 185	..
2.2.3	Securities issued by residents	910	910	167	743	..
2.2.4	Securities issued by non-residents	557	557	19	538	..
2.3	Loans	86	86	0	86	..
2.3.1	Short-term loans	86	86	..	86	..
2.3.2	Long-term loans	0	0	..	0	..
2.3.3	Loans granted to residents	79	79	..	79	..
2.3.4	Loans granted to non-residents	7	7	..	7	..
2.4	Shares and other equity	708	708	0	708	..
2.4.1	Shares issued by residents	450	450	0	450	..
2.4.2	Shares issued by non-residents	258	258	0	258	..
2.5	Other, not elsewhere classified	9	9	1	8	..

		Total	Insurance corporations and autonomous pension funds: Insurance corporations: Total	Life insurance corporations	Non-life insurance corporations	Autonomous pension funds: Total
2	Financial assets	11 733	5 950	778	21	5 783
2.1	Currency and deposits	1 978	355	30	1	1 623
2.2	Securities other than shares, except financial derivatives	8 062	4 101	415	15	3 961
2.2.1	Short-term securities	630	38	0	0	592
2.2.2	Long-term securities	7 432	4 063	415	15	3 369
2.2.3	Securities issued by residents	4 270	2 281	268	14	1 989
2.2.4	Securities issued by non-residents	3 792	1 820	147	1	1 972
2.3	Loans	95	95	1	0	0
2.3.1	Short-term loans	1	1	1	..	..
2.3.2	Long-term loans	94	94	0	..	..
2.3.3	Loans granted to residents	24	24	1	..	..
2.3.4	Loans granted to non-residents	70	70	0	..	..
2.4	Shares and other equity	1 193	995	309	0	198
2.4.1	Shares issued by residents	555	467	69	..	88
2.4.2	Shares issued by non-residents	638	528	240	0	110
2.5	Other, not elsewhere classified	404	403	23	5	1

Note: Detailed metadata at: http://metalinks.oecd.org/instinv/20141203/4b13

Table 2. Financial assets of investment funds

Million EUR (2009 SKK euro)

		2006	2007	2008	2009	2010	2011	2012	2013
	Investment funds								
2	Financial assets	3 627	4 484	3 123	3 425	3 805	3 247	..	..
2.1	Currency and deposits	782	1 194	708	977	1 211	977	..	..
2.2	Securities other than shares, except financial derivatives	1 907	2 228	1 874	1 792	1 768	1 467	..	..
2.2.1	Short-term securities	97	114	58	133	172	126	..	..
2.2.2	Long-term securities	1 811	2 114	1 816	1 659	1 596	1 341	..	..
2.2.3	Securities issued by residents	1 087	1 452	1 336	1 093	1 104	910	..	..
2.2.4	Securities issued by non-residents	820	776	539	699	664	557	..	..
2.3	Loans	0	0	0	0	0	86	..	..
2.3.1	Short-term loans	..	..	..	..	..	86	..	..
2.3.2	Long-term loans	..	..	..	..	..	0	..	..
2.3.3	Loans granted to residents	..	..	..	..	..	79	..	..
2.3.4	Loans granted to non-residents	..	..	..	..	..	7	..	..
2.4	Shares and other equity	874	1 001	490	652	811	708	..	..
2.4.1	Shares issued by residents	258	365	306	314	416	450	..	..
2.4.2	Shares issued by non-residents	616	636	183	338	395	258	..	..
2.5	Other, not elsewhere classified	63	61	52	4	15	9	..	..
	Open-end companies (mutual funds)								
2	Financial assets	3 595	4 340	2 976	3 425	3 805	3 247	..	..
2.1	Currency and deposits	777	1 134	666	977	1 211	977	..	..
2.2	Securities other than shares, except financial derivatives	1 890	2 197	1 845	1 792	1 768	1 467	..	..
2.2.1	Short-term securities	97	113	58	133	172	126	..	..
2.2.2	Long-term securities	1 794	2 084	1 787	1 659	1 596	1 341	..	..
2.2.3	Securities issued by residents	1 083	1 434	1 322	1 093	1 104	910	..	..
2.2.4	Securities issued by non-residents	807	763	523	699	664	557	..	..
2.3	Loans	0	0	0	0	0	86	..	..
2.3.1	Short-term loans	..	..	..	..	..	86	..	..
2.3.2	Long-term loans	..	..	..	..	..	0	..	..
2.3.3	Loans granted to residents	..	..	..	..	..	79	..	..
2.3.4	Loans granted to non-residents	..	..	..	..	..	7	..	..
2.4	Shares and other equity	865	963	416	652	811	708	..	..
2.4.1	Shares issued by residents	252	331	246	314	416	450	..	..
2.4.2	Shares issued by non-residents	613	632	169	338	395	258	..	..
2.5	Other, not elsewhere classified	62	46	48	4	15	9	..	..
	Money market funds								
2	Financial assets	1 617	2 136	1 453	1 769	1 756	384	..	..
2.1	Currency and deposits	597	851	358	631	791	197	..	..
2.2	Securities other than shares, except financial derivatives	998	1 260	1 074	1 093	925	186	..	..
2.2.1	Short-term securities	64	75	29	83	96	30	..	..
2.2.2	Long-term securities	933	1 185	1 045	1 010	829	156	..	..
2.2.3	Securities issued by residents	623	874	814	676	639	167	..	..
2.2.4	Securities issued by non-residents	375	386	260	417	286	19	..	..
2.3	Loans	0	0	0	0	0	0	..	..
2.3.1	Short-term loans	..	..	..	..	..	..	..	..
2.3.2	Long-term loans	..	..	..	..	..	..	..	..
2.3.3	Loans granted to residents	..	..	..	..	..	..	..	..
2.3.4	Loans granted to non-residents	..	..	..	..	..	..	..	..
2.4	Shares and other equity	0	3	3	43	37	0	..	..
2.4.1	Shares issued by residents	0	0	0	0	24	0	..	..
2.4.2	Shares issued by non-residents	0	3	3	43	13	0	..	..
2.5	Other, not elsewhere classified	22	21	17	2	3	1	..	..
	Other mutual funds								
2	Financial assets	1 978	2 205	1 523	1 656	2 049	2 863	..	..
2.1	Currency and deposits	180	283	308	346	420	780	..	..
2.2	Securities other than shares, except financial derivatives	892	937	771	699	843	1 281	..	..
2.2.1	Short-term securities	32	38	29	50	76	96	..	..
2.2.2	Long-term securities	860	899	742	649	767	1 185	..	..
2.2.3	Securities issued by residents	460	560	508	417	465	743	..	..
2.2.4	Securities issued by non-residents	432	377	264	282	378	538	..	..
2.3	Loans	0	0	0	0	0	86	..	..
2.3.1	Short-term loans	..	..	..	..	..	86	..	..
2.3.2	Long-term loans	..	..	..	..	..	0	..	..
2.3.3	Loans granted to residents	..	..	..	..	..	79	..	..
2.3.4	Loans granted to non-residents	..	..	..	..	..	7	..	..
2.4	Shares and other equity	865	959	413	609	774	708	..	..
2.4.1	Shares issued by residents	252	331	246	314	392	450	..	..
2.4.2	Shares issued by non-residents	613	629	166	295	382	258	..	..
2.5	Other, not elsewhere classified	41	25	31	2	12	8	..	..

Table 2. Financial assets of investment funds *(cont.)*

Million EUR (2009 SKK euro)

		2006	2007	2008	2009	2010	2011	2012	2013
	Closed-end companies								
2	Financial assets	32	144	147	..	..	..	..	..
2.1	Currency and deposits	5	60	41	..	..	..	..	..
2.2	Securities other than shares, except financial derivatives	17	31	29	..	..	..	..	..
2.2.1	Short-term securities	0	1	0	..	..	..	..	..
2.2.2	Long-term securities	17	30	29	..	..	..	..	..
2.2.3	Securities issued by residents	4	18	14	..	..	..	..	..
2.2.4	Securities issued by non-residents	13	13	15	..	..	..	..	..
2.3	Loans	0	0	0	..	..	..	..	..
2.3.1	Short-term loans	..	..	..	..	..	..	..	..
2.3.2	Long-term loans	..	..	..	..	..	..	..	..
2.3.3	Loans granted to residents	..	..	..	..	..	..	..	..
2.3.4	Loans granted to non-residents	..	..	..	..	..	..	..	..
2.4	Shares and other equity	9	39	74	..	..	..	..	..
2.4.1	Shares issued by residents	6	34	60	..	..	..	..	..
2.4.2	Shares issued by non-residents	4	4	14	..	..	..	..	..
2.5	Other, not elsewhere classified	1	14	4	..	..	..	..	..

Note: Detailed metadata at: http://metalinks.oecd.org/instinv/20141203/4b13

Table 3. Financial assets of insurance corporations and autonomous pension funds

Million EUR (2009 SKK euro)

		2006	2007	2008	2009	2010	2011	2012	2013
	Insurance corporations and autonomous pension funds								
2	Financial assets	5 178	6 165	8 298	9 339	11 186	11 733	..	..
2.1	Currency and deposits	1 018	985	1 358	1 562	1 670	1 978	..	..
2.2	Securities other than shares, except financial derivatives	3 045	3 593	5 717	6 658	7 508	8 062	..	..
2.2.1	Short-term securities	26	74	127	1 058	1 069	630	..	..
2.2.2	Long-term securities	3 019	3 519	5 590	5 600	6 437	7 432	..	..
2.2.3	Securities issued by residents	..	..	3 776	3 391	3 727	4 270	..	..
2.2.4	Securities issued by non-residents	..	..	1 941	3 267	3 173	3 792	..	..
2.3	Loans	14	28	78	88	87	95	..	..
2.3.1	Short-term loans	..	5	8	7	1	1	..	..
2.3.2	Long-term loans	..	23	70	81	86	94	..	..
2.3.3	Loans granted to residents	..	0	78	27	24	24	..	..
2.3.4	Loans granted to non-residents	..	0	0	61	63	70	..	..
2.4	Shares and other equity	717	788	651	580	1 153	1 193	..	..
2.4.1	Shares issued by residents	0	0	362	404	505	555	..	..
2.4.2	Shares issued by non-residents	0	0	289	176	648	638	..	..
2.5	Other, not elsewhere classified	385	770	495	451	768	404	..	..
	Insurance corporations								
2	Financial assets	4 234	5 324	5 124	5 400	6 012	5 950	..	..
2.1	Currency and deposits	576	634	580	403	411	355	..	..
2.2	Securities other than shares, except financial derivatives	2 690	3 137	3 559	3 935	4 167	4 101	..	..
2.2.1	Short-term securities	..	45	9	35	10	38	..	..
2.2.2	Long-term securities	..	3 093	3 549	3 900	4 155	4 063	..	..
2.2.3	Securities issued by residents	..	..	2 194	2 311	2 289	2 281	..	..
2.2.4	Securities issued by non-residents	..	..	1 365	1 624	1 878	1 820	..	..
2.3	Loans	14	28	78	88	87	95	..	..
2.3.1	Short-term loans	..	5	8	7	1	1	..	..
2.3.2	Long-term loans	..	23	70	81	86	94	..	..
2.3.3	Loans granted to residents	..	..	78	27	24	24	..	..
2.3.4	Loans granted to non-residents	..	..	0	61	63	70	..	..
2.4	Shares and other equity	574	756	476	571	919	995	..	..
2.4.1	Shares issued by residents	..	..	360	399	423	467	..	..
2.4.2	Shares issued by non-residents	..	..	116	172	496	528	..	..
2.5	Other, not elsewhere classified	380	769	432	403	428	403	..	..
	Life insurance corporations								
2	Financial assets	537	642	472	532	786	778	..	..
2.1	Currency and deposits	33	40	46	46	33	30	..	..
2.2	Securities other than shares, except financial derivatives	264	313	347	388	399	415	..	..
2.2.1	Short-term securities	..	0	2	4	3	0	..	..
2.2.2	Long-term securities	..	313	345	384	396	415	..	..
2.2.3	Securities issued by residents	..	..	258	254	261	268	..	..
2.2.4	Securities issued by non-residents	..	..	89	130	138	147	..	..
2.3	Loans	1	2	1	1	1	1	..	..
2.3.1	Short-term loans	..	0	1	1	1	1	..	..
2.3.2	Long-term loans	..	1	0	0	0	0	..	..
2.3.3	Loans granted to residents	..	..	1	1	1	1	..	..
2.3.4	Loans granted to non-residents	..	..	0	0	0	0	..	..
2.4	Shares and other equity	227	260	59	81	331	309	..	..
2.4.1	Shares issued by residents	..	..	52	68	71	69	..	..
2.4.2	Shares issued by non-residents	..	..	8	13	260	240	..	..
2.5	Other, not elsewhere classified	13	28	18	16	22	23	..	..
	Non-life insurance corporations								
2	Financial assets	36	62	103	17	19	21	..	..
2.1	Currency and deposits	18	26	69	4	3	1	..	..
2.2	Securities other than shares, except financial derivatives	12	18	23	10	11	15	..	..
2.2.1	Short-term securities	..	1	1	2	0	0	..	..
2.2.2	Long-term securities	..	18	21	8	11	15	..	..
2.2.3	Securities issued by residents	..	..	22	10	10	14	..	..
2.2.4	Securities issued by non-residents	..	..	1	0	1	1	..	..
2.3	Loans	0	0	0	0	0	0	..	..
2.3.1	Short-term loans	..	..	..	..	..	..	..	..
2.3.2	Long-term loans	..	..	..	..	..	..	..	..
2.3.3	Loans granted to residents	..	..	..	..	..	..	..	..
2.3.4	Loans granted to non-residents	..	..	..	..	..	..	..	..
2.4	Shares and other equity	0	0	0	0	1	0	..	..
2.4.1	Shares issued by residents	..	..	..	..	..	..	..	..
2.4.2	Shares issued by non-residents	..	..	0	0	1	0	..	..
2.5	Other, not elsewhere classified	7	17	11	3	4	5	..	..

Table 3. Financial assets of insurance corporations and autonomous pension funds *(cont.)*

Million EUR (2009 SKK euro)

		2006	2007	2008	2009	2010	2011	2012	2013
	Autonomous pension funds								
2	Financial assets	944	840	3 174	3 939	5 174	5 783	..	..
2.1	Currency and deposits	442	351	778	1 159	1 259	1 623	..	..
2.2	Securities other than shares, except financial derivatives	355	456	2 158	2 723	3 341	3 961	..	..
2.2.1	Short-term securities	26	30	118	1 023	1 059	592	..	..
2.2.2	Long-term securities	329	426	2 040	1 700	2 282	3 369	..	..
2.2.3	Securities issued by residents	..	..	1 582	1 080	1 438	1 989	..	..
2.2.4	Securities issued by non-residents	..	..	576	1 643	1 295	1 972	..	..
2.3	Loans	0	0	0	0	0	0	..	..
2.3.1	Short-term loans	..	..	..	..	..	..	..	..
2.3.2	Long-term loans	..	..	..	..	..	..	..	..
2.3.3	Loans granted to residents	..	..	..	..	..	..	..	..
2.3.4	Loans granted to non-residents	..	..	..	..	..	..	..	..
2.4	Shares and other equity	142	32	175	9	234	198	..	..
2.4.1	Shares issued by residents	..	..	2	5	82	88	..	..
2.4.2	Shares issued by non-residents	..	..	173	4	152	110	..	..
2.5	Other, not elsewhere classified	5	1	63	48	340	1	..	..

Note: Detailed metadata at: http://metalinks.oecd.org/instinv/20141203/4b13

Table 4. Portfolio composition by type of investor

Percentage of total financial assets

Per cent

		2006	2007	2008	2009	2010	2011	2012	2013
	Investment funds								
2	Financial assets	100.0	100.0	100.0	100.0	100.0	100.0	..	..
2.1	Currency and deposits	21.6	26.6	22.7	28.5	31.8	30.1	..	..
2.2	Securities other than shares, except financial derivatives	52.6	49.7	60.0	52.3	46.5	45.2	..	..
2.2.1	Short-term securities	2.7	2.6	1.9	3.9	4.5	3.9	..	..
2.2.2	Long-term securities	49.9	47.1	58.1	48.4	42.0	41.3	..	..
2.2.3	Securities issued by residents	30.0	32.4	42.8	31.9	29.0	28.0	..	..
2.2.4	Securities issued by non-residents	22.6	17.3	17.2	20.4	17.5	17.1	..	..
2.3	Loans	0.0	0.0	0.0	0.0	0.0	2.6	..	..
2.3.1	Short-term loans	..	..	..	..	..	2.6	..	..
2.3.2	Long-term loans	..	..	..	..	..	0.0	..	..
2.3.3	Loans granted to residents	..	..	..	..	..	2.4	..	..
2.3.4	Loans granted to non-residents	..	..	..	..	..	0.2	..	..
2.4	Shares and other equity	24.1	22.3	15.7	19.0	21.3	21.8	..	..
2.4.1	Shares issued by residents	7.1	8.1	9.8	9.2	10.9	13.9	..	..
2.4.2	Shares issued by non-residents	17.0	14.2	5.9	9.9	10.4	7.9	..	..
2.5	Other, not elsewhere classified	1.7	1.4	1.7	0.1	0.4	0.3	..	..
	Insurance corporations								
2	Financial assets	100.0	100.0	100.0	100.0	100.0	100.0	..	..
2.1	Currency and deposits	13.6	11.9	11.3	7.5	6.8	6.0	..	..
2.2	Securities other than shares, except financial derivatives	63.5	58.9	69.4	72.9	69.3	68.9	..	..
2.2.1	Short-term securities	..	0.8	0.2	0.6	0.2	0.6	..	..
2.2.2	Long-term securities	..	58.1	69.3	72.2	69.1	68.3	..	..
2.2.3	Securities issued by residents	..	..	42.8	42.8	38.1	38.3	..	..
2.2.4	Securities issued by non-residents	..	..	26.6	30.1	31.2	30.6	..	..
2.3	Loans	0.3	0.5	1.5	1.6	1.4	1.6	..	..
2.3.1	Short-term loans	..	0.1	0.1	0.1	0.0	0.0	..	..
2.3.2	Long-term loans	..	0.4	1.4	1.5	1.4	1.6	..	..
2.3.3	Loans granted to residents	..	..	1.5	0.5	0.4	0.4	..	..
2.3.4	Loans granted to non-residents	..	..	0.0	1.1	1.0	1.2	..	..
2.4	Shares and other equity	13.6	14.2	9.3	10.6	15.3	16.7	..	..
2.4.1	Shares issued by residents	..	..	7.0	7.4	7.0	7.8	..	..
2.4.2	Shares issued by non-residents	..	..	2.3	3.2	8.3	8.9	..	..
2.5	Other, not elsewhere classified	9.0	14.4	8.4	7.5	7.1	6.8	..	..
	Autonomous pension funds								
2	Financial assets	100.0	100.0	100.0	100.0	100.0	100.0	..	..
2.1	Currency and deposits	46.8	41.8	24.5	29.4	24.3	28.1	..	..
2.2	Securities other than shares, except financial derivatives	37.6	54.3	68.0	69.1	64.6	68.5	..	..
2.2.1	Short-term securities	2.7	3.5	3.7	26.0	20.5	10.2	..	..
2.2.2	Long-term securities	34.8	50.7	64.3	43.2	44.1	58.3	..	..
2.2.3	Securities issued by residents	..	..	49.9	27.4	27.8	34.4	..	..
2.2.4	Securities issued by non-residents	..	..	18.1	41.7	25.0	34.1	..	..
2.3	Loans	0.0	0.0	0.0	0.0	0.0	0.0	..	..
2.3.1	Short-term loans	..	..	..	..	..	..	..	..
2.3.2	Long-term loans	..	..	..	..	..	..	..	..
2.3.3	Loans granted to residents	..	..	..	..	..	..	..	..
2.3.4	Loans granted to non-residents	..	..	..	..	..	..	..	..
2.4	Shares and other equity	15.1	3.9	5.5	0.2	4.5	3.4	..	..
2.4.1	Shares issued by residents	..	..	0.1	0.1	1.6	1.5	..	..
2.4.2	Shares issued by non-residents	..	..	5.4	0.1	2.9	1.9	..	..
2.5	Other, not elsewhere classified	0.5	0.1	2.0	1.2	6.6	0.0	..	..

Note: Detailed metadata at: http://metalinks.oecd.org/instinv/20141203/f729

SLOVENIA

Table 1. Financial assets of institutional investors, 2013

Million EUR (2007 SIT euro)

		Investment funds				
		Total	Open-end companies (mutual funds)			Closed-end companies
			Total	Money market funds	Other mutual funds	Total
2	Financial assets	1 855	1 855	37	1 819	..
2.1	Currency and deposits	110	110	23	87	..
2.2	Securities other than shares, except financial derivatives	220	220	14	206	..
2.2.1	Short-term securities	19	19	13	6	..
2.2.2	Long-term securities	202	202	1	201	..
2.2.3	Securities issued by residents	55	55	8	47	..
2.2.4	Securities issued by non-residents	165	165	6	160	..
2.3	Loans	..	..	..	..	..
2.3.1	Short-term loans	..	..	..	..	..
2.3.2	Long-term loans	..	..	..	..	..
2.3.3	Loans granted to residents	..	..	..	..	..
2.3.4	Loans granted to non-residents	..	..	..	..	..
2.4	Shares and other equity	1 516	1 516	..	1 516	..
2.4.1	Shares issued by residents	202	202	..	202	..
2.4.2	Shares issued by non-residents	1 314	1 314	..	1 314	..
2.5	Other, not elsewhere classified	9	9	0	9	..

		Insurance corporations and autonomous pension funds				
		Total	Insurance corporations			Autonomous pension funds
			Total	Life insurance corporations	Non-life insurance corporations	Total
2	Financial assets	8 614	6 527	..	..	2 087
2.1	Currency and deposits	686	386	..	..	300
2.2	Securities other than shares, except financial derivatives	4 882	3 628	..	..	1 254
2.2.1	Short-term securities	235	100	..	..	134
2.2.2	Long-term securities	4 647	3 527	..	..	1 120
2.2.3	Securities issued by residents	2 184	1 325	..	..	859
2.2.4	Securities issued by non-residents	2 698	2 302	..	..	395
2.3	Loans	166	112	..	..	54
2.3.1	Short-term loans	21	21	..	..	..
2.3.2	Long-term loans	145	91	..	..	54
2.3.3	Loans granted to residents	142	88	..	..	54
2.3.4	Loans granted to non-residents	24	24	..	..	0
2.4	Shares and other equity	2 307	1 850	..	..	457
2.4.1	Shares issued by residents	1 307	1 190	..	..	117
2.4.2	Shares issued by non-residents	1 000	660	..	..	340
2.5	Other, not elsewhere classified	573	551	..	..	22

Note: Detailed metadata at: http://metalinks.oecd.org/instinv/20141203/7550

SLOVENIA

Table 2. Financial assets of investment funds

Million EUR (2007 SIT euro)

		2006	2007	2008	2009	2010	2011	2012	2013
	Investment funds								
2	Financial assets	2 950	4 151	1 912	2 234	2 289	1 779	1 831	1 855
2.1	Currency and deposits	264	384	201	190	163	130	136	110
2.2	Securities other than shares, except financial derivatives	291	322	223	223	234	229	250	220
2.2.1	Short-term securities	31	9	2	0	0	0	19	19
2.2.2	Long-term securities	260	313	221	223	234	229	231	202
2.2.3	Securities issued by residents	223	201	134	115	102	83	85	55
2.2.4	Securities issued by non-residents	68	121	89	108	132	146	165	165
2.3	Loans	0	0	0	0	0	0	0	..
2.3.1	Short-term loans	..	..	..	..	..	..	..	..
2.3.2	Long-term loans	..	..	..	..	..	..	..	..
2.3.3	Loans granted to residents	..	..	..	..	..	..	..	..
2.3.4	Loans granted to non-residents	..	..	..	..	..	..	..	..
2.4	Shares and other equity	2 385	3 433	1 482	1 814	1 881	1 409	1 433	1 516
2.4.1	Shares issued by residents	1 311	1 664	664	659	509	339	247	202
2.4.2	Shares issued by non-residents	1 074	1 769	818	1 155	1 372	1 071	1 187	1 314
2.5	Other, not elsewhere classified	9	12	6	7	11	10	12	9
	Open-end companies (mutual funds)								
2	Financial assets	1 927	2 925	1 513	1 856	2 048	1 810	1 831	1 855
2.1	Currency and deposits	152	293	169	169	140	147	136	110
2.2	Securities other than shares, except financial derivatives	240	247	192	197	222	248	250	220
2.2.1	Short-term securities	17	9	2	0	0	6	19	19
2.2.2	Long-term securities	222	238	190	197	222	242	231	202
2.2.3	Securities issued by residents	177	145	103	89	90	86	85	55
2.2.4	Securities issued by non-residents	63	102	89	108	132	161	165	165
2.3	Loans	0	0	0	0	0	0	0	..
2.3.1	Short-term loans	..	..	..	..	..	..	..	..
2.3.2	Long-term loans	..	..	..	..	..	..	..	..
2.3.3	Loans granted to residents	..	..	..	..	..	..	..	..
2.3.4	Loans granted to non-residents	..	..	..	..	..	..	..	..
2.4	Shares and other equity	1 532	2 376	1 148	1 484	1 675	1 407	1 433	1 516
2.4.1	Shares issued by residents	608	857	361	365	330	322	247	202
2.4.2	Shares issued by non-residents	924	1 519	787	1 119	1 345	1 085	1 187	1 314
2.5	Other, not elsewhere classified	4	9	5	6	11	9	12	9
	Money market funds								
2	Financial assets	7	11	17	14	12	26	26	37
2.1	Currency and deposits	6	11	17	14	12	20	15	23
2.2	Securities other than shares, except financial derivatives	0	0	0	0	0	6	10	14
2.2.1	Short-term securities	0	0	0	0	0	5	10	13
2.2.2	Long-term securities	0	0	0	0	0	1	0	1
2.2.3	Securities issued by residents	0	0	0	0	0	1	4	8
2.2.4	Securities issued by non-residents	0	0	0	0	0	5	6	6
2.3	Loans	0	0	0	0	0	0	0	..
2.3.1	Short-term loans	..	..	..	..	..	..	..	..
2.3.2	Long-term loans	..	..	..	..	..	..	..	..
2.3.3	Loans granted to residents	..	..	..	..	..	..	..	..
2.3.4	Loans granted to non-residents	..	..	..	..	..	..	..	..
2.4	Shares and other equity	0	0	0	0	0	0	0	..
2.4.1	Shares issued by residents	..	..	..	..	..	..	..	..
2.4.2	Shares issued by non-residents	..	..	..	..	..	..	..	..
2.5	Other, not elsewhere classified	0	0	0	0	0	0	0	0
	Other mutual funds								
2	Financial assets	1 920	2 914	1 496	1 842	2 036	1 785	1 805	1 819
2.1	Currency and deposits	146	282	152	155	127	127	121	87
2.2	Securities other than shares, except financial derivatives	239	246	191	197	222	242	239	206
2.2.1	Short-term securities	17	9	2	0	0	1	9	6
2.2.2	Long-term securities	222	238	190	197	222	241	231	201
2.2.3	Securities issued by residents	176	145	103	89	90	86	81	47
2.2.4	Securities issued by non-residents	63	102	88	108	132	157	159	160
2.3	Loans	0	0	0	0	0	0	0	..
2.3.1	Short-term loans	..	..	..	..	..	..	..	..
2.3.2	Long-term loans	..	..	..	..	..	..	..	..
2.3.3	Loans granted to residents	..	..	..	..	..	..	..	..
2.3.4	Loans granted to non-residents	..	..	..	..	..	..	..	..
2.4	Shares and other equity	1 532	2 376	1 148	1 484	1 675	1 407	1 433	1 516
2.4.1	Shares issued by residents	608	857	361	365	330	322	247	202
2.4.2	Shares issued by non-residents	924	1 519	787	1 119	1 345	1 085	1 187	1 314
2.5	Other, not elsewhere classified	4	9	5	6	11	9	12	9

Table 2. Financial assets of investment funds *(cont.)*

Million EUR (2007 SIT euro)

		2006	2007	2008	2009	2010	2011	2012	2013
	Closed-end companies								
2	Financial assets	1 023	1 226	398	377	240	..	..	..
2.1	Currency and deposits	112	91	33	21	23	..	..	..
2.2	Securities other than shares, except financial derivatives	52	75	31	26	11	..	..	..
2.2.1	Short-term securities	14	0	0	0	0	..	..	..
2.2.2	Long-term securities	38	75	31	26	11	..	..	..
2.2.3	Securities issued by residents	47	56	31	26	11	..	..	..
2.2.4	Securities issued by non-residents	5	19	0	0	0	..	..	..
2.3	Loans	0	0	0	0	0	..	..	..
2.3.1	Short-term loans	..	..	..	..	..	..	..	..
2.3.2	Long-term loans	..	..	..	..	..	..	..	..
2.3.3	Loans granted to residents	..	..	..	..	..	..	..	..
2.3.4	Loans granted to non-residents	..	..	..	..	..	..	..	..
2.4	Shares and other equity	854	1 057	334	330	206	..	..	..
2.4.1	Shares issued by residents	704	807	303	294	179	..	..	..
2.4.2	Shares issued by non-residents	150	250	31	36	27	..	..	..
2.5	Other, not elsewhere classified	5	3	1	1	0	..	..	..

Note: Detailed metadata at: http://metalinks.oecd.org/instinv/20141203/7550

Table 3. Financial assets of insurance corporations and autonomous pension funds

Million EUR (2007 SIT euro)

		2006	2007	2008	2009	2010	2011	2012	2013
	Insurance corporations and autonomous pension funds								
2	Financial assets	4 858	5 999	5 908	6 705	7 344	7 539	8 275	8 614
2.1	Currency and deposits	412	529	701	739	967	1 151	950	686
2.2	Securities other than shares, except financial derivatives	2 815	3 186	3 303	3 700	3 938	3 928	4 440	4 882
2.2.1	Short-term securities	120	71	36	82	8	34	151	235
2.2.2	Long-term securities	2 695	3 115	3 268	3 618	3 930	3 894	4 289	4 647
2.2.3	Securities issued by residents	2 067	1 985	1 948	2 192	2 093	1 919	2 011	2 184
2.2.4	Securities issued by non-residents	748	1 201	1 355	1 507	1 844	2 009	2 429	2 698
2.3	Loans	26	38	54	145	151	196	174	166
2.3.1	Short-term loans	9	5	5	5	22	21	18	21
2.3.2	Long-term loans	17	32	49	139	129	175	156	145
2.3.3	Loans granted to residents	25	32	47	127	137	173	148	142
2.3.4	Loans granted to non-residents	0	6	6	18	14	22	26	24
2.4	Shares and other equity	1 208	1 824	1 345	1 634	1 830	1 808	2 153	2 307
2.4.1	Shares issued by residents	912	1 273	894	1 065	1 113	1 076	1 251	1 307
2.4.2	Shares issued by non-residents	296	551	452	569	717	732	902	1 000
2.5	Other, not elsewhere classified	398	422	505	488	458	457	558	573
	Insurance corporations								
2	Financial assets	3 669	4 598	4 479	4 961	5 348	5 324	6 237	6 527
2.1	Currency and deposits	209	242	320	368	490	570	515	386
2.2	Securities other than shares, except financial derivatives	2 106	2 423	2 443	2 601	2 792	2 750	3 288	3 628
2.2.1	Short-term securities	92	46	26	82	3	10	74	100
2.2.2	Long-term securities	2 014	2 377	2 417	2 519	2 790	2 739	3 214	3 527
2.2.3	Securities issued by residents	1 539	1 497	1 406	1 514	1 418	1 272	1 295	1 325
2.2.4	Securities issued by non-residents	568	926	1 038	1 087	1 375	1 478	1 993	2 302
2.3	Loans	25	37	45	96	105	131	122	112
2.3.1	Short-term loans	9	4	3	5	22	21	18	21
2.3.2	Long-term loans	16	32	43	91	82	110	104	91
2.3.3	Loans granted to residents	24	31	39	78	91	109	97	88
2.3.4	Loans granted to non-residents	0	6	7	18	14	22	26	24
2.4	Shares and other equity	934	1 476	1 172	1 411	1 508	1 428	1 761	1 850
2.4.1	Shares issued by residents	688	1 017	776	934	973	936	1 130	1 190
2.4.2	Shares issued by non-residents	246	459	397	477	535	492	631	660
2.5	Other, not elsewhere classified	395	420	498	484	454	445	550	551
	Life insurance corporations								
2	Financial assets	..	..	..	..	..	..	..	..
2.1	Currency and deposits	..	..	..	..	..	..	..	..
2.2	Securities other than shares, except financial derivatives	..	..	..	..	..	..	..	..
2.2.1	Short-term securities	..	..	..	..	..	..	..	..
2.2.2	Long-term securities	..	..	..	..	..	..	..	..
2.2.3	Securities issued by residents	..	..	..	..	..	..	..	..
2.2.4	Securities issued by non-residents	..	..	..	..	..	..	..	..
2.3	Loans	..	..	..	..	..	..	..	..
2.3.1	Short-term loans	..	..	..	..	..	..	..	..
2.3.2	Long-term loans	..	..	..	..	..	..	..	..
2.3.3	Loans granted to residents	..	..	..	..	..	..	..	..
2.3.4	Loans granted to non-residents	..	..	..	..	..	..	..	..
2.4	Shares and other equity	..	..	..	..	..	..	..	..
2.4.1	Shares issued by residents	..	..	..	..	..	..	..	..
2.4.2	Shares issued by non-residents	..	..	..	..	..	..	..	..
2.5	Other, not elsewhere classified	..	..	..	..	..	..	..	..
	Non-life insurance corporations								
2	Financial assets	..	..	..	..	..	..	..	..
2.1	Currency and deposits	..	..	..	..	..	..	..	..
2.2	Securities other than shares, except financial derivatives	..	..	..	..	..	..	..	..
2.2.1	Short-term securities	..	..	..	..	..	..	..	..
2.2.2	Long-term securities	..	..	..	..	..	..	..	..
2.2.3	Securities issued by residents	..	..	..	..	..	..	..	..
2.2.4	Securities issued by non-residents	..	..	..	..	..	..	..	..
2.3	Loans	..	..	..	..	..	..	..	..
2.3.1	Short-term loans	..	..	..	..	..	..	..	..
2.3.2	Long-term loans	..	..	..	..	..	..	..	..
2.3.3	Loans granted to residents	..	..	..	..	..	..	..	..
2.3.4	Loans granted to non-residents	..	..	..	..	..	..	..	..
2.4	Shares and other equity	..	..	..	..	..	..	..	..
2.4.1	Shares issued by residents	..	..	..	..	..	..	..	..
2.4.2	Shares issued by non-residents	..	..	..	..	..	..	..	..
2.5	Other, not elsewhere classified	..	..	..	..	..	..	..	..

Table 3. Financial assets of insurance corporations and autonomous pension funds *(cont.)*

Million EUR (2007 SIT euro)

		2006	2007	2008	2009	2010	2011	2012	2013
	Autonomous pension funds								
2	Financial assets	1 189	1 401	1 428	1 744	1 996	2 216	2 039	2 087
2.1	Currency and deposits	203	287	380	371	478	580	434	300
2.2	Securities other than shares, except financial derivatives	708	762	860	1 099	1 145	1 179	1 152	1 254
2.2.1	Short-term securities	28	24	9	0	5	24	77	134
2.2.2	Long-term securities	680	738	851	1 099	1 140	1 154	1 075	1 120
2.2.3	Securities issued by residents	528	488	543	678	676	647	716	859
2.2.4	Securities issued by non-residents	180	275	317	421	469	531	436	395
2.3	Loans	1	1	8	48	47	65	52	54
2.3.1	Short-term loans	0	1	2	0	0	0	0	..
2.3.2	Long-term loans	1	0	7	48	47	65	52	54
2.3.3	Loans granted to residents	1	1	9	48	47	65	52	54
2.3.4	Loans granted to non-residents	0	0	0	0	0	0	0	0
2.4	Shares and other equity	274	348	173	223	322	380	392	457
2.4.1	Shares issued by residents	224	256	118	131	140	140	121	117
2.4.2	Shares issued by non-residents	50	92	55	92	182	240	271	340
2.5	Other, not elsewhere classified	2	2	7	3	4	12	9	22

Note: Detailed metadata at: http://metalinks.oecd.org/instinv/20141203/7550

Table 4. Portfolio composition by type of investor

Percentage of total financial assets

Per cent

		2006	2007	2008	2009	2010	2011	2012	2013
	Investment funds								
2	Financial assets	100.0	100.0	100.0	100.0	100.0	100.0	100.0	100.0
2.1	Currency and deposits	8.9	9.2	10.5	8.5	7.1	7.3	7.4	5.9
2.2	Securities other than shares, except financial derivatives	9.9	7.7	11.6	10.0	10.2	12.9	13.6	11.9
2.2.1	Short-term securities	1.1	0.2	0.1	0.0	0.0	0.0	1.0	1.0
2.2.2	Long-term securities	8.8	7.5	11.5	10.0	10.2	12.9	12.6	10.9
2.2.3	Securities issued by residents	7.6	4.8	7.0	5.1	4.4	4.7	4.6	3.0
2.2.4	Securities issued by non-residents	2.3	2.9	4.6	4.8	5.8	8.2	9.0	8.9
2.3	Loans	0.0	0.0	0.0	0.0	0.0	0.0	0.0	..
2.3.1	Short-term loans	..	..	..	..	..	..	..	..
2.3.2	Long-term loans	..	..	..	..	..	..	..	..
2.3.3	Loans granted to residents	..	..	..	..	..	..	..	..
2.3.4	Loans granted to non-residents	..	..	..	..	..	..	..	..
2.4	Shares and other equity	80.9	82.7	77.5	81.2	82.2	79.2	78.3	81.7
2.4.1	Shares issued by residents	44.4	40.1	34.7	29.5	22.2	19.0	13.5	10.9
2.4.2	Shares issued by non-residents	36.4	42.6	42.8	51.7	59.9	60.2	64.8	70.8
2.5	Other, not elsewhere classified	0.3	0.3	0.3	0.3	0.5	0.6	0.7	0.5
	Insurance corporations								
2	Financial assets	100.0	100.0	100.0	100.0	100.0	100.0	100.0	100.0
2.1	Currency and deposits	5.7	5.3	7.2	7.4	9.2	10.7	8.3	5.9
2.2	Securities other than shares, except financial derivatives	57.4	52.7	54.5	52.4	52.2	51.6	52.7	55.6
2.2.1	Short-term securities	2.5	1.0	0.6	1.7	0.1	0.2	1.2	1.5
2.2.2	Long-term securities	54.9	51.7	54.0	50.8	52.2	51.5	51.5	54.0
2.2.3	Securities issued by residents	41.9	32.6	31.4	30.5	26.5	23.9	20.8	20.3
2.2.4	Securities issued by non-residents	15.5	20.1	23.2	21.9	25.7	27.8	32.0	35.3
2.3	Loans	0.7	0.8	1.0	1.9	2.0	2.5	2.0	1.7
2.3.1	Short-term loans	0.2	0.1	0.1	0.1	0.4	0.4	0.3	0.3
2.3.2	Long-term loans	0.4	0.7	0.9	1.8	1.5	2.1	1.7	1.4
2.3.3	Loans granted to residents	0.7	0.7	0.9	1.6	1.7	2.0	1.6	1.3
2.3.4	Loans granted to non-residents	0.0	0.1	0.1	0.4	0.3	0.4	0.4	0.4
2.4	Shares and other equity	25.4	32.1	26.2	28.4	28.2	26.8	28.2	28.3
2.4.1	Shares issued by residents	18.7	22.1	17.3	18.8	18.2	17.6	18.1	18.2
2.4.2	Shares issued by non-residents	6.7	10.0	8.9	9.6	10.0	9.2	10.1	10.1
2.5	Other, not elsewhere classified	10.8	9.1	11.1	9.8	8.5	8.4	8.8	8.4
	Autonomous pension funds								
2	Financial assets	100.0	100.0	100.0	100.0	100.0	100.0	100.0	100.0
2.1	Currency and deposits	17.1	20.5	26.6	21.2	23.9	26.2	21.3	14.4
2.2	Securities other than shares, except financial derivatives	59.6	54.4	60.2	63.0	57.4	53.2	56.5	60.1
2.2.1	Short-term securities	2.4	1.7	0.7	0.0	0.2	1.1	3.8	6.4
2.2.2	Long-term securities	57.2	52.7	59.6	63.0	57.1	52.1	52.7	53.7
2.2.3	Securities issued by residents	44.4	34.8	38.0	38.9	33.9	29.2	35.1	41.1
2.2.4	Securities issued by non-residents	15.2	19.6	22.2	24.1	23.5	24.0	21.4	18.9
2.3	Loans	0.1	0.1	0.6	2.8	2.3	2.9	2.5	2.6
2.3.1	Short-term loans	0.0	0.1	0.1	0.0	0.0	0.0	0.0	..
2.3.2	Long-term loans	0.1	0.0	0.5	2.8	2.3	2.9	2.5	2.6
2.3.3	Loans granted to residents	0.1	0.1	0.6	2.8	2.3	2.9	2.5	2.6
2.3.4	Loans granted to non-residents	0.0	0.0	0.0	0.0	0.0	0.0	0.0	0.0
2.4	Shares and other equity	23.1	24.9	12.1	12.8	16.1	17.1	19.2	21.9
2.4.1	Shares issued by residents	18.9	18.3	8.3	7.5	7.0	6.3	6.0	5.6
2.4.2	Shares issued by non-residents	4.2	6.5	3.8	5.3	9.1	10.8	13.3	16.3
2.5	Other, not elsewhere classified	0.2	0.1	0.5	0.2	0.2	0.5	0.4	1.0

Note: Detailed metadata at: http://metalinks.oecd.org/instinv/20141203/f729

SPAIN

Table 1. Financial assets of institutional investors, 2013

Million EUR (1999 ESP euro)

		Total	Investment funds			
			Open-end companies (mutual funds)			Closed-end companies
			Total	Money market funds	Other mutual funds	Total
2	Financial assets	180 485	186 533	8 448	178 086	351
2.1	Currency and deposits	39 500	39 250	2 695	36 555	250
2.2	Securities other than shares, except financial derivatives	98 663	98 662	5 644	93 018	1
2.2.1	Short-term securities	5 840	5 839	1 739	4 100	1
2.2.2	Long-term securities	92 823	92 823	3 905	88 918	0
2.2.3	Securities issued by residents	86 489	86 488	4 644	81 844	1
2.2.4	Securities issued by non-residents	12 174	12 174	1 000	11 174	0
2.3	Loans	230	230	1	229	0
2.3.1	Short-term loans	230	230	1	229	0
2.3.2	Long-term loans	0	0	0	0	0
2.3.3	Loans granted to residents	230	230	1	229	0
2.3.4	Loans granted to non-residents	0	0	0	0	0
2.4	Shares and other equity	39 273	45 244	3	45 242	12
2.4.1	Shares issued by residents	7 251	13 223	3	13 220	12
2.4.2	Shares issued by non-residents	32 022	32 022	0	32 022	0
2.5	Other, not elsewhere classified	2 819	3 147	104	3 043	88

		Insurance corporations and autonomous pension funds				
		Total	Insurance corporations			Autonomous pension funds
			Total	Life insurance corporations	Non-life insurance corporations	Total
2	Financial assets	393 030	276 669	..	..	116 361
2.1	Currency and deposits	63 159	47 481	..	..	15 679
2.2	Securities other than shares, except financial derivatives	234 258	167 494	..	..	66 764
2.2.1	Short-term securities	6 489	4 392	..	..	2 097
2.2.2	Long-term securities	227 769	163 102	..	..	64 667
2.2.3	Securities issued by residents	160 042	107 622	..	..	52 420
2.2.4	Securities issued by non-residents	74 216	59 872	..	..	14 344
2.3	Loans	6 237	6 219	..	..	18
2.3.1	Short-term loans	2 369	2 367	..	..	1
2.3.2	Long-term loans	3 868	3 852	..	..	16
2.3.3	Loans granted to residents	4 688	4 670	..	..	18
2.3.4	Loans granted to non-residents	1 549	1 549	..	..	0
2.4	Shares and other equity	50 926	27 100	..	..	23 827
2.4.1	Shares issued by residents	27 328	19 459	..	..	7 868
2.4.2	Shares issued by non-residents	23 599	7 640	..	..	15 958
2.5	Other, not elsewhere classified	38 449	28 375	..	..	10 074

Note: Detailed metadata at: http://metalinks.oecd.org/instinv/20141203/acc5

Table 2. Financial assets of investment funds

Million EUR (1999 ESP euro)

		2006	2007	2008	2009	2010	2011	2012	2013
	Investment funds								
2	Financial assets	286 264	270 404	193 325	188 837	163 903	149 994	145 389	180 485
2.1	Currency and deposits	48 122	54 208	56 523	44 570	37 142	28 326	27 387	39 500
2.2	Securities other than shares, except financial derivatives	149 503	144 752	112 054	112 614	92 205	94 285	87 273	98 663
2.2.1	Short-term securities	37 471	48 623	27 257	17 047	7 756	7 016	5 323	5 840
2.2.2	Long-term securities	112 033	96 129	84 797	95 567	84 449	87 269	81 950	92 823
2.2.3	Securities issued by residents	67 270	76 083	61 313	62 517	62 658	77 121	75 064	86 489
2.2.4	Securities issued by non-residents	82 233	68 669	50 742	50 097	29 548	17 164	12 209	12 174
2.3	Loans	1 595	1 264	1 400	1 199	595	377	266	230
2.3.1	Short-term loans	1 595	1 264	1 400	1 199	595	377	266	230
2.3.2	Long-term loans	0	0	0	0	0	0	0	0
2.3.3	Loans granted to residents	1 595	1 264	1 400	1 199	595	377	266	230
2.3.4	Loans granted to non-residents	0	0	0	0	0	0	0	0
2.4	Shares and other equity	79 026	62 624	20 157	27 561	31 855	25 595	28 605	39 273
2.4.1	Shares issued by residents	20 345	17 689	6 420	7 135	6 152	5 028	4 819	7 251
2.4.2	Shares issued by non-residents	58 682	44 935	13 737	20 426	25 703	20 567	23 786	32 022
2.5	Other, not elsewhere classified	8 017	7 556	3 191	2 893	2 106	1 411	1 857	2 819
	Open-end companies (mutual funds)								
2	Financial assets	302 607	289 765	204 479	199 505	172 486	156 816	149 790	186 533
2.1	Currency and deposits	46 453	53 114	55 840	44 390	36 967	28 213	27 246	39 250
2.2	Securities other than shares, except financial derivatives	148 586	144 309	111 981	112 597	92 202	94 282	87 273	98 662
2.2.1	Short-term securities	36 807	48 244	27 226	17 030	7 752	7 013	5 323	5 839
2.2.2	Long-term securities	111 779	96 066	84 755	95 567	84 449	87 269	81 950	92 823
2.2.3	Securities issued by residents	66 353	75 640	61 239	62 513	62 654	77 118	75 064	86 488
2.2.4	Securities issued by non-residents	82 233	68 669	50 742	50 084	29 548	17 164	12 209	12 174
2.3	Loans	1 595	1 264	1 400	1 199	595	377	266	230
2.3.1	Short-term loans	1 595	1 264	1 400	1 199	595	377	266	230
2.3.2	Long-term loans	0	0	0	0	0	0	0	0
2.3.3	Loans granted to residents	1 595	1 264	1 400	1 199	595	377	266	230
2.3.4	Loans granted to non-residents	0	0	0	0	0	0	0	0
2.4	Shares and other equity	97 377	82 742	31 715	38 165	40 349	32 179	32 795	45 244
2.4.1	Shares issued by residents	38 695	37 807	17 978	17 739	14 646	11 613	9 008	13 223
2.4.2	Shares issued by non-residents	58 682	44 935	13 737	20 426	25 703	20 567	23 786	32 022
2.5	Other, not elsewhere classified	8 595	8 336	3 543	3 155	2 374	1 765	2 211	3 147
	Money market funds								
2	Financial assets	107	0	28 263	13 567	8 174	8 071	7 007	8 448
2.1	Currency and deposits	17	0	9 238	5 030	3 952	2 855	1 825	2 695
2.2	Securities other than shares, except financial derivatives	90	0	17 937	8 293	4 071	5 104	5 055	5 644
2.2.1	Short-term securities	4	0	8 930	3 511	1 554	2 874	2 156	1 739
2.2.2	Long-term securities	86	0	9 007	4 783	2 517	2 230	2 899	3 905
2.2.3	Securities issued by residents	10	0	12 706	5 207	2 726	4 228	3 859	4 644
2.2.4	Securities issued by non-residents	80	0	5 231	3 086	1 345	876	1 195	1 000
2.3	Loans	0	0	2	18	67	10	23	1
2.3.1	Short-term loans	0	0	2	18	67	10	23	1
2.3.2	Long-term loans	0	0	0	0	0	0	0	0
2.3.3	Loans granted to residents	0	0	2	18	67	10	23	1
2.3.4	Loans granted to non-residents	0	0	0	0	0	0	0	0
2.4	Shares and other equity	0	0	910	0	0	0	1	3
2.4.1	Shares issued by residents	0	0	910	0	0	0	1	3
2.4.2	Shares issued by non-residents	0	0	0	0	0	0	0	0
2.5	Other, not elsewhere classified	0	0	176	225	84	102	104	104
	Other mutual funds								
2	Financial assets	302 500	289 765	176 216	185 938	164 312	148 745	142 784	178 086
2.1	Currency and deposits	46 437	53 114	46 601	39 359	33 015	25 358	25 421	36 555
2.2	Securities other than shares, except financial derivatives	148 496	144 309	94 044	104 304	88 131	89 178	82 218	93 018
2.2.1	Short-term securities	36 803	48 244	18 296	13 519	6 199	4 139	3 167	4 100
2.2.2	Long-term securities	111 693	96 066	75 748	90 784	81 932	85 039	79 051	88 918
2.2.3	Securities issued by residents	66 343	75 640	48 534	57 306	59 929	72 890	71 205	81 844
2.2.4	Securities issued by non-residents	82 153	68 669	45 511	46 998	28 202	16 288	11 013	11 174
2.3	Loans	1 595	1 264	1 398	1 181	528	367	244	229
2.3.1	Short-term loans	1 595	1 264	1 398	1 181	528	367	244	229
2.3.2	Long-term loans	0	0	0	0	0	0	0	0
2.3.3	Loans granted to residents	1 595	1 264	1 398	1 181	528	367	244	229
2.3.4	Loans granted to non-residents	0	0	0	0	0	0	0	0
2.4	Shares and other equity	97 377	82 742	30 805	38 165	40 349	32 179	32 794	45 242
2.4.1	Shares issued by residents	38 695	37 807	17 068	17 739	14 646	11 613	9 008	13 220
2.4.2	Shares issued by non-residents	58 682	44 935	13 737	20 426	25 703	20 567	23 786	32 022
2.5	Other, not elsewhere classified	8 595	8 336	3 367	2 929	2 290	1 663	2 107	3 043

Table 2. Financial assets of investment funds *(cont.)*

Million EUR (1999 ESP euro)

		2006	2007	2008	2009	2010	2011	2012	2013
	Closed-end companies								
2	Financial assets	2 761	1 607	820	359	336	179	205	351
2.1	Currency and deposits	1 669	1 094	683	181	175	113	142	250
2.2	Securities other than shares, except financial derivatives	917	443	73	17	4	3	0	1
2.2.1	Short-term securities	663	379	31	17	4	3	0	1
2.2.2	Long-term securities	254	64	42	0	0	0	0	0
2.2.3	Securities issued by residents	917	443	73	4	4	3	0	1
2.2.4	Securities issued by non-residents	0	0	0	13	0	0	0	0
2.3	Loans	0	0	0	0	0	0	0	0
2.3.1	Short-term loans	0	0	0	0	0	0	0	0
2.3.2	Long-term loans	0	0	0	0	0	0	0	0
2.3.3	Loans granted to residents	0	0	0	0	0	0	0	0
2.3.4	Loans granted to non-residents	0	0	0	0	0	0	0	0
2.4	Shares and other equity	0	0	0	6	9	0	0	12
2.4.1	Shares issued by residents	0	0	0	6	9	0	0	12
2.4.2	Shares issued by non-residents	0	0	0	0	0	0	0	0
2.5	Other, not elsewhere classified	175	70	65	154	148	62	63	88

Note: Detailed metadata at: http://metalinks.oecd.org/instinv/20141203/acc5

Table 3. Financial assets of insurance corporations and autonomous pension funds

Million EUR (1999 ESP euro)

		2006	2007	2008	2009	2010	2011	2012	2013
	Insurance corporations and autonomous pension funds								
2	Financial assets	323 468	330 552	328 395	344 642	343 925	351 752	366 310	393 030
2.1	Currency and deposits	52 238	58 800	68 697	65 132	65 370	63 969	63 153	63 159
2.2	Securities other than shares, except financial derivatives	172 655	177 306	180 944	199 242	195 207	206 102	215 296	234 258
2.2.1	Short-term securities	13 643	10 568	6 890	4 697	4 055	8 471	9 159	6 489
2.2.2	Long-term securities	159 012	166 737	174 054	194 546	191 152	197 631	206 137	227 769
2.2.3	Securities issued by residents	71 740	72 204	70 696	86 089	102 965	133 730	146 947	160 042
2.2.4	Securities issued by non-residents	100 915	105 102	110 248	113 153	92 242	72 372	68 349	74 216
2.3	Loans	3 821	3 534	4 471	5 509	7 455	7 704	7 730	6 237
2.3.1	Short-term loans	1 842	1 838	2 116	2 317	2 403	2 418	2 369	2 369
2.3.2	Long-term loans	1 979	1 697	2 355	3 192	5 052	5 286	5 361	3 868
2.3.3	Loans granted to residents	3 306	2 774	3 585	4 581	6 169	6 365	6 227	4 688
2.3.4	Loans granted to non-residents	515	760	886	927	1 285	1 339	1 503	1 549
2.4	Shares and other equity	60 968	55 854	39 689	43 385	43 468	41 111	43 714	50 926
2.4.1	Shares issued by residents	36 288	32 106	24 653	23 076	21 601	22 821	23 165	27 328
2.4.2	Shares issued by non-residents	24 680	23 748	15 035	20 309	21 866	18 290	20 549	23 599
2.5	Other, not elsewhere classified	33 786	35 057	34 595	31 374	32 427	32 866	36 418	38 449
	Insurance corporations								
2	Financial assets	223 342	224 436	231 207	239 755	237 651	246 893	257 035	276 669
2.1	Currency and deposits	37 118	42 711	49 509	48 057	47 426	50 504	48 155	47 481
2.2	Securities other than shares, except financial derivatives	123 612	123 614	128 046	139 708	137 628	143 699	154 110	167 494
2.2.1	Short-term securities	8 759	5 134	2 415	2 180	605	2 562	4 059	4 392
2.2.2	Long-term securities	114 854	118 480	125 630	137 528	137 023	141 137	150 051	163 102
2.2.3	Securities issued by residents	49 221	45 469	45 765	55 550	68 442	88 978	100 193	107 622
2.2.4	Securities issued by non-residents	74 392	78 145	82 280	84 158	69 186	54 721	53 917	59 872
2.3	Loans	3 180	3 010	4 137	5 240	7 301	7 626	7 689	6 219
2.3.1	Short-term loans	1 725	1 746	2 052	2 265	2 376	2 405	2 362	2 367
2.3.2	Long-term loans	1 455	1 265	2 084	2 975	4 925	5 221	5 327	3 852
2.3.3	Loans granted to residents	2 665	2 250	3 251	4 313	6 016	6 288	6 186	4 670
2.3.4	Loans granted to non-residents	515	760	886	927	1 285	1 339	1 503	1 549
2.4	Shares and other equity	36 140	30 578	24 953	25 239	23 357	23 047	21 831	27 100
2.4.1	Shares issued by residents	27 377	22 901	17 463	15 541	14 721	15 829	15 947	19 459
2.4.2	Shares issued by non-residents	8 763	7 677	7 490	9 697	8 636	7 218	5 884	7 640
2.5	Other, not elsewhere classified	23 292	24 523	24 563	21 511	21 938	22 018	25 250	28 375
	Life insurance corporations								
2	Financial assets	..	..	..	..	..	..	..	..
2.1	Currency and deposits	..	..	..	..	..	..	..	..
2.2	Securities other than shares, except financial derivatives	..	..	..	..	..	..	..	..
2.2.1	Short-term securities	..	..	..	..	..	..	..	..
2.2.2	Long-term securities	..	..	..	..	..	..	..	..
2.2.3	Securities issued by residents	..	..	..	..	..	..	..	..
2.2.4	Securities issued by non-residents	..	..	..	..	..	..	..	..
2.3	Loans	..	..	..	..	..	..	..	..
2.3.1	Short-term loans	..	..	..	..	..	..	..	..
2.3.2	Long-term loans	..	..	..	..	..	..	..	..
2.3.3	Loans granted to residents	..	..	..	..	..	..	..	..
2.3.4	Loans granted to non-residents	..	..	..	..	..	..	..	..
2.4	Shares and other equity	..	..	..	..	..	..	..	..
2.4.1	Shares issued by residents	..	..	..	..	..	..	..	..
2.4.2	Shares issued by non-residents	..	..	..	..	..	..	..	..
2.5	Other, not elsewhere classified	..	..	..	..	..	..	..	..
	Non-life insurance corporations								
2	Financial assets	..	..	..	..	..	..	..	..
2.1	Currency and deposits	..	..	..	..	..	..	..	..
2.2	Securities other than shares, except financial derivatives	..	..	..	..	..	..	..	..
2.2.1	Short-term securities	..	..	..	..	..	..	..	..
2.2.2	Long-term securities	..	..	..	..	..	..	..	..
2.2.3	Securities issued by residents	..	..	..	..	..	..	..	..
2.2.4	Securities issued by non-residents	..	..	..	..	..	..	..	..
2.3	Loans	..	..	..	..	..	..	..	..
2.3.1	Short-term loans	..	..	..	..	..	..	..	..
2.3.2	Long-term loans	..	..	..	..	..	..	..	..
2.3.3	Loans granted to residents	..	..	..	..	..	..	..	..
2.3.4	Loans granted to non-residents	..	..	..	..	..	..	..	..
2.4	Shares and other equity	..	..	..	..	..	..	..	..
2.4.1	Shares issued by residents	..	..	..	..	..	..	..	..
2.4.2	Shares issued by non-residents	..	..	..	..	..	..	..	..
2.5	Other, not elsewhere classified	..	..	..	..	..	..	..	..

Table 3. Financial assets of insurance corporations and autonomous pension funds *(cont.)*

Million EUR (1999 ESP euro)

		2006	2007	2008	2009	2010	2011	2012	2013
	Autonomous pension funds								
2	Financial assets	100 126	106 116	97 188	104 887	106 274	104 858	109 275	116 361
2.1	Currency and deposits	15 120	16 090	19 188	17 074	17 943	13 465	14 997	15 679
2.2	Securities other than shares, except financial derivatives	49 043	53 692	52 898	59 534	57 579	62 403	61 186	66 764
2.2.1	Short-term securities	4 884	5 435	4 475	2 516	3 450	5 909	5 100	2 097
2.2.2	Long-term securities	44 159	48 257	48 423	57 018	54 129	56 494	56 086	64 667
2.2.3	Securities issued by residents	22 520	26 735	24 931	30 539	34 523	44 752	46 754	52 420
2.2.4	Securities issued by non-residents	26 523	26 956	27 967	28 995	23 056	17 651	14 432	14 344
2.3	Loans	641	524	334	269	153	77	40	18
2.3.1	Short-term loans	116	92	64	52	27	13	6	1
2.3.2	Long-term loans	525	432	271	217	126	65	34	16
2.3.3	Loans granted to residents	641	524	334	269	153	77	40	18
2.3.4	Loans granted to non-residents	0	0	0	0	0	0	0	0
2.4	Shares and other equity	24 828	25 276	14 736	18 147	20 111	18 064	21 883	23 827
2.4.1	Shares issued by residents	8 911	9 206	7 190	7 535	6 881	6 992	7 218	7 868
2.4.2	Shares issued by non-residents	15 917	16 071	7 546	10 612	13 230	11 072	14 665	15 958
2.5	Other, not elsewhere classified	10 494	10 534	10 032	9 864	10 488	10 849	11 169	10 074

Note: Detailed metadata at: http://metalinks.oecd.org/instinv/20141203/acc5

Table 4. Portfolio composition by type of investor

Percentage of total financial assets

Per cent

		2006	2007	2008	2009	2010	2011	2012	2013
	Investment funds								
2	Financial assets	100.0	100.0	100.0	100.0	100.0	100.0	100.0	100.0
2.1	Currency and deposits	16.8	20.0	29.2	23.6	22.7	18.9	18.8	21.9
2.2	Securities other than shares, except financial derivatives	52.2	53.5	58.0	59.6	56.3	62.9	60.0	54.7
2.2.1	Short-term securities	13.1	18.0	14.1	9.0	4.7	4.7	3.7	3.2
2.2.2	Long-term securities	39.1	35.6	43.9	50.6	51.5	58.2	56.4	51.4
2.2.3	Securities issued by residents	23.5	28.1	31.7	33.1	38.2	51.4	51.6	47.9
2.2.4	Securities issued by non-residents	28.7	25.4	26.2	26.5	18.0	11.4	8.4	6.7
2.3	Loans	0.6	0.5	0.7	0.6	0.4	0.3	0.2	0.1
2.3.1	Short-term loans	0.6	0.5	0.7	0.6	0.4	0.3	0.2	0.1
2.3.2	Long-term loans	0.0	0.0	0.0	0.0	0.0	0.0	0.0	0.0
2.3.3	Loans granted to residents	0.6	0.5	0.7	0.6	0.4	0.3	0.2	0.1
2.3.4	Loans granted to non-residents	0.0	0.0	0.0	0.0	0.0	0.0	0.0	0.0
2.4	Shares and other equity	27.6	23.2	10.4	14.6	19.4	17.1	19.7	21.8
2.4.1	Shares issued by residents	7.1	6.5	3.3	3.8	3.8	3.4	3.3	4.0
2.4.2	Shares issued by non-residents	20.5	16.6	7.1	10.8	15.7	13.7	16.4	17.7
2.5	Other, not elsewhere classified	2.8	2.8	1.7	1.5	1.3	0.9	1.3	1.6
	Insurance corporations								
2	Financial assets	100.0	100.0	100.0	100.0	100.0	100.0	100.0	100.0
2.1	Currency and deposits	16.6	19.0	21.4	20.0	20.0	20.5	18.7	17.2
2.2	Securities other than shares, except financial derivatives	55.3	55.1	55.4	58.3	57.9	58.2	60.0	60.5
2.2.1	Short-term securities	3.9	2.3	1.0	0.9	0.3	1.0	1.6	1.6
2.2.2	Long-term securities	51.4	52.8	54.3	57.4	57.7	57.2	58.4	59.0
2.2.3	Securities issued by residents	22.0	20.3	19.8	23.2	28.8	36.0	39.0	38.9
2.2.4	Securities issued by non-residents	33.3	34.8	35.6	35.1	29.1	22.2	21.0	21.6
2.3	Loans	1.4	1.3	1.8	2.2	3.1	3.1	3.0	2.2
2.3.1	Short-term loans	0.8	0.8	0.9	0.9	1.0	1.0	0.9	0.9
2.3.2	Long-term loans	0.7	0.6	0.9	1.2	2.1	2.1	2.1	1.4
2.3.3	Loans granted to residents	1.2	1.0	1.4	1.8	2.5	2.5	2.4	1.7
2.3.4	Loans granted to non-residents	0.2	0.3	0.4	0.4	0.5	0.5	0.6	0.6
2.4	Shares and other equity	16.2	13.6	10.8	10.5	9.8	9.3	8.5	9.8
2.4.1	Shares issued by residents	12.3	10.2	7.6	6.5	6.2	6.4	6.2	7.0
2.4.2	Shares issued by non-residents	3.9	3.4	3.2	4.0	3.6	2.9	2.3	2.8
2.5	Other, not elsewhere classified	10.4	10.9	10.6	9.0	9.2	8.9	9.8	10.3
	Autonomous pension funds								
2	Financial assets	100.0	100.0	100.0	100.0	100.0	100.0	100.0	100.0
2.1	Currency and deposits	15.1	15.2	19.7	16.3	16.9	12.8	13.7	13.5
2.2	Securities other than shares, except financial derivatives	49.0	50.6	54.4	56.8	54.2	59.5	56.0	57.4
2.2.1	Short-term securities	4.9	5.1	4.6	2.4	3.2	5.6	4.7	1.8
2.2.2	Long-term securities	44.1	45.5	49.8	54.4	50.9	53.9	51.3	55.6
2.2.3	Securities issued by residents	22.5	25.2	25.7	29.1	32.5	42.7	42.8	45.0
2.2.4	Securities issued by non-residents	26.5	25.4	28.8	27.6	21.7	16.8	13.2	12.3
2.3	Loans	0.6	0.5	0.3	0.3	0.1	0.1	0.0	0.0
2.3.1	Short-term loans	0.1	0.1	0.1	0.0	0.0	0.0	0.0	0.0
2.3.2	Long-term loans	0.5	0.4	0.3	0.2	0.1	0.1	0.0	0.0
2.3.3	Loans granted to residents	0.6	0.5	0.3	0.3	0.1	0.1	0.0	0.0
2.3.4	Loans granted to non-residents	0.0	0.0	0.0	0.0	0.0	0.0	0.0	0.0
2.4	Shares and other equity	24.8	23.8	15.2	17.3	18.9	17.2	20.0	20.5
2.4.1	Shares issued by residents	8.9	8.7	7.4	7.2	6.5	6.7	6.6	6.8
2.4.2	Shares issued by non-residents	15.9	15.1	7.8	10.1	12.4	10.6	13.4	13.7
2.5	Other, not elsewhere classified	10.5	9.9	10.3	9.4	9.9	10.3	10.2	8.7

Note: Detailed metadata at: http://metalinks.oecd.org/instinv/20141203/f729

SWEDEN

Table 1. Financial assets of institutional investors, 2013

Million SEK

			Investment funds			
		Total	Open-end companies (mutual funds)			Closed-end companies
			Total	Money market funds	Other mutual funds	Total
2	Financial assets	2 307 071	2 366 593	108 526	2 258 067	..
2.1	Currency and deposits	68 292	68 292	1 523	66 769	..
2.2	Securities other than shares, except financial derivatives	488 594	488 594	103 156	385 438	..
2.2.1	Short-term securities	34 956	34 956	18 760	16 196	..
2.2.2	Long-term securities	453 638	453 638	84 396	369 242	..
2.2.3	Securities issued by residents	355 683	355 683	95 257	260 426	..
2.2.4	Securities issued by non-residents	132 911	132 911	7 899	125 012	..
2.3	Loans	0	0	0	0	..
2.3.1	Short-term loans	0	0	0	0	..
2.3.2	Long-term loans	0	0	0	0	..
2.3.3	Loans granted to residents	0	0	0	0	..
2.3.4	Loans granted to non-residents	0	0	0	0	..
2.4	Shares and other equity	1 638 579	1 697 683	3 669	1 694 014	..
2.4.1	Shares issued by residents	544 643	603 747	3 669	600 078	..
2.4.2	Shares issued by non-residents	1 093 936	1 093 936	0	1 093 936	..
2.5	Other, not elsewhere classified	111 606	112 024	178	111 846	..

			Insurance corporations and autonomous pension funds			
		Total	Insurance corporations			Autonomous pension funds
			Total	Life insurance corporations	Non-life insurance corporations	Total
2	Financial assets	4 102 410	3 391 770	..	..	785 149
2.1	Currency and deposits	126 167	124 540	..	..	1 627
2.2	Securities other than shares, except financial derivatives	1 324 128	1 247 642	..	..	76 486
2.2.1	Short-term securities	41 619	39 248	..	..	2 371
2.2.2	Long-term securities	1 282 509	1 208 394	..	..	74 115
2.2.3	Securities issued by residents	988 830	912 344	..	..	76 486
2.2.4	Securities issued by non-residents	335 298	335 298	..	..	0
2.3	Loans	79 625	78 609	..	..	1 016
2.3.1	Short-term loans	0	0	..	..	0
2.3.2	Long-term loans	79 625	78 609	..	..	1 016
2.3.3	Loans granted to residents	54 134	53 118	..	..	1 016
2.3.4	Loans granted to non-residents	25 491	25 491	..	..	0
2.4	Shares and other equity	2 499 880	1 848 442	..	..	704 933
2.4.1	Shares issued by residents	1 551 054	1 004 077	..	..	600 472
2.4.2	Shares issued by non-residents	948 826	844 365	..	..	104 461
2.5	Other, not elsewhere classified	72 610	92 537	..	..	1 087

Note: Detailed metadata at: http://metalinks.oecd.org/instinv/20141203/fed1

SWEDEN

Table 2. Financial assets of investment funds

Million SEK

		2006	2007	2008	2009	2010	2011	2012	2013
	Investment funds								
2	Financial assets	1 442 028	1 544 004	1 085 924	1 509 985	1 767 531	1 602 807	1 839 782	2 307 071
2.1	Currency and deposits	53 349	55 633	51 325	49 042	47 895	56 493	64 448	68 292
2.2	Securities other than shares, except financial derivatives	315 584	320 054	304 846	344 665	370 452	396 512	401 142	488 594
2.2.1	Short-term securities	77 111	68 331	73 021	45 336	43 499	49 098	39 515	34 956
2.2.2	Long-term securities	238 473	251 723	231 825	299 329	326 953	347 414	361 627	453 638
2.2.3	Securities issued by residents	278 945	276 298	269 775	282 817	316 899	349 143	332 216	355 683
2.2.4	Securities issued by non-residents	36 639	43 756	35 071	61 848	53 553	47 369	68 926	132 911
2.3	Loans	0	0	0	0	0	0	0	0
2.3.1	Short-term loans	0	0	0	0	0	0	0	0
2.3.2	Long-term loans	0	0	0	0	0	0	0	0
2.3.3	Loans granted to residents	0	0	0	0	0	0	0	0
2.3.4	Loans granted to non-residents	0	0	0	0	0	0	0	0
2.4	Shares and other equity	1 057 275	1 097 706	687 449	1 048 131	1 263 181	1 080 860	1 271 731	1 638 579
2.4.1	Shares issued by residents	457 404	418 326	243 507	403 656	501 308	402 385	438 103	544 643
2.4.2	Shares issued by non-residents	599 871	679 380	443 942	644 475	761 873	678 475	833 628	1 093 936
2.5	Other, not elsewhere classified	15 820	70 611	42 304	68 147	86 003	68 942	102 461	111 606
	Open-end companies (mutual funds)								
2	Financial assets	1 455 350	1 560 749	1 099 578	1 527 845	1 790 567	1 640 445	1 893 240	2 366 593
2.1	Currency and deposits	53 349	55 633	51 325	49 042	47 895	56 493	64 448	68 292
2.2	Securities other than shares, except financial derivatives	315 584	320 054	304 846	344 665	370 452	396 512	401 142	488 594
2.2.1	Short-term securities	77 111	68 331	73 021	45 336	43 499	49 098	39 515	34 956
2.2.2	Long-term securities	238 473	251 723	231 825	299 329	326 953	347 414	361 627	453 638
2.2.3	Securities issued by residents	278 945	276 298	269 775	282 817	316 899	349 143	332 216	355 683
2.2.4	Securities issued by non-residents	36 639	43 756	35 071	61 848	53 553	47 369	68 926	132 911
2.3	Loans	0	0	0	0	0	0	0	0
2.3.1	Short-term loans	0	0	0	0	0	0	0	0
2.3.2	Long-term loans	0	0	0	0	0	0	0	0
2.3.3	Loans granted to residents	0	0	0	0	0	0	0	0
2.3.4	Loans granted to non-residents	0	0	0	0	0	0	0	0
2.4	Shares and other equity	1 070 392	1 114 305	700 342	1 065 971	1 286 192	1 118 462	1 325 172	1 697 683
2.4.1	Shares issued by residents	470 521	434 925	256 400	421 496	524 319	439 987	491 544	603 747
2.4.2	Shares issued by non-residents	599 871	679 380	443 942	644 475	761 873	678 475	833 628	1 093 936
2.5	Other, not elsewhere classified	16 025	70 757	43 065	68 167	86 028	68 978	102 478	112 024
	Money market funds								
2	Financial assets	79 025	85 973	93 399	70 996	71 707	100 308	90 903	108 526
2.1	Currency and deposits	1 227	1 348	1 848	1 330	1 066	2 235	1 908	1 523
2.2	Securities other than shares, except financial derivatives	73 838	82 841	90 341	69 473	70 214	97 925	86 009	103 156
2.2.1	Short-term securities	32 650	29 553	39 520	16 851	14 605	27 162	21 882	18 760
2.2.2	Long-term securities	41 188	53 288	50 821	52 622	55 609	70 763	64 127	84 396
2.2.3	Securities issued by residents	66 583	75 187	86 061	66 145	68 323	94 856	81 770	95 257
2.2.4	Securities issued by non-residents	7 255	7 654	4 280	3 328	1 891	3 069	4 239	7 899
2.3	Loans	0	0	0	0	0	0	0	0
2.3.1	Short-term loans	0	0	0	0	0	0	0	0
2.3.2	Long-term loans	0	0	0	0	0	0	0	0
2.3.3	Loans granted to residents	0	0	0	0	0	0	0	0
2.3.4	Loans granted to non-residents	0	0	0	0	0	0	0	0
2.4	Shares and other equity	3 648	871	882	103	155	39	2 698	3 669
2.4.1	Shares issued by residents	3 648	871	882	103	155	39	2 698	3 669
2.4.2	Shares issued by non-residents	0	0	0	0	0	0	0	0
2.5	Other, not elsewhere classified	312	913	328	90	272	109	288	178
	Other mutual funds								
2	Financial assets	1 376 325	1 474 776	1 006 179	1 456 849	1 718 860	1 540 137	1 802 337	2 258 067
2.1	Currency and deposits	52 122	54 285	49 477	47 712	46 829	54 258	62 540	66 769
2.2	Securities other than shares, except financial derivatives	241 746	237 213	214 505	275 192	300 238	298 587	315 133	385 438
2.2.1	Short-term securities	44 461	38 778	33 501	28 485	28 894	21 936	17 633	16 196
2.2.2	Long-term securities	197 285	198 435	181 004	246 707	271 344	276 651	297 500	369 242
2.2.3	Securities issued by residents	212 362	201 111	183 714	216 672	248 576	254 287	250 446	260 426
2.2.4	Securities issued by non-residents	29 384	36 102	30 791	58 520	51 662	44 300	64 687	125 012
2.3	Loans	0	0	0	0	0	0	0	0
2.3.1	Short-term loans	0	0	0	0	0	0	0	0
2.3.2	Long-term loans	0	0	0	0	0	0	0	0
2.3.3	Loans granted to residents	0	0	0	0	0	0	0	0
2.3.4	Loans granted to non-residents	0	0	0	0	0	0	0	0
2.4	Shares and other equity	1 066 744	1 113 434	699 460	1 065 868	1 286 037	1 118 423	1 322 474	1 694 014
2.4.1	Shares issued by residents	466 873	434 054	255 518	421 393	524 164	439 948	488 846	600 078
2.4.2	Shares issued by non-residents	599 871	679 380	443 942	644 475	761 873	678 475	833 628	1 093 936
2.5	Other, not elsewhere classified	15 713	69 844	42 737	68 077	85 756	68 869	102 190	111 846

Table 2. Financial assets of investment funds *(cont.)*

Million SEK

		2006	2007	2008	2009	2010	2011	2012	2013
	Closed-end companies								
2	Financial assets	..	..	..	..	..	..	..	..
2.1	Currency and deposits	..	..	..	..	..	..	..	..
2.2	Securities other than shares, except financial derivatives	..	..	..	..	..	..	..	..
2.2.1	Short-term securities	..	..	..	..	..	..	..	..
2.2.2	Long-term securities	..	..	..	..	..	..	..	..
2.2.3	Securities issued by residents	..	..	..	..	..	..	..	..
2.2.4	Securities issued by non-residents	..	..	..	..	..	..	..	..
2.3	Loans	..	..	..	..	..	..	..	..
2.3.1	Short-term loans	..	..	..	..	..	..	..	..
2.3.2	Long-term loans	..	..	..	..	..	..	..	..
2.3.3	Loans granted to residents	..	..	..	..	..	..	..	..
2.3.4	Loans granted to non-residents	..	..	..	..	..	..	..	..
2.4	Shares and other equity	..	..	..	..	..	..	..	..
2.4.1	Shares issued by residents	..	..	..	..	..	..	..	..
2.4.2	Shares issued by non-residents	..	..	..	..	..	..	..	..
2.5	Other, not elsewhere classified	..	..	..	..	..	..	..	..

Note: Detailed metadata at: http://metalinks.oecd.org/instinv/20141203/fed1

Table 3. Financial assets of insurance corporations and autonomous pension funds

Million SEK

		2006	2007	2008	2009	2010	2011	2012	2013
	Insurance corporations and autonomous pension funds								
2	Financial assets	2 904 716	3 049 778	2 754 129	3 187 305	3 443 205	3 439 252	3 722 011	4 102 410
2.1	Currency and deposits	106 795	112 302	121 801	98 109	117 829	136 065	124 075	126 167
2.2	Securities other than shares, except financial derivatives	1 134 688	1 193 108	1 299 579	1 244 521	1 190 185	1 318 125	1 359 356	1 324 128
2.2.1	Short-term securities	109 400	112 428	61 533	48 248	29 875	33 004	52 185	41 619
2.2.2	Long-term securities	1 025 288	1 080 680	1 238 046	1 196 273	1 160 310	1 285 121	1 307 171	1 282 509
2.2.3	Securities issued by residents	863 684	881 999	907 198	901 524	858 055	958 876	1 019 839	988 830
2.2.4	Securities issued by non-residents	271 004	311 109	392 381	342 997	332 130	359 249	339 517	335 298
2.3	Loans	46 558	49 026	49 742	54 080	58 898	63 628	71 689	79 625
2.3.1	Short-term loans	0	0	0	0	0	0	0	0
2.3.2	Long-term loans	46 558	49 026	49 742	54 080	58 898	63 628	71 689	79 625
2.3.3	Loans granted to residents	43 526	44 405	41 377	44 061	49 264	52 847	58 818	54 134
2.3.4	Loans granted to non-residents	3 032	4 621	8 365	10 019	9 634	10 781	12 871	25 491
2.4	Shares and other equity	1 557 913	1 636 053	1 193 553	1 723 972	2 000 658	1 827 272	2 070 295	2 499 880
2.4.1	Shares issued by residents	1 030 554	1 059 735	741 607	1 055 839	1 233 487	1 135 020	1 265 142	1 551 054
2.4.2	Shares issued by non-residents	527 359	576 318	451 946	668 133	767 171	692 252	805 153	948 826
2.5	Other, not elsewhere classified	58 762	59 289	89 454	66 623	75 635	94 162	96 596	72 610
	Insurance corporations								
2	Financial assets	2 514 205	2 617 575	2 429 233	2 736 251	2 950 129	2 930 267	3 152 534	3 391 770
2.1	Currency and deposits	97 756	100 616	109 886	87 813	115 035	133 127	120 987	124 540
2.2	Securities other than shares, except financial derivatives	1 045 301	1 106 045	1 223 554	1 164 537	1 131 600	1 248 990	1 284 289	1 247 642
2.2.1	Short-term securities	92 233	95 357	44 879	31 538	28 086	30 893	49 893	39 248
2.2.2	Long-term securities	953 068	1 010 688	1 178 675	1 132 999	1 103 514	1 218 097	1 234 396	1 208 394
2.2.3	Securities issued by residents	774 297	794 936	831 173	821 540	799 470	889 741	944 772	912 344
2.2.4	Securities issued by non-residents	271 004	311 109	392 381	342 997	332 130	359 249	339 517	335 298
2.3	Loans	45 057	47 738	48 873	53 652	58 322	61 984	70 320	78 609
2.3.1	Short-term loans	10	1	613	0	0	0	0	0
2.3.2	Long-term loans	45 047	47 737	48 260	53 652	58 322	61 984	70 320	78 609
2.3.3	Loans granted to residents	42 025	43 117	40 508	43 633	48 688	51 203	57 449	53 118
2.3.4	Loans granted to non-residents	3 032	4 621	8 365	10 019	9 634	10 781	12 871	25 491
2.4	Shares and other equity	1 252 512	1 285 586	936 433	1 343 186	1 550 922	1 374 155	1 561 907	1 848 442
2.4.1	Shares issued by residents	779 602	775 996	529 048	752 693	876 116	754 305	845 554	1 004 077
2.4.2	Shares issued by non-residents	472 910	509 590	407 385	590 493	674 806	619 850	716 353	844 365
2.5	Other, not elsewhere classified	73 579	77 590	110 487	87 063	94 250	112 011	115 031	92 537
	Life insurance corporations								
2	Financial assets								
2.1	Currency and deposits	..	..	..	..	..	..	..	..
2.2	Securities other than shares, except financial derivatives	..	..	..	..	..	..	..	..
2.2.1	Short-term securities	..	..	..	..	..	..	..	..
2.2.2	Long-term securities	..	..	..	..	..	..	..	..
2.2.3	Securities issued by residents	..	..	..	..	..	..	..	..
2.2.4	Securities issued by non-residents	..	..	..	..	..	..	..	..
2.3	Loans	..	..	..	..	..	..	..	..
2.3.1	Short-term loans	..	..	..	..	..	..	..	..
2.3.2	Long-term loans	..	..	..	..	..	..	..	..
2.3.3	Loans granted to residents	..	..	..	..	..	..	..	..
2.3.4	Loans granted to non-residents	..	..	..	..	..	..	..	..
2.4	Shares and other equity	..	..	..	..	..	..	..	..
2.4.1	Shares issued by residents	..	..	..	..	..	..	..	..
2.4.2	Shares issued by non-residents	..	..	..	..	..	..	..	..
2.5	Other, not elsewhere classified	..	..	..	..	..	..	..	..
	Non-life insurance corporations								
2	Financial assets								
2.1	Currency and deposits	..	..	..	..	..	..	..	..
2.2	Securities other than shares, except financial derivatives	..	..	..	..	..	..	..	..
2.2.1	Short-term securities	..	..	..	..	..	..	..	..
2.2.2	Long-term securities	..	..	..	..	..	..	..	..
2.2.3	Securities issued by residents	..	..	..	..	..	..	..	..
2.2.4	Securities issued by non-residents	..	..	..	..	..	..	..	..
2.3	Loans	..	..	..	..	..	..	..	..
2.3.1	Short-term loans	..	..	..	..	..	..	..	..
2.3.2	Long-term loans	..	..	..	..	..	..	..	..
2.3.3	Loans granted to residents	..	..	..	..	..	..	..	..
2.3.4	Loans granted to non-residents	..	..	..	..	..	..	..	..
2.4	Shares and other equity	..	..	..	..	..	..	..	..
2.4.1	Shares issued by residents	..	..	..	..	..	..	..	..
2.4.2	Shares issued by non-residents	..	..	..	..	..	..	..	..
2.5	Other, not elsewhere classified	..	..	..	..	..	..	..	..

Table 3. Financial assets of insurance corporations and autonomous pension funds *(cont.)*

Million SEK

		2006	2007	2008	2009	2010	2011	2012	2013
	Autonomous pension funds								
2	Financial assets	422 329	467 187	362 169	492 235	536 550	547 957	639 326	785 149
2.1	Currency and deposits	9 039	11 686	11 915	10 296	2 794	2 938	3 088	1 627
2.2	Securities other than shares, except financial derivatives	89 387	87 063	76 025	79 984	58 585	69 135	75 067	76 486
2.2.1	Short-term securities	17 167	17 071	16 654	16 710	1 789	2 111	2 292	2 371
2.2.2	Long-term securities	72 220	69 992	59 371	63 274	56 796	67 024	72 775	74 115
2.2.3	Securities issued by residents	89 387	87 063	76 025	79 984	58 585	69 135	75 067	76 486
2.2.4	Securities issued by non-residents	0	0	0	0	0	0	0	0
2.3	Loans	1 511	1 289	1 482	428	576	1 644	1 369	1 016
2.3.1	Short-term loans	0	0	0	0	0	0	0	0
2.3.2	Long-term loans	1 511	1 289	1 482	428	576	1 644	1 369	1 016
2.3.3	Loans granted to residents	1 511	1 289	1 482	428	576	1 644	1 369	1 016
2.3.4	Loans granted to non-residents	0	0	0	0	0	0	0	0
2.4	Shares and other equity	321 073	365 731	271 638	400 109	473 592	473 066	558 571	704 933
2.4.1	Shares issued by residents	266 624	299 003	227 077	322 469	381 227	400 664	469 771	600 472
2.4.2	Shares issued by non-residents	54 449	66 728	44 561	77 640	92 365	72 402	88 800	104 461
2.5	Other, not elsewhere classified	1 319	1 418	1 109	1 418	1 003	1 174	1 231	1 087

Note: Detailed metadata at: http://metalinks.oecd.org/instinv/20141203/fed1

Table 4. Portfolio composition by type of investor

Percentage of total financial assets

Per cent

		2006	2007	2008	2009	2010	2011	2012	2013
	Investment funds								
2	Financial assets	100.0	100.0	100.0	100.0	100.0	100.0	100.0	100.0
2.1	Currency and deposits	3.7	3.6	4.7	3.2	2.7	3.5	3.5	3.0
2.2	Securities other than shares, except financial derivatives	21.9	20.7	28.1	22.8	21.0	24.7	21.8	21.2
2.2.1	Short-term securities	5.3	4.4	6.7	3.0	2.5	3.1	2.1	1.5
2.2.2	Long-term securities	16.5	16.3	21.3	19.8	18.5	21.7	19.7	19.7
2.2.3	Securities issued by residents	19.3	17.9	24.8	18.7	17.9	21.8	18.1	15.4
2.2.4	Securities issued by non-residents	2.5	2.8	3.2	4.1	3.0	3.0	3.7	5.8
2.3	Loans	0.0	0.0	0.0	0.0	0.0	0.0	0.0	0.0
2.3.1	Short-term loans	0.0	0.0	0.0	0.0	0.0	0.0	0.0	0.0
2.3.2	Long-term loans	0.0	0.0	0.0	0.0	0.0	0.0	0.0	0.0
2.3.3	Loans granted to residents	0.0	0.0	0.0	0.0	0.0	0.0	0.0	0.0
2.3.4	Loans granted to non-residents	0.0	0.0	0.0	0.0	0.0	0.0	0.0	0.0
2.4	Shares and other equity	73.3	71.1	63.3	69.4	71.5	67.4	69.1	71.0
2.4.1	Shares issued by residents	31.7	27.1	22.4	26.7	28.4	25.1	23.8	23.6
2.4.2	Shares issued by non-residents	41.6	44.0	40.9	42.7	43.1	42.3	45.3	47.4
2.5	Other, not elsewhere classified	1.1	4.6	3.9	4.5	4.9	4.3	5.6	4.8
	Insurance corporations								
2	Financial assets	100.0	100.0	100.0	100.0	100.0	100.0	100.0	100.0
2.1	Currency and deposits	3.9	3.8	4.5	3.2	3.9	4.5	3.8	3.7
2.2	Securities other than shares, except financial derivatives	41.6	42.3	50.4	42.6	38.4	42.6	40.7	36.8
2.2.1	Short-term securities	3.7	3.6	1.8	1.2	1.0	1.1	1.6	1.2
2.2.2	Long-term securities	37.9	38.6	48.5	41.4	37.4	41.6	39.2	35.6
2.2.3	Securities issued by residents	30.8	30.4	34.2	30.0	27.1	30.4	30.0	26.9
2.2.4	Securities issued by non-residents	10.8	11.9	16.2	12.5	11.3	12.3	10.8	9.9
2.3	Loans	1.8	1.8	2.0	2.0	2.0	2.1	2.2	2.3
2.3.1	Short-term loans	0.0	0.0	0.0	0.0	0.0	0.0	0.0	0.0
2.3.2	Long-term loans	1.8	1.8	2.0	2.0	2.0	2.1	2.2	2.3
2.3.3	Loans granted to residents	1.7	1.6	1.7	1.6	1.7	1.7	1.8	1.6
2.3.4	Loans granted to non-residents	0.1	0.2	0.3	0.4	0.3	0.4	0.4	0.8
2.4	Shares and other equity	49.8	49.1	38.5	49.1	52.6	46.9	49.5	54.5
2.4.1	Shares issued by residents	31.0	29.6	21.8	27.5	29.7	25.7	26.8	29.6
2.4.2	Shares issued by non-residents	18.8	19.5	16.8	21.6	22.9	21.2	22.7	24.9
2.5	Other, not elsewhere classified	2.9	3.0	4.5	3.2	3.2	3.8	3.6	2.7
	Autonomous pension funds								
2	Financial assets	100.0	100.0	100.0	100.0	100.0	100.0	100.0	100.0
2.1	Currency and deposits	2.1	2.5	3.3	2.1	0.5	0.5	0.5	0.2
2.2	Securities other than shares, except financial derivatives	21.2	18.6	21.0	16.2	10.9	12.6	11.7	9.7
2.2.1	Short-term securities	4.1	3.7	4.6	3.4	0.3	0.4	0.4	0.3
2.2.2	Long-term securities	17.1	15.0	16.4	12.9	10.6	12.2	11.4	9.4
2.2.3	Securities issued by residents	21.2	18.6	21.0	16.2	10.9	12.6	11.7	9.7
2.2.4	Securities issued by non-residents	0.0	0.0	0.0	0.0	0.0	0.0	0.0	0.0
2.3	Loans	0.4	0.3	0.4	0.1	0.1	0.3	0.2	0.1
2.3.1	Short-term loans	0.0	0.0	0.0	0.0	0.0	0.0	0.0	0.0
2.3.2	Long-term loans	0.4	0.3	0.4	0.1	0.1	0.3	0.2	0.1
2.3.3	Loans granted to residents	0.4	0.3	0.4	0.1	0.1	0.3	0.2	0.1
2.3.4	Loans granted to non-residents	0.0	0.0	0.0	0.0	0.0	0.0	0.0	0.0
2.4	Shares and other equity	76.0	78.3	75.0	81.3	88.3	86.3	87.4	89.8
2.4.1	Shares issued by residents	63.1	64.0	62.7	65.5	71.1	73.1	73.5	76.5
2.4.2	Shares issued by non-residents	12.9	14.3	12.3	15.8	17.2	13.2	13.9	13.3
2.5	Other, not elsewhere classified	0.3	0.3	0.3	0.3	0.2	0.2	0.2	0.1

Note: Detailed metadata at: http://metalinks.oecd.org/instinv/20141203/f729

SWITZERLAND

Table 1. Financial assets of institutional investors, 2013

Million CHF

		Investment funds				
		Total	Open-end companies (mutual funds)			Closed-end companies
			Total	Money market funds	Other mutual funds	Total
2	Financial assets	..	548 383	..	..	..
2.1	Currency and deposits	..	15 899	..	..	..
2.2	Securities other than shares, except financial derivatives	..	281 150	..	..	..
2.2.1	Short-term securities	..	15 439	..	..	..
2.2.2	Long-term securities	..	265 711	..	..	..
2.2.3	Securities issued by residents	..	85 097	..	..	..
2.2.4	Securities issued by non-residents	..	196 053	..	..	..
2.3	Loans	..	0	..	..	..
2.3.1	Short-term loans	..	0	..	..	..
2.3.2	Long-term loans	..	0	..	..	..
2.3.3	Loans granted to residents	..	0	..	..	..
2.3.4	Loans granted to non-residents	..	0	..	..	..
2.4	Shares and other equity	..	251 334	..	..	..
2.4.1	Shares issued by residents	..	124 063	..	..	..
2.4.2	Shares issued by non-residents	..	127 271	..	..	..
2.5	Other, not elsewhere classified	..	0	..	..	..

		Insurance corporations and autonomous pension funds				
		Total	Insurance corporations			Autonomous pension funds
			Total	Life insurance corporations	Non-life insurance corporations	Total
2	Financial assets	1 205 893	550 463	..	..	655 430
2.1	Currency and deposits	80 327	28 970	..	..	51 357
2.2	Securities other than shares, except financial derivatives	322 601	188 201	..	..	134 400
2.2.1	Short-term securities	12 869	10 392	..	..	2 477
2.2.2	Long-term securities	309 732	177 809	..	..	131 923
2.2.3	Securities issued by residents	122 400	58 149	..	..	64 251
2.2.4	Securities issued by non-residents	200 201	130 052	..	..	70 149
2.3	Loans	63 432	52 922	..	..	10 510
2.3.1	Short-term loans	..	..	..	..	..
2.3.2	Long-term loans	..	..	..	..	..
2.3.3	Loans granted to residents	41 690	31 180	..	..	10 510
2.3.4	Loans granted to non-residents	21 742	21 742	..	..	0
2.4	Shares and other equity	732 107	280 370	..	..	451 737
2.4.1	Shares issued by residents	458 109	105 478	..	..	352 631
2.4.2	Shares issued by non-residents	273 998	174 892	..	..	99 106
2.5	Other, not elsewhere classified	7 426	..	..	..	7 426

Note: Detailed metadata at: http://metalinks.oecd.org/instinv/20141203/47d1

Table 2. Financial assets of investment funds

Million CHF

		2006	2007	2008	2009	2010	2011	2012	2013
	Investment funds								
2	Financial assets	..	..	..	..	..	..	..	..
2.1	Currency and deposits	..	..	..	..	..	..	..	..
2.2	Securities other than shares, except financial derivatives	..	..	..	..	..	..	..	..
2.2.1	Short-term securities	..	..	..	..	..	..	..	..
2.2.2	Long-term securities	..	..	..	..	..	..	..	..
2.2.3	Securities issued by residents	..	..	..	..	..	..	..	..
2.2.4	Securities issued by non-residents	..	..	..	..	..	..	..	..
2.3	Loans	..	..	..	..	..	..	..	..
2.3.1	Short-term loans	..	..	..	..	..	..	..	..
2.3.2	Long-term loans	..	..	..	..	..	..	..	..
2.3.3	Loans granted to residents	..	..	..	..	..	..	..	..
2.3.4	Loans granted to non-residents	..	..	..	..	..	..	..	..
2.4	Shares and other equity	..	..	..	..	..	..	..	..
2.4.1	Shares issued by residents	..	..	..	..	..	..	..	..
2.4.2	Shares issued by non-residents	..	..	..	..	..	..	..	..
2.5	Other, not elsewhere classified	..	..	..	..	..	..	..	..
	Open-end companies (mutual funds)								
2	Financial assets	373 289	415 707	321 727	388 874	422 397	437 898	489 668	548 383
2.1	Currency and deposits	11 780	13 553	12 479	10 860	11 934	16 499	16 939	15 899
2.2	Securities other than shares, except financial derivatives	166 135	189 941	188 060	217 822	235 611	253 149	268 060	281 150
2.2.1	Short-term securities	11 606	20 619	29 609	23 583	18 861	18 044	15 648	15 439
2.2.2	Long-term securities	154 529	169 322	158 451	194 239	216 750	235 105	252 412	265 711
2.2.3	Securities issued by residents	48 958	53 571	54 854	63 113	73 225	75 905	81 918	85 097
2.2.4	Securities issued by non-residents	117 177	136 370	133 206	154 709	162 386	177 244	186 142	196 053
2.3	Loans	0	0	0	0	0	0	0	0
2.3.1	Short-term loans	0	0	0	0	0	0	0	0
2.3.2	Long-term loans	0	0	0	0	0	0	0	0
2.3.3	Loans granted to residents	0	0	0	0	0	0	0	0
2.3.4	Loans granted to non-residents	0	0	0	0	0	0	0	0
2.4	Shares and other equity	195 374	212 213	121 188	160 192	174 852	168 250	204 669	251 334
2.4.1	Shares issued by residents	69 870	76 479	57 003	72 465	79 990	78 150	96 565	124 063
2.4.2	Shares issued by non-residents	125 504	135 734	64 185	87 727	94 862	90 100	108 104	127 271
2.5	Other, not elsewhere classified	0	0	0	0	0	0	0	0
	Money market funds								
2	Financial assets	..	..	..	..	..	..	..	..
2.1	Currency and deposits	..	..	..	..	..	..	..	..
2.2	Securities other than shares, except financial derivatives	..	..	..	..	..	..	..	..
2.2.1	Short-term securities	..	..	..	..	..	..	..	..
2.2.2	Long-term securities	..	..	..	..	..	..	..	..
2.2.3	Securities issued by residents	..	..	..	..	..	..	..	..
2.2.4	Securities issued by non-residents	..	..	..	..	..	..	..	..
2.3	Loans	..	..	..	..	..	..	..	..
2.3.1	Short-term loans	..	..	..	..	..	..	..	..
2.3.2	Long-term loans	..	..	..	..	..	..	..	..
2.3.3	Loans granted to residents	..	..	..	..	..	..	..	..
2.3.4	Loans granted to non-residents	..	..	..	..	..	..	..	..
2.4	Shares and other equity	..	..	..	..	..	..	..	..
2.4.1	Shares issued by residents	..	..	..	..	..	..	..	..
2.4.2	Shares issued by non-residents	..	..	..	..	..	..	..	..
2.5	Other, not elsewhere classified	..	..	..	..	..	..	..	..
	Other mutual funds								
2	Financial assets	..	..	..	..	..	..	..	..
2.1	Currency and deposits	..	..	..	..	..	..	..	..
2.2	Securities other than shares, except financial derivatives	..	..	..	..	..	..	..	..
2.2.1	Short-term securities	..	..	..	..	..	..	..	..
2.2.2	Long-term securities	..	..	..	..	..	..	..	..
2.2.3	Securities issued by residents	..	..	..	..	..	..	..	..
2.2.4	Securities issued by non-residents	..	..	..	..	..	..	..	..
2.3	Loans	..	..	..	..	..	..	..	..
2.3.1	Short-term loans	..	..	..	..	..	..	..	..
2.3.2	Long-term loans	..	..	..	..	..	..	..	..
2.3.3	Loans granted to residents	..	..	..	..	..	..	..	..
2.3.4	Loans granted to non-residents	..	..	..	..	..	..	..	..
2.4	Shares and other equity	..	..	..	..	..	..	..	..
2.4.1	Shares issued by residents	..	..	..	..	..	..	..	..
2.4.2	Shares issued by non-residents	..	..	..	..	..	..	..	..
2.5	Other, not elsewhere classified	..	..	..	..	..	..	..	..

Table 2. Financial assets of investment funds (*cont.*)

Million CHF

		2006	2007	2008	2009	2010	2011	2012	2013
	Closed-end companies								
2	Financial assets	..	..	..	..	..	..	..	..
2.1	Currency and deposits	..	..	..	..	..	..	..	..
2.2	Securities other than shares, except financial derivatives	..	..	..	..	..	..	..	..
2.2.1	Short-term securities	..	..	..	..	..	..	..	..
2.2.2	Long-term securities	..	..	..	..	..	..	..	..
2.2.3	Securities issued by residents	..	..	..	..	..	..	..	..
2.2.4	Securities issued by non-residents	..	..	..	..	..	..	..	..
2.3	Loans	..	..	..	..	..	..	..	..
2.3.1	Short-term loans	..	..	..	..	..	..	..	..
2.3.2	Long-term loans	..	..	..	..	..	..	..	..
2.3.3	Loans granted to residents	..	..	..	..	..	..	..	..
2.3.4	Loans granted to non-residents	..	..	..	..	..	..	..	..
2.4	Shares and other equity	..	..	..	..	..	..	..	..
2.4.1	Shares issued by residents	..	..	..	..	..	..	..	..
2.4.2	Shares issued by non-residents	..	..	..	..	..	..	..	..
2.5	Other, not elsewhere classified	..	..	..	..	..	..	..	..

Note: Detailed metadata at: http://metalinks.oecd.org/instinv/20141203/47d1

Table 3. Financial assets of insurance corporations and autonomous pension funds

Million CHF

		2006	2007	2008	2009	2010	2011	2012	2013
	Insurance corporations and autonomous pension funds								
2	Financial assets	964 266	1 011 359	916 577	1 008 219	1 049 813	1 078 324	1 150 295	1 205 893
2.1	Currency and deposits	67 389	64 674	63 649	64 400	65 026	71 652	77 436	80 327
2.2	Securities other than shares, except financial derivatives	328 273	349 542	341 521	329 472	324 772	327 333	338 110	322 601
2.2.1	Short-term securities	18 089	19 292	14 879	20 105	17 005	11 076	15 557	12 869
2.2.2	Long-term securities	310 184	330 250	326 642	309 367	307 767	316 257	322 553	309 732
2.2.3	Securities issued by residents	134 717	136 631	136 085	122 189	125 125	121 619	125 245	122 400
2.2.4	Securities issued by non-residents	193 556	212 911	205 436	207 283	199 647	205 714	212 865	200 201
2.3	Loans	68 391	67 515	60 604	63 109	62 012	61 588	61 731	63 432
2.3.1	Short-term loans	..	..	..	..	..	..	..	..
2.3.2	Long-term loans	..	..	..	..	..	..	..	..
2.3.3	Loans granted to residents	44 595	40 939	40 408	40 500	40 580	41 201	40 709	41 690
2.3.4	Loans granted to non-residents	23 796	26 576	20 196	22 609	21 432	20 387	21 022	21 742
2.4	Shares and other equity	497 355	526 755	436 052	542 446	590 811	608 081	665 592	732 107
2.4.1	Shares issued by residents	282 726	318 207	250 397	319 951	364 562	370 454	412 357	458 109
2.4.2	Shares issued by non-residents	214 629	208 548	185 655	222 495	226 249	237 627	253 235	273 998
2.5	Other, not elsewhere classified	2 858	2 873	14 751	8 792	7 192	9 670	7 426	7 426
	Insurance corporations								
2	Financial assets	436 447	472 808	436 822	474 006	488 932	511 936	542 900	550 463
2.1	Currency and deposits	29 651	31 000	30 024	29 758	28 957	32 444	33 581	28 970
2.2	Securities other than shares, except financial derivatives	162 578	182 968	187 823	176 539	182 548	186 009	198 874	188 201
2.2.1	Short-term securities	8 118	5 649	7 921	14 296	10 492	7 081	12 498	10 392
2.2.2	Long-term securities	154 460	177 319	179 902	162 243	172 056	178 928	186 376	177 809
2.2.3	Securities issued by residents	58 591	65 255	64 156	53 311	57 189	56 578	60 025	58 149
2.2.4	Securities issued by non-residents	103 987	117 713	123 667	123 228	125 359	129 431	138 849	130 052
2.3	Loans	50 217	52 696	46 425	49 679	49 591	49 740	51 221	52 922
2.3.1	Short-term loans	..	..	..	..	..	..	..	..
2.3.2	Long-term loans	..	..	..	..	..	..	..	..
2.3.3	Loans granted to residents	26 421	26 120	26 229	27 070	28 159	29 353	30 199	31 180
2.3.4	Loans granted to non-residents	23 796	26 576	20 196	22 609	21 432	20 387	21 022	21 742
2.4	Shares and other equity	194 001	206 144	172 550	218 030	227 836	243 743	259 224	280 370
2.4.1	Shares issued by residents	66 956	88 095	49 407	76 123	86 168	89 052	97 217	105 478
2.4.2	Shares issued by non-residents	127 045	118 049	123 143	141 907	141 668	154 691	162 007	174 892
2.5	Other, not elsewhere classified	0	0	0	0	0	0	0	..
	Life insurance corporations								
2	Financial assets	..	..	..	..	..	..	..	..
2.1	Currency and deposits	..	..	..	..	..	..	..	..
2.2	Securities other than shares, except financial derivatives	..	..	..	..	..	..	..	..
2.2.1	Short-term securities	..	..	..	..	..	..	..	..
2.2.2	Long-term securities	..	..	..	..	..	..	..	..
2.2.3	Securities issued by residents	..	..	..	..	..	..	..	..
2.2.4	Securities issued by non-residents	..	..	..	..	..	..	..	..
2.3	Loans	..	..	..	..	..	..	..	..
2.3.1	Short-term loans	..	..	..	..	..	..	..	..
2.3.2	Long-term loans	..	..	..	..	..	..	..	..
2.3.3	Loans granted to residents	..	..	..	..	..	..	..	..
2.3.4	Loans granted to non-residents	..	..	..	..	..	..	..	..
2.4	Shares and other equity	..	..	..	..	..	..	..	..
2.4.1	Shares issued by residents	..	..	..	..	..	..	..	..
2.4.2	Shares issued by non-residents	..	..	..	..	..	..	..	..
2.5	Other, not elsewhere classified	..	..	..	..	..	..	..	..
	Non-life insurance corporations								
2	Financial assets	..	..	..	..	..	..	..	..
2.1	Currency and deposits	..	..	..	..	..	..	..	..
2.2	Securities other than shares, except financial derivatives	..	..	..	..	..	..	..	..
2.2.1	Short-term securities	..	..	..	..	..	..	..	..
2.2.2	Long-term securities	..	..	..	..	..	..	..	..
2.2.3	Securities issued by residents	..	..	..	..	..	..	..	..
2.2.4	Securities issued by non-residents	..	..	..	..	..	..	..	..
2.3	Loans	..	..	..	..	..	..	..	..
2.3.1	Short-term loans	..	..	..	..	..	..	..	..
2.3.2	Long-term loans	..	..	..	..	..	..	..	..
2.3.3	Loans granted to residents	..	..	..	..	..	..	..	..
2.3.4	Loans granted to non-residents	..	..	..	..	..	..	..	..
2.4	Shares and other equity	..	..	..	..	..	..	..	..
2.4.1	Shares issued by residents	..	..	..	..	..	..	..	..
2.4.2	Shares issued by non-residents	..	..	..	..	..	..	..	..
2.5	Other, not elsewhere classified	..	..	..	..	..	..	..	..

Table 3. Financial assets of insurance corporations and autonomous pension funds *(cont.)*

Million CHF

		2006	2007	2008	2009	2010	2011	2012	2013
	Autonomous pension funds								
2	Financial assets	527 819	538 551	479 755	534 213	560 881	566 388	607 395	655 430
2.1	Currency and deposits	37 738	33 674	33 625	34 642	36 069	39 208	43 855	51 357
2.2	Securities other than shares, except financial derivatives	165 695	166 574	153 698	152 933	142 224	141 324	139 236	134 400
2.2.1	Short-term securities	9 971	13 643	6 958	5 809	6 513	3 995	3 059	2 477
2.2.2	Long-term securities	155 724	152 931	146 740	147 124	135 711	137 329	136 177	131 923
2.2.3	Securities issued by residents	76 126	71 376	71 929	68 878	67 936	65 041	65 220	64 251
2.2.4	Securities issued by non-residents	89 569	95 198	81 769	84 055	74 288	76 283	74 016	70 149
2.3	Loans	18 174	14 819	14 179	13 430	12 421	11 848	10 510	10 510
2.3.1	Short-term loans	..	..	..	..	..	..	..	..
2.3.2	Long-term loans	..	..	..	..	..	..	..	..
2.3.3	Loans granted to residents	18 174	14 819	14 179	13 430	12 421	11 848	10 510	10 510
2.3.4	Loans granted to non-residents	0	0	0	0	0	0	0	0
2.4	Shares and other equity	303 354	320 611	263 502	324 416	362 975	364 338	406 368	451 737
2.4.1	Shares issued by residents	215 770	230 112	200 990	243 828	278 394	281 402	315 140	352 631
2.4.2	Shares issued by non-residents	87 584	90 499	62 512	80 588	84 581	82 936	91 228	99 106
2.5	Other, not elsewhere classified	2 858	2 873	14 751	8 792	7 192	9 670	7 426	7 426

Note: Detailed metadata at: http://metalinks.oecd.org/instinv/20141203/47d1

Table 4. Portfolio composition by type of investor

Percentage of total financial assets

Per cent

		2006	2007	2008	2009	2010	2011	2012	2013
	Investment funds								
2	Financial assets	..	..	..	..	..	..	..	..
2.1	Currency and deposits	..	..	..	..	..	..	..	..
2.2	Securities other than shares, except financial derivatives	..	..	..	..	..	..	..	..
2.2.1	Short-term securities	..	..	..	..	..	..	..	..
2.2.2	Long-term securities	..	..	..	..	..	..	..	..
2.2.3	Securities issued by residents	..	..	..	..	..	..	..	..
2.2.4	Securities issued by non-residents	..	..	..	..	..	..	..	..
2.3	Loans	..	..	..	..	..	..	..	..
2.3.1	Short-term loans	..	..	..	..	..	..	..	..
2.3.2	Long-term loans	..	..	..	..	..	..	..	..
2.3.3	Loans granted to residents	..	..	..	..	..	..	..	..
2.3.4	Loans granted to non-residents	..	..	..	..	..	..	..	..
2.4	Shares and other equity	..	..	..	..	..	..	..	..
2.4.1	Shares issued by residents	..	..	..	..	..	..	..	..
2.4.2	Shares issued by non-residents	..	..	..	..	..	..	..	..
2.5	Other, not elsewhere classified	..	..	..	..	..	..	..	..
	Insurance corporations								
2	Financial assets	100.0	100.0	100.0	100.0	100.0	100.0	100.0	100.0
2.1	Currency and deposits	6.8	6.6	6.9	6.3	5.9	6.3	6.2	5.3
2.2	Securities other than shares, except financial derivatives	37.3	38.7	43.0	37.2	37.3	36.3	36.6	34.2
2.2.1	Short-term securities	1.9	1.2	1.8	3.0	2.1	1.4	2.3	1.9
2.2.2	Long-term securities	35.4	37.5	41.2	34.2	35.2	35.0	34.3	32.3
2.2.3	Securities issued by residents	13.4	13.8	14.7	11.2	11.7	11.1	11.1	10.6
2.2.4	Securities issued by non-residents	23.8	24.9	28.3	26.0	25.6	25.3	25.6	23.6
2.3	Loans	11.5	11.1	10.6	10.5	10.1	9.7	9.4	9.6
2.3.1	Short-term loans	..	..	..	..	..	..	..	..
2.3.2	Long-term loans	..	..	..	..	..	..	..	..
2.3.3	Loans granted to residents	6.1	5.5	6.0	5.7	5.8	5.7	5.6	5.7
2.3.4	Loans granted to non-residents	5.5	5.6	4.6	4.8	4.4	4.0	3.9	3.9
2.4	Shares and other equity	44.5	43.6	39.5	46.0	46.6	47.6	47.7	50.9
2.4.1	Shares issued by residents	15.3	18.6	11.3	16.1	17.6	17.4	17.9	19.2
2.4.2	Shares issued by non-residents	29.1	25.0	28.2	29.9	29.0	30.2	29.8	31.8
2.5	Other, not elsewhere classified	0.0	0.0	0.0	0.0	0.0	0.0	0.0	..
	Autonomous pension funds								
2	Financial assets	100.0	100.0	100.0	100.0	100.0	100.0	100.0	100.0
2.1	Currency and deposits	7.1	6.3	7.0	6.5	6.4	6.9	7.2	7.8
2.2	Securities other than shares, except financial derivatives	31.4	30.9	32.0	28.6	25.4	25.0	22.9	20.5
2.2.1	Short-term securities	1.9	2.5	1.5	1.1	1.2	0.7	0.5	0.4
2.2.2	Long-term securities	29.5	28.4	30.6	27.5	24.2	24.2	22.4	20.1
2.2.3	Securities issued by residents	14.4	13.3	15.0	12.9	12.1	11.5	10.7	9.8
2.2.4	Securities issued by non-residents	17.0	17.7	17.0	15.7	13.2	13.5	12.2	10.7
2.3	Loans	3.4	2.8	3.0	2.5	2.2	2.1	1.7	1.6
2.3.1	Short-term loans	..	..	..	..	..	..	..	..
2.3.2	Long-term loans	..	..	..	..	..	..	..	..
2.3.3	Loans granted to residents	3.4	2.8	3.0	2.5	2.2	2.1	1.7	1.6
2.3.4	Loans granted to non-residents	0.0	0.0	0.0	0.0	0.0	0.0	0.0	0.0
2.4	Shares and other equity	57.5	59.5	54.9	60.7	64.7	64.3	66.9	68.9
2.4.1	Shares issued by residents	40.9	42.7	41.9	45.6	49.6	49.7	51.9	53.8
2.4.2	Shares issued by non-residents	16.6	16.8	13.0	15.1	15.1	14.6	15.0	15.1
2.5	Other, not elsewhere classified	0.5	0.5	3.1	1.6	1.3	1.7	1.2	1.1

Note: Detailed metadata at: http://metalinks.oecd.org/instinv/20141203/f729

Table 1. Financial assets of institutional investors, 2012

Million TRY

		Total	Investment funds			
			Open-end companies (mutual funds)			Closed-end companies
			Total	Money market funds	Other mutual funds	Total
2	Financial assets	32 130	29 688	17 289	12 399	2 442
2.1	Currency and deposits	3 516	2 302	1 967	335	1 214
2.2	Securities other than shares, except financial derivatives	18 270	17 474	15 322	2 152	796
2.2.1	Short-term securities	15 589	15 322	15 322	0	267
2.2.2	Long-term securities	2 681	2 152	0	2 152	529
2.2.3	Securities issued by residents	18 154	17 358	15 322	2 036	796
2.2.4	Securities issued by non-residents	116	116	0	116	0
2.3	Loans	0	0	0	0	0
2.3.1	Short-term loans	..	..	..	..	..
2.3.2	Long-term loans	..	..	..	..	..
2.3.3	Loans granted to residents	..	..	..	..	..
2.3.4	Loans granted to non-residents	..	..	..	..	..
2.4	Shares and other equity	1 873	1 468	0	1 468	406
2.4.1	Shares issued by residents	1 867	1 461	0	1 461	406
2.4.2	Shares issued by non-residents	7	7	0	7	0
2.5	Other, not elsewhere classified	8 472	8 445	0	8 445	27

		Total	Insurance corporations and autonomous pension funds			
			Insurance corporations			Autonomous pension funds
			Total	Life insurance corporations	Non-life insurance corporations	Total
2	Financial assets	31 202	21 232	2 272	18 960	9 970
2.1	Currency and deposits	11 762	8 282	994	7 288	3 480
2.2	Securities other than shares, except financial derivatives	8 976	3 550	358	3 192	5 425
2.2.1	Short-term securities	8 973	3 549	358	3 191	5 424
2.2.2	Long-term securities	2	1	0	1	1
2.2.3	Securities issued by residents	..	..	..	..	..
2.2.4	Securities issued by non-residents	..	..	..	..	..
2.3	Loans	240	2	2	0	238
2.3.1	Short-term loans	96	2	2	0	94
2.3.2	Long-term loans	144	0	0	0	144
2.3.3	Loans granted to residents	..	..	..	..	..
2.3.4	Loans granted to non-residents	..	..	..	..	..
2.4	Shares and other equity	1 942	1 579	463	1 116	363
2.4.1	Shares issued by residents	..	..	..	..	..
2.4.2	Shares issued by non-residents	..	..	..	..	..
2.5	Other, not elsewhere classified	8 282	7 819	455	7 364	464

Note: Detailed metadata at: http://metalinks.oecd.org/instinv/20141203/369c

Table 2. Financial assets of investment funds

Million TRY

		2006	2007	2008	2009	2010	2011	2012	2013
	Investment funds								
2	Financial assets	23 812	28 463	24 820	30 889	34 280	30 221	32 130	..
2.1	Currency and deposits	249	802	1 318	1 868	4 745	3 474	3 516	..
2.2	Securities other than shares, except financial derivatives	22 671	26 620	22 824	27 559	26 307	23 936	18 270	..
2.2.1	Short-term securities	21 155	20 775	19 759	22 138	21 836	22 071	15 589	..
2.2.2	Long-term securities	1 516	5 846	3 066	5 420	4 472	1 864	2 681	..
2.2.3	Securities issued by residents	22 653	26 608	22 814	27 525	26 204	23 836	18 154	..
2.2.4	Securities issued by non-residents	18	12	10	34	103	100	116	..
2.3	Loans	0	0	0	0	0	0	0	..
2.3.1	Short-term loans	..	..	..	..	..	..	..	..
2.3.2	Long-term loans	..	..	..	..	..	..	..	..
2.3.3	Loans granted to residents	..	..	..	..	..	..	..	..
2.3.4	Loans granted to non-residents	..	..	..	..	..	..	..	..
2.4	Shares and other equity	885	971	550	1 047	1 454	1 171	1 873	..
2.4.1	Shares issued by residents	885	971	550	1 045	1 449	1 167	1 867	..
2.4.2	Shares issued by non-residents	0	0	0	2	5	4	7	..
2.5	Other, not elsewhere classified	6	70	128	415	1 773	1 641	8 472	..
	Open-end companies (mutual funds)								
2	Financial assets	23 021	26 961	23 747	29 606	30 980	27 051	29 688	..
2.1	Currency and deposits	233	800	1 021	1 504	2 476	2 475	2 302	..
2.2	Securities other than shares, except financial derivatives	22 175	25 427	22 259	26 888	25 624	22 100	17 474	..
2.2.1	Short-term securities	21 034	20 599	19 505	21 957	21 700	21 700	15 322	..
2.2.2	Long-term securities	1 141	4 829	2 754	4 931	3 924	400	2 152	..
2.2.3	Securities issued by residents	22 157	25 415	22 250	26 856	25 522	22 001	17 358	..
2.2.4	Securities issued by non-residents	18	12	9	32	102	99	116	..
2.3	Loans	0	0	0	0	0	0	0	..
2.3.1	Short-term loans	..	..	..	..	..	..	..	..
2.3.2	Long-term loans	..	..	..	..	..	..	..	..
2.3.3	Loans granted to residents	..	..	..	..	..	..	..	..
2.3.4	Loans granted to non-residents	..	..	..	..	..	..	..	..
2.4	Shares and other equity	608	668	359	805	1 179	965	1 468	..
2.4.1	Shares issued by residents	607	668	359	804	1 174	961	1 461	..
2.4.2	Shares issued by non-residents	0	0	0	1	4	4	7	..
2.5	Other, not elsewhere classified	5	66	108	409	1 702	1 511	8 445	..
	Money market funds								
2	Financial assets	18 816	21 220	20 322	22 943	23 173	20 550	17 289	..
2.1	Currency and deposits	222	768	1 014	1 496	2 401	1 880	1 967	..
2.2	Securities other than shares, except financial derivatives	18 594	20 452	19 308	21 447	20 772	18 670	15 322	..
2.2.1	Short-term securities	18 594	20 452	19 308	21 447	20 772	18 670	15 322	..
2.2.2	Long-term securities	0	0	0	0	0	0	0	..
2.2.3	Securities issued by residents	18 594	20 452	19 308	21 447	20 772	18 670	15 322	..
2.2.4	Securities issued by non-residents	0	0	0	0	0	0	0	..
2.3	Loans	0	0	0	0	0	0	0	..
2.3.1	Short-term loans	..	..	..	..	..	..	..	..
2.3.2	Long-term loans	..	..	..	..	..	..	..	..
2.3.3	Loans granted to residents	..	..	..	..	..	..	..	..
2.3.4	Loans granted to non-residents	..	..	..	..	..	..	..	..
2.4	Shares and other equity	0	0	0	0	0	0	0	..
2.4.1	Shares issued by residents	0	0	0	0	0	0	0	..
2.4.2	Shares issued by non-residents	0	0	0	0	0	0	0	..
2.5	Other, not elsewhere classified	0	0	0	0	0	0	0	..
	Other mutual funds								
2	Financial assets	4 205	5 741	3 424	6 663	7 807	6 501	12 399	..
2.1	Currency and deposits	11	31	7	8	75	595	335	..
2.2	Securities other than shares, except financial derivatives	3 581	4 976	2 950	5 441	4 852	3 430	2 152	..
2.2.1	Short-term securities	2 440	147	197	510	928	3 030	0	..
2.2.2	Long-term securities	1 141	4 829	2 754	4 931	3 924	400	2 152	..
2.2.3	Securities issued by residents	3 563	4 964	2 941	5 409	4 750	3 331	2 036	..
2.2.4	Securities issued by non-residents	18	12	9	32	102	99	116	..
2.3	Loans	0	0	0	0	0	0	0	..
2.3.1	Short-term loans	..	..	..	..	..	..	..	..
2.3.2	Long-term loans	..	..	..	..	..	..	..	..
2.3.3	Loans granted to residents	..	..	..	..	..	..	..	..
2.3.4	Loans granted to non-residents	..	..	..	..	..	..	..	..
2.4	Shares and other equity	608	668	359	805	1 179	965	1 468	..
2.4.1	Shares issued by residents	607	668	359	804	1 174	961	1 461	..
2.4.2	Shares issued by non-residents	0	0	0	1	4	4	7	..
2.5	Other, not elsewhere classified	5	66	108	409	1 702	1 511	8 445	..

Table 2. Financial assets of investment funds *(cont.)*

Million TRY

		2006	2007	2008	2009	2010	2011	2012	2013
	Closed-end companies								
2	Financial assets	791	1 502	1 073	1 283	3 300	3 170	2 442	..
2.1	Currency and deposits	16	3	297	364	2 270	999	1 214	..
2.2	Securities other than shares, except financial derivatives	496	1 193	565	670	683	1 836	796	..
2.2.1	Short-term securities	121	176	253	181	136	371	267	..
2.2.2	Long-term securities	375	1 017	312	489	548	1 464	529	..
2.2.3	Securities issued by residents	496	1 193	565	669	683	1 835	796	..
2.2.4	Securities issued by non-residents	0	0	0	1	1	1	0	..
2.3	Loans	0	0	0	0	0	0	0	..
2.3.1	Short-term loans	..	..	..	..	..	..	..	..
2.3.2	Long-term loans	..	..	..	..	..	..	..	..
2.3.3	Loans granted to residents	..	..	..	..	..	..	..	..
2.3.4	Loans granted to non-residents	..	..	..	..	..	..	..	..
2.4	Shares and other equity	277	303	191	242	276	205	406	..
2.4.1	Shares issued by residents	277	303	191	241	275	205	406	..
2.4.2	Shares issued by non-residents	0	0	0	1	1	0	0	..
2.5	Other, not elsewhere classified	2	4	20	6	71	130	27	..

Note: Detailed metadata at: http://metalinks.oecd.org/instinv/20141203/369c

TURKEY

Table 3. Financial assets of insurance corporations and autonomous pension funds

Million TRY

		2006	2007	2008	2009	2010	2011	2012	2013
	Insurance corporations and autonomous pension funds								
2	Financial assets	13 917	17 363	19 713	22 317	22 881	25 930	31 202	..
2.1	Currency and deposits	2 385	3 176	4 678	4 874	7 125	8 840	11 762	..
2.2	Securities other than shares, except financial derivatives	5 505	6 920	7 726	8 514	8 098	8 130	8 976	..
2.2.1	Short-term securities	5 503	6 918	7 717	8 503	8 087	8 128	8 973	..
2.2.2	Long-term securities	2	1	10	11	11	2	2	..
2.2.3	Securities issued by residents	..	..	..	..	..	..	..	..
2.2.4	Securities issued by non-residents	..	..	..	..	..	..	..	..
2.3	Loans	77	170	275	234	217	239	240	..
2.3.1	Short-term loans	75	169	273	107	78	82	96	..
2.3.2	Long-term loans	1	1	1	127	139	157	144	..
2.3.3	Loans granted to residents	..	..	..	..	..	..	..	..
2.3.4	Loans granted to non-residents	..	..	..	..	..	..	..	..
2.4	Shares and other equity	2 685	3 305	2 259	3 469	1 364	1 629	1 942	..
2.4.1	Shares issued by residents	..	..	..	..	..	..	..	..
2.4.2	Shares issued by non-residents	..	..	..	..	..	..	..	..
2.5	Other, not elsewhere classified	3 266	3 792	4 775	5 225	6 077	7 092	8 282	..
	Insurance corporations								
2	Financial assets	9 862	12 376	14 057	15 905	15 235	16 230	21 232	..
2.1	Currency and deposits	1 929	2 586	3 652	3 592	5 154	5 609	8 282	..
2.2	Securities other than shares, except financial derivatives	2 208	2 931	3 567	3 990	3 324	3 105	3 550	..
2.2.1	Short-term securities	2 207	2 929	3 566	3 988	3 321	3 104	3 549	..
2.2.2	Long-term securities	2	1	2	3	3	1	1	..
2.2.3	Securities issued by residents	..	..	..	..	..	..	..	..
2.2.4	Securities issued by non-residents	..	..	..	..	..	..	..	..
2.3	Loans	59	68	145	88	11	0	2	..
2.3.1	Short-term loans	57	67	143	87	10	0	2	..
2.3.2	Long-term loans	1	1	1	1	1	0	0	..
2.3.3	Loans granted to residents	..	..	..	..	..	..	..	..
2.3.4	Loans granted to non-residents	..	..	..	..	..	..	..	..
2.4	Shares and other equity	2 504	3 129	2 119	3 272	1 088	899	1 579	..
2.4.1	Shares issued by residents	..	..	..	..	..	..	..	..
2.4.2	Shares issued by non-residents	..	..	..	..	..	..	..	..
2.5	Other, not elsewhere classified	3 161	3 662	4 574	4 963	5 658	6 617	7 819	..
	Life insurance corporations								
2	Financial assets	553	678	828	829	1 027	252	2 272	..
2.1	Currency and deposits	121	117	194	177	278	249	994	..
2.2	Securities other than shares, except financial derivatives	301	378	413	462	470	0	358	..
2.2.1	Short-term securities	301	378	413	461	469	0	358	..
2.2.2	Long-term securities	0	0	0	1	1	0	0	..
2.2.3	Securities issued by residents	..	..	..	..	..	..	..	..
2.2.4	Securities issued by non-residents	..	..	..	..	..	..	..	..
2.3	Loans	54	65	88	31	11	0	2	..
2.3.1	Short-term loans	52	63	86	29	10	0	2	..
2.3.2	Long-term loans	1	1	1	1	1	0	0	..
2.3.3	Loans granted to residents	..	..	..	..	..	..	..	..
2.3.4	Loans granted to non-residents	..	..	..	..	..	..	..	..
2.4	Shares and other equity	2	8	3	3	2	0	463	..
2.4.1	Shares issued by residents	..	..	..	..	..	..	..	..
2.4.2	Shares issued by non-residents	..	..	..	..	..	..	..	..
2.5	Other, not elsewhere classified	75	110	130	156	266	3	455	..
	Non-life insurance corporations								
2	Financial assets	9 309	11 698	13 229	15 076	14 208	15 978	18 960	..
2.1	Currency and deposits	1 808	2 469	3 458	3 415	4 876	5 360	7 288	..
2.2	Securities other than shares, except financial derivatives	1 908	2 552	3 154	3 528	2 854	3 105	3 192	..
2.2.1	Short-term securities	1 906	2 551	3 152	3 527	2 853	3 104	3 191	..
2.2.2	Long-term securities	2	1	2	2	2	1	1	..
2.2.3	Securities issued by residents	..	..	..	..	..	..	..	..
2.2.4	Securities issued by non-residents	..	..	..	..	..	..	..	..
2.3	Loans	5	3	57	57	0	0	0	..
2.3.1	Short-term loans	5	3	57	57	0	0	0	..
2.3.2	Long-term loans	0	0	0	0	0	0	0	..
2.3.3	Loans granted to residents	..	..	..	..	..	..	..	..
2.3.4	Loans granted to non-residents	..	..	..	..	..	..	..	..
2.4	Shares and other equity	2 502	3 121	2 116	3 269	1 085	899	1 116	..
2.4.1	Shares issued by residents	..	..	..	..	..	..	..	..
2.4.2	Shares issued by non-residents	..	..	..	..	..	..	..	..
2.5	Other, not elsewhere classified	3 086	3 552	4 444	4 807	5 392	6 614	7 364	..

Table 3. Financial assets of insurance corporations and autonomous pension funds *(cont.)*

Million TRY

		2006	2007	2008	2009	2010	2011	2012	2013
	Autonomous pension funds								
2	Financial assets	4 056	4 987	5 656	6 412	7 646	9 700	9 970	..
2.1	Currency and deposits	456	590	1 026	1 283	1 971	3 232	3 480	..
2.2	Securities other than shares, except financial derivatives	3 296	3 989	4 159	4 524	4 774	5 026	5 425	..
2.2.1	Short-term securities	3 296	3 989	4 151	4 516	4 766	5 025	5 424	..
2.2.2	Long-term securities	0	0	8	8	8	1	1	..
2.2.3	Securities issued by residents	..	..	..	..	..	..	..	..
2.2.4	Securities issued by non-residents	..	..	..	..	..	..	..	..
2.3	Loans	18	102	130	146	206	239	238	..
2.3.1	Short-term loans	18	102	130	21	67	82	94	..
2.3.2	Long-term loans	0	0	0	126	138	157	144	..
2.3.3	Loans granted to residents	..	..	..	..	..	..	..	..
2.3.4	Loans granted to non-residents	..	..	..	..	..	..	..	..
2.4	Shares and other equity	181	176	140	197	276	730	363	..
2.4.1	Shares issued by residents	..	..	..	..	..	..	..	..
2.4.2	Shares issued by non-residents	..	..	..	..	..	..	..	..
2.5	Other, not elsewhere classified	105	130	200	262	419	475	464	..

Note: Detailed metadata at: http://metalinks.oecd.org/instinv/20141203/369c

Table 4. Portfolio composition by type of investor

Percentage of total financial assets

Per cent

		2006	2007	2008	2009	2010	2011	2012	2013
	Investment funds								
2	Financial assets	100.0	100.0	100.0	100.0	100.0	100.0	100.0	..
2.1	Currency and deposits	1.0	2.8	5.3	6.0	13.8	11.5	10.9	..
2.2	Securities other than shares, except financial derivatives	95.2	93.5	92.0	89.2	76.7	79.2	56.9	..
2.2.1	Short-term securities	88.8	73.0	79.6	71.7	63.7	73.0	48.5	..
2.2.2	Long-term securities	6.4	20.5	12.4	17.5	13.0	6.2	8.3	..
2.2.3	Securities issued by residents	95.1	93.5	91.9	89.1	76.4	78.9	56.5	..
2.2.4	Securities issued by non-residents	0.1	0.0	0.0	0.1	0.3	0.3	0.4	..
2.3	Loans	0.0	0.0	0.0	0.0	0.0	0.0	0.0	..
2.3.1	Short-term loans	..	..	..	..	..	..	..	..
2.3.2	Long-term loans	..	..	..	..	..	..	..	..
2.3.3	Loans granted to residents	..	..	..	..	..	..	..	..
2.3.4	Loans granted to non-residents	..	..	..	..	..	..	..	..
2.4	Shares and other equity	3.7	3.4	2.2	3.4	4.2	3.9	5.8	..
2.4.1	Shares issued by residents	3.7	3.4	2.2	3.4	4.2	3.9	5.8	..
2.4.2	Shares issued by non-residents	0.0	0.0	0.0	0.0	0.0	0.0	0.0	..
2.5	Other, not elsewhere classified	0.0	0.2	0.5	1.3	5.2	5.4	26.4	..
	Insurance corporations								
2	Financial assets	100.0	100.0	100.0	100.0	100.0	100.0	100.0	..
2.1	Currency and deposits	19.6	20.9	26.0	22.6	33.8	34.6	39.0	..
2.2	Securities other than shares, except financial derivatives	22.4	23.7	25.4	25.1	21.8	19.1	16.7	..
2.2.1	Short-term securities	22.4	23.7	25.4	25.1	21.8	19.1	16.7	..
2.2.2	Long-term securities	0.0	0.0	0.0	0.0	0.0	0.0	0.0	..
2.2.3	Securities issued by residents	..	..	..	..	..	..	..	..
2.2.4	Securities issued by non-residents	..	..	..	..	..	..	..	..
2.3	Loans	0.6	0.5	1.0	0.6	0.1	0.0	0.0	..
2.3.1	Short-term loans	0.6	0.5	1.0	0.5	0.1	0.0	0.0	..
2.3.2	Long-term loans	0.0	0.0	0.0	0.0	0.0	0.0	0.0	..
2.3.3	Loans granted to residents	..	..	..	..	..	..	..	..
2.3.4	Loans granted to non-residents	..	..	..	..	..	..	..	..
2.4	Shares and other equity	25.4	25.3	15.1	20.6	7.1	5.5	7.4	..
2.4.1	Shares issued by residents	..	..	..	..	..	..	..	..
2.4.2	Shares issued by non-residents	..	..	..	..	..	..	..	..
2.5	Other, not elsewhere classified	32.1	29.6	32.5	31.2	37.1	40.8	36.8	..
	Autonomous pension funds								
2	Financial assets	100.0	100.0	100.0	100.0	100.0	100.0	100.0	..
2.1	Currency and deposits	11.2	11.8	18.1	20.0	25.8	33.3	34.9	..
2.2	Securities other than shares, except financial derivatives	81.3	80.0	73.5	70.6	62.4	51.8	54.4	..
2.2.1	Short-term securities	81.3	80.0	73.4	70.4	62.3	51.8	54.4	..
2.2.2	Long-term securities	0.0	0.0	0.1	0.1	0.1	0.0	0.0	..
2.2.3	Securities issued by residents	..	..	..	..	..	..	..	..
2.2.4	Securities issued by non-residents	..	..	..	..	..	..	..	..
2.3	Loans	0.4	2.1	2.3	2.3	2.7	2.5	2.4	..
2.3.1	Short-term loans	0.4	2.1	2.3	0.3	0.9	0.8	0.9	..
2.3.2	Long-term loans	0.0	0.0	0.0	2.0	1.8	1.6	1.4	..
2.3.3	Loans granted to residents	..	..	..	..	..	..	..	..
2.3.4	Loans granted to non-residents	..	..	..	..	..	..	..	..
2.4	Shares and other equity	4.5	3.5	2.5	3.1	3.6	7.5	3.6	..
2.4.1	Shares issued by residents	..	..	..	..	..	..	..	..
2.4.2	Shares issued by non-residents	..	..	..	..	..	..	..	..
2.5	Other, not elsewhere classified	2.6	2.6	3.5	4.1	5.5	4.9	4.7	..

Note: Detailed metadata at: http://metalinks.oecd.org/instinv/20141203/f729

Table 1. Financial assets of institutional investors, 2012

Million GBP

		Investment funds				
		Total	Open-end companies (mutual funds)			Closed-end companies
			Total	Money market funds	Other mutual funds	Total
2	Financial assets	797 456	735 163	..	..	62 293
2.1	Currency and deposits	22 560	20 864	..	..	1 696
2.2	Securities other than shares, except financial derivatives	196 822	193 483	..	..	3 339
2.2.1	Short-term securities	11 987	11 355	..	..	632
2.2.2	Long-term securities	184 835	182 128	..	..	2 707
2.2.3	Securities issued by residents	111 822	110 073	..	..	1 749
2.2.4	Securities issued by non-residents	85 000	83 410	..	..	1 590
2.3	Loans	..	..	..	..	..
2.3.1	Short-term loans	..	..	..	..	..
2.3.2	Long-term loans	..	..	..	..	..
2.3.3	Loans granted to residents	..	..	..	..	..
2.3.4	Loans granted to non-residents	..	..	..	..	..
2.4	Shares and other equity	465 059	414 674	..	..	50 385
2.4.1	Shares issued by residents	218 596	198 969	..	..	19 627
2.4.2	Shares issued by non-residents	246 463	215 705	..	..	30 758
2.5	Other, not elsewhere classified	113 015	106 142	..	..	6 873

		Insurance corporations and autonomous pension funds				
		Total	Insurance corporations			Autonomous pension funds
			Total	Life insurance corporations	Non-life insurance corporations	Total
2	Financial assets	3 049 335	1 476 748	1 353 049	123 699	1 572 587
2.1	Currency and deposits	105 039	66 688	54 062	12 626	38 351
2.2	Securities other than shares, except financial derivatives	976 631	605 181	544 587	60 594	371 450
2.2.1	Short-term securities	39 178	24 135	18 962	5 173	15 043
2.2.2	Long-term securities	937 453	581 046	525 625	55 421	356 407
2.2.3	Securities issued by residents	697 189	414 350	385 786	28 564	282 839
2.2.4	Securities issued by non-residents	279 442	190 831	158 801	32 030	88 611
2.3	Loans	37 948	36 635	29 928	6 707	1 313
2.3.1	Short-term loans	..	..	..	..	..
2.3.2	Long-term loans	..	..	..	..	..
2.3.3	Loans granted to residents	..	..	..	..	..
2.3.4	Loans granted to non-residents	..	..	..	..	..
2.4	Shares and other equity	625 218	348 164	336 931	11 233	277 054
2.4.1	Shares issued by residents	283 594	171 681	162 949	8 732	111 913
2.4.2	Shares issued by non-residents	341 624	176 483	173 982	2 501	165 141
2.5	Other, not elsewhere classified	1 304 499	420 080	387 541	32 539	884 419

Note: Detailed metadata at: http://metalinks.oecd.org/instinv/20141203/e23d

UNITED KINGDOM

Table 2. Financial assets of investment funds

Million GBP

		2006	2007	2008	2009	2010	2011	2012	2013
	Investment funds								
2	Financial assets	506 027	559 302	477 278	570 365	715 293	691 394	797 456	..
2.1	Currency and deposits	15 019	19 504	20 054	17 223	21 431	21 396	22 560	..
2.2	Securities other than shares, except financial derivatives	98 045	105 312	108 253	122 027	154 280	165 768	196 822	..
2.2.1	Short-term securities	4 989	5 351	5 918	4 417	7 001	9 259	11 987	..
2.2.2	Long-term securities	93 056	99 961	102 335	117 610	147 279	156 509	184 835	..
2.2.3	Securities issued by residents	67 979	69 899	69 759	70 421	92 854	100 072	111 822	..
2.2.4	Securities issued by non-residents	30 066	35 413	38 494	51 606	61 426	65 696	85 000	..
2.3	Loans	..	..	..	..	..	..	..	..
2.3.1	Short-term loans	..	..	..	..	..	..	..	..
2.3.2	Long-term loans	..	..	..	..	..	..	..	..
2.3.3	Loans granted to residents	..	..	..	..	..	..	..	..
2.3.4	Loans granted to non-residents	..	..	..	..	..	..	..	..
2.4	Shares and other equity	354 214	382 486	287 258	356 719	449 402	412 860	465 059	..
2.4.1	Shares issued by residents	205 146	214 480	155 206	181 991	220 033	196 063	218 596	..
2.4.2	Shares issued by non-residents	149 068	168 006	132 052	174 728	229 369	216 797	246 463	..
2.5	Other, not elsewhere classified	38 749	52 000	61 713	74 396	90 180	91 370	113 015	..
	Open-end companies (mutual funds)								
2	Financial assets	454 092	500 551	434 947	520 032	657 496	632 331	735 163	..
2.1	Currency and deposits	12 960	17 514	17 819	15 969	20 050	19 677	20 864	..
2.2	Securities other than shares, except financial derivatives	94 861	101 407	104 563	118 767	151 139	162 535	193 483	..
2.2.1	Short-term securities	4 154	4 609	4 702	3 602	6 600	8 834	11 355	..
2.2.2	Long-term securities	90 707	96 798	99 861	115 165	144 539	153 701	182 128	..
2.2.3	Securities issued by residents	65 638	67 356	67 571	68 869	91 571	98 568	110 073	..
2.2.4	Securities issued by non-residents	29 223	34 051	36 992	49 898	59 568	63 967	83 410	..
2.3	Loans	..	..	..	..	..	..	..	..
2.3.1	Short-term loans	..	..	..	..	..	..	..	..
2.3.2	Long-term loans	..	..	..	..	..	..	..	..
2.3.3	Loans granted to residents	..	..	..	..	..	..	..	..
2.3.4	Loans granted to non-residents	..	..	..	..	..	..	..	..
2.4	Shares and other equity	310 665	334 667	255 145	315 818	402 373	365 795	414 674	..
2.4.1	Shares issued by residents	183 256	192 456	141 478	164 955	202 345	178 081	198 969	..
2.4.2	Shares issued by non-residents	127 409	142 211	113 667	150 863	200 028	187 714	215 705	..
2.5	Other, not elsewhere classified	35 606	46 963	57 420	69 478	83 934	84 324	106 142	..
	Money market funds								
2	Financial assets	..	..	..	..	..	..	..	..
2.1	Currency and deposits	..	..	..	..	..	..	..	..
2.2	Securities other than shares, except financial derivatives	..	..	..	..	..	..	..	..
2.2.1	Short-term securities	..	..	..	..	..	..	..	..
2.2.2	Long-term securities	..	..	..	..	..	..	..	..
2.2.3	Securities issued by residents	..	..	..	..	..	..	..	..
2.2.4	Securities issued by non-residents	..	..	..	..	..	..	..	..
2.3	Loans	..	..	..	..	..	..	..	..
2.3.1	Short-term loans	..	..	..	..	..	..	..	..
2.3.2	Long-term loans	..	..	..	..	..	..	..	..
2.3.3	Loans granted to residents	..	..	..	..	..	..	..	..
2.3.4	Loans granted to non-residents	..	..	..	..	..	..	..	..
2.4	Shares and other equity	..	..	..	..	..	..	..	..
2.4.1	Shares issued by residents	..	..	..	..	..	..	..	..
2.4.2	Shares issued by non-residents	..	..	..	..	..	..	..	..
2.5	Other, not elsewhere classified	..	..	..	..	..	..	..	..
	Other mutual funds								
2	Financial assets	..	..	..	..	..	..	..	..
2.1	Currency and deposits	..	..	..	..	..	..	..	..
2.2	Securities other than shares, except financial derivatives	..	..	..	..	..	..	..	..
2.2.1	Short-term securities	..	..	..	..	..	..	..	..
2.2.2	Long-term securities	..	..	..	..	..	..	..	..
2.2.3	Securities issued by residents	..	..	..	..	..	..	..	..
2.2.4	Securities issued by non-residents	..	..	..	..	..	..	..	..
2.3	Loans	..	..	..	..	..	..	..	..
2.3.1	Short-term loans	..	..	..	..	..	..	..	..
2.3.2	Long-term loans	..	..	..	..	..	..	..	..
2.3.3	Loans granted to residents	..	..	..	..	..	..	..	..
2.3.4	Loans granted to non-residents	..	..	..	..	..	..	..	..
2.4	Shares and other equity	..	..	..	..	..	..	..	..
2.4.1	Shares issued by residents	..	..	..	..	..	..	..	..
2.4.2	Shares issued by non-residents	..	..	..	..	..	..	..	..
2.5	Other, not elsewhere classified	..	..	..	..	..	..	..	..

Table 2. Financial assets of investment funds *(cont.)*

Million GBP

		2006	2007	2008	2009	2010	2011	2012	2013
	Closed-end companies								
2	Financial assets	51 935	58 751	42 331	50 333	57 797	59 063	62 293	..
2.1	Currency and deposits	2 059	1 990	2 235	1 254	1 381	1 719	1 696	..
2.2	Securities other than shares, except financial derivatives	3 184	3 905	3 690	3 260	3 141	3 233	3 339	..
2.2.1	Short-term securities	835	742	1 216	815	401	425	632	..
2.2.2	Long-term securities	2 349	3 163	2 474	2 445	2 740	2 808	2 707	..
2.2.3	Securities issued by residents	2 341	2 543	2 188	1 552	1 283	1 504	1 749	..
2.2.4	Securities issued by non-residents	843	1 362	1 502	1 708	1 858	1 729	1 590	..
2.3	Loans	..	..	..	..	..	..	..	..
2.3.1	Short-term loans	..	..	..	..	..	..	..	..
2.3.2	Long-term loans	..	..	..	..	..	..	..	..
2.3.3	Loans granted to residents	..	..	..	..	..	..	..	..
2.3.4	Loans granted to non-residents	..	..	..	..	..	..	..	..
2.4	Shares and other equity	43 549	47 819	32 113	40 901	47 029	47 065	50 385	..
2.4.1	Shares issued by residents	21 890	22 024	13 728	17 036	17 688	17 982	19 627	..
2.4.2	Shares issued by non-residents	21 659	25 795	18 385	23 865	29 341	29 083	30 758	..
2.5	Other, not elsewhere classified	3 143	5 037	4 293	4 918	6 246	7 046	6 873	..

Note: Detailed metadata at: http://metalinks.oecd.org/instinv/20141203/e23d

UNITED KINGDOM

Table 3. Financial assets of insurance corporations and autonomous pension funds

Million GBP

		2006	2007	2008	2009	2010	2011	2012	2013
	Insurance corporations and autonomous pension funds								
2	Financial assets	2 408 883	2 510 356	2 210 934	2 444 877	2 625 984	2 783 262	3 049 335	..
2.1	Currency and deposits	73 802	93 293	92 367	110 086	96 700	100 182	105 039	..
2.2	Securities other than shares, except financial derivatives	731 834	778 087	792 632	824 686	831 277	919 750	976 631	..
2.2.1	Short-term securities	58 580	72 829	65 567	45 863	37 921	44 368	39 178	..
2.2.2	Long-term securities	673 254	705 258	727 065	778 823	793 356	875 382	937 453	..
2.2.3	Securities issued by residents	560 984	578 174	560 742	571 948	585 387	666 296	697 189	..
2.2.4	Securities issued by non-residents	170 850	199 913	231 890	252 738	245 890	253 454	279 442	..
2.3	Loans	18 691	17 756	26 415	25 681	28 456	36 254	37 948	..
2.3.1	Short-term loans	17 917	16 985	24 866	..	..	..	..	..
2.3.2	Long-term loans	774	771	1 549	..	..	..	..	..
2.3.3	Loans granted to residents	17 521	16 481	23 822	..	..	..	..	..
2.3.4	Loans granted to non-residents	1 170	1 275	2 593	..	..	..	..	..
2.4	Shares and other equity	850 465	789 457	573 413	647 718	667 378	591 808	625 218	..
2.4.1	Shares issued by residents	518 328	454 709	309 502	336 665	339 378	294 546	283 594	..
2.4.2	Shares issued by non-residents	332 137	334 748	263 911	311 053	328 000	297 262	341 624	..
2.5	Other, not elsewhere classified	734 091	831 763	726 107	836 706	1 002 173	1 135 268	1 304 499	..
	Insurance corporations								
2	Financial assets	1 325 237	1 409 710	1 265 074	1 345 572	1 367 072	1 372 234	1 476 748	..
2.1	Currency and deposits	46 563	61 120	67 583	74 467	63 136	64 300	66 688	..
2.2	Securities other than shares, except financial derivatives	508 466	523 629	552 465	560 853	553 509	584 992	605 181	..
2.2.1	Short-term securities	49 483	58 831	51 505	34 113	23 962	25 030	24 135	..
2.2.2	Long-term securities	458 983	464 798	500 960	526 740	529 547	559 962	581 046	..
2.2.3	Securities issued by residents	392 016	393 680	392 895	384 886	389 154	418 837	414 350	..
2.2.4	Securities issued by non-residents	116 450	129 949	159 570	175 967	164 355	166 155	190 831	..
2.3	Loans	18 649	17 339	25 897	23 913	26 113	34 598	36 635	..
2.3.1	Short-term loans	17 875	16 568	24 348	..	..	..	..	..
2.3.2	Long-term loans	774	771	1 549	..	..	..	..	..
2.3.3	Loans granted to residents	17 515	16 469	23 822	..	..	..	..	..
2.3.4	Loans granted to non-residents	1 134	870	2 075	..	..	..	..	..
2.4	Shares and other equity	449 014	467 811	335 317	375 431	384 453	333 539	348 164	..
2.4.1	Shares issued by residents	309 855	302 661	198 931	219 955	217 496	185 915	171 681	..
2.4.2	Shares issued by non-residents	139 159	165 150	136 386	155 476	166 957	147 624	176 483	..
2.5	Other, not elsewhere classified	302 545	339 811	283 812	310 908	339 861	354 805	420 080	..
	Life insurance corporations								
2	Financial assets	1 199 434	1 289 491	1 131 635	1 221 988	1 263 176	1 266 652	1 353 049	..
2.1	Currency and deposits	35 809	50 781	55 593	60 626	50 868	52 615	54 062	..
2.2	Securities other than shares, except financial derivatives	438 992	461 088	481 090	494 017	505 348	534 376	544 587	..
2.2.1	Short-term securities	35 347	43 580	37 251	26 117	21 173	21 631	18 962	..
2.2.2	Long-term securities	403 645	417 508	443 839	467 900	484 175	512 745	525 625	..
2.2.3	Securities issued by residents	351 206	352 252	351 131	349 031	363 072	391 990	385 786	..
2.2.4	Securities issued by non-residents	87 786	108 836	129 959	144 986	142 276	142 386	158 801	..
2.3	Loans	15 330	13 655	21 926	19 580	20 960	28 233	29 928	..
2.3.1	Short-term loans	14 814	13 050	20 851	..	..	..	..	..
2.3.2	Long-term loans	516	605	1 075	..	..	..	..	..
2.3.3	Loans granted to residents	14 251	13 248	20 174	..	..	..	..	..
2.3.4	Loans granted to non-residents	1 079	407	1 752	..	..	..	..	..
2.4	Shares and other equity	436 369	456 904	322 641	363 492	373 187	323 412	336 931	..
2.4.1	Shares issued by residents	299 717	293 655	188 430	209 992	207 971	177 480	162 949	..
2.4.2	Shares issued by non-residents	136 652	163 249	134 211	153 500	165 216	145 932	173 982	..
2.5	Other, not elsewhere classified	272 934	307 063	250 385	284 273	312 813	328 016	387 541	..
	Non-life insurance corporations								
2	Financial assets	125 803	120 219	133 439	123 584	103 896	105 582	123 699	..
2.1	Currency and deposits	10 754	10 339	11 990	13 841	12 268	11 685	12 626	..
2.2	Securities other than shares, except financial derivatives	69 474	62 541	71 375	66 836	48 161	50 616	60 594	..
2.2.1	Short-term securities	14 136	15 251	14 254	7 996	2 789	3 399	5 173	..
2.2.2	Long-term securities	55 338	47 290	57 121	58 840	45 372	47 217	55 421	..
2.2.3	Securities issued by residents	40 810	41 428	41 764	35 855	26 082	26 847	28 564	..
2.2.4	Securities issued by non-residents	28 664	21 113	29 611	30 981	22 079	23 769	32 030	..
2.3	Loans	3 319	3 684	3 971	4 333	5 153	6 365	6 707	..
2.3.1	Short-term loans	3 061	3 518	3 497	..	..	..	..	..
2.3.2	Long-term loans	258	166	474	..	..	..	..	..
2.3.3	Loans granted to residents	3 264	3 221	3 648	..	..	..	..	..
2.3.4	Loans granted to non-residents	55	463	323	..	..	..	..	..
2.4	Shares and other equity	12 645	10 907	12 676	11 939	11 266	10 127	11 233	..
2.4.1	Shares issued by residents	10 138	9 006	10 501	9 963	9 525	8 435	8 732	..
2.4.2	Shares issued by non-residents	2 507	1 901	2 175	1 976	1 741	1 692	2 501	..
2.5	Other, not elsewhere classified	29 611	32 748	33 427	26 635	27 048	26 789	32 539	..

Table 3. Financial assets of insurance corporations and autonomous pension funds *(cont.)*

Million GBP

		2006	2007	2008	2009	2010	2011	2012	2013
	Autonomous pension funds								
2	Financial assets	1 083 646	1 100 646	945 860	1 099 305	1 258 912	1 411 028	1 572 587	..
2.1	Currency and deposits	27 239	32 173	24 784	35 619	33 564	35 882	38 351	..
2.2	Securities other than shares, except financial derivatives	223 368	254 458	240 167	263 833	277 768	334 758	371 450	..
2.2.1	Short-term securities	9 097	13 998	14 062	11 750	13 959	19 338	15 043	..
2.2.2	Long-term securities	214 271	240 460	226 105	252 083	263 809	315 420	356 407	..
2.2.3	Securities issued by residents	168 968	184 494	167 847	187 062	196 233	247 459	282 839	..
2.2.4	Securities issued by non-residents	54 400	69 964	72 320	76 771	81 535	87 299	88 611	..
2.3	Loans	42	417	518	1 768	2 343	1 656	1 313	..
2.3.1	Short-term loans	42	417	518	..	..	..	..	..
2.3.2	Long-term loans	0	0	0	..	..	..	..	..
2.3.3	Loans granted to residents	6	12	0	..	..	..	..	..
2.3.4	Loans granted to non-residents	36	405	518	..	..	..	..	..
2.4	Shares and other equity	401 451	321 646	238 096	272 287	282 925	258 269	277 054	..
2.4.1	Shares issued by residents	208 473	152 048	110 571	116 710	121 882	108 631	111 913	..
2.4.2	Shares issued by non-residents	192 978	169 598	127 525	155 577	161 043	149 638	165 141	..
2.5	Other, not elsewhere classified	431 546	491 952	442 295	525 798	662 312	780 463	884 419	..

Note: Detailed metadata at: http://metalinks.oecd.org/instinv/20141203/e23d

Table 4. Portfolio composition by type of investor

Percentage of total financial assets

Per cent

		2006	2007	2008	2009	2010	2011	2012	2013
	Investment funds								
2	Financial assets	100.0	100.0	100.0	100.0	100.0	100.0	100.0	..
2.1	Currency and deposits	3.0	3.5	4.2	3.0	3.0	3.1	2.8	..
2.2	Securities other than shares, except financial derivatives	19.4	18.8	22.7	21.4	21.6	24.0	24.7	..
2.2.1	Short-term securities	1.0	1.0	1.2	0.8	1.0	1.3	1.5	..
2.2.2	Long-term securities	18.4	17.9	21.4	20.6	20.6	22.6	23.2	..
2.2.3	Securities issued by residents	13.4	12.5	14.6	12.3	13.0	14.5	14.0	..
2.2.4	Securities issued by non-residents	5.9	6.3	8.1	9.0	8.6	9.5	10.7	..
2.3	Loans	..	..	..	..	..	..	..	..
2.3.1	Short-term loans	..	..	..	..	..	..	..	..
2.3.2	Long-term loans	..	..	..	..	..	..	..	..
2.3.3	Loans granted to residents	..	..	..	..	..	..	..	..
2.3.4	Loans granted to non-residents	..	..	..	..	..	..	..	..
2.4	Shares and other equity	70.0	68.4	60.2	62.5	62.8	59.7	58.3	..
2.4.1	Shares issued by residents	40.5	38.3	32.5	31.9	30.8	28.4	27.4	..
2.4.2	Shares issued by non-residents	29.5	30.0	27.7	30.6	32.1	31.4	30.9	..
2.5	Other, not elsewhere classified	7.7	9.3	12.9	13.0	12.6	13.2	14.2	..
	Insurance corporations								
2	Financial assets	100.0	100.0	100.0	100.0	100.0	100.0	100.0	..
2.1	Currency and deposits	3.5	4.3	5.3	5.5	4.6	4.7	4.5	..
2.2	Securities other than shares, except financial derivatives	38.4	37.1	43.7	41.7	40.5	42.6	41.0	..
2.2.1	Short-term securities	3.7	4.2	4.1	2.5	1.8	1.8	1.6	..
2.2.2	Long-term securities	34.6	33.0	39.6	39.1	38.7	40.8	39.3	..
2.2.3	Securities issued by residents	29.6	27.9	31.1	28.6	28.5	30.5	28.1	..
2.2.4	Securities issued by non-residents	8.8	9.2	12.6	13.1	12.0	12.1	12.9	..
2.3	Loans	1.4	1.2	2.0	1.8	1.9	2.5	2.5	..
2.3.1	Short-term loans	1.3	1.2	1.9	..	..	..	..	..
2.3.2	Long-term loans	0.1	0.1	0.1	..	..	..	..	..
2.3.3	Loans granted to residents	1.3	1.2	1.9	..	..	..	..	..
2.3.4	Loans granted to non-residents	0.1	0.1	0.2	..	..	..	..	..
2.4	Shares and other equity	33.9	33.2	26.5	27.9	28.1	24.3	23.6	..
2.4.1	Shares issued by residents	23.4	21.5	15.7	16.3	15.9	13.5	11.6	..
2.4.2	Shares issued by non-residents	10.5	11.7	10.8	11.6	12.2	10.8	12.0	..
2.5	Other, not elsewhere classified	22.8	24.1	22.4	23.1	24.9	25.9	28.4	..
	Autonomous pension funds								
2	Financial assets	100.0	100.0	100.0	100.0	100.0	100.0	100.0	..
2.1	Currency and deposits	2.5	2.9	2.6	3.2	2.7	2.5	2.4	..
2.2	Securities other than shares, except financial derivatives	20.6	23.1	25.4	24.0	22.1	23.7	23.6	..
2.2.1	Short-term securities	0.8	1.3	1.5	1.1	1.1	1.4	1.0	..
2.2.2	Long-term securities	19.8	21.8	23.9	22.9	21.0	22.4	22.7	..
2.2.3	Securities issued by residents	15.6	16.8	17.7	17.0	15.6	17.5	18.0	..
2.2.4	Securities issued by non-residents	5.0	6.4	7.6	7.0	6.5	6.2	5.6	..
2.3	Loans	0.0	0.0	0.1	0.2	0.2	0.1	0.1	..
2.3.1	Short-term loans	0.0	0.0	0.1	..	..	..	..	..
2.3.2	Long-term loans	0.0	0.0	0.0	..	..	..	..	..
2.3.3	Loans granted to residents	0.0	0.0	0.0	..	..	..	..	..
2.3.4	Loans granted to non-residents	0.0	0.0	0.1	..	..	..	..	..
2.4	Shares and other equity	37.0	29.2	25.2	24.8	22.5	18.3	17.6	..
2.4.1	Shares issued by residents	19.2	13.8	11.7	10.6	9.7	7.7	7.1	..
2.4.2	Shares issued by non-residents	17.8	15.4	13.5	14.2	12.8	10.6	10.5	..
2.5	Other, not elsewhere classified	39.8	44.7	46.8	47.8	52.6	55.3	56.2	..

Note: Detailed metadata at: http://metalinks.oecd.org/instinv/20141203/f729

UNITED STATES

Table 1. Financial assets of institutional investors, 2013

Billion USD

			Investment funds			
		Total	Open-end companies (mutual funds)			Closed-end companies
			Total	Money market funds	Other mutual funds	Total
2	Financial assets	16 822	15 894	2 678	13 215	929
2.1	Currency and deposits	576	542	542	..	34
2.2	Securities other than shares, except financial derivatives	6 524	6 055	1 612	4 443	468
2.2.1	Short-term securities	780	780	642	139	..
2.2.2	Long-term securities	5 743	5 275	970	4 305	468
2.2.3	Securities issued by residents	..	..	..	..	..
2.2.4	Securities issued by non-residents	..	..	..	..	..
2.3	Loans	1 193	994	493	501	199
2.3.1	Short-term loans	994	994	493	501	..
2.3.2	Long-term loans	199	..	..	..	199
2.3.3	Loans granted to residents	..	..	..	..	..
2.3.4	Loans granted to non-residents	..	..	..	..	..
2.4	Shares and other equity	8 394	8 279	0	8 279	114
2.4.1	Shares issued by residents	..	..	..	..	..
2.4.2	Shares issued by non-residents	..	..	..	..	..
2.5	Other, not elsewhere classified	136	23	32	-8	113

			Insurance corporations and autonomous pension funds			
		Total	Insurance corporations			Autonomous pension funds
			Total	Life insurance corporations	Non-life insurance corporations	Total
2	Financial assets	24 403	7 511	5 977	1 534	16 892
2.1	Currency and deposits	173	77	47	30	96
2.2	Securities other than shares, except financial derivatives	7 442	3 879	2 934	945	3 563
2.2.1	Short-term securities	171	85	53	32	86
2.2.2	Long-term securities	7 271	3 794	2 881	914	3 477
2.2.3	Securities issued by residents	..	..	2 373	..	..
2.2.4	Securities issued by non-residents	..	..	561	..	..
2.3	Loans	570	535	526	10	35
2.3.1	Short-term loans	170	164	162	2	6
2.3.2	Long-term loans	399	371	363	8	28
2.3.3	Loans granted to residents	..	..	..	..	..
2.3.4	Loans granted to non-residents	..	..	..	..	..
2.4	Shares and other equity	11 086	2 523	2 069	454	8 563
2.4.1	Shares issued by residents	..	..	..	..	..
2.4.2	Shares issued by non-residents	..	..	..	..	..
2.5	Other, not elsewhere classified	5 131	496	401	95	4 635

Note: Detailed metadata at: http://metalinks.oecd.org/instinv/20141203/b8ac

UNITED STATES

Table 2. Financial assets of investment funds

Billion USD

		2006	2007	2008	2009	2010	2011	2012	2013
	Investment funds								
2	Financial assets	10 422	12 098	10 130	11 444	12 161	12 230	14 151	16 822
2.1	Currency and deposits	310	413	508	713	604	493	531	576
2.2	Securities other than shares, except financial derivatives	3 775	4 405	5 113	4 976	5 014	5 498	6 238	6 524
2.2.1	Short-term securities	779	926	1 149	909	725	688	744	780
2.2.2	Long-term securities	2 996	3 479	3 964	4 067	4 290	4 810	5 494	5 743
2.2.3	Securities issued by residents	..	..	..	..	..	..	..	..
2.2.4	Securities issued by non-residents	..	..	..	..	..	..	..	..
2.3	Loans	710	944	838	755	736	749	978	1 193
2.3.1	Short-term loans	574	820	762	709	691	693	913	994
2.3.2	Long-term loans	136	123	76	46	45	56	64	199
2.3.3	Loans granted to residents	..	..	..	..	..	..	..	..
2.3.4	Loans granted to non-residents	..	..	..	..	..	..	..	..
2.4	Shares and other equity	5 513	6 196	3 560	4 894	5 714	5 387	6 303	8 394
2.4.1	Shares issued by residents	..	..	..	..	..	..	..	..
2.4.2	Shares issued by non-residents	..	..	..	..	..	..	..	..
2.5	Other, not elsewhere classified	113	141	110	107	93	103	102	136
	Open-end companies (mutual funds)								
2	Financial assets	9 784	11 463	9 676	10 952	11 615	11 556	13 300	15 894
2.1	Currency and deposits	292	396	490	682	579	466	495	542
2.2	Securities other than shares, except financial derivatives	3 473	4 110	4 881	4 714	4 701	5 078	5 688	6 055
2.2.1	Short-term securities	779	926	1 149	909	725	688	744	780
2.2.2	Long-term securities	2 695	3 185	3 732	3 805	3 977	4 390	4 944	5 275
2.2.3	Securities issued by residents	..	..	..	..	..	..	..	..
2.2.4	Securities issued by non-residents	..	..	..	..	..	..	..	..
2.3	Loans	574	820	762	709	691	693	913	994
2.3.1	Short-term loans	574	820	762	709	691	693	913	994
2.3.2	Long-term loans	0	0	0	0	0	0	0	..
2.3.3	Loans granted to residents	..	..	..	..	..	..	..	..
2.3.4	Loans granted to non-residents	..	..	..	..	..	..	..	..
2.4	Shares and other equity	5 392	6 051	3 488	4 806	5 617	5 291	6 203	8 279
2.4.1	Shares issued by residents	..	..	..	..	..	..	..	..
2.4.2	Shares issued by non-residents	..	..	..	..	..	..	..	..
2.5	Other, not elsewhere classified	54	86	55	42	26	28	1	23
	Money market funds								
2	Financial assets	2 296	3 033	3 757	3 259	2 755	2 643	2 650	2 678
2.1	Currency and deposits	292	396	490	682	579	466	495	542
2.2	Securities other than shares, except financial derivatives	1 570	1 962	2 690	2 070	1 673	1 664	1 581	1 612
2.2.1	Short-term securities	664	811	1 097	829	629	618	624	642
2.2.2	Long-term securities	906	1 151	1 593	1 241	1 045	1 046	957	970
2.2.3	Securities issued by residents	..	..	..	..	..	..	..	..
2.2.4	Securities issued by non-residents	..	..	..	..	..	..	..	..
2.3	Loans	395	606	542	480	479	491	545	493
2.3.1	Short-term loans	395	606	542	480	479	491	545	493
2.3.2	Long-term loans	0	0	0	0	0	0	0	..
2.3.3	Loans granted to residents	..	..	..	..	..	..	..	..
2.3.4	Loans granted to non-residents	..	..	..	..	..	..	..	..
2.4	Shares and other equity	0	0	0	0	0	0	0	0
2.4.1	Shares issued by residents	..	..	..	..	..	..	..	..
2.4.2	Shares issued by non-residents	..	..	..	..	..	..	..	..
2.5	Other, not elsewhere classified	40	69	35	27	24	23	29	32
	Other mutual funds								
2	Financial assets	7 488	8 430	5 919	7 694	8 860	8 913	10 650	13 215
2.1	Currency and deposits	0	0	0	0	0	0	0	..
2.2	Securities other than shares, except financial derivatives	1 903	2 148	2 191	2 644	3 028	3 415	4 107	4 443
2.2.1	Short-term securities	115	114	52	80	96	70	120	139
2.2.2	Long-term securities	1 789	2 034	2 140	2 564	2 932	3 344	3 987	4 305
2.2.3	Securities issued by residents	..	..	..	..	..	..	..	..
2.2.4	Securities issued by non-residents	..	..	..	..	..	..	..	..
2.3	Loans	179	215	220	229	212	202	368	501
2.3.1	Short-term loans	179	215	220	229	212	202	368	501
2.3.2	Long-term loans	0	0	0	0	0	0	0	..
2.3.3	Loans granted to residents	..	..	..	..	..	..	..	..
2.3.4	Loans granted to non-residents	..	..	..	..	..	..	..	..
2.4	Shares and other equity	5 392	6 051	3 488	4 806	5 617	5 291	6 203	8 279
2.4.1	Shares issued by residents	..	..	..	..	..	..	..	..
2.4.2	Shares issued by non-residents	..	..	..	..	..	..	..	..
2.5	Other, not elsewhere classified	14	17	20	15	3	6	-27	-8

Table 2. Financial assets of investment funds *(cont.)*

Billion USD

		2006	2007	2008	2009	2010	2011	2012	2013
	Closed-end companies								
2	Financial assets	638	635	453	491	545	674	851	929
2.1	Currency and deposits	18	17	18	31	25	28	35	34
2.2	Securities other than shares, except financial derivatives	302	294	232	262	313	420	550	468
2.2.1	Short-term securities	0	0	0	0	0	0	0	..
2.2.2	Long-term securities	302	294	232	262	313	420	550	468
2.2.3	Securities issued by residents	..	..	..	..	..	..	..	..
2.2.4	Securities issued by non-residents	..	..	..	..	..	..	..	..
2.3	Loans	136	123	76	46	45	56	64	199
2.3.1	Short-term loans	..	..	..	..	..	..	..	..
2.3.2	Long-term loans	136	123	76	46	45	56	64	199
2.3.3	Loans granted to residents	..	..	..	..	..	..	..	..
2.3.4	Loans granted to non-residents	..	..	..	..	..	..	..	..
2.4	Shares and other equity	122	145	72	87	97	96	101	114
2.4.1	Shares issued by residents	..	..	..	..	..	..	..	..
2.4.2	Shares issued by non-residents	..	..	..	..	..	..	..	..
2.5	Other, not elsewhere classified	60	55	55	65	66	75	100	113

Note: Detailed metadata at: http://metalinks.oecd.org/instinv/20141203/b8ac

Table 3. Financial assets of insurance corporations and autonomous pension funds

Billion USD

		2006	2007	2008	2009	2010	2011	2012	2013
	Insurance corporations and autonomous pension funds								
2	Financial assets	18 202	19 156	17 922	19 370	21 074	21 633	22 777	24 403
2.1	Currency and deposits	161	185	186	155	168	171	181	173
2.2	Securities other than shares, except financial derivatives	5 742	5 912	5 942	6 158	6 540	6 867	7 138	7 442
2.2.1	Short-term securities	163	158	167	169	157	156	155	171
2.2.2	Long-term securities	5 579	5 754	5 775	5 989	6 383	6 711	6 983	7 271
2.2.3	Securities issued by residents	..	..	..	..	..	..	..	..
2.2.4	Securities issued by non-residents	..	..	..	..	..	..	..	..
2.3	Loans	499	542	573	528	521	538	551	570
2.3.1	Short-term loans	144	159	184	162	161	167	166	170
2.3.2	Long-term loans	355	383	389	367	360	371	384	399
2.3.3	Loans granted to residents	..	..	..	..	..	..	..	..
2.3.4	Loans granted to non-residents	..	..	..	..	..	..	..	..
2.4	Shares and other equity	8 628	9 185	6 200	7 644	8 593	8 308	9 200	11 086
2.4.1	Shares issued by residents	..	..	..	..	..	..	..	..
2.4.2	Shares issued by non-residents	..	..	..	..	..	..	..	..
2.5	Other, not elsewhere classified	3 171	3 331	5 021	4 885	5 251	5 748	5 708	5 131
	Insurance corporations								
2	Financial assets	6 021	6 336	5 820	6 204	6 528	6 720	7 057	7 511
2.1	Currency and deposits	86	101	111	78	84	78	93	77
2.2	Securities other than shares, except financial derivatives	3 211	3 264	3 223	3 438	3 602	3 740	3 801	3 879
2.2.1	Short-term securities	84	74	88	89	75	70	75	85
2.2.2	Long-term securities	3 127	3 190	3 134	3 349	3 528	3 670	3 727	3 794
2.2.3	Securities issued by residents	..	..	..	..	..	..	..	..
2.2.4	Securities issued by non-residents	..	..	..	..	..	..	..	..
2.3	Loans	444	483	526	486	477	498	511	535
2.3.1	Short-term loans	137	152	178	156	155	160	161	164
2.3.2	Long-term loans	307	331	347	331	322	337	350	371
2.3.3	Loans granted to residents	..	..	..	..	..	..	..	..
2.3.4	Loans granted to non-residents	..	..	..	..	..	..	..	..
2.4	Shares and other equity	1 911	2 087	1 523	1 793	1 978	1 966	2 185	2 523
2.4.1	Shares issued by residents	..	..	..	..	..	..	..	..
2.4.2	Shares issued by non-residents	..	..	..	..	..	..	..	..
2.5	Other, not elsewhere classified	369	400	438	409	387	439	467	496
	Life insurance corporations								
2	Financial assets	4 685	4 950	4 514	4 824	5 168	5 340	5 615	5 977
2.1	Currency and deposits	56	58	83	51	52	54	56	47
2.2	Securities other than shares, except financial derivatives	2 350	2 399	2 374	2 556	2 716	2 819	2 879	2 934
2.2.1	Short-term securities	33	44	58	64	51	44	53	53
2.2.2	Long-term securities	2 317	2 355	2 316	2 492	2 665	2 775	2 826	2 881
2.2.3	Securities issued by residents	2 023	2 047	2 003	2 121	2 229	2 272	2 336	2 373
2.2.4	Securities issued by non-residents	327	352	372	435	487	546	543	561
2.3	Loans	439	475	516	477	469	491	503	526
2.3.1	Short-term loans	135	149	174	151	152	159	159	162
2.3.2	Long-term loans	304	326	342	326	317	332	344	363
2.3.3	Loans granted to residents	..	..	..	..	..	..	..	..
2.3.4	Loans granted to non-residents	..	..	..	..	..	..	..	..
2.4	Shares and other equity	1 558	1 702	1 190	1 415	1 628	1 625	1 801	2 069
2.4.1	Shares issued by residents	..	..	..	..	..	..	..	..
2.4.2	Shares issued by non-residents	..	..	..	..	..	..	..	..
2.5	Other, not elsewhere classified	282	315	351	326	303	351	375	401
	Non-life insurance corporations								
2	Financial assets	1 336	1 386	1 306	1 380	1 360	1 380	1 442	1 534
2.1	Currency and deposits	30	43	28	28	33	24	36	30
2.2	Securities other than shares, except financial derivatives	861	865	848	882	886	922	922	945
2.2.1	Short-term securities	51	29	30	26	23	26	21	32
2.2.2	Long-term securities	810	835	819	857	863	896	901	914
2.2.3	Securities issued by residents	..	..	..	..	..	..	..	..
2.2.4	Securities issued by non-residents	..	..	..	..	..	..	..	..
2.3	Loans	5	8	9	9	8	7	7	10
2.3.1	Short-term loans	2	4	4	5	4	2	2	2
2.3.2	Long-term loans	3	5	5	4	4	5	6	8
2.3.3	Loans granted to residents	..	..	..	..	..	..	..	..
2.3.4	Loans granted to non-residents	..	..	..	..	..	..	..	..
2.4	Shares and other equity	353	385	333	378	350	340	384	454
2.4.1	Shares issued by residents	..	..	..	..	..	..	..	..
2.4.2	Shares issued by non-residents	..	..	..	..	..	..	..	..
2.5	Other, not elsewhere classified	87	85	87	83	84	87	92	95

Table 3. Financial assets of insurance corporations and autonomous pension funds *(cont.)*

Billion USD

		2006	2007	2008	2009	2010	2011	2012	2013
	Autonomous pension funds								
2	Financial assets	12 181	12 820	12 103	13 166	14 545	14 913	15 720	16 892
2.1	Currency and deposits	75	84	76	76	84	94	88	96
2.2	Securities other than shares, except financial derivatives	2 531	2 648	2 719	2 720	2 938	3 127	3 337	3 563
2.2.1	Short-term securities	79	84	79	80	82	87	80	86
2.2.2	Long-term securities	2 452	2 564	2 641	2 641	2 856	3 040	3 256	3 477
2.2.3	Securities issued by residents	..	..	..	..	..	..	..	..
2.2.4	Securities issued by non-residents	..	..	..	..	..	..	..	..
2.3	Loans	54	59	47	42	44	40	40	35
2.3.1	Short-term loans	7	7	6	6	6	6	6	6
2.3.2	Long-term loans	48	52	41	36	38	34	34	28
2.3.3	Loans granted to residents	..	..	..	..	..	..	..	..
2.3.4	Loans granted to non-residents	..	..	..	..	..	..	..	..
2.4	Shares and other equity	6 717	7 097	4 677	5 851	6 615	6 343	7 015	8 563
2.4.1	Shares issued by residents	..	..	..	..	..	..	..	..
2.4.2	Shares issued by non-residents	..	..	..	..	..	..	..	..
2.5	Other, not elsewhere classified	2 802	2 931	4 584	4 476	4 865	5 310	5 241	4 635

Note: Detailed metadata at: http://metalinks.oecd.org/instinv/20141203/b8ac

Table 4. Portfolio composition by type of investor

Percentage of total financial assets

Per cent

		2006	2007	2008	2009	2010	2011	2012	2013
	Investment funds								
2	Financial assets	100.0	100.0	100.0	100.0	100.0	100.0	100.0	100.0
2.1	Currency and deposits	3.0	3.4	5.0	6.2	5.0	4.0	3.7	3.4
2.2	Securities other than shares, except financial derivatives	36.2	36.4	50.5	43.5	41.2	45.0	44.1	38.8
2.2.1	Short-term securities	7.5	7.7	11.3	7.9	6.0	5.6	5.3	4.6
2.2.2	Long-term securities	28.7	28.8	39.1	35.5	35.3	39.3	38.8	34.1
2.2.3	Securities issued by residents	..	..	..	..	..	..	..	..
2.2.4	Securities issued by non-residents	..	..	..	..	..	..	..	..
2.3	Loans	6.8	7.8	8.3	6.6	6.1	6.1	6.9	7.1
2.3.1	Short-term loans	5.5	6.8	7.5	6.2	5.7	5.7	6.5	5.9
2.3.2	Long-term loans	1.3	1.0	0.8	0.4	0.4	0.5	0.5	1.2
2.3.3	Loans granted to residents	..	..	..	..	..	..	..	..
2.3.4	Loans granted to non-residents	..	..	..	..	..	..	..	..
2.4	Shares and other equity	52.9	51.2	35.1	42.8	47.0	44.0	44.5	49.9
2.4.1	Shares issued by residents	..	..	..	..	..	..	..	..
2.4.2	Shares issued by non-residents	..	..	..	..	..	..	..	..
2.5	Other, not elsewhere classified	1.1	1.2	1.1	0.9	0.8	0.8	0.7	0.8
	Insurance corporations								
2	Financial assets	100.0	100.0	100.0	100.0	100.0	100.0	100.0	100.0
2.1	Currency and deposits	1.4	1.6	1.9	1.3	1.3	1.2	1.3	1.0
2.2	Securities other than shares, except financial derivatives	53.3	51.5	55.4	55.4	55.2	55.7	53.9	51.6
2.2.1	Short-term securities	1.4	1.2	1.5	1.4	1.1	1.0	1.1	1.1
2.2.2	Long-term securities	51.9	50.4	53.9	54.0	54.0	54.6	52.8	50.5
2.2.3	Securities issued by residents	..	..	..	..	..	..	..	..
2.2.4	Securities issued by non-residents	..	..	..	..	..	..	..	..
2.3	Loans	7.4	7.6	9.0	7.8	7.3	7.4	7.2	7.1
2.3.1	Short-term loans	2.3	2.4	3.1	2.5	2.4	2.4	2.3	2.2
2.3.2	Long-term loans	5.1	5.2	6.0	5.3	4.9	5.0	5.0	4.9
2.3.3	Loans granted to residents	..	..	..	..	..	..	..	..
2.3.4	Loans granted to non-residents	..	..	..	..	..	..	..	..
2.4	Shares and other equity	31.7	32.9	26.2	28.9	30.3	29.2	31.0	33.6
2.4.1	Shares issued by residents	..	..	..	..	..	..	..	..
2.4.2	Shares issued by non-residents	..	..	..	..	..	..	..	..
2.5	Other, not elsewhere classified	6.1	6.3	7.5	6.6	5.9	6.5	6.6	6.6
	Autonomous pension funds								
2	Financial assets	100.0	100.0	100.0	100.0	100.0	100.0	100.0	100.0
2.1	Currency and deposits	0.6	0.7	0.6	0.6	0.6	0.6	0.6	0.6
2.2	Securities other than shares, except financial derivatives	20.8	20.7	22.5	20.7	20.2	21.0	21.2	21.1
2.2.1	Short-term securities	0.6	0.7	0.7	0.6	0.6	0.6	0.5	0.5
2.2.2	Long-term securities	20.1	20.0	21.8	20.1	19.6	20.4	20.7	20.6
2.2.3	Securities issued by residents	..	..	..	..	..	..	..	..
2.2.4	Securities issued by non-residents	..	..	..	..	..	..	..	..
2.3	Loans	0.4	0.5	0.4	0.3	0.3	0.3	0.3	0.2
2.3.1	Short-term loans	0.1	0.1	0.0	0.0	0.0	0.0	0.0	0.0
2.3.2	Long-term loans	0.4	0.4	0.3	0.3	0.3	0.2	0.2	0.2
2.3.3	Loans granted to residents	..	..	..	..	..	..	..	..
2.3.4	Loans granted to non-residents	..	..	..	..	..	..	..	..
2.4	Shares and other equity	55.1	55.4	38.6	44.4	45.5	42.5	44.6	50.7
2.4.1	Shares issued by residents	..	..	..	..	..	..	..	..
2.4.2	Shares issued by non-residents	..	..	..	..	..	..	..	..
2.5	Other, not elsewhere classified	23.0	22.9	37.9	34.0	33.4	35.6	33.3	27.4

Note: Detailed metadata at: http://metalinks.oecd.org/instinv/20141203/f729

Table 1. Financial assets of institutional investors, 2013

Million RUB

		Total	Investment funds				
			Open-end companies (mutual funds)			Closed-end companies
			Total	Money market funds	Other mutual funds	Total
2	Financial assets	1 178 948	125 343	8 849	116 494	1 053 605
2.1	Currency and deposits	233 794	15 317	7 248	8 070	218 476
2.2	Securities other than shares, except financial derivatives	112 612	63 562	991	62 571	49 050
2.2.1	Short-term securities	..	..	..	..	..
2.2.2	Long-term securities	..	..	..	..	..
2.2.3	Securities issued by residents	93 728	53 359	991	52 367	40 369
2.2.4	Securities issued by non-residents	18 884	10 204	0	10 204	8 681
2.3	Loans	5 573	0	0	0	5 573
2.3.1	Short-term loans	..	..	..	..	..
2.3.2	Long-term loans	..	..	..	..	..
2.3.3	Loans granted to residents	5 573	0	0	0	5 573
2.3.4	Loans granted to non-residents	..	..	..	..	..
2.4	Shares and other equity	553 341	37 104	0	37 104	516 237
2.4.1	Shares issued by residents	523 453	33 071	0	33 071	490 381
2.4.2	Shares issued by non-residents	29 888	4 032	0	4 032	25 856
2.5	Other, not elsewhere classified	273 629	9 360	610	8 750	264 269

		Total	Insurance corporations and autonomous pension funds			
			Insurance corporations			Autonomous pension funds
			Total	Life insurance corporations	Non-life insurance corporations	Total
2	Financial assets	3 424 890	1 199 092	..	..	2 225 798
2.1	Currency and deposits	1 116 399	377 029	..	..	739 370
2.2	Securities other than shares, except financial derivatives	1 167 626	303 110	..	..	864 516
2.2.1	Short-term securities	..	..	..	..	..
2.2.2	Long-term securities	..	..	..	..	..
2.2.3	Securities issued by residents	1 107 362	262 987	..	..	844 375
2.2.4	Securities issued by non-residents	60 264	40 123	..	..	20 141
2.3	Loans	12 145	11 963	..	..	182
2.3.1	Short-term loans	..	..	..	..	..
2.3.2	Long-term loans	..	..	..	..	..
2.3.3	Loans granted to residents	7 708	7 526	..	..	182
2.3.4	Loans granted to non-residents	4 437	4 437	..	..	0
2.4	Shares and other equity	714 447	137 714	..	..	576 733
2.4.1	Shares issued by residents	695 614	129 042	..	..	566 571
2.4.2	Shares issued by non-residents	18 833	8 672	..	..	10 161
2.5	Other, not elsewhere classified	414 272	369 276	..	..	44 996

Note: Detailed metadata at: http://metalinks.oecd.org/instinv/20141203/e91d

Table 2. Financial assets of investment funds

Million RUB

		2006	2007	2008	2009	2010	2011	2012	2013
	Investment funds								
2	Financial assets	392 446	665 899	470 759	599 906	762 432	841 278	1 004 450	1 178 948
2.1	Currency and deposits	26 755	62 874	56 513	70 599	96 172	105 313	153 160	233 794
2.2	Securities other than shares, except financial derivatives	38 730	57 367	41 232	53 528	48 521	65 362	89 613	112 612
2.2.1	Short-term securities	..	..	..	..	..	..	..	..
2.2.2	Long-term securities	..	..	..	..	..	..	..	..
2.2.3	Securities issued by residents	38 605	57 365	41 226	53 324	48 403	60 076	76 535	93 728
2.2.4	Securities issued by non-residents	125	2	6	204	117	5 286	13 079	18 884
2.3	Loans	0	0	0	1 743	6 297	6 518	4 485	5 573
2.3.1	Short-term loans	..	..	..	..	..	..	..	..
2.3.2	Long-term loans	..	..	..	..	..	..	..	..
2.3.3	Loans granted to residents	0	0	0	1 743	6 297	6 518	4 485	5 573
2.3.4	Loans granted to non-residents	..	..	..	..	..	..	..	..
2.4	Shares and other equity	300 460	500 596	287 664	388 050	482 265	499 573	571 058	553 341
2.4.1	Shares issued by residents	300 460	500 596	287 664	388 037	481 786	496 558	551 234	523 453
2.4.2	Shares issued by non-residents	0	0	0	14	479	3 015	19 824	29 888
2.5	Other, not elsewhere classified	26 502	45 063	85 350	85 986	129 178	164 511	186 133	273 629
	Open-end companies (mutual funds)								
2	Financial assets	155 251	189 639	62 081	96 734	121 414	99 846	101 875	125 343
2.1	Currency and deposits	5 425	5 078	5 439	4 132	3 141	3 875	7 073	15 317
2.2	Securities other than shares, except financial derivatives	23 743	28 693	15 820	18 758	23 503	28 001	39 497	63 562
2.2.1	Short-term securities	..	..	..	..	..	..	..	..
2.2.2	Long-term securities	..	..	..	..	..	..	..	..
2.2.3	Securities issued by residents	23 618	28 691	15 819	18 680	23 443	27 924	34 229	53 359
2.2.4	Securities issued by non-residents	125	2	1	78	60	77	5 268	10 204
2.3	Loans	0	0	0	0	0	0	0	0
2.3.1	Short-term loans	..	..	..	..	..	..	..	..
2.3.2	Long-term loans	..	..	..	..	..	..	..	..
2.3.3	Loans granted to residents	0	0	0	0	0	0	0	0
2.3.4	Loans granted to non-residents	..	..	..	..	..	..	..	..
2.4	Shares and other equity	119 089	144 306	33 938	67 256	86 613	59 389	47 788	37 104
2.4.1	Shares issued by residents	119 089	144 306	33 938	67 242	86 134	57 374	45 249	33 071
2.4.2	Shares issued by non-residents	0	0	0	14	479	2 015	2 539	4 032
2.5	Other, not elsewhere classified	6 994	11 561	6 884	6 588	8 157	8 580	7 517	9 360
	Money market funds								
2	Financial assets	297	404	717	390	901	1 439	1 374	8 849
2.1	Currency and deposits	209	189	341	196	580	674	807	7 248
2.2	Securities other than shares, except financial derivatives	80	104	244	87	243	652	478	991
2.2.1	Short-term securities	..	..	..	..	..	..	..	..
2.2.2	Long-term securities	..	..	..	..	..	..	..	..
2.2.3	Securities issued by residents	80	104	244	87	243	652	478	991
2.2.4	Securities issued by non-residents	0	0	0	0	0	0	0	0
2.3	Loans	0	0	0	0	0	0	0	0
2.3.1	Short-term loans	..	..	..	..	..	..	..	..
2.3.2	Long-term loans	..	..	..	..	..	..	..	..
2.3.3	Loans granted to residents	0	0	0	0	0	0	0	0
2.3.4	Loans granted to non-residents	..	..	..	..	..	..	..	..
2.4	Shares and other equity	0	107	80	61	42	24	24	0
2.4.1	Shares issued by residents	0	107	80	61	42	24	24	0
2.4.2	Shares issued by non-residents	0	0	0	0	0	0	0	0
2.5	Other, not elsewhere classified	8	4	51	46	36	89	65	610
	Other mutual funds								
2	Financial assets	154 954	189 235	61 365	96 344	120 514	98 407	100 501	116 494
2.1	Currency and deposits	5 216	4 889	5 098	3 936	2 561	3 202	6 266	8 070
2.2	Securities other than shares, except financial derivatives	23 663	28 589	15 576	18 670	23 260	27 350	39 020	62 571
2.2.1	Short-term securities	..	..	..	..	..	..	..	..
2.2.2	Long-term securities	..	..	..	..	..	..	..	..
2.2.3	Securities issued by residents	23 538	28 587	15 575	18 592	23 200	27 273	33 751	52 367
2.2.4	Securities issued by non-residents	125	2	1	78	60	77	5 268	10 204
2.3	Loans	0	0	0	0	0	0	0	0
2.3.1	Short-term loans	..	..	..	..	..	..	..	..
2.3.2	Long-term loans	..	..	..	..	..	..	..	..
2.3.3	Loans granted to residents	0	0	0	0	0	0	0	0
2.3.4	Loans granted to non-residents	..	..	..	..	..	..	..	..
2.4	Shares and other equity	119 089	144 200	33 858	67 195	86 571	59 365	47 763	37 104
2.4.1	Shares issued by residents	119 089	144 200	33 858	67 181	86 093	57 350	45 224	33 071
2.4.2	Shares issued by non-residents	0	0	0	14	479	2 015	2 539	4 032
2.5	Other, not elsewhere classified	6 986	11 558	6 833	6 543	8 120	8 491	7 452	8 750

Table 2. Financial assets of investment funds *(cont.)*

Million RUB

		2006	2007	2008	2009	2010	2011	2012	2013
	Closed-end companies								
2	Financial assets	237 195	476 260	408 678	503 173	641 018	741 432	902 576	1 053 605
2.1	Currency and deposits	21 330	57 796	51 074	66 467	93 031	101 438	146 088	218 476
2.2	Securities other than shares, except financial derivatives	14 987	28 673	25 412	34 771	25 017	37 361	50 116	49 050
2.2.1	Short-term securities	..	..	..	..	..	..	..	..
2.2.2	Long-term securities	..	..	..	..	..	..	..	..
2.2.3	Securities issued by residents	14 987	28 673	25 407	34 644	24 960	32 152	42 306	40 369
2.2.4	Securities issued by non-residents	0	0	5	126	57	5 209	7 810	8 681
2.3	Loans	0	0	0	1 743	6 297	6 518	4 485	5 573
2.3.1	Short-term loans	..	..	..	..	..	..	..	..
2.3.2	Long-term loans	..	..	..	..	..	..	..	..
2.3.3	Loans granted to residents	0	0	0	1 743	6 297	6 518	4 485	5 573
2.3.4	Loans granted to non-residents	..	..	..	..	..	..	..	..
2.4	Shares and other equity	181 370	356 289	253 726	320 794	395 652	440 184	523 271	516 237
2.4.1	Shares issued by residents	181 370	356 289	253 726	320 794	395 652	439 184	505 986	490 381
2.4.2	Shares issued by non-residents	0	0	0	0	0	1 000	17 285	25 856
2.5	Other, not elsewhere classified	19 508	33 502	78 466	79 398	121 021	155 931	178 616	264 269

Note: Detailed metadata at: http://metalinks.oecd.org/instinv/20141203/e91d

Table 3. Financial assets of insurance corporations and autonomous pension funds

Million RUB

		2006	2007	2008	2009	2010	2011	2012	2013
	Insurance corporations and autonomous pension funds								
2	Financial assets	1 142 885	1 298 600	1 365 737	1 569 827	1 754 805	2 133 672	2 601 855	3 424 890
2.1	Currency and deposits	200 706	292 588	329 951	426 888	459 955	613 417	842 539	1 116 399
2.2	Securities other than shares, except financial derivatives	288 495	327 594	410 033	446 486	456 295	633 920	775 828	1 167 626
2.2.1	Short-term securities	..	..	..	..	..	..	..	..
2.2.2	Long-term securities	..	..	..	..	..	..	..	..
2.2.3	Securities issued by residents	284 272	320 708	401 372	441 416	444 567	600 914	742 449	1 107 362
2.2.4	Securities issued by non-residents	4 223	6 885	8 660	5 070	11 728	33 006	33 378	60 264
2.3	Loans	9 539	7 677	18 262	14 593	8 635	15 048	10 524	12 145
2.3.1	Short-term loans	..	..	..	..	..	..	..	..
2.3.2	Long-term loans	..	..	..	..	..	..	..	..
2.3.3	Loans granted to residents	9 520	7 277	17 449	14 353	8 388	11 041	8 464	7 708
2.3.4	Loans granted to non-residents	18	400	813	240	247	4 007	2 060	4 437
2.4	Shares and other equity	419 250	445 827	331 457	406 619	541 295	570 887	625 053	714 447
2.4.1	Shares issued by residents	418 064	444 783	329 870	401 805	538 959	558 102	607 418	695 614
2.4.2	Shares issued by non-residents	1 187	1 043	1 587	4 813	2 336	12 785	17 635	18 833
2.5	Other, not elsewhere classified	224 895	224 914	276 035	275 242	288 625	300 400	347 912	414 272
	Insurance corporations								
2	Financial assets	632 247	703 240	793 259	836 355	857 179	940 684	1 056 102	1 199 092
2.1	Currency and deposits	147 851	196 506	222 127	253 326	258 372	323 804	351 372	377 029
2.2	Securities other than shares, except financial derivatives	158 061	197 684	227 435	205 332	200 130	230 489	265 342	303 110
2.2.1	Short-term securities	..	..	..	..	..	..	..	..
2.2.2	Long-term securities	..	..	..	..	..	..	..	..
2.2.3	Securities issued by residents	153 839	190 862	218 971	200 874	189 183	206 404	242 780	262 987
2.2.4	Securities issued by non-residents	4 223	6 822	8 464	4 457	10 947	24 085	22 562	40 123
2.3	Loans	8 790	6 542	17 148	13 015	7 652	12 897	9 044	11 963
2.3.1	Short-term loans	..	..	..	..	..	..	..	..
2.3.2	Long-term loans	..	..	..	..	..	..	..	..
2.3.3	Loans granted to residents	8 771	6 142	16 335	12 776	7 404	8 890	6 984	7 526
2.3.4	Loans granted to non-residents	18	400	813	240	247	4 007	2 060	4 437
2.4	Shares and other equity	114 484	91 711	73 036	110 866	116 887	100 385	115 204	137 714
2.4.1	Shares issued by residents	113 709	91 001	71 782	106 422	114 625	87 674	97 569	129 042
2.4.2	Shares issued by non-residents	775	710	1 253	4 444	2 262	12 711	17 635	8 672
2.5	Other, not elsewhere classified	203 061	210 796	253 514	253 816	274 139	273 108	315 140	369 276
	Life insurance corporations								
2	Financial assets	..	..	..	..	..	..	..	..
2.1	Currency and deposits	..	..	..	..	..	..	..	..
2.2	Securities other than shares, except financial derivatives	..	..	..	..	..	..	..	..
2.2.1	Short-term securities	..	..	..	..	..	..	..	..
2.2.2	Long-term securities	..	..	..	..	..	..	..	..
2.2.3	Securities issued by residents	..	..	..	..	..	..	..	..
2.2.4	Securities issued by non-residents	..	..	..	..	..	..	..	..
2.3	Loans	..	..	..	..	..	..	..	..
2.3.1	Short-term loans	..	..	..	..	..	..	..	..
2.3.2	Long-term loans	..	..	..	..	..	..	..	..
2.3.3	Loans granted to residents	..	..	..	..	..	..	..	..
2.3.4	Loans granted to non-residents	..	..	..	..	..	..	..	..
2.4	Shares and other equity	..	..	..	..	..	..	..	..
2.4.1	Shares issued by residents	..	..	..	..	..	..	..	..
2.4.2	Shares issued by non-residents	..	..	..	..	..	..	..	..
2.5	Other, not elsewhere classified	..	..	..	..	..	..	..	..
	Non-life insurance corporations								
2	Financial assets	..	..	..	..	..	..	..	..
2.1	Currency and deposits	..	..	..	..	..	..	..	..
2.2	Securities other than shares, except financial derivatives	..	..	..	..	..	..	..	..
2.2.1	Short-term securities	..	..	..	..	..	..	..	..
2.2.2	Long-term securities	..	..	..	..	..	..	..	..
2.2.3	Securities issued by residents	..	..	..	..	..	..	..	..
2.2.4	Securities issued by non-residents	..	..	..	..	..	..	..	..
2.3	Loans	..	..	..	..	..	..	..	..
2.3.1	Short-term loans	..	..	..	..	..	..	..	..
2.3.2	Long-term loans	..	..	..	..	..	..	..	..
2.3.3	Loans granted to residents	..	..	..	..	..	..	..	..
2.3.4	Loans granted to non-residents	..	..	..	..	..	..	..	..
2.4	Shares and other equity	..	..	..	..	..	..	..	..
2.4.1	Shares issued by residents	..	..	..	..	..	..	..	..
2.4.2	Shares issued by non-residents	..	..	..	..	..	..	..	..
2.5	Other, not elsewhere classified	..	..	..	..	..	..	..	..

Table 3. Financial assets of insurance corporations and autonomous pension funds *(cont.)*

Million RUB

		2006	2007	2008	2009	2010	2011	2012	2013
	Autonomous pension funds								
2	Financial assets	510 638	595 360	572 478	733 472	897 626	1 192 988	1 545 753	2 225 798
2.1	Currency and deposits	52 855	96 082	107 824	173 562	201 583	289 612	491 167	739 370
2.2	Securities other than shares, except financial derivatives	130 433	129 909	182 598	241 154	256 165	403 431	510 486	864 516
2.2.1	Short-term securities	..	..	..	..	..	..	..	..
2.2.2	Long-term securities	..	..	..	..	..	..	..	..
2.2.3	Securities issued by residents	130 433	129 846	182 401	240 542	255 384	394 511	499 669	844 375
2.2.4	Securities issued by non-residents	0	63	197	612	781	8 921	10 816	20 141
2.3	Loans	749	1 135	1 114	1 577	983	2 151	1 480	182
2.3.1	Short-term loans	..	..	..	..	..	..	..	..
2.3.2	Long-term loans	..	..	..	..	..	..	..	..
2.3.3	Loans granted to residents	749	1 135	1 114	1 577	983	2 151	1 480	182
2.3.4	Loans granted to non-residents	0	0	0	0	0	0	0	0
2.4	Shares and other equity	304 766	354 116	258 421	295 753	424 409	470 502	509 849	576 733
2.4.1	Shares issued by residents	304 355	353 783	258 088	295 384	424 334	470 428	509 849	566 571
2.4.2	Shares issued by non-residents	411	333	333	369	74	74	0	10 161
2.5	Other, not elsewhere classified	21 834	14 118	22 521	21 426	14 486	27 291	32 772	44 996

Note: Detailed metadata at: http://metalinks.oecd.org/instinv/20141203/e91d

Table 4. Portfolio composition by type of investor

Percentage of total financial assets

Per cent

		2006	2007	2008	2009	2010	2011	2012	2013
	Investment funds								
2	Financial assets	100.0	100.0	100.0	100.0	100.0	100.0	100.0	100.0
2.1	Currency and deposits	6.8	9.4	12.0	11.8	12.6	12.5	15.2	19.8
2.2	Securities other than shares, except financial derivatives	9.9	8.6	8.8	8.9	6.4	7.8	8.9	9.6
2.2.1	Short-term securities	..	..	..	..	..	..	..	..
2.2.2	Long-term securities	..	..	..	..	..	..	..	..
2.2.3	Securities issued by residents	9.8	8.6	8.8	8.9	6.3	7.1	7.6	8.0
2.2.4	Securities issued by non-residents	0.0	0.0	0.0	0.0	0.0	0.6	1.3	1.6
2.3	Loans	0.0	0.0	0.0	0.3	0.8	0.8	0.4	0.5
2.3.1	Short-term loans	..	..	..	..	..	..	..	..
2.3.2	Long-term loans	..	..	..	..	..	..	..	..
2.3.3	Loans granted to residents	0.0	0.0	0.0	0.3	0.8	0.8	0.4	0.5
2.3.4	Loans granted to non-residents	..	..	..	..	..	..	..	..
2.4	Shares and other equity	76.6	75.2	61.1	64.7	63.3	59.4	56.9	46.9
2.4.1	Shares issued by residents	76.6	75.2	61.1	64.7	63.2	59.0	54.9	44.4
2.4.2	Shares issued by non-residents	0.0	0.0	0.0	0.0	0.1	0.4	2.0	2.5
2.5	Other, not elsewhere classified	6.8	6.8	18.1	14.3	16.9	19.6	18.5	23.2
	Insurance corporations								
2	Financial assets	100.0	100.0	100.0	100.0	100.0	100.0	100.0	100.0
2.1	Currency and deposits	23.4	27.9	28.0	30.3	30.1	34.4	33.3	31.4
2.2	Securities other than shares, except financial derivatives	25.0	28.1	28.7	24.6	23.3	24.5	25.1	25.3
2.2.1	Short-term securities	..	..	..	..	..	..	..	..
2.2.2	Long-term securities	..	..	..	..	..	..	..	..
2.2.3	Securities issued by residents	24.3	27.1	27.6	24.0	22.1	21.9	23.0	21.9
2.2.4	Securities issued by non-residents	0.7	1.0	1.1	0.5	1.3	2.6	2.1	3.3
2.3	Loans	1.4	0.9	2.2	1.6	0.9	1.4	0.9	1.0
2.3.1	Short-term loans	..	..	..	..	..	..	..	..
2.3.2	Long-term loans	..	..	..	..	..	..	..	..
2.3.3	Loans granted to residents	1.4	0.9	2.1	1.5	0.9	0.9	0.7	0.6
2.3.4	Loans granted to non-residents	0.0	0.1	0.1	0.0	0.0	0.4	0.2	0.4
2.4	Shares and other equity	18.1	13.0	9.2	13.3	13.6	10.7	10.9	11.5
2.4.1	Shares issued by residents	18.0	12.9	9.0	12.7	13.4	9.3	9.2	10.8
2.4.2	Shares issued by non-residents	0.1	0.1	0.2	0.5	0.3	1.4	1.7	0.7
2.5	Other, not elsewhere classified	32.1	30.0	32.0	30.3	32.0	29.0	29.8	30.8
	Autonomous pension funds								
2	Financial assets	100.0	100.0	100.0	100.0	100.0	100.0	100.0	100.0
2.1	Currency and deposits	10.4	16.1	18.8	23.7	22.5	24.3	31.8	33.2
2.2	Securities other than shares, except financial derivatives	25.5	21.8	31.9	32.9	28.5	33.8	33.0	38.8
2.2.1	Short-term securities	..	..	..	..	..	..	..	..
2.2.2	Long-term securities	..	..	..	..	..	..	..	..
2.2.3	Securities issued by residents	25.5	21.8	31.9	32.8	28.5	33.1	32.3	37.9
2.2.4	Securities issued by non-residents	0.0	0.0	0.0	0.1	0.1	0.7	0.7	0.9
2.3	Loans	0.1	0.2	0.2	0.2	0.1	0.2	0.1	0.0
2.3.1	Short-term loans	..	..	..	..	..	..	..	..
2.3.2	Long-term loans	..	..	..	..	..	..	..	..
2.3.3	Loans granted to residents	0.1	0.2	0.2	0.2	0.1	0.2	0.1	0.0
2.3.4	Loans granted to non-residents	0.0	0.0	0.0	0.0	0.0	0.0	0.0	0.0
2.4	Shares and other equity	59.7	59.5	45.1	40.3	47.3	39.4	33.0	25.9
2.4.1	Shares issued by residents	59.6	59.4	45.1	40.3	47.3	39.4	33.0	25.5
2.4.2	Shares issued by non-residents	0.1	0.1	0.1	0.1	0.0	0.0	0.0	0.5
2.5	Other, not elsewhere classified	4.3	2.4	3.9	2.9	1.6	2.3	2.1	2.0

Note: Detailed metadata at: http://metalinks.oecd.org/instinv/20141203/f729

ORGANISATION FOR ECONOMIC CO-OPERATION AND DEVELOPMENT

The OECD is a unique forum where governments work together to address the economic, social and environmental challenges of globalisation. The OECD is also at the forefront of efforts to understand and to help governments respond to new developments and concerns, such as corporate governance, the information economy and the challenges of an ageing population. The Organisation provides a setting where governments can compare policy experiences, seek answers to common problems, identify good practice and work to co-ordinate domestic and international policies.

The OECD member countries are: Australia, Austria, Belgium, Canada, Chile, the Czech Republic, Denmark, Estonia, Finland, France, Germany, Greece, Hungary, Iceland, Ireland, Israel, Italy, Japan, Korea, Luxembourg, Mexico, the Netherlands, New Zealand, Norway, Poland, Portugal, the Slovak Republic, Slovenia, Spain, Sweden, Switzerland, Turkey, the United Kingdom and the United States. The European Union takes part in the work of the OECD.

OECD Publishing disseminates widely the results of the Organisation's statistics gathering and research on economic, social and environmental issues, as well as the conventions, guidelines and standards agreed by its members.

OECD PUBLISHING, 2, rue André-Pascal, 75775 PARIS CEDEX 16
(01 2014 24 1 P) ISBN 978-92-64-22582-4 – 2014-07

www.ingramcontent.com/pod-product-compliance
Lightning Source LLC
Chambersburg PA
CBHW061209240926
51846CB00006B/1162
9789264225824